Slavery and Sentiment

Becoming Modern: New Nineteenth-Century Studies

SERIES EDITORS

Sarah Way Sherman
Department of English
University of New Hampshire

Janet Aikins Yount
Department of English
University of New Hampshire

Rohan McWilliam
Anglia Ruskin University
Cambridge, England

Janet Polasky
Department of History
University of New Hampshire

This book series maps the complexity of historical change and assesses the formation of ideas, movements, and institutions crucial to our own time by publishing books that examine the emergence of modernity in North America and Europe. Set primarily but not exclusively in the nineteenth century, the series shifts attention from modernity's twentieth-century forms to its earlier moments of uncertain and often disputed construction. Seeking books of interest to scholars on both sides of the Atlantic, it thereby encourages the expansion of nineteenth-century studies and the exploration of more global patterns of development.

For a complete list of books that are available in this series, see www.upne.com

Christine Levecq, *Slavery and Sentiment: The Politics of Feeling in Black Atlantic Antislavery Writing, 1770–1850*

Jennifer J. Popiel, *Rousseau's Daughters: Domesticity, Education, and Autonomy in Modern France*

Paula Young Lee, editor, *Meat, Modernity, and the Rise of the Slaughterhouse*

Duncan Faherty, *Remodeling the Nation: The Architecture of American Identity, 1776–1858*

Jennifer Hall-Witt, *Fashionable Acts: Opera and Elite Culture in London, 1780–1880*

Scott Molloy, *Trolley Wars: Streetcar Workers on the Line*

William C. Dowling, *Oliver Wendell Holmes in Paris: Medicine, Theology, and the Autocrat of the Breakfast Table*

Betsy Klimasmith, *At Home in the City: Urban Domesticity in American Literature and Culture, 1850–1930*

Sarah Luria, *Capital Speculations: Writing and Building Washington, D.C.*

David L. Richards, *Poland Spring: A Tale of the Gilded Age, 1860–1900*

Angela Sorby, *Schoolroom Poets: Childhood, Performance, and the Place of American Poetry, 1865–1917*

William M. Morgan, *Philanthropists in Disguise: Gender, Humanitarianism, and Complicity in U.S. Literary Realism*

Piya Pal-Lapinski, *The Exotic Woman in Nineteenth-Century British Fiction and Culture: A Reconsideration*

Patrick H. Vincent, *The Romantic Poetess: European Culture, Politics, and Gender, 1820–1840*

Edward S. Cutler, *Recovering the New: Transatlantic Roots of Modernism*

Margaret M. Mulrooney, *Black Powder, White Lace: The du Pont Irish and Cultural Identity in Nineteenth-Century America*

Stephen Carl Arch, *After Franklin: The Emergence of Autobiography in Post-Revolutionary America, 1780–1830*

Justin D. Edwards, *Exotic Journeys: Exploring the Erotics of U.S. Travel Literature, 1840–1930*

Christine Levecq

Slavery and Sentiment

The Politics of Feeling in Black Atlantic Antislavery Writing, 1770–1850

University of New Hampshire Press
Durham, New Hampshire

PUBLISHED BY UNIVERSITY PRESS OF NEW ENGLAND
HANOVER AND LONDON

University of New Hampshire Press
Published by University Press of New England,
One Court Street, Lebanon, NH 03766
www.upne.com

© 2008 by University of New Hampshire Press

Printed in the United States of America
5 4 3 2 1

All rights reserved. No part of this book may be reproduced in any form or by any electronic or mechanical means, including storage and retrieval systems, without permission in writing from the publisher, except by a reviewer, who may quote brief passages in a review. Members of educational institutions and organizations wishing to photocopy any of the work for classroom use, or authors and publishers who would like to obtain permission for any of the material in the work, should contact Permissions, University Press of New England, One Court Street, Lebanon, NH 03766.

Library of Congress Cataloging-in-Publication Data
Levecq, Christine.
Slavery and sentiment : the politics of feeling in Black Atlantic antislavery writing, 1770–1850 / Christine Levecq.
  p. cm. — (Becoming modern : new nineteenth-century studies)
Includes bibliographical references and index.
ISBN 978-1-58465-734-7 (cloth : alk. paper)
 1. American literature—African American authors—History and criticism. 2. American literature—19th century—History and criticism. 3. Didactic fiction, American—History and criticism. 4. Slavery in literature. 5. African Americans—Intellectual life—19th century. 6. Literature and society—United States—History—19th century. 7. Antislavery movements in literature. 8. Antislavery movements—United States—History—19th century. I. Title.
PS153.N5L455 2008
810.9'896073009034—dc22   2008029050

 University Press of New England is a member of the Green Press Initiative. The paper used in this book meets their minimum requirement for recycled paper.

*A mes parents,
avec tout mon amour
et toute ma gratitude*

Contents

Preface ix
Acknowledgments xi
Introduction 1
Chapter 1 Interiority, Aesthetics, and Antislavery Sentiment 33
Chapter 2 Trade, Sailors, National Agency, and World Citizenship 84
Chapter 3 Brotherhood, Radicalism, and Antislavery 139
Chapter 4 Blood, Bodies, and the Antebellum Slave Narrative 190
Chapter 5 The Case of Frederick Douglass 226
Epilogue Transnationalism and Black Studies 241

Notes 249
Works Cited 273
Index 293

Preface

This book aims to show that the anglophone literature about slavery in the eighteenth and the early nineteenth centuries made an important contribution to the history of emotion, and that black writers in particular pushed feeling's ability to express a political vision. Texts on slavery, including slave narratives, invariably contained an appeal to the reader's sympathy. By engaging readers emotionally, narrators hoped to shake them into a recognition of the slaves' plight, and to bring about a change in the slaves' lives. This book posits, though, that sympathy and sentiment in antislavery texts were not just about slavery, or even about the particular thoughts and feelings of black men and women, but about conveying an encompassing political ideology. Black writers, I argue, were profoundly engaged with the ideologies and the literatures of their times, and they used sentiment in their writings to perform that engagement. Feeling, in effect, became a means to promote of a particular vision of society, including of post-emancipation society.[1]

In a way, this book offers one possible investigation of the insight that Black Atlantic writers were men and women of their times. Although it is hard to track down their reading habits, it is clear that many of them, including Phillis Wheatley, Olaudah Equiano, Lemuel Haynes, John Marrant, Frederick Douglass, were well read and knowledgeable about immediately surrounding as well as international cultural and political currents. While many of the readings proposed here emphasize the originality and the unique radicalism of their texts, they also encourage making connections between black and white texts as co-participants in the ideologies of their times.

Two major worldviews emanate from the appeals to feeling analyzed here. Commonly referred to as "liberalism" and "republicanism," they are anchored respectively in an individual and in a civic or communal definition of ethical, social, and political ideals. As Philip Pettit puts it, "liberalism hails a distinctively isolationist, and republicanism a distinctively communal, ideal" (180). The historiographical debate about the presence and the nature of liberalism and republicanism in the eighteenth and the nineteenth centuries has found no resolution, and this book does not enter that debate at length. The debate revealed the extent to which the terms *liberalism* and *republicanism* only describe a prevailing attitude. They do not allow us to make precise predictions about the thoughts or the intentions or even the political programs of those who claim loyalty to them. This book recognizes the complexity of values and intentions. Still, the concepts can helpfully distinguish the substance and the interactions of important cultural values. Indeed, I argue that they provide considerable new insight into the political world of Black Atlantic writers, and that they help put these writers on modernity's political map.

This book is based on the assumption that the broad opposition of individualism and communalism describes a fundamental ethical dilemma of all social life. While the norm is to care most intensely for those closest to us, a culture's myths and practices can expand the self-sustaining community to very large numbers of people with whom contact is only conceptual. In fact, it is a characteristic of modernity that societies have an aversion to the suffering of people who are far distant from their immediate contacts. The point of the dichotomy is not to differentiate individualist and communalist writers by those labels, but to put the study of their complexity into the context in which it was most important to them. Focusing on the emotional and political tendencies of the texts, moreover, is valuable because together they constitute the culture's ethics. American culture became markedly liberal and individualistic in comparison to other cultures, including the one from which its sprang. While the term *republicanism* is no longer embraced in contemporary political theory,[2] it remains the best descriptive term by which to understand the communal ethic of some abolitionists as well as of contemporary leftists in the West. Whatever label people of social conscience in the West attach to their concern that government operate for the common good, that impulse is in the tradition of republicanism, and the history of that ethic can tell us much about how we have arrived at our current condition.

Acknowledgments

This book has benefited from the incisive comments of several readers, at both the proposal and manuscript stages. I am deeply grateful to Madhu Dubey, Kirsten Fermaglich, Rich Manderfield, Carine Mardorossian, Phillip Richards, John Saillant, Ned Watts. Many thanks also to my anonymous readers at the University Press of New England, as well as to Phyllis Deutsch and the editors of the Becoming Modern series, whose comments and advice led to a dramatic transformation of the manuscript.

Many other people have made the existence of this book possible, even if indirectly, and I want to thank them here.

The journey toward this book started a long time ago. I thank the college professors who sparked and fed my intellectual curiosity when I was an undergraduate at the University of Liège in Belgium: Louis Gillet, Hena Maes-Jelinek, Pierre Michel.

My graduate years at the University of Illinois in Urbana-Champaign were life changing. Nina Baym remains one of my uppermost models in scholarship and pedagogy, and she has been steadfast in her support throughout the years. I also learned much from Bob Parker's teaching and guidance. Chester Fontenot gave me, through his lectures, a passionate and eloquent introduction to African American literature. Mireille Rosello encouraged me to give my first conference paper. Bruce Michelson made my coming to the States possible by helping to set up an exchange program between the two universities.

Several years later I was very fortunate to spend a year as a Resident Fellow at the W.E.B. Du Bois Institute for Afro-American Research at Harvard University. I warmly thank Henry Louis Gates, Jr., for his generosity and his encouragements, and for welcoming me into such a friendly and intellectually stimulating community. I also benefited from conversations with Glenn Hendler at the University of Notre Dame, and with Chris Castiglia at Loyola University Chicago. Reading their work sparked the interest in sentiment that led to this book.

A few persons have given me that very special combination of professional help and loving affection. Madhu Dubey has my enduring gratitude. Her work has been a constant source of inspiration, and her help at every stage of my professional development has been invaluable. Barbara McCaskill has been immensely generous in her support, and in sharing her knowledge and her good cheer. Luc Herman opened up a cultural and intellectual world I hardly knew existed.

My parents, Fabien and Francine, have given me everything from inspiration, energy, and love to laughs and *blanc cassis*. This book is dedicated to them. My sisters, Brigitte and Nathalie, have given me much encouragement and heartwarming hospitality. I also thank the Manderfield family for their affectionate generosity.

A number of friends have enriched my intellectual life, and have given me their unfailing support throughout the years: Cécile Blase, Ulric Chung, Steve and Angie Elliston, Michiel van Kempen, Elisabeth Leijnse, Jean Mainil, Carine Mardorossian, Andrew Norris, Marija Rac, Hélène Varsamidou. Thanks in particular to Yves Clemmen, who has been a steady companion for many years. A very special thanks, also, to Hazel Rowley, who daily inspires me.

My deepest thanks are to Rich Manderfield, who has had the most profound impact on this book. His critical readings and his constant intellectual challenge have helped me become, I hope, a better thinker. I thank him even more for taking me away from my books.

Slavery and Sentiment

Introduction

> The common good was lost in the pursuit of private interest.
> —ROYALL TYLER, *The Contrast* (1787)

In February 1782, an African-born woman named Belinda addressed a petition to the Massachusetts legislature, appealing for her readers' sympathy. In the petition she first describes a happy childhood in a paradisiacal African environment, suddenly interrupted by a brutal invasion by white men into the "sacred grove" where she was praying, "with each hand in that of a tender parent." In spite of "the tears, the sighs, the supplications," she was "ravished from the bosom of her country," and separated from her parents forever. The ravishment and the suggestion of rape in this scene, together with the emphasis on familial attachment and separation, mark the text as sentimental: the reader is made to feel for the plight of a victim who suffers in her individual integrity as a person, a daughter, and a woman. The reader's personal identification is actually encouraged from the beginning of the piece, where the author invites us into the early impressions of "her mind" and "her affrighted imagination" (Belinda 142). We then follow her in her horrifying journey across the ocean and into slavery. At this point, using the vocabulary of natural rights theory, she directs the reader's sympathy to the fact that "the laws rendered her incapable of receiving property," even though she is a "free moral agent, accountable for her own actions." Indeed, "freedom" has been "intended for all the human race." She enjoins the legislature to let her enjoy part of "the immense wealth" of her former and now dead owner, "a part whereof hath been accumulated by her own industry" (143). In this text, individual victimization leads to a plea for personal sympathy based on the liberal idea of a natural right to freedom and to property, suggesting that the author knew such a combination to be a coherent and effective strategy.[1]

The Story of Quashi, the first version of which appeared in 1793 in the *Massachusetts Magazine*, appeals to a different sort of emotion. Here the protagonist proceeds, not from a desire for individual freedom, but from a communal identity defined both by his fellow slaves and by his master. Quashi grew up with his master as a "play-fellow," and, to him, this "boyish intimacy" (*Story of Quashi* 5) was the sign of an egalitarian relationship. When, years later, the master threatens to whip him, Quashi, now a man who "takes pride in what he calls the smoothness of his skin" (6), feels the "wound to his honour" (7). He tries to reason with the master, but they end up in a fatal struggle, "in which each had several times been uppermost." Quashi "got firmly seated on his master's breast, now panting and out of breath, and with his weight, his thighs, and one hand, secured him motionless." Reproaching the master for planning "'a punishment of which I must ever have borne the disgraceful marks'" (9), he cuts his own throat. While the reader is made to feel for Quashi's individual plight, his suicide symbolizes the destruction of the communal ethic that threatens not only him but all members of the community. Defined through male bonding and communal life, Quashi appears fully as a human being, endowed with feelings of tenderness, but also with a body that the text lovingly dwells on, and which makes him an equal, even a superior, during the fight.[2] Here, the body is not the difference that creates individuals, but the equalizer that creates communities. In its emphasis on community and honor, in its intimation of an egalitarian relationship between two men despite the official hierarchy of slavery, in its free depiction of the entanglements of black and white bodies, the text reflects a republican sensibility, one that prepares readers to accept, not just free agency, but equal citizenship.

The difference in the ways these stories appeal to the reader's feelings is the subject of this book. Through their respective emphases on individual and community, on interiority and physicality, on personal property and brotherhood, and more generally on freedom and the common good, these texts express feelings with different political meanings. This book's intended critical contribution is the idea that expressions of feeling in eighteenth- and nineteenth-century transatlantic texts about slavery and the slave trade appealed not just to individual readers' moral feelings but to their political assumptions as well. When abolitionist writers represented, or appealed to, various kinds of sentiment in their rhetoric—whether it was benevolence, sympathy, or, more generally, feeling—they did not just aim at eliciting an emotional response but also promoted political ideas, even a political ideology. These texts said something more and more important than that slavery was "wrong." Their authors made arguments from the social and political ideologies that grounded their moral and social lives. These writers had to consider how their world might be moved to care more broadly, and they did so by projecting a particular vision of society's ideal future.

More specifically, as is the case for Belinda's petition and *The Story of Quashi*, I argue that these texts expressed feelings that conveyed varying combinations of liberal and republican worldviews, and that while the overall story is one of increased liberalization of ideology on both sides of the Atlantic, the analysis proposed here also shows a persistent, sometimes separate, sometimes integrated, presence of republican ideals. By "liberalism," I mean an ideology that did not yet bear that name at the time, but that commonly denotes a Lockean philosophy grounded in the individual, freedom, and natural rights, and that is further associated with entrepreneurship and the free pursuit of self-interest.[3] "Republicanism" designates the civic humanist emphasis on civic responsibility and a devotion to the common good. While, as we will see, historians have argued about the degree to which these worldviews played a role in Anglo-American political ideology, most agree that liberalism and republicanism led a complex and always evolving coexistence on both sides of the Atlantic in the eighteenth and early nineteenth centuries. By identifying the liberal and republican leanings of sentiment in British and American antislavery writings up to 1850, this book makes a new contribution to that debate.

While both black and white texts are included in my discussion, I argue that the political ideology espoused by Black Atlantic texts not only reflected ideologies present in their time and place but also provided an original and a radical extension of them, thanks to what I see as a unique, republican-inspired black cosmopolitanism. When placed in a transatlantic, comparative context, as is the case in this book, black-authored texts are revealed to have adhered, to an important extent, to the configurations in political philosophy that immediately surrounded them. Putting

Afro-British and African American texts side by side allows me, for example, to uncover significant differences in the way black authors expressed political feeling on each side of the Atlantic. Yet all these texts are also shown, in varying degrees, to have made a more radical use of political sentiment. As my readings suggest, writers from Phillis Wheatley, Ignatius Sancho, and Olaudah Equiano, up to the major antebellum authors of slave narratives, such as Frederick Douglass and Mary Prince, had a radical dimension that was largely shaped by what was at the time an idiosyncratic cosmopolitan outlook.

Slavery and Sentiment offers a new look at the relationship between sentiment and politics in antislavery writings. Sentiment has enjoyed a critical revival in the past two decades, much of it focused on the political implications of texts by women writers that aim at eliciting sympathy for women in distress.[4] While the political is often an important component in those approaches, this book aims at reinvigorating specific aspects of politics that they tend to neglect. Important feminist work on sentiment has certainly revealed the ways in which the personal is political. Moreover, because the looming influence of *Uncle Tom's Cabin*, published in the early 1850s, shaped much subsequent antislavery discourse, it has helped direct the critical discussion on the collaboration of sentiment and abolitionism toward issues of female sympathy and domesticity. But the focus on gender politics has caused critics to downplay a certain dimension of the political that I would like to put forward in my work, one that is important to the understanding of abolitionist texts. Because slavery and the slave trade were intimately bound up with issues of property and trade, the role of the state, national identity, and international relations, expressions of feeling in texts about slavery often carried political implications. Ending my inquiry in 1850, a year before *Uncle Tom's Cabin* began to appear in the *National Era*, I show that writing about slavery addressed those aspects of political thought more systematically than the sentimental literature that has been analyzed for political content so far, and that it allows for the politics of sentiment to be theorized more clearly than would be the case for texts with political intentions of a different kind.[5]

Because of its transnational focus, my analysis also situates itself within another recent trend that emphasizes the multiple connections and similarities in antislavery thought and methods throughout the anglophone transatlantic world. In 1972 already, Betty Fladeland studied the many forms of collaboration that existed between British and American abolitionists, and emphasized how they were motivated by "similar intellectual and social trends," "developed similar theories," and "borrowed strategy and tactics from one another" (x). In his recent study, when discussing the use of sentiment in eighteenth-century abolitionist texts, Philip Gould asserts that "between the 1760s and 1810s British and American reformers engaged in the same rhetorical tactics" (*Barbaric Traffic* 4). He aims at placing the United States more squarely within "comparative, transatlantic, and even multilingual contexts" (7), and his discussions focus on cross-pollination and mutual exchange. My study certainly contributes to this trend, by highlighting similarities in thought and arguments among many transatlantic texts.

But by placing these writers within an international context, *Slavery and Sentiment* also helps uncover ways in which their texts partly reflected national ideological trends. Indeed, British and American cultures became more and more differentiated in the course of the eighteenth century, and political ideology was an important signal of this process. To the British and their colonies, liberty had long been an ideal of the social and political system, but it had always shared the ideological terrain with the notion of common good. Having rights did not mean the freedom to do as one pleases, but entailed duties in the service of a well-ordered world. Then, and relatively suddenly, the American Revolution turned liberty in the colonies into a dynamic political concept associated with change and individual agency in the construction of a national identity. American writers in the latter part of the eighteenth century showed a definite embrace of the idea of liberty as a natural right, and only occasionally retained the more communitarian vision anchored in the common good. In Britain, liberty had also been on everyone's lips throughout the century, but as we will see, it was always blended with notions of order and balance. This ideological divergence is crucial to the texts examined in this book.

These differences particularly mark expressions of feeling in the mainstream antislavery discourse that developed on both continents in the eighteenth and early nineteenth centuries. Whether it evolved from moral philosophy, secular philosophy, or evangelicalism, sentiment revealed its political infrastructure, explicitly or implicitly. On both sides of the Atlantic, people assembled liberalism and republicanism into social philosophies that ranged from profound individualism to exclusive devotion to the common good. But the British and the American emphases were different. A complex interplay of benevolence and natural law informed the abolitionist strategy used in Britain, while in America a sharper reliance on agency and natural rights led to an appeal for sympathy on the basis of individual humanity. It is as if the British attempt at equilibrium became shattered in its colony at the onset of the Revolution. The expression of feeling in British texts, while never devoid of individualism, often combined it with a wider social and economic consciousness. Many American abolitionists made the individual human core the cornerstone of their liberal sentimental appeal.

These differences in emotional rhetoric shaped the way abolitionist texts dealt with racial difference. Liberalism promotes pluralism in principle, but it relegates difference to the private, prepolitical realm. While theoretically acceptable, cultural or bodily difference is actually suppressed, in order to ease the process of reaching a common ground. The historical reality has been that liberalism has been unable to accommodate difference in its pursuit of that common ground, leaving women and nonwhites without access to freedom and equality. I argue that, in its practice, liberal sympathy has grounded its supposedly humanistic appeal in body or blood similarity, and that, while it did promote a necessary focus on individual dignity, it had limited conceptual means to resist illiberal tendencies because its individualism hampered the development of a larger, heterogeneous social vision. The republican emphasis on the common good traditionally led to an emphasis on order and hierarchy. But it was also able to take on forms that encompassed difference and, in some hands, became more radical. This type of republicanism attempted to acknowledge difference, cultivating a capacity for caring about large groups of diverse elements.

The politics of sentiment in Black Atlantic texts reveals that they were significantly informed by these national trends. African Americans like Wheatley or Briton Hammon relied on what I show to be predominantly liberal strategies, even as they and others also laced their writings with republican feelings drawn from more communitarian pockets in the culture. The emphasis on similarity in the idea of a common human core prevailed in these writings, but it regularly competed with a republican worldview presented as separate. Black American writers pursued a similar strategy in the nineteenth century, as can be seen in authors from William Grimes and Charles Ball to Douglass. Aiming rather at an integration of freedom and the common good, Afro-British writers such as Sancho, Quobna Ottobah Cugoano, and Equiano reflected a search for balance. These British writers used sentiment as a way to promote forms of sensibility that combined individual sympathy with a sense of social order and well-distributed public good. In some important ways, then,

Slavery and Sentiment shows a substantial degree of adherence, on the part of black writers, to aspects of the culture that immediately surrounded them. These writers drew important concepts from it, even as this culture was rejecting their own right to belong in it.

Their development also partly reflects the evolution of political thought during the turbulent eighty-year period from 1770 to 1850. Liberalism and republicanism changed as thinkers and writers adapted them to new social, political, and economic challenges. The eighteenth-century texts show what can be seen as different manifestations of liberalism, from a focus on individual interiority (as in Wheatley and Sancho), through a reflection on national identity (as in Hammon, Equiano, and Cugoano), to a concern with middle-class values (as in the Freemasons). Liberalism then became "full-blown" in antebellum texts adamant about freedom of choice and participation in an entrepreneurial, capitalist economy. Republicanism, based on the more ancient concept of common good, was virtually fighting for its life in the mainstream culture, but it emerges in these black texts in various guises, ranging from aesthetic appreciation of the body to radical visions of brotherhood. While the opposition of liberalism and republicanism cannot contain all the ideological dynamism present in the texts, it does convey important changes in political ideals that took place during this time period.

Many black writers occupied an even more complex ideological position, however, in that they not only appropriated surrounding and evolving political discourses but also managed to radicalize those ideas, a radical bent that was made possible largely by their republican-inspired cosmopolitan, cross-cultural outlook. Diasporic experience and cross-national consciousness spurred eighteenth- and nineteenth-century black writers to envision large communities in all their diversity. These writers found inspiration in such alternative worlds as the international culture of sailors, or the transhistorical and transcontinental cultural repository of Freemasonry. Many nineteenth-century slave narrators developed their political outlook from their own personal experience of travel and displacement. These mobile writers scanned cultures, and assembled from the transatlantic repertoire of political and emotional tropes a new rhetoric of sympathy anchored in their own brand of republican transnationalism. Republicanism found expression mostly in a cosmopolitan worldview that began in a transcultural model, gradually became a more political global vision, peaked in forms of international brotherhood at the end of the eighteenth century, and made intermittent appeals to community in the nineteenth century. In Black Atlantic texts, sentimental themes such as interiority, beauty, and brotherhood were placed in subtle connection with larger political ideas such as freedom and the common good, the individual and the state, nationalism and internationalism, in such a way as to convey new international visions of liberation and solidarity. In this sense, eighteenth- and nineteenth-century black writers occupy a unique ideological position, defined by their capacity both to take in elements of a national culture and to combine it with radical elements inspired by their idiosyncratic form of cosmopolitanism.

This book's critical enterprise contributes to the new emphasis on transnationalism that marks the field of literary studies, and I believe that it does so in two important ways. It shows that when critics take a step back and adopt a wider, transnational perspective, they can use it to highlight the extent to which black literary traditions are actually embedded in national ideologies. It also shows, on the other hand, that looking at writers' international leanings in particular can help uncover how they often managed to move beyond their national embeddedness, and thus to radicalize various aspects of the culture. This book tries to build on the contribution made by Paul Gilroy in *The Black Atlantic*, in identifying particular components of black "double consciousness" at a specific historical moment, and in allocating equal importance to the national and the international, as well as to the British and the American, configurations of the Black Atlantic. In this way, it shows the particular political configurations of black texts as they made their entry into modernity.

Liberalism and Republicanism

What Eric Foner says about late-eighteenth-century Philadelphia seems to have been true of the Anglo-American political world as a whole: there was a conflict between "a Lockean emphasis on natural rights, which seemed to posit a society composed of competitive individuals, each engaged in the pursuit of his own happiness, and the notion of the general good, which seemed to hark back to an earlier corporate notion of society" (*Tom Paine* 88). In the past few decades, indeed, historians have highlighted the presence in seventeenth- and eighteenth-century England and its colonies of two different political visions, which manifested themselves both separately and in combination. While some of their threads are hard to untangle, these theories are still marked by different approaches to social and political life. One, usually referred to as "liberalism," emphasizes individual rights, a contractarian view of social relations, and a concept of freedom as the absence of impediment to the pursuit of one's interests. The other, "republicanism," harks back to the politics of ancient Rome and northern Italian republics in the Renaissance, and sees the individual within a civic context, displaying civic virtue and pursuing the common good.[6] These political philosophies, while they do not account for the whole spectrum of political ideas on both sides of the Atlantic, played an important role in the growth of political ideology at the time and, I will argue, suffused the work of Black Atlantic writers as well, as they defended their rightful place in society as free human beings and as citizens.

The birth of liberalism is usually attributed to John Locke. Major aspects of Locke's ideas as put down in *The Second Treatise of Government* (1689) include his depiction of the original state of nature as one of freedom, equality, and independence, his insistence on the role of consent in the formation of a political society, his intimation of certain natural rights, and his thesis that unjust governments can be dissolved by the people. Locke also stressed the connection of labor and ownership. Starting from the premise that "every man has a 'property' in his own 'person,'" he deduces that "whatsoever, then, he removes out of the state that Nature hath provided and left it in, he hath mixed his labour with it, and joined to it something that is his own, and thereby makes it his property" (20). Indeed, "government has no other end but the preservation of property" (53–54), which, in the state of nature, is "very unsafe, very insecure" (69). It is no wonder Locke has come to stand for aggressive individualism and the pursuit of wealth. According to this ideology, human beings define themselves primarily through their separateness and their autonomy, and the main function of society is to provide them with the maximum amount of freedom possible to achieve and preserve this autonomy without detriment to others. A society built on liberal principles aims to provide its members with, in the term made famous by Isaiah Berlin, "negative" freedom, the principle that "there ought to exist a certain minimum area of personal freedom which must on no account be violated" (124). To be free, for a liberal, means to be free from interference.

English republicanism has more recently been associated by historians with the so-called Real Whigs who, from the Restoration to the end of the eighteenth century, provided a critical commentary on social and political events.[7] To J. G. A. Pocock, these Whigs were profoundly republican, all influenced by James Harrington who, with *Oceana* (1656), produced a civic humanist breakthrough in his vision of the independent, property-holding citizen-soldier as essential to a citizenship grounded in public action and civic virtue. During the Restoration, says Pocock, virtue became opposed less to fortune, in the sense of the accidents of timebound history, than to corruption. Around the turn of the century, a slow revolution in the political economy of English society meant that it relied increasingly on trade, finance, and credit, and sparked civic humanist calls for a revival of civic virtue against the corruption of luxury and dependence. These calls characterized the so-called Country ideology, which was anchored both in "a presumption of real property"—as opposed to the imaginary, fictitious, irrational world of finance and mobile property where people became subservient to their own passions—and in "an ethos of the civic life . . . perpetually threatened by corruption operating through private appetites and false consciousness" (Pocock, *Machiavellian* 486). Civic humanists were out to resist both the conservative impulses of parliamentary tradition, and the corrupting effects of an increasingly commercial and socially mobile society. To Pocock, the Real Whigs represent this civic humanist trend. To Michael P. Zuckert and Isaac Kramnick, these thinkers were predominantly liberal, in their defense of liberal freedom and of natural rights. Caroline Robbins, whose book originally came out in 1959, calls them liberal.

Though, as Robbins points out, the Real Whigs never brought about any concrete achievements in England, the political system reflected the mix of ideologies that these different interpretations suggest. Indeed, historians have emphasized the balanced ideology, the "wholesome equilibrium" (Robbins 129), that grew out of England's eventful seventeenth century. The Glorious Revolution of 1688–89 led to the establishment of a mixed government whose moderateness reflected a desire for political balance. The English Bill of Rights marked a step forward from the divine rights monarchy, but it lacked what would be essential components of the American Declaration of Independence, such as "equality," the notion of "government as artifact," "natural rights as the foundation and end of politics," "consent," and "the right of revolution" (Zuckert 6). Even though Locke published his *Two Treatises of Government* in 1690, the Whigs who wrote in defense of the Glorious Revolution were, as Zuckert reminds us, more influenced by Hugo Grotius than by Locke. To many British, liberty and natural law entailed duties as well as rights. As Knud Haakonssen explains, the theory of natural law prevalent in the eighteenth-century anglophone world was "less individualistic and antiauthoritarian than it has later been taken to be" (20). Rights were seen as the flip side of duties, rather than as properties inherent to human beings in search of their own self-interest in a conflicted, chaotic movement toward uncertain harmony. Eighteenth-century British political culture retained a unique emphasis on the qualities of mixed government and balance, on the blending of freedom and the common good, issued from the Glorious Revolution.

The various entanglements of liberalism and republicanism that characterized British political culture in the eighteenth century may be said to reflect the particular form of Enlightenment it is associated with. The notion of a British Enlightenment has been hotly debated. Of course, as Roy Porter shows, the British enjoyed a degree of freedom almost unprecedented in Europe: enlightened persons in Britain "waved the liberty banner, legitimizing such claims through Lockean liberalism" (15). According to Pocock, however, the British Enlightenment also exhibited a desire to control the sort of excesses associated with the religious and political wars that had marked the previous century: it had to do with "the protection of sovereign authority and personal security against religious fanaticism and civil war" ("Conservative" 83). The reaction against all manners of "enthusiasm" was of a modern rather than of a traditionalist kind, and promoted freedoms such as "'manners,' 'politeness,' and 'sociability,'" reflecting a society now based on "circulation and exchange" (90). Being enlightened meant being willing and able to participate in this system, whose emphasis on "consumption and exchange" should be differentiated from that on "mere acquisitive individualism" (91). The British Enlightenment thus combined authority, moderation, and stoicism for the sake of the common good, with the freedom to exchange commodities as part of a modern commercial society. This combination and this attempt at balance characterized British political values that still held sway in the last decades of the eighteenth century.

The growth of the nation into an empire in the course of the eighteenth century contributed to this idea of a balance to be achieved between freedom and the common good. The theoretical discussion of this concern found its inspiration in classical authors, who were models for the development of political theory at the time. While political writings contain various definitions of what constituted liberty or the common good, Peter N. Miller shows that, up until the revolt of the American colonies, there was widespread agreement on the primacy of the public good as the source of guidance for political thought and action throughout the empire. While its ultimate goal was maintaining the liberty of individual citizens, the concept of the common good could also be used to justify measures deemed necessary for society as a whole, rather than for its individual members. The growth of commerce, and the territorial and maritime expansion that accompanied the rise of the British Empire, demanded an even stronger defense of the traditional complementarity of liberty and security. To many in England, the economic and political dependence of the colonies on the metropolis was a small price to pay for the protection afforded them by the motherland. This does not necessarily mean that Britain was automatically more conservative. Indeed, the "subjecthood" involved in empire sometimes offered more liberty than the "citizenship" at the heart of, for example, American identity. As T. H. Breen points out, "the rhetoric of subjecthood . . . was categorically nonhierarchical and inclusive; it encouraged egalitarian thinking" (399). To some extent, the ideology of empire would give British parliamentarians the power to move toward abolition that American representatives did not have.

The historiography concerning the role played by liberalism and republicanism in the American colonies in the eighteenth century is more controversial. In the past few decades a number of historians have been keen to emphasize the republican heritage of the American revolutionary generation.[8] Though he hardly ever uses the term, the American historian Bernard Bailyn is often seen as having launched the republican thesis about the American Revolution, by arguing that the fear of corruption by power and conspiracy was the primary concern that the Real Whigs impressed on the revolutionary generation.[9] Gordon S. Wood also sees a republican paradigm at the heart of the American Revolution. To him, republicanism contained "a moral dimension, a utopian depth" (47), which aimed at a reordering of American society on the basis of such qualities as "restraint, temperance, fortitude, dignity, and independence" (50). Key to this vision was a "sacrifice of individual interests to the greater good of the whole" (53). To him, the revolutionary generation believed that common interest should always trump the private interests of the individuals who make up the community because "ideally, republicanism obliterated the individual." Individual liberty consisted less in "the private rights of individuals" than in "the public rights of the collective people" (61). The sacrifice of private interests demanded an essential republican quality, public virtue, which was in turn stimulated by the exercise of private virtues. To Wood and the promoters of this republican viewpoint such as Pocock, Locke's role in the American Revolution has been consistently overstated, and only the republican influence can account for that era's events and their ideological underpinnings.

Indeed, by stressing the republican heritage of the American Revolution, Bailyn, Wood, and Pocock were reversing a long historiographical tradition anchored in liberalism and the writings of Locke. For a long time, Locke seemed emblematic of the ideals of the American Revolution, and the liberal notion of freedom has long been considered a mainstay of American political ideology. The defenders of the republican paradigm in American historiography—which, as Daniel T. Rodgers shows, has extended to areas such as labor history, women's history, and Southern history—were reacting against the consensus school predominant in the 1950s, best represented by Louis Hartz' book *The Liberal Tradition in America* (1955). According to Hartz, the fact that America has never known a feudal stage had profound implications for its political ideology: "One of the central characteristics of a nonfeudal society is that it lacks a genuine revolutionary tradition" (5), so that it accepts the middle ground as the basic idea, rejecting extremes on both the right and the left ends of the political spectrum. This ubiquitous presence of liberalism has become "a nationalist articulation" (11) so widespread that it even escapes consciousness.

While each of these ideologies, republicanism and liberalism, has liberatory potential, republicanism keeps attracting historians and literary critics because of the possible associations many see with radicalism and egalitarianism. It is this sort of republicanism that prompted the tavern keeper William Thompson to demand that republican leaders be "*good, able, useful,* and *friends to social equality*" (qtd. In Shalhope 63). Nevertheless, one can often only speculate on the ideological roots of radical movements at the time. As Alfred F. Young points out, his collection shows "not a single radicalism but multiple radicalisms," which do not stem from "one all-pervasive idea or ideology" (Young, 1993, 332). Farmers, urban artisans, merchant seamen, apprentices, women, and slaves were moved by different objectives and used different strategies to try to better their lot. Quite often, their complaints about their difficult access to property ownership or their references to their natural right to freedom sound downright liberal. These oppositional voices often show the radical possibilities, not of republicanism, but of liberal thought—an idea which I hope resonates throughout this book, even as it emphasizes the weaknesses of liberalism. Joyce Appleby has shown over and over that the liberal idea of human beings as autonomous, self-governing individuals involved in a rational pursuit of their own interests sounded radical at the time compared with the mixture of liberty and authority offered by classical republicanism.[10] Still, many see in republicanism a communal perspective that opens the way to radical egalitarianism in a way that individual liberalism does not.[11]

The debate about the relative importance of liberalism and republicanism in American ideology has raged for several decades, and some historians, seemingly tired of the argument, now tend to dismiss it. Ultimately, writers about the period end up positing "a world of complex currents, interlaced strands, a handful of powerful texts and systematic thinkers, and beyond a loosely structured, confused, and altogether familiar muddle" (Rodgers 37). In his own overview, Philip Gould concludes that most historians tend to emphasize "synthesis, pluralism, and even multivalence" (*Covenant and Republic* 26). There is no question that one should avoid positing clear-cut separations or unchanging concepts. Such, at the time ubiquitous, terms as "virtue" or "liberty," for example, do not automatically translate into a particular ideology, and need to be interpreted in context.

Nevertheless, the distinction between republicanism and liberalism has remained essential, even in our contemporary political world. As Rodgers points out, both were filling very real interpretive needs at some point, and they still are.[12] They did not turn out to be Kuhnian paradigms, it is true. What I refer to as "liberalism," for example, evolved throughout the time period examined here; it did not, in the eighteenth century, imply the unchecked pursuit of self-interest and the primacy of entrepreneurship it would connote in the next century. Nonetheless, the two concepts do convey critical differences in the individual's relationship to community and national identity. They may not be as sharply delineated and opposed as some historians made them out to be, and they should not be used as monolithic icons with all-encompassing explanatory power, but they do convey different political visions, and they can still help provide an entry into a complex ideological world.

Understanding the differences between the two ideologies can also be useful when comparing the political thought on each side of the Atlantic because they highlight a number of differences that might otherwise be subsumed under the notion of an Anglo-American political world. Seen from this perspective, the British and the American texts discussed in this book often behave differently. Out of the analysis provided here emerges a British search for integration and balance that often contrasts with more sharply divided ideas at the heart of the American Revolution. The American texts contain often invigorating appeals to individualism and natural rights; occasionally and separately, they also present a more communitarian vision inspired by republicanism as a valid alternative or as a philosophy of equal weight.[13] Many British texts eschew outright liberalism, which at the time was still considered radical, but offer interesting and sometimes even more progressive combinations of individualism and concern for community. In Britain, liberty and the common good remained tied together. The opposite sides seem to have less sharply separated in Britain, which kept blending liberalism and civic humanism well into the nineteenth century, than in the United States, where the separation between liberal and republican worldviews led to an increased predominance of the one and a gradual disappearance of the other.[14]

Finally, this book is based on the premise that observing the late eighteenth and the early nineteenth centuries through the lenses of liberalism and republicanism can help throw a new light on Black Atlantic texts, which have rarely been inserted into that debate even though they were very much a part of the ideological ferment of the time. Indeed, while this book refers regularly to social and economic contexts, as well as to particular experiences that occasioned or accompanied the writing of black texts, it interprets those texts mainly as the expressions of a political and ideological consciousness. In other words, it places black authors not just within a history of oppression and of resistance to that oppression but also, and most importantly, within the development of a political language from pre-revolutionary days to the middle of the nineteenth century. The close readings I offer show that liberalism and republicanism often combined in subtle ways, so that the approach helps underscore the political complexity at the heart of Black Atlantic texts. Inserting Black Atlantic texts within the debate on liberalism and republicanism can actually help rejuvenate that debate by showing how the ideologies were absorbed into their idiosyncratic, cosmopolitan visions. Ultimately, the presence of a political project at the heart of an antislavery appeal provides important clues as to the nature of the post-emancipation society the authors envisioned.

The Politics of Sentiment

This book argues that the political ideologies of liberalism and republicanism played an important role in shaping eighteenth- and nineteenth-century appeals to, and expressions of, sentiment about people who were suffering, and particularly about people who were enslaved. When sensibility became a major component of Anglo-American culture in the eighteenth century, it provided writers with an emotional rhetoric for the political ideas they wanted to convey. Because they involved particular conceptualizations of the human subject's relationship to other individual subjects, a group, a community, a state, or an international horizon, these political theories inevitably drew on the language of human connection and association. Tracing literary emotion in eighteenth- and nineteenth-century texts as they depict individual and communal experience can reveal how the culture integrated political and emotional discourses. By making the relations between an individual and other individuals or groups the subject of an affective encounter, the authors discussed in this book invariably established links between various aspects of feeling and their own political thought.

Because sentimental appeals rely on a reader's imagining of others' emotional and physical experience, the political valence of emotion in the texts discussed here was often couched in particular representations of interiority and corporeality. Thomas W. Laqueur, among other critics, has emphasized how the "humanitarian narrative" that developed in the eighteenth and nineteenth centuries "relies on the personal body" (177) as it zooms in on the lacerations, diseases, and death suffered by individual bodies. I argue that this attention to the body, when read closely, reveals a number of subtle implications about what the writer thinks the reader should see or imagine. If, as Laqueur says, "the flesh speaks" (179), it speaks in different languages.[15] The way a writer mobilizes emotion for others' feelings and bodies reveals specific convictions on how this "other" relates to the viewer, as well as to the wider community that both do or do not belong to. In other words, at the very moment when the reader is made to imagine a suffering other, his or her imagination is made to stretch to encompass the way the sufferer relates to him or her, and to the surrounding community. It is the peculiar configuration of interiority and bodily attributes that guides this process, and it is the new multiplicity of forms of sensibility in the eighteenth century that made it possible.

Indeed, sensibility in the eighteenth century reflected new ways of conceptualizing the human body. Ann Jessie Van Sant points out that the psychological aspects we associate with the sentimental tradition developed out of, and borrowed metaphors from, a new emphasis on physiology and concurrently on an epistemology of sensation. According to G. S. Rousseau, the writings of Thomas Willis, especially his *Anatomy of the Brain* (1664) and *Pathology of the Brain* (1667), both translated from Latin in the early 1680s, were the first "clearly and loudly to posit that the seat of the soul is strictly limited to the brain, nowhere else" (144). Since most physiologists at the time already assumed that nerves were in essential ways collaborating with the brain, this new theory spurred a new interest in the nature and function of nerves, which led to new theories of sensory perception and of knowledge. This trend made John Locke's *Essay Concerning Human Understanding* (1690) possible, with its notions of the mind as a blank slate, gradually inscribed with ideas originating in sensation. The late seventeenth and the eighteenth centuries then spawned various physiological schemes to account for mental processes, such as Isaac Newton's idea of fluids or David Hartley's concept of vibrations to explain the associations of ideas. Even though René Descartes had, about a century earlier, tried to locate the mind within the pineal gland, the new physiology meant a revolutionary displacement of the Cartesian mind/body dualism: the nervous system "began to emerge, both ontologically and methodologically, as the common matrix" (Figlio 177). This matrix became the fount of a new cultural enthusiasm for human sensibility, which could refer to both the nervous system and the soul.

While sensibility received its big push from this new interest in nerves and fibers, however, in the course of the eighteenth century the mental and spiritual elements of sensibility came to define it. The concept of "sympathy" in particular went through a complex process of transformation. It first re-entered medical discourse with the new interest in the nervous system. Sympathy already had a long history by then, grounded in theories of universal correspondence between the elements. These theories underlay not only medieval alchemy but highly original medical experiments such as those of Paracelsus in the sixteenth century and Sir Kenelm Digby in the seventeenth century.[16] Eighteenth-century Edinburgh physicians started using the word "sympathy" to refer to "the communication of feeling between different bodily organs," thus as "a special case of sensibility" (Lawrence 27). Since those organs could be the eyes and ears, sympathy came to include the effects of witnessing affecting scenes, hence merging with sentiment and psychology. Sympathy's transfer from the occult to the biological to the realm of feeling mirrors reappraisals of the body in the rapidly changing world of the Enlightenment. Not allowed to stay in the spotlight for very long, the body gradually became less prominent in sensibility. Of course characters in the sentimental novel kept blushing and trembling, and this physicality is often used as evidence of the prominence of the body in the genre. But the body was often relegated to epiphenomena of expressions, while inner emotional processes came to receive emphasis.[17]

A similar relationship of feeling and the body entered eighteenth-century ethical discourse, and Adam Smith represents the climax of this trend, in his dissection of the psychological and emotional components in human sympathy. Smith presents sympathy as a momentary connection between two individual, interior states. Here is the locus classicus of his *Theory of Moral Sentiments* (1759):

> As we have no immediate experience of what other men feel, we can form no idea of the manner in which they are affected, but by conceiving what we ourselves should feel in the like situation. Though our brother is upon the rack, as long as we ourselves are at our ease, our senses will never inform us of what he suffers. They never did, and never can, carry us beyond our own person, and it is by the imagination only that we can form any conception of what are his sensations. . . . By the imagination we place ourselves in his situation, we conceive ourselves enduring all the same torments, we enter as it were into his body, and become in some measure the same person with him, and thence form some idea of his sensations, and even feel something which, though weaker in degree, is not altogether unlike them. (3–4)

Sympathy requires work of the imagination on the part of the observer, who attempts to duplicate the feelings of the suffering person under observation within his or her own interior state. Only this interior connection between the two human beings can activate the observer's dormant supply of compassion. The sufferer's body becomes an obstacle to be removed, or a fortress to be penetrated, so as to make the imaginative communication possible. Observer and observed are "changing places in fancy" (4), the observer relinquishing his or her focus as an onlooker to adopt the vantage point of the observed.

Smith's model is thoroughly based on interiority. Even though he allows that we sometimes sympathize with visible displays of grief or joy without knowing their cause, in which case the passion is "transfused" from one person to another, he still accounts for this phenomenon by relating it to an interior state, explaining that such displays of emotion "suggest to us the general idea of some good or bad fortune" (6). In other words, Smith says, sympathy "does not arise so much from the view of the passion, as from that of the situation which excites it" (7). In order to help this process the sufferer, in order to elicit sympathy, needs to make that leap of the imagination possible. Only if the spectator and sufferer find themselves "in perfect concord" (14) can such a process take place. Indeed, the sufferer "can only hope to obtain this by lowering his passion to that pitch, in which the spectators are capable of going along with him. He must flatten, if I may be allowed to say so, the sharpness of its natural tone, in order to reduce it to harmony and concord with the emotions of those who are about him" (23). The sufferer must modulate his or her feelings, tune them in to the observer's because, Smith says of the latter, "if the passion is too high, or if it is too low, he cannot enter into it" (31). Sympathy will not take place without this alignment of two interior states. The sufferer, by downplaying his or her bodily affect, or by adjusting it to the sympathizing ability of the sympathizer, makes sure that the corporeal does not interfere with the process through which the sympathizer imagines himself or herself reaching into the sufferer's interiority. Here we see a direct result of the model's anchoring in interiority.[18]

Through its focus on one-on-one interactions in which the body needs to be downplayed, Smith's theory of sentiment typifies the liberal outlook. Smith makes the process of sympathy extremely selective by qualifications he imposes on the capacity to sympathize. He keeps advocating "lowering" and "bringing down" the display of emotions to elicit sympathy. The sufferer needs to show "self-denial," "self-government," "command of the passions" (26). Overall, "moderation" (29) will ensure the "propriety" (31) of emotion. It is "indecent to express any strong degree of those passions which arise from a certain situation or disposition of the body" (33), such as hunger and sex, because they do not involve the imagination. Because of these restrictions, John Dwyer argues that Scottish ideas of sympathy have more to do with stoicism and with "the classical language of virtue than with the rise of affective individualism or the evolution of the modern self" (96). But stoicism implies a desire to reach harmony with the whole natural and cosmic order, ideas that do not seem to be part of Smith's primary motivation. Dwyer does acknowledge that Smith's emphasis on "small-scale, day-to-day exchanges between actors and spectators" brought the ethical focus away from the public arena, and that he replaced "an abstract devotion to duty" with "an imperative for politeness and flexibility" (102).[19] It is this small-scale, intersubjective focus that unhooks Smith from the civic humanist tradition. His emphasis on self-command and self-discipline does not in any way detract from his liberal standpoint—it contributes to it by controlling the body as part of an imaginative, interpersonal exchange.[20]

Toward the other end of the ideological spectrum covered by sentiment in the eighteenth and nineteenth centuries is republican feeling, which, unlike Smith's sympathy, does not rely, or at least not solely or predominantly, on an interpersonal, interior exchange.[21] Republicanism is founded on a different concept of how humans are motivated to care for others. It began with the ancient recognition of the human ability to extend the altruistic impulse beyond the personal, familial, and tribal to larger political and cultural communities. Just as Smith's liberal politics are reflected in his individualist psychology, so the more communitarian psychology of republicanism suggests an inclusive communitarian sympathy that exceeds the limitations of Smith's interpersonal model. Republicanism is built on the conviction that sympathy is not limited to interpersonal contact. The republican appeal calls on the cultural optimism of the ability of sympathy to respond to images of the individual's embeddedness in communities. The aim is not to suppress a consciousness of the body in order to access an individual interiority, but to trigger an expansion of consciousness toward a feeling for a whole community, a feeling that includes the corporeal. This is what republican feeling does, in an expansion of the sympathetic impulse from a direct interaction with the individual other to a feeling for community.

Different forms of sentiment are found along the entire continuum between Smithian sympathy and republican feeling. In his posthumously published *System of Moral Philosophy* (1755), Francis Hutcheson was much inspired by the Scottish moral sense school, which can be seen as blending liberalism and republicanism.[22] Searching for an explanation of human behavior that would offer an alternative to "*self-love*" or "one's *desire of his own happiness*" (vol. 1, 39), he held that "our nature is susceptible of affections truly disinterested in the strictest sense, and not directly subordinated to self-love, or aiming at private interest of any kind" (49). Indeed, we live under "two grand determinations, one toward our own greatest happiness, the other toward the greatest general good, each independent on the other" (50); these two principles "seem to draw different ways" (51). Our innate moral sense, which aims at moral goodness independent from our own pleasure or happiness, ensures that we act not out of selfish principles alone. "Mere desire of one's own happiness" is morally insufficient, and needs to be supplemented by affections such as benevolence. While Hutcheson conceives of it as an innate sense rather than as a cultural construction, his concept of benevolence provides the image of a bridge between the natural liberty that Hutcheson cherishes and the common good, the ideal end that trumps all other ends. Benevolence can still ensure individual liberty, but it is different from Smith's model in that it involves a search for a general happiness. Several texts discussed in this book evoke this politically balanced version of sentiment.

The interdependence of the political and the emotional in eighteenth- and nineteenth-century texts can thus be traced in allusions to individual freedom or the common good, to interpersonal exchange or communal consciousness, to interiorities or bodies. These are the images that motivated readers to endorse specific political visions. Some of the writers of these texts were vocal on both the affective and the political fronts. The fact that Smith, for example, authored both a moral study of sentiment and a book of liberal, free-market economics, *The Wealth of Nations*, suggests that his theory of individually negotiated emotional exchange is ideally suited to naturalize the individualism at the heart of his political philosophy. But even when the connection cannot be so easily substantiated, the readings I propose in this book show that feeling was a particularly faithful reflection of the political. The interaction of sentiment and politics was stronger than the normal interactions of cultural spheres, all the more so when it came to abolitionist writings. The writers did not necessarily intend to make those connections, but sentiment became the conduit through which those notions reached their intended audience. In liberalism à la Smith, sympathy acted on an individual level. In moral philosophy, especially of the Scottish kind, the concept of benevolence acted as a bridge between natural law and the common good. Republicanism elicited feelings that proceeded from a larger communitarian concept. The presence of sentiment in a text was not just about eliciting feeling from the readers. It inevitably revealed a particular political ideology, and induced an acceptance of its aims and limitations. Calling feeling "sentiment" underlines this combination of emotional and political content.

This approach allows me to draw specific links between political theory and the sentimental novel, a genre whose political dimensions have been highlighted by many critics, albeit in a broader sense.[23] Because the sentimental novel focused on the private sphere, its political dimension was often not obvious or explicit, but that the personal was not only moral but also social and political in these eighteenth- and nineteenth-century texts is borne out by close reading.[24] Bypassing the debate engendered by the works of Ann Douglas and Jane Tompkins about the progressive or the conservative dimensions of the sentimental, I focus on the interplay between liberalism and republicanism in these works.[25] In novels like *The Power of Sympathy*, *Charlotte Temple*, *The Coquette*, the novels of Charles Brockden Brown, and novels by Catharine Maria Sedgwick and Lydia Maria Child, themes related to freedom and the common good, or interiority and the body, such as marriage, homosocial bonding, and even incest, all play a role in the ideological landscape of the work.[26] The death of Little Eva in *Uncle Tom's Cabin*, Harriet Beecher Stowe's 1852 best seller, is heartbreaking, Cato's suicide in Joseph Addison's 1713 play is meant to elicit an emotional reaction that blends poignancy and admiration, and Richardson, as Leslie Fiedler puts it, "exacts from his reader the supreme tribute of tears" (72). All are appeals to sympathy, but they are so in different ways, appealing to readers who are predisposed by political ideologies to respond to different emotional situations.

The British and the American uses of sentiment, moreover, reflect the political differences sketched out earlier.[27] The British texts show a profound anchoring in a republicanism that only slowly opened up to absorb more liberal influences. The British seventeenth-century Roman plays held on to stoic ideals such as civic virtue, even if the private sphere watered down some of their communitarian messages. Male bonding, an important republican theme, lived side by side with heterosexual marriage, and these two forms of emotional attachment became entangled. Even Richardson and Laurence Sterne kept sentiment within the realm of duty and community. In the American novel, sentiment and sympathy helped express a gradual shift, in the years between the Revolution and the Civil War, from a republican to a liberal outlook, even as both philosophies remained present, but competed rather than blended with each other. The eighteenth-century sentimental novel in particular staged a debate between those views through the struggles and feelings of its characters, the result being not always clear-cut.[28]

Political Sentiment and the Black Atlantic

Liberalism and republicanism have intricate relationships with racism and difference. Because America, often seen as fundamentally liberal, has not lived up to its promise of justice and freedom, liberalism has invited two kinds of appraisal. One is part of a history of progress, which argues that liberalism implies egalitarianism, and that the nation is steadily moving in the right direction, however slowly and grudgingly. This version often uses terms such as "contradiction" and "hypocrisy" to account for the country's history of violent racism. The other sees liberalism as fundamentally alien to the egalitarian promise, often arguing that its form of thought inevitably produces illiberalism.[29] Both recognize that, in its practice, liberalism has grounded its humanistic appeal in inner and outer similarity. Lauren Berlant formulates the liberal creed appropriately when she explains how "white male privilege has been veiled by the rhetoric of the bodiless citizen," and how such a model has set up "a peculiar dialectic between embodiment and abstraction in the post-Enlightenment body politic" (112). Indeed, she adds, "American women and African-Americans have never had the privilege to suppress the body" (113).[30] Liberalism has thus swerved between a rhetoric of abstraction or neutral interiority, and an actual rejection of bodily difference.[31] Like liberalism, republicanism had traditionally relied on similarity. Because only propertied white men participated in public virtue, they were really similar. Racist, sexist, and classist customs pervaded republican cultures. Many commentators during the Revolution referred worryingly to Montesquieu's idea that a republic could survive only on the condition that it remain small and homogeneous, since the idea of a republic could obviously not apply to an expanding and increasingly diverse America. For different reasons, then, the republican public sphere had historically also tended to de-emphasize difference.

But the texts discussed in this book show that a republican mind-set had the potential to take on forms that encompassed and accepted difference. While liberal theory contains a suggestion of equality in its natural rights doctrine, its deference to the limitations of the individual imagination easily short-circuits in practice the inclusiveness of its theory. Republicanism, on the other hand, begins with an interest in the needs of communities, and challenges individual imaginations to achieve "virtue," defined as the ability to sacrifice for the common good. Republicanism does not interject an individualist ethic between its theory and its practice as liberalism does. In practice, then, while the notion of common good could lead to an emphasis on the primacy of unity and order in a racially homogeneous nation, it could also transform itself to encourage the presence and the acceptance of different bodies. This recognition of the body tries to combine a republican abstract acceptance of community with a real, concrete, horizontal look at the members of that community.[32] These differences are echoed in the different notions of nationalism that derive from liberalism and this type of republicanism. While liberalism cannot conceive of a nation horizontally, because it cannot possibly imagine all the individuals composing it, republicanism is removed enough from individualism to conceive of national, even international, communities extensively. It is mostly in black-authored texts that this type of republican vision informed the appeal to sentiment couched in representations of slavery.[33]

Many black writers used a liberal humanist approach in order to reach their readers' hearts and encourage identification, creating interior links while de-emphasizing their own blackness.[34] Recognition through interior connection is a leitmotif, as these texts often display a nervous avoidance of a corporeal difference that can pop up at any time and ruin the sympathetic process. Some critics have identified this limitation. Susan M. Ryan refers to the model's "tension between the erasure of difference and its stubborn resurgence" (18). As Glenn Hendler puts it, "if I have to *be* like you and *feel* like you in order for you to feel *for* me, sympathy reaches its limits at the moment you are reminded that I am not quite like you" (8). The concurrent growth of liberal feeling and disembodiment made the attendant politics both liberatory and constricting, and these political subtleties inform many black texts about slavery.[35]

Charging liberal sentiment with political ambiguity is certainly not new, but while this charge has been repeatedly made against white humanitarianism as embodied in, say, *Uncle Tom's Cabin*, it has not been clearly made against slave narratives. Thomas L. Haskell, for example, argues that humanitarianism developed not out of self-interest or a desire for social control, as Michel Foucault and David Brion Davis have theorized to various degrees, but as a natural consequence of new "cognitive structures" ("Capitalism" 111) that arose from the expansion of capitalism, such as a sense of personal responsibility and a desire to attend the long-term consequences of one's actions. If Haskell is right, this ambient ideology must have suffused the whole culture, affecting blacks and whites alike. This phenomenon would partly account for the way in which liberalism played an increasingly significant role in black-authored texts.

But using liberal sympathy is not the only way in which black texts appealed to readers' feelings. Many texts also show an attempt to acknowledge and represent difference, and to appeal to readers on that basis. In this republican sentiment, sympathy does not depend solely on an individual, interior connection of similarity; it acknowledges the separateness of identity and needs. While in texts such sympathy may be enacted in moments of intersubjective identification, its ideological ramifications extend from the individual to a community. Just as republicanism is open to radicalization through an extension of the notion of common good, many of the texts discussed in this book extend the possibilities of imagination, using feeling to initiate in readers a kind of imaginary process unlike the one involved in Smithian sympathy. This form of feeling gathers its tropes from realms of egalitarian connection, such as the male bonding of sailors or Freemasons, or simply from the language of community and citizenship. John Saillant, for example, looks at texts that enact a particular form of relationship between black men and white men; those texts were "not antirepublican, but rather the result of a different understanding of the connections among race, sentiment, and republicanism" ("Black Body" 91). This form of feeling resisted disembodiment, and provided black writers with a language that allowed them to fight slavery with more radical tools.[36]

The interdependence of emotional and political rhetorics is especially important and visible in Black Atlantic texts because the suffering and the necessary political change were so great. Texts about slavery and the slave trade regularly appealed to feelings about individuality, autonomy, and family, which were indirectly related to such issues as the role of the state, free trade, and international relations. Slavery forced writers to define or redefine basic concepts such as freedom and the law, and to envisage a future for their society after abolition. Feeling in black abolitionist texts was thus an extremely sensitive barometer of black political thought. This thought also showed significant differences between black writers on each continent, a distinction that partly reflects different racial attitudes in America and in England. African Americans like James Albert Ukawsaw Gronniosaw, Wheatley, or Hammon predominantly relied on liberal sentiment, but some also included in their writings isolated moments of republican sentiment. In the nineteenth century, the influence of liberal individualism on the American writers became even stronger, as can be seen in slave narratives by authors ranging from William Grimes and Charles Ball to Douglass. Afro-British writers such as Sancho, Cugoano, Equiano, and Mary Prince reflected a British search for a more coherent integration of freedom and the common good than the Americans sought.

Black Atlantic Sentiment and Cosmopolitanism

The radical possibilities of republicanism, I argue, most often took shape in an international or cosmopolitan outlook that was unique to Black Atlantic texts. Black writers did know some form of national feeling—whether it was Wheatley, who strongly identified with a nation in the making, or Equiano, who felt significantly British—and it is a major part of this book's argument that they found much of their political inspiration in the national culture. Most of these writers, however, were conscious of their link to the world outside the national space, and some of them traveled to investigate it. Many nineteenth-century slave narratives lost some of this larger perspective, as the prominence of the Mason and Dixon line indirectly reinforced national thinking, but even with these writers the transcultural element in their knowledge and experience lent a certain radical dimension to their political vision. The intention here is not to celebrate a transnational consciousness, forgetting that it was often acquired through the violence of the Middle Passage, but to identify the political perspective it afforded these writers.

Associating eighteenth-century black writers with cosmopolitanism may seem ill-advised. Enlightenment cosmopolitanism is often denigrated either for its passivity, as it calls up the image of leisurely *flâneurs* traveling the world with phlegmatic detachment, or for its ethnocentrism, since the notion of a global humanity united by a common rationality suffered from the biases of Enlightenment thought. Inspired by both classical stoicism, which encouraged seeing oneself primarily as a "citizen of the world," and by the liberal values anchored in individualism and natural rights, members of a Western social and intellectual elite tended to project their own values onto the world. Their cultural sensitivity and their defense of individual dignity are a positive result of the growth of liberal thought in the eighteenth century. But it was also abstract, detached, and blind to the real effects of power. Samuel Johnson's dictionary defined a cosmopolitan plainly as "a citizen of the world; one who is at home in every place." The French *Encyclopédie* apparently saw something funny in it: "On se sert quelquefois de ce nom en plaisantant, pour signifier *un homme qui n'a point de demeure fixe*, ou bien *un homme qui n'est étranger nulle part*."[37] To some extent, this kind of cosmopolitanism was part of black writers' cultural and political makeup, less in the sense that they felt at home in the world—they did not, and part of my argument is that their cosmopolitanism precisely did away with the fraught concept of "home"—than in that their perspective was worldly.[38]

I argue, however, that most often the cosmopolitan feeling displayed by these writers was unique in its expansiveness and its inclusiveness, and that this inclusiveness was made possible by their republicanism.[39] The black writers discussed here had multiple anchorings, and a consciousness and knowledge of the diverse world outside the nation and across the Atlantic, which allowed them imaginatively to step outside national boundaries and look back critically at their own condition. These writers perceived an international community rather than an extension of liberal national feeling. The international for them was not a repository of alien or foreign entities, or a hierarchical chain of nations, at least not to the same extent that it was for mainstream white writers. Because their national feeling was unstable and politically complex, it dissolved easily when set in the context of an international space. For some, their international identity was the primary one. If Prince Hall, whom I discuss in chapter 3, thoroughly adhered to American middle-class values, his Freemason's ideals reinforced a primary identity that reached across space and time toward his "brothers." A republican identity that has already embraced the diversity of the nation can also embrace the increased diversity of the transnational as a change in degree and not in kind. What we saw as the psychology of republican sentiment can be extended wholesale across borders, and this is what many of the black writers did as they envisioned the world as a myriad of differences.[40]

I want to briefly turn to Bruce Robbins' 1999 book *Feeling Global: Internationalism in Distress* because it deals with this particular challenge of thinking through an internationalism anchored in feeling. Robbins starts by criticizing traditional internationalism, which is based on rational universality. Instead, he advocates one in which "forms of global feeling are continuous with forms of national feeling" (282). To him, globalism should spring from feeling, and one cannot feel for the world unless one sees the world as an extension of the nation. He criticizes Susan Sontag for her 1995 article in the *Nation*, "A Lament for Bosnia," in which she tries to elicit action in solidarity with the sufferers in Bosnia at the time. Pointing out that her piece was received with mixed feelings and was found preachy, he deplores her "cold" appeal to "self-transcendence" (22). His own concept of internationalism, which he calls "cultural cosmopolitanism" because of its "emphasis on individuals rather than collectivities" (17), starts from the premise that "for better or worse, internationalism demands feeling as well as knowing" (16). Yet it acknowledges and accepts the fact that people cannot easily be made to feel for distant others. So he develops a concept in tandem with the recent rehabilitation of nationalism, which aims at integrating "the emotional power of culture" (18) into a cosmopolitanism that has heretofore been seen as remote from local cultural manifestations. According to Robbins, we should find a way to make cosmopolitanism feel like "an extension of existing interests, affections, and loyalties" (22). Robbins' vocabulary typically associates the Sontag type of internationalism with transcendence, elevation, distance, while his own concept speaks to notions of extension, continuity, displacement. The opposition may sound familiar to literary critics, and indeed, in a later chapter, he refers to each concept of cosmopolitanism respectively as "metaphor" and "metonymy" (86).

But those associations are misplaced. In fact, I wish to argue, Robbins' model relies much more on liberal forms of transcendence than the universal model represented by Sontag. According to Robbins, we need "an internationalist ethics of the everyday," one that is "rooted in routine duties and pleasures," "made part of ordinary culture" (23) because "internationalism properly conceived does not require a fight to the death with the new nationalism" (24). Rather than using the discourse of disinterestedness, the new internationalism could use self-interest profitably.[41] Robbins attempts to extend the liberal individualist psychology of sentiment to an international scale. This politics proposes to elicit an interior emotional connection with an individual or a concept. But contrary to his assertions, Robbins' model is not horizontal. Precisely because it starts from the concept of compassion, it needs individual transcendence in order to travel. Sontag does not advocate this kind of emotional transcendence. She bases her appeal on a sense of duty and, more importantly, a feeling of solidarity. She presents the need for Western intellectuals' involvement in Bosnia to effect the comprehensive construction of a just and democratic Europe. Her references to twentieth-century European history, whether to the Spanish Civil War or to the two world wars, underscore this extensive vision. What some readers of her piece may experience as a certain smugness on her part, in the way she indirectly highlights her own courage, should not detract from her main message that "no one can be unaware that the Bosnian cause is that of Europe: democracy, and a society composed of citizens, not of the members of a tribe" (819). Her repeated links between "here" and "there" reveal the republican horizontality of her universalism: to her, nationalist complacency undermines international solidarity and world citizenship. There is much feeling in her piece, but not of the kind that Robbins advocates.

Cosmopolitanism can be anchored in some kind of feeling while avoiding the limitations of liberal individualism. What Robbins sees as the religious fervor of international environmentalism, for example, can be based on a sense of urgency provoked by a scientific assessment of the earth's present and future resources, and is thus a more "horizontal" feeling than an approach that seeks to establish an alliance between individual or national hedonism and ecology.[42] More specifically, emphasizing Martha Nussbaum's reference to love in the last sentence of her essay "Patriotism and Cosmopolitanism" thoroughly misrepresents her argument. In her plea for a cosmopolitan curriculum Nussbaum appeals to notions such as "a reasonable and principled cosmopolitanism," an "allegiance to what is morally good" (3), the "point of view of justice and the good" (4), and an attitude that "puts right before country, and universal reason before the symbols of national belonging" (6). When, in the endnote referencing Nussbaum's article, Robbins adds that her "defense of 'universal reason' does not seem necessary to her defense of cosmopolitanism" (189), he again misreads what is an essential ingredient of her project. Nussbaum advocates a cosmopolitanism partly based on reason and duty—and this includes, among others, an ecologism that "requires global planning, global knowledge, and the recognition of a shared future" (6). In fact, she is very critical of a nationalism that "substitutes a colorful idol for the substantive universal values of justice and right" (3). Her theory does indeed give feeling pride of place, but her feeling is one of horizontal and englobing solidarity rather than the vertical emotion of idolatry, and her concept of love is more complex than the one Robbins relies on, both because it focuses on the global rather than the local[43] and because it directly leads to her more recent critique of contractarianism as applied to global issues.[44]

When I present the black writers discussed in this book as exhibiting cosmopolitan feeling, I emphasize their search for a complex form of "love" that can effect a republican transcendence by envisioning the world with its complex differences. These authors do realize that trying to elicit feeling for beings who are different and far away is a difficult task. So it is often in their representation of small interactions that they place the germs of their wider vision. When Gronniosaw describes the beauty of a French gentleman made prisoner by the captain, he describes a single individual, but the scene has larger implications. The real look at the face of the other offers a model of global thinking that goes beyond the vague, neutral pieties of liberal cosmopolitanism. It proposes an active form of "love." When Equiano develops a notion of diasporic identity as anchored in negotiation and exchange, in an attempt to squeeze out of both colonialist discourses and romantic notions of African purity, he attempts to create a new form of cosmopolitanism, anchored in forms of caring and giving that also imply a recognition of difference and of equality. When Marrant and Hall use brotherhood as a rallying concept, its internationalization allows them to develop new visions of interracial, global communities. Afro-British Robert Wedderburn even pushes brotherhood to its radical limits in his mixture of abolitionism and cosmopolitan, interracial communism. The black writers who people the following pages show a formidable imagination fostered by a unique social, cultural, and political status. They constitute a highly idiosyncratic strand in the era's movement toward "becoming modern."

The book follows a roughly chronological order, tracing the development of liberal and republican sentiment in texts about slavery on both sides of the Atlantic, and broadly showing how this double ideological presence (in chapters 1, 2, and 3) led to a predominance of liberalism (in chapters 4 and 5). It sketches out a subtle development in the manifestations of each political philosophy, by focusing on what I found to be prominent images and themes, which usually come through wrapped in the language of sentiment: liberalism found its expression in themes that range from human interiority, to individual and national agency, to contractarianism and individual entrepreneurship; republicanism can be detected in images of physical beauty, world citizenship, and, more radically, communist brotherhood. A cross-racial, cosmopolitan consciousness informs many of the republican moments. Because these images and themes also appeared, though often with less egalitarian implications, in mainstream culture, I start each chapter by briefly examining their manifestations there, as a way to paint a broad canvas against which the black texts will stand out. Each chapter deals with African American and Afro-British texts consecutively.[45]

Chapter 1 focuses on the interplay between a sentimental discourse of interiority, as can be found in some religious appeals as well as in emotional appeals to natural rights, and a discourse of exteriority expressed through aesthetic feeling. It argues that Gronniosaw and Wheatley, while mostly adhering to liberal forms of interiority, also occasionally happen to display a feeling for exterior beauty that suggests an alternative world of republican, cross-racial and cross-cultural recognition and equality, even if they do not ultimately reconcile their aesthetic visions with their fundamental outlook. Afro-Briton Sancho, on the other hand, integrates his sense of an aesthetic realm into visions of balance and exchange that, through his interracial view of community, sound new and sometimes even radical.

Chapter 2 uncovers an alternation between a liberal feeling for a national identity, expressed through an emphasis on individual agency, and a hankering for a self-identification as a world citizen. Interestingly, this debate takes place in three black writers who were very much acquainted with international trade as well as with the world of sailors, the latter being a breeding ground for internationalized identities and cross-racial egalitarianism. While it is fleeting in Hammon's narrative, this cosmopolitan feeling informs the works of Equiano and Cugoano in a way that makes their global vision unique at the time.

Chapter 3 examines the high point of republican radicalism at the turn from the eighteenth to the nineteenth centuries, as it found expression in a special form of emotion, the sense of brotherhood. It looks at cosmopolitan ideologies of brotherhood that developed among black American Freemasons, on the one hand, and in the writings of Robert Wedderburn, a black man from Jamaica who spoke for communal land ownership, on the other. While the Americans mostly retained middle-class ideals typical of Freemasons, and endowed brotherhood with a sometimes unpredictable alternation of liberal and republican meanings, Wedderburn pushed the British combination of freedom and the common good to radical extremes.

Chapter 4 shows that sentiment in the nineteenth-century slave narrative became increasingly liberal as the authors tried to negotiate the representation of bodily pain either through suppression, as in William Grimes and Charles Ball, or through objectification, as in Moses Roper and James Williams, of the human body. These authors also emphasized themes linked to a liberal viewpoint, such as social contracts and blood ties. Still, in this transitional period before *Uncle Tom's Cabin*, republicanism keeps reappearing sporadically in several African American narratives, in moments that force the reader to feel and think beyond the by then predominant liberal ethos. Narratives by Lewis and Milton Clarke, Josiah Henson, Henry Box Brown, and James W. Pennington all show this difficult negotiation of liberalism and a more communitarian vision. Mary Prince conveys a British mixture of the two ideologies, but like black Afro-Britons before her, she also radicalizes the combination.

Chapter 5 shows the prominent role of liberal feeling in the writings of this era's foremost African American thinker, even as it identifies some remnants of republicanism before his major publications of the 1850s. Through the almost exclusive emphasis on individual and natural rights, Douglass ushered in the liberal standpoint that would mark the politics of race relations for many years to come.

Chapter 1

Interiority, Aesthetics, and Antislavery Sentiment

This chapter explores the simultaneous presence of the themes of interiority and aesthetics in the sentimental rhetoric of American and British antislavery appeals, and it reads them as respectively invoking different political ideas. Placing interiority and aesthetics at opposite angles may seem surprising, considering our modern association of aesthetics with subjective experience.[1] But the interpretations offered here show that expressions of aesthetic feeling in antislavery texts often contributed to redirecting the gaze beyond the individual self toward a fuller perception of the outside world. The liberal emphasis on interiority in antislavery writings, through a discourse anchored either in notions of a similar human core and of universal natural rights, or in some expressions of religious sentiment, helped to counter racist assertions that highlighted bodily difference. Yet it also revealed its weakness and its limitations precisely because of its supposed inattention to outwardness, the exterior, the surface. Over against this focus on interiority, one occasionally finds an aesthetic discourse that directed the gaze at exterior or physical beauty. Better equipped against the almost irresistible forces of illiberalism, especially in an age when aesthetics played a significant role in the dynamics of racism, this aesthetic streak could have a progressive political effect by providing readers with a concrete, positive glimpse of a republican, multiracial, multicultural community.[2]

Observed through these themes, the white novel of sentiment on both sides of the Atlantic may be said to have shown a clear investment in the workings of interior liberal sympathy, even as it left some room for republican solidarity. In spite of their official endorsement of a republican worldview, the American novels conveyed enthusiasm for the possibilities of liberal individualism surging up in the new nation, and the authors seemed unable or reluctant to merge those political philosophies. Sympathy, which in Adam Smith functioned as a correspondence between two interior worlds, reached delirious, and even incestuous, heights, as it transported its subjects into a world of intensity and passion. The British culture of sentiment seemed more open to an integration of liberal and republican tendencies, or to a combination of interior worlds and exterior forces.

Three black writers used the themes of interiority and aesthetics explicitly in their appeals to feeling, but they offered an idiosyncratic take on those themes. Two African American writers, James Albert Ukawsaw Gronniosaw and Phillis Wheatley, were obviously inspired by both religious belief and the discourse of natural rights, and anchored many of their emotional appeals in the logic of interiority inherent in those ideologies. While Gronniosaw gives an extensive description of his religious conversion, Wheatley offers grand visions of the religious sublime. But my analysis also highlights points of divergence from that kind of emotionality, and especially the ways in which, for both writers, modes of aesthetic feeling helped to smuggle in a different political consciousness. Directing the reader's emotion toward the outward features and appearance of both nature and human beings, these writers attempted to create an appreciation of the other that is not based exclusively on interior similarity, but makes possible a recognition of external difference. The association of this external difference with beauty, and its integration into the reader's emotional world, suggest a politics of recognition and inclusion, and an acceptance of otherness within a communitarian vision. Gronniosaw and Wheatley occasionally forced the reader to move from interior to exterior, hence proposing a vision more complex than the liberal one, and better equipped to deal with the vagaries of difference. It is the writers' international and cosmopolitan experience, moreover, that allowed them to develop this ideology, and the feelings to express it. Unlike in the writings of the Afro-British writer Ignatius Sancho, however, the liberal and republican impulses tended to remain separate, and did not lead to a coherent whole. Sancho, on the other hand, strove to achieve a unique "balancing act."

Interiority, Aesthetics, and the White Novel of Sentiment

In William Hill Brown's *The Power of Sympathy* (1789) Worthy and Myra, the ideal republican couple, are linked by an aesthetic sensibility that suggests that worldview. When Worthy remarks to Mrs. Holmes on the beauty of nature, she points out to him that Myra used to admire those very scenes, and that a "secret sympathy" makes them "entertain the same predilection." She then mentions a piece of embroidery in the temple that she has seen him observe many times, reminding him that "'it was executed by the hand of *Myra*'" (W. Brown 30). Worthy continues his letter to Myra: "I ACKNOWLEDGE I have often *gazed* upon it (as Mrs. Holmes terms it) but did not recollect it to be a piece of your work. I stole an opportunity to revisit it by myself, and I instantly remembered it—I remembered when you finished it" (30–31). He concludes: "I CONSIDERED the work as coming from your hand, and was delighted the more with it. A piece of steel that has been rubbed with a loadstone, retains the power of attracting small bodies of iron: So the beauties of this embroidery, springing from your hands, continue to draw my attention, and fill the mind with ideas of the artist." In this passage, Worthy displays a searching quality in his perception of beauty, in his focus on the beauty of the piece itself and on its emotional significance. Both observing its outward shapes and retracing their origin,[3] he expands his emotional world toward the aesthetic qualities of the object he observes. His image for the force that binds him to Myra is that of magnetism, an apt metaphor for the attraction that brings different bodies closer together. Here the perception of beauty leads to an appreciation of both the similarities that connect and the differences that make attraction elating. The singular, exterior beauty of the embroidery in particular spurs an appreciative interrogation of appearance, suggesting an ethic able to celebrate difference rather than repress it.

The novel contrasts this republican sensibility with another, more complacent, less open to difference, and rather suggestive of liberal sympathy. In his very first letter Harrington announces himself as a reader of bodies, one who can interpret a blush, and for whom a look or a glance provides "more divine information to the soul of sensibility, than can be contained in myriads of volumes" (9–10). For Harrington the body is a mere sign, which provides easy access to an inside realm. He is applying the lessons of physiognomy, which sees the body as a direct and faithful reflection of its interior.[4] In another significant passage, Harrington tells of a trip to South Carolina, during which he asked a female slave about the origin of a scar on her shoulder. When she explained that she chose to receive punishment in order to protect her child, Harrington praised her, hoping that her "soul be ever disposed to SYMPATHIZE with thy children, and with thy brethren and sisters in calamity." He continues: "I WAS sensibly relieved as I pronounced these words, and I felt my heart glow with feelings of exquisite delight." Indeed, "what delightful sensations are those in which the heart is interested!" He concludes with an encomium to sensibility: "HAIL *Sensibility*! Sweetener of the joys of life! . . . *Sensibility* is the good *Samaritan*" (62). Harrington is elated by the rewards of his Smithian sympathy. He enjoys the righteousness of his own feelings, unencumbered by the reality of the slave mother's suffering. He does not share her suffering; he shares only in what he sees to be the nobility of her self-sacrifice for her children. Because his sympathy is strictly based on a correspondence between two interiorities, the essence of his identity subsumes the real experience of this woman. The focus on interiority even threatens to devolve into narcissism.

The predominance of interiority and self-referentiality in Harrington's sentimental experience also characterizes his love story with Harriot — a story that constitutes the tragic and forceful element at the heart of the novel, and represents the "power of sympathy" referred to in the title. Their story supposedly acts as a warning against the perils of seduction, since Harriot was born of Harrington's father's relationship with her mother. The sheer power of their love, however, subtly sends a different message, urging the readers to feel sympathy for an incestuous couple. Suddenly interiority and similarity go hand in hand, and sentiment keeps them together. Cathy N. Davidson warns that here sympathy has a "menacing underside," embodied in the "irresistible and ultimately tragic attraction" of incest (*Revolution* 109). Elizabeth Barnes explains that this "dangerous capacity" of sympathy "to undermine the democratic principles it ostensibly means to reinforce" is based on "a politics of affinity," and that sentimental literature "relies on likeness and thereby reinforces homogeneity" (4). Barnes' comment nicely captures the political implications of Smithian sympathy. An obsessive focus on internal similarity as a ground for caring can have dangerous consequences. Unlike republican homosocial homogeneity, which relies on a notion of the communal good and can be expanded to heterogeneous communities, liberal sameness finds its root at the core of the individual and cannot be shaken easily. The love between Worthy and Myra was part of a wider statement about a perfect republican society.⁵ The power of liberal sympathy in the case of Harrington and Harriot represents, not the magnetic power that brings different bodies closer, but the attraction of same to same on an interior, individual level.⁶

Through these differences in the quality of their sentimental experience, the two couples represent two separate political visions with little apparent common ground, and the two ideologies imply different aesthetic receptivities. Worthy and Myra are associated with life at Belleview, a beautiful property away from the "bustle and parade" (W. Brown 15) of the city, which mirrors a combination of a healthy enjoyment of the countryside with the intellectual stimulation of conversation. It symbolizes the "real charms of economy and simplicity" (74), which should lead people, especially impressionable young women, away from the superficial pleasures of a fashionable life and put them on the right path to virtue. And virtue here has republican connotations, as it refers more to a dedication to the common good than to the strictly moral concept it would soon develop into.⁷ Harrington and Harriot are motivated by an ethic that is ruled by the power of individual, inner attraction, and it is this form of feeling that constitutes the core of the more engrossing plotline of the novel. Brown seems to have felt, as Robert D. Arner points out, some "confusion concerning the role of emotion" (122) in his novel. Arner opposes Richardsonian emotion, which is morally informed, to Sternean sensibility, which "revelled in emotions for their own sake" (121), equating this opposition with that between the head and the heart. Whether or not Brown was aware of this split, and whether or not Arner's characterization of Samuel Richardson and Laurence Sterne is correct, the novel does reveal separate emotional and political strands in the early American novel.⁸

The split between interiority and aesthetics—which signals this division in the political valence of sentiment in the eighteenth century—and the appreciation of the former over the latter, would remain an important feature of American sentimental culture well into the nineteenth century. The increased focus on interiority was an effect of Enlightenment interest in human nature. As Roy Porter puts it, "the understanding of selfhood in general and of the individual self in particular meant prioritizing interiority" (163).⁹ Karen Halttunen has demonstrated the importance of the concept of sincerity to antebellum sentimentalists, and how this concept shaped views of beauty and appearance. To *Godey's Lady's Book*, the most famous American women's magazine of the time, "the concept of personal beauty" was "the sentimental ideal of transparency" (Halttunen 71). Following the rules of physiognomy, a woman's dress had to directly reflect her inner character; it had to make the viewer forget about the physical shell, and give direct access to the inner self. "Whereas classical dress had focused attention on the body," says Halttunen, "sentimental dress effaced it" (79). Notions of beauty were directly connected to the idea of interiority: "true beauty, according to the sentimentalists, came from within" (82). Dress had to "translate purely the inner character into outward forms" (90). American sentimental culture clearly valued interiority at the expense of sensual, aesthetic pleasure.[10]

But the eighteenth century also saw the birth of aesthetics as both a distinct discipline and a popular cultural interest, and while it affected sentimental culture on both sides of the Atlantic, it seems to have found a better integration into British culture at the time.[11] Of course, aesthetics involved a degree of preoccupation with interiority, especially since its theoreticians, such as Francis Hutcheson and David Hume, tended increasingly to explain perceptions of beauty as subjective phenomena. But beauty for its own sake, the sheer interest in shapes and colors, acquired admirers. In England, aesthetics received a boost thanks to the birth of the picturesque as promoted by William Gilpin. Nature and landscapes were no longer appreciated exclusively for their moral connotations or emblematic significance, but became sources of sheer aesthetic and sensual pleasure as well. While British culture certainly promoted the discourse of interiority, it seemed more open to a combination of it with an appreciation of exterior beauty, and one can see in this mix the reflection of a search for emotional and political balance that marks many other British texts of that time period.

Interiority and White American Antislavery Writing

Through its frequent emotional appeals to both religious values and natural rights, eighteenth-century white American antislavery writing was replete with discourses of interiority. While helping to promote abolition, however, these discourses also contained the weaknesses of a supposedly neutral liberal humanism that can easily slip into illiberalism. Natural rights theory proved useful but also limited because its anchoring in the idea of a presocial state could relieve it of responsibility in issues of contemporary society. Both Hugo Grotius and Samuel Pufendorf had been able to reconcile natural law with an acceptance of slavery as, though "not a product of nature" (D. Davis, *Western Culture* 115), still compatible with "external right" (115–16). Another major source of inspiration for antislavery thought, religion was also most often grounded in individual interiority.[12] For many centuries the conviction that spiritual freedom transcended slavery of the body underlay an acceptance of slavery by many Christians. Only in the seventeenth century did the notion of "spiritual equality" and "inward purity" as opposed to "external distinctions" (338) spark the desire to change human institutions. Initially several Protestant commentators, such as Morgan Godwyn, argued the spiritual equality of blacks and whites, not in support of the abolition of slavery, but to demand the Christianization of slaves. The curbing of slaveholders' liberty aimed less at the establishment of a new social order than at promoting the individual spiritual well-being of enslaved persons. In the end, both religious and rights-based white antislavery discourses used feeling and sympathy in order to advocate liberty for blacks, but they rarely involved a call for solidarity and equality.

In the first white American antislavery text of the eighteenth century, Samuel Sewall displays a strikingly liberal attitude, as he combines an emotional appeal to natural rights with contractual language. He begins *The Selling of Joseph: A Memorial* (1700) with a ringing endorsement of liberty: "*Forasmuch as* Liberty *is in real value next unto* Life: *None ought to part with it themselves, or deprive others of it, but upon most mature Consideration.*"[13] All men, he continues, "have equal Right unto Liberty, and all other outward Comforts of Life" (7).[14] Adam received a "Title" from God which "doth infinitely better Mens Estates," and "grants them a most beneficial and inviolable Lease under the Broad Seal of Heaven, who were before only Tenants at Will"; through God's indulgence after the fall, "the outward Estate of all and every of their Children, remains the Same, as to one another." Because of this generous contractual agreement with God, "Originally, and Naturally, there is no such thing as Slavery" (8). The sellers of Joseph were wrong, since "there is no proportion between Twenty Pieces of Silver, and LIBERTY. The Commodity it self is the Claimer" (9). Sewall seems to espouse a Lockean view, in which the producer cannot logically be a product of his or her own labor, and the use of commodities constitutes an important part of what makes humans free agents. In order to make that view quite clear for his reader, Sewall cannot quote the biblical statement that "*God hath given the Earth . . .*

unto the Sons of Adam" without inserting the additional clarification "[with all its Commodities]" (8). The biggest font is reserved for his warning "Caveat Emptor!" or "Let the buyer beware!"—an appeal to the slaveholder's conscience as a shopper and consumer of human commodities.

But the appeal to interior as well as contractual rights cannot hide the emotional conservatism attendant to these liberal ideals, and the pamphlet is also suffused with anti-egalitarianism. Sewall acknowledges that former slaves "can seldom use their freedom well." Hovering between their aspirations for liberty and their inability to use their freedom responsibly, the blacks occupy a space both created and looked down on by a liberal individualist outlook. Moreover, "there is such a disparity in their Conditions, Colour & Hair, that they can never embody with us, and grow up into orderly Families, to the Peopling of the Land: but still remain in our Body Politick as a kind of extravasat Blood" (10).[15] There is a logic of similarity at work in this apparent discourse of pity that clearly sees the black body as alien to the white "Body Politick," and unable to achieve citizenship. Smithian sympathy, through its embeddedness in the work of imagination, simultaneously encourages an interior sense of compassion and humanity, and prevents the expansion of that sensibility into an all-encompassing, multiracial national realm. In a view that anticipates the logic of liberal sentiment that will culminate in *Uncle Tom's Cabin*, which famously ends by sending its main characters off to Africa, black people who are not enslaved need to be expelled from the white nation.

Most of the white-authored eighteenth-century antislavery texts used the appeal to sympathy in both human rights and religious arguments to emphasize an inner similarity in people, simultaneously avoiding the issue of racial difference. Many of these arguments were so often blended together that Winthrop D. Jordan points out "the impossibility of getting them thoroughly disentangled." Especially striking, though, is the "commingling of natural rights theory with religious affirmations of equality." The minutes of a Methodist conference in Virginia in 1784, for example, assert that they view slavery as "'contrary to the Golden Law of God on which hang all the Law and the Prophets, and the unalienable Rights of Mankind, as well as every Principle of the Revolution.'" At the same time, Jordan adds, "a theme of humanitarian empathy could easily accompany orthodox natural rights theory" (293). By the time of the Revolution, "the right to liberty was normally spoken of as God's gratuitous gift to mankind, as an endowment by the Creator" (294). It is the emphasis on interiority that made these two arguments overlap so easily. The emotional energy mobilized in both approaches privileged and trusted the interior, leaving the exterior vulnerable to immediate or unconscious illiberal tendencies.

It is mainly among the Quakers that we find the first stirrings of this liberal antislavery feeling.[16] With the Quakers, interiority played an important role: the Inner Light might strike anyone regardless of race; moreover, getting rid of slavery slowly became synonymous with an internal purification of the sect.[17] Some very early Quaker voices, even as they based their antislavery stance on Christian compassion, sounded an already strikingly liberal message of sympathy. Fiery George Keith built his 1693 pamphlet on the notion that, since Jesus Christ had been sent to redeem humankind, all humans deserved "Liberty both inward and outward"; true Christians should show "*Love, Mercy, Goodness, and Compassion*" toward the oppressed, and refuse to traffic in slaves. At the heart of his faith-based plea is the Golden Rule, "*To do to others what we would have others do to us*" (Bruns 6). A similar message had already informed a historic petition signed by several Germantown Friends in 1688. Here, though, the authors more clearly appealed to the readers' feelings, reminding them of "how fearful and fainthearted are many on sea, when they see a strange vessel," a sign that Turks might be about to catch and enslave them. Similarly, how would the readers feel if they saw their families separated as do these poor creatures? The appeal to sympathy is here harnessed to resonant declarations of natural rights: Africans are "brought hither against their will and consent"; a country that values "liberty of conscience, wch is right and reasonable," should also practice "liberty of ye body"; honest people deserve a similar treatment, "making no difference of what generation, descent or colour they are" (Bruns 3).[18]

In Robert Piles' 1698 "Paper about Negroes," the avoidance of racial exterior difference by appeals to interior similarity manifests both strengths and weaknesses from a liberationist perspective. Piles describes his moral hesitation following his decision to "buy a negro" (9). At one point he has a dream in which, traveling on a road with a friend, he sees a black pot by the wayside. Refusing to share it with his friend, he carries the pot until he comes upon a ladder standing upright. He realizes he will need both hands to climb it. When he wakes up, he decides to "lett black negroes or pots alone" (10). In this variation on Jacob's ladder, blacks represent what prevents the white man from reaching his own salvation, so that his motivation is self-interest disguised as benevolence. Piles' imaginative rejection of the black man who is symbolized by the pot precludes him from buying a slave but also signifies a rejection of blacks as equal. Black freedom is acceptable, but the image of blacks as personal companions on the way to heaven is not. When he suggests that blacks be encouraged to convert, he does show a desire to extend the benefits of the spiritual community to blacks. While the pot, whose blackness is a burden to him directly, leads to his decision to leave blacks "alone," his responsibility for their spiritual welfare motivates him to include them in that community. This duality of sentiment foreshadows Quaker attitudes toward blacks throughout the eighteenth century. The Friends would encourage black meetings and, in the South, provide slaves with means of escape and survival, but their own meetings would long remain segregated, and membership of blacks in white Quaker meetings would be deterred in subtle ways.[19] While the recourse to a higher law led some Quakers to a more radical stance, this early distinction between liberation and integration shows their alignment with a liberal abolitionist strategy.

A similar strategy characterizes the evangelical movements that grew in the eighteenth century. The New Divinity school of the Congregationalists (with adherents such as Samuel Hopkins and Jonathan Edwards, Jr.) as well as the Methodists (whether George Whitefield and the Huntingdon Connexion or John Wesley) all attracted huge numbers of blacks, and preached the general equality of blacks and whites in the eyes of their god. They had a "nominally egalitarian theology, rejecting race as a sign of Calvinist election or inelection" (Brooks, *American Lazarus* 31). Whitefield had personal connections with, and influence on, many African Americans. Yet Whitefield and the Huntingdon Connexion were proslavery; when they set up an orphanage in Georgia (after lobbying Parliament for the introduction of slavery in the colony), they bought slaves for it. American Methodists decreased their emphasis on antislavery rhetoric after they separated from the Church of England. Continued segregation and the refusal to ordain black preachers led to walkouts and the founding of separate black churches. New Divinity adherents evolved a "dispensationalist" vision of history, according to which slavery was part of a grand design toward godly perfection.[20] Overall, the religious emphasis on inner equality and humanity made some, but no decisive, inroads against racism.[21]

The last decades of the eighteenth century, which witnessed a remarkable increase in antislavery writings, saw a deepening of the liberal sensibility, but while the liberal theory of natural rights was argued to its logical, liberationist conclusion, it left unchanged the population's fundamental inability to care about black bodies. As Jordan shows, the notion of human rights combined with a relatively new way of thinking, environmentalism, in an attempt both to account for Africans' apparent lower state of civilization and to make mental equality between blacks and whites more visible. Benjamin Rush summarized that approach perfectly: "Human nature is the same in all Ages and Countries; and all the difference we perceive in its Characters in respect to Virtue and Vice, Knowledge and Ignorance, may be accounted for from Climate, Country, Degrees of Civilization, form of Government, or other accidental causes" (qtd. in Jordan 287). The idea became especially attractive at the time in that "this postulation of quintessential human nature formed the critical point of contact between environmentalist thinking and the political ideology of the Revolution" (289). Humanism, however, did not necessarily mean an acceptance of difference. Ever since Montesquieu had applied his sarcastic skills to the question, alleging that "one cannot get into one's mind that god, who is a very wise being, should have put a soul, above all a good soul, into a body that was entirely black" (*Spirit of the Laws* 250), several writers had discussed the specific issue of color prejudice. But, Jordan points out, the argument soon dried up, as "extending liberty to Negroes was enormously difficult simply because they did not look like other Americans" (279). So abolitionists turned their back on issues of the body rather than face the notion that "blackness meant that slavery could never really end" (280). Liberal sympathy had them backed into a corner.

That the incompatibility of natural rights and slavery could not be applied to both blacks and whites during the revolutionary period is therefore evidence, less of the hypocrisy of double standards, than of the feeble power wielded by the common interior denominator understood by "natural right," as principle was repeatedly trampled by real practice. In *The Rights of the British Colonies Asserted and Proved* (1764), James Otis, while defending the "natural rights of the colonists," acknowledges that it "is rather an abstract way of considering men," since "men come into the world and into society at the same time." Only through this "abstract consideration of men" have thinkers been able to "imagine some real general state of nature agreeable to this abstract conception, antecedent to and independent of society" (Bruns 103). The belief in natural rights results from an intellectual process of construction, or even of re-creation, that has its starting point in the social order, and posits those rights as existing prior to society. Otis' description conveys the stunning insight that natural rights might actually not be antecedent to society, but are rather the product of a highly sophisticated abstraction of thought.

This thought process painstakingly separates "society" from the natural state human beings are supposedly born into, gradually moving from outward social circumstances toward what constitutes a human interior core. In effect, it creates a nonsocial standard by which to judge social affairs. Otis' description accounts for the easy collaboration of natural rights with Smithian sympathy since it privileges the emotionality of the interior, the presocial. It also accounts for how, in its fragility and abstraction, the process became easy to assail.[22]

Most white antislavery writings during the revolutionary period show an awareness of this vulnerability, as they present accumulations of arguments, using liberal sympathy as the glue. In his 1767 essay, Arthur Lee selects passages from Montesquieu's *Spirit of the Laws* that tally with his own argument based on natural law. Montesquieu starts his chapter on slavery by refuting Aristotle's three arguments in favor of slavery: captivity through war; consenting to sell oneself; and being a slave's offspring. Lee focuses on the argument in which Montesquieu asserts that "it is not true that a freeman can sell himself." Africans do not "consent to be our slaves," since "the British Merchants obtain them from Africa by violence, artifice & treachery." Even though an act of Parliament allows it, it "could not of right assume even a shadow of authority" over them. "There cannot be in nature," he continues, "there is not in all history, an instance in which every right of men is more flagrantly violated." To these legal arguments anchored in natural law, Lee then adds the role of religion: Christians should be "humanized by its benevolence," and by its "Meekness, Charity, love, and justice to mankind." He tells the reader to "ask then your own Heart" and to "remember that God knoweth the heart," and that punishment awaits those who do not follow his will (109). Ultimately, "your temporal, your eternal wellfare" (110) depends on the abolition of slavery. He concludes the essay with apocalyptic warnings about slave rebellions. The arguments follow a common succession, where an awareness of the slave's inherent, interior right to freedom needs to be complemented by an appeal to the reader's feelings, interior state, and welfare. The strategy shows natural rights and liberal sympathy tied together through a web of interiority, supposed to hold strong against outside threats of rebellion.

Occasionally, one finds an approach with more republican overtones. In his 1773 *Address to the Inhabitants of the British Settlements in America upon Slave-Keeping*, Benjamin Rush takes pains to establish the equality of blacks and whites despite their differences in skin color, and, interestingly, he ventures into the realm of aesthetics. Speaking of blacks, he points out that "the ravages of heat, diseases and time, appear less in their faces than in a white one" (225). It is a very unusual statement for the time, obviously meant to induce an appreciation for the beauty and youthfulness of black skin. Since it appears in the middle of a social and political essay, this passage seems meant to encourage a vision of a multiracial community based on mutual recognition and appreciation. His comment on black faces is meant to defuse the white repugnance at the appearance of black skin, by associating that skin color with vitality and resilience. He understands that most whites have a visceral association of black skin with "darkness," and that any appeal he makes for equality through Smithian sympathy will only invite this immediate reaction. Only when his readers lose their learned reaction to black skin can they imagine blacks within their community of caring. In other words, if whites can suspend the imaginative reaction that Smithian ethics sanction, they can use imagination to expand their conception of community, as the republican ethic encourages.

Ultimately Rush thinks we need to "exclude variety of color from our ideas of Beauty" (225) before we can establish racial equality. Still, envisioning a society without slaves, he predicts that "the general product would be greater, although the profits to individuals would be less,—a circumstance this, which by diminishing opulence in a few, would suppress Luxury and Vice, and promote that equal distribution of property, which appears best calculated to promote the welfare of Society" (226). He advises to emancipate young blacks, give them instruction, and "entitle them to all the privileges of free-born British subjects" (229). His change of tone immediately thereafter, in his depiction of heart-wrenching scenes of separation and cruelty, serves the idea of mixed citizenship he has just expressed. He ends by advising readers to avoid laws "which allow exclusive privileges to men of one color in preference to another" (230), supporting his arguments with references to the Somerset decision and the English Constitution.[23] With this communitarian and transatlantic consciousness, Rush points to the possibilities of a more republican approach.

Black Variations on Interiority

Many texts written by black Americans during this period generally display emotional appeals to liberal individualist values. A January 1773 African American petition signed "Felix," and addressed to Governor of Massachusetts Thomas Hutchinson, the Council, and the House of Representatives, starts with a form of authentication by referring to the abolitionist agitation rising at the time both in England and in the colonies. Reminding the readers that God "is no respecter of Persons," he points out that that same God "hath lately put it into the Hearts of Multitudes on both Sides of the Water, to bear our Burthens, some of whom are Men of great Note and Influence; who have pleaded our cause with Arguments which we hope will have their weight with this Honorable Court." He then grounds his petition in a clearly liberal appeal to the readers' feelings about law, liberty, property, and nation. He first points out that blacks should be judged by laws like any other citizen, emphasizing that most of them are "discreet, sober, honest, and industrious," a plea that leads to an emotional climax: "We have no Property! We have no Wives! No Children! We have no City! No Country!" (Felix 6). Here the appeal to familial sentiment is framed by allegiance to the ideology of ownership as well as to national identity. At the same time, he reassures the reader that the petitioners have all intention to remain "obedient to our Masters," and that they "pray for such Relief only, which by no Possibility can ever be productive of the least Wrong or Injury to our Masters" (7).

The self-conceptualization of the petitioners as a "we," however, points to a black political framework that is slightly different from, and more communal than, the interiority of liberal individualism. An April 20, 1773, petition by four men, Peter Bestes, Sambo Freeman, Felix Holbrook, and Chester Joie, seems to adopt a liberal mindframe when its authors insist that they are devoted to "peaceable and lawful attempts to gain our freedom," suggesting that they are willing to work and earn the money necessary for their own purchase. Here they appeal to the reader's individual identification with their moral virtue, hoping that the sympathizer will recognize his or her own respect for law in it, and can then feel the suffering of someone denied justice under the law. But they end the petition by declaring their intention to resettle in Africa. As we will see throughout this book, black emigration (to Nova Scotia, to Sierra Leone) occurred for various reasons and in various circumstances, and so its political significance varies and each case needs to be evaluated individually. Since these petitioners do not offer a specific motivation or objective, apart from the desire to set up "a settlement," the emigration scheme almost sounds like an obvious, natural conclusion: "We are willing to submit to such regulations and laws, as may be made relative to us, until we leave the province" (Bestes et al. 8). This conclusion conveys the power of contractarianism, and a sense of respect for the "regulations and laws" that constitutes the foundation of a liberal state. Still, the desire to emigrate also stems from the goal of equality, and it evinces a certain cosmopolitan consciousness, and a more republican approach to the notion of freedom. We cannot track the ideology of this particular group more specifically, but this petition shows that while many black authors found they had to adopt the language of liberalism in order to pursue their goals, they also inserted a specific political difference.

The emotional invocation of freedom in texts written by black abolitionists in the late eighteenth and early nineteenth centuries contains a similar desire to move beyond liberal interiority. While, as we have seen, many white texts combined religious arguments with references to natural rights, black texts repeatedly displayed the tendency to enlarge the concept of freedom. An 1808 anonymous piece, "The Sons of Africans: An Essay on Freedom," written by a member of the African Society in Boston, starts with a long exegesis of relevant passages in Genesis, such as the selling of Joseph and the tyranny of Pharaoh. The author then refers to the ideals of the Revolution, as well as to the golden rule, a by then fairly conventional strategy: "Did not America think it [freedom] was a privilege truly desirable to be enjoyed, when her mother nation was about to invade her land, and bring her under their dominion" ("Sons" 18). But he then expands on the reasons why "freedom is desirable," by asserting that "a bound man, or slave, is prohibited from being beneficial to society," and that "we are social beings, and much of our happiness consisteth in those friendly interviews with each other" (19). While the former reason may smack of typical liberal arguments that appeal to a reader's sense of profitability rather than of justice, the context shows that the writer conceives of freedom as being part of a fundamentally social or communal ethic. Freedom is desirable, not just because it is the inner appurtenance of all human beings, but because it makes a shared social life possible. This remarkable text indicates that black writers in the late eighteenth and early nineteenth centuries found original ways to break out of the liberal mind-set, even as they used it to their advantage.[24]

The New England black preacher Lemuel Haynes similarly displays partly liberal tendencies. His essay "Liberty Further Extended," which dates from the second half of the 1770s, asserts the fundamental liberal principles of the Declaration of Independence, which he quotes at the beginning of the essay. These principles assume the similarity of people in some spiritual or natural essence. Haynes urges his audience to "turn one Eye into our own Breast" (17) and see that "Liberty, & freedom" are "an innate principle, which is unmovebly placed in the human Species," conforming to the "Laws of nature." This right is indifferent to color or national origin. Indeed, "Even an affrican, has Equally as good a right to his Liberty in common with Englishmen" (18). In order emotionally to convey this right, Haynes evokes scenes of separation of families, asking his reader to listen to the parents' "plaintive noats": "Do not I really hear the fond mother Expressing her Sorrows, in accents that mite well peirce the most obdurate heart?" (22). He also counters arguments in favor of slavery based on the Old Testament by arguing that the coming of Jesus Christ changed that old dispensation by internalizing the nature of religious belief. "Under the *Law*," he says, "their were many External Cerimonies that were tipecal of Spiritual things" (24). Thanks to Christ, the spirit has replaced undue attention to the external.[25] By ending with an appeal to "pity, and compassion," as well as to "Disinterested Benevolence" (29), Haynes establishes a close link between sentiment and the liberal ideals expressed throughout the essay.

But Haynes exhibits a somewhat different political personality in "The Nature and Importance of True Republicanism," a speech he delivered on July 4, 1801. Here Haynes makes clear that although the value of liberty remains fundamental, it needs to be complemented with what he calls a "generous regard to the community at large" (78). A man can be called great only if he shows a genuine love for the "interest of the commonwealth" and a "proper regard for the general good" (78). Haynes is keen to point out the difference between liberty and "licentiousness." His aim is to expound the ideas "that we ought to connect with Independence, Republicanism, Liberty." The ideal conveyed through those terms is "to defend and secure the natural rights of men."[26] But in order to maintain those rights, "we are to view them in their relation to society at large." Liberty can be achieved only within the object of the "*general good*" (79). Here Haynes shows an extremely sharp consciousness of the contemporary political debates. While he advocates a notion of liberty based on interiority, he also attaches to it the communal and social values that turn his philosophy into "true republicanism." Not only natural rights but also a genuine pursuit of "equality" (78) need to drive political thought. The republican feeling is here conveyed through the "bonds of friendship" (80), a form of sentiment that suits a political world that goes beyond the isolation of liberal interiority.

James Albert Ukawsaw Gronniosaw

James Albert Ukawsaw Gronniosaw's 1772 *Narrative* tells the story of a peripatetic life, with a protagonist—the author himself—who initially seems rather acculturated, an impression that the use of liberal sentiment helps confirm.[27] Gronniosaw appeals to sentiment in a sustained yet understated way, in order to elicit the reader's Smithian sympathy for both his physical hardships and his personal, religious struggle. He describes how, as a child in West Africa, he was made restless because of his personal intimations of the existence of a god, feelings that kept him isolated from his family and community. We also feel for him when, as a slave in New York, he struggles daily with his sense of undeservedness, until the final moment of rebirth and full conversion. After he moves to England, his economic hardships cannot but evoke compassion and a desire to help. This continuous reliance on the reader's sense of humanity follows a liberal logic of sympathy.

Liberal sympathy also suffuses the first important moment of transition in Gronniosaw's life, which occurs during childhood. After he is taken to the coast of Guinea, Gronniosaw has heard he will be put to death by the king. But as he is walking up to the king's throne, "it pleased God to melt the heart of the King, who sat with his scimitar in his hand ready to behead me; yet, being himself so affected, he dropped it out of his hand, and took me upon his knee and wept over me. I put my right hand round his neck, and pressed him to my heart" (39). The king decides the child will live, and be sold as a slave. The passage strongly implies that, through some divine inner power, the child has magically arrested the king's action. This upsurge of affect illustrates the transformative power of the child, the strength of his interior world—even if, ironically, it also marks his passage into slavery. The focus on the magical moment of connection between him and the king, rather than on its consequence, announces a shift toward an interiorization of his experience.

Similarly, the next segment of Gronniosaw's life, which takes place in New York, concentrates less on the exterior manifestations of the slavery establishment than on his intimate struggle with religious conversion. He pictures himself trying to find interior connections. When Mr. Freelandhouse, his master in New York, tells him that there is a god who "created all the world, and every person and thing in it" (Gronniosaw 42), Gronniosaw is filled with joy: "I was exceedingly pleased with this information of my master's, because it corresponded so well with my own opinion" (42), the one he had developed as a child in Africa. This sudden correspondence between his master's inner life and his own African one confirms for him the usefulness of searching his inner self, as well as personal connection. The moment confirms the value of Western individualism, which he had sensed as a child.

But the narrative also contains moments with a different sort of sensibility, one that forms a counterpart to his reliance on interiority. The trope of the Talking Book is a case in point.[28] The trope refers to a scene on the ship taking Gronniosaw as a child away from his homeland, when he sees the captain read from the Bible in public and fancies that he "saw the book talk to my master" (40). Later on, "when nobody saw me, I opened it and put my ear down close upon it, in great hope that it would say something to me; but [I] was very sorry and greatly disappointed when I found it would not speak; this thought immediately presented itself to me, that everybody and everything despised me because I was black" (40–41). To Henry Louis Gates, Jr., the text "does not 'recognize' Gronniosaw's presence and so refuses to share its secrets or decipher its coded message" (18). Because Gronniosaw is black, the text cannot see him, conveying the image of blackness as absence. Consequently, "this desire for recognition of his 'self' in the text of Western letters motivates Gronniosaw's creation of a text" (19), the narrative we are reading. Such a narrative is the black person's way of impelling recognition of himself or herself as a human presence, to "demonstrate her or his own membership in the human community" (9). I agree that the trope indirectly humanizes Gronniosaw. But when he thinks the book hates him because he is black, he presents himself less as an absence than as a despised presence, whose blackness he actually puts in the foreground. The gesture is not merely humanist; it forces the reader of Gronniosaw's narrative to confront the author's racial difference, and to go beyond an immediate negative reaction to it. It pushes the reader to access a republican sensibility in the culture, one that places white reader and black author within the same community without either of them relinquishing his or her sense of difference.

The gesture that forces readers to acknowledge difference is part of a pattern in the narrative that shifts the reader's feelings from interior to exterior, and more particularly to exterior beauty. When, in New York, Gronniosaw holds private conversations with God under an oak tree, the scene calls up a contrast between these sessions and his description of the

Interiority, Aesthetics, and Antislavery Sentiment 51

Africans' meetings under palm trees in the first segment of his life. In the African descriptions, although Gronniosaw consciously emphasizes his spiritual search, it is above all his aesthetic sensibility that comes through, with his references to the "beauty" of those "high and majestic" (35) trees, to the "very delicious" wine they give off, to the "silky nature" of their leaves, to their nuts whose milk is "very pleasant to the taste" and whose shell is "of a hard substance, and of a very beautiful appearance" (36). Similarly, as he is making the trek toward the coast with strangers, he cannot help noticing "a valley of marble that we came through which is unspeakably beautiful," where "some of the pieces of marble are of prodigious length and breadth but of different sizes and color, and shaped in a variety of forms, in a wonderful manner," some having "striking and beautiful colors," and the whole forming "as pleasing a sight as can be imagined" (38). This intense appreciation for the sheer beauty of forms and colors fades away in the westernized part of his life, as if the king's tears had marked a passage from consciousness and love of exterior signs toward a preoccupation with inner affect. But it highlights his capacity for an aesthetic vision that directs the gaze toward an awareness and an acceptance of the outward shape of things. While paradisiacal accounts of Africa were common in travel narratives, here the gaze seems to move away from liberal interiority, and to provide an aesthetic pleasure that could be harnessed to other cultural and political purposes.

Indeed, the second important transition in Gronniosaw's life, the one from America to England, contains a similarly suggestive affective moment, but one in which the aesthetic expansiveness he has created now applies to human appearance, and suggests a particular form of human community. Before reaching England, Gronniosaw spends time working as a cook on a British warship, during which they have several engagements with the French. At some point he interrupts his narrative to bemoan the cruelty of his captain toward "one young Gentleman" taken prisoner, whose treatment "grieved me to the heart." He emphasizes that the young man "appeared very amiable" and "was strikingly handsome." The captain stole his money, "took the buckles of his shoes, and untied his hair, which was very fine, and long." When Gronniosaw gave the gentleman something to eat and drink, "he was so thankful and pretty in his manner that my heart bled for him" (48). When he heard that the captain took the prisoner ashore and shot him, "this circumstance affected me exceedingly; I could not put him out of my mind [for] a long while" (48–49). While some critics see this episode as revealing Gronniosaw's infatuation with things white and Western, I think it can also be meant to convey that complex, full recognition of the other that remains fleeting in many narratives. This is not a case of simple charity, of the Good Samaritan, of individual sympathy. To Gronniosaw, the young gentleman is a complete package, whose form and color are as pleasing as the beautiful interior he surmises exists underneath them, and who provokes in him feelings more complex than sheer benevolence. These feelings imply a sensitivity for difference, as well as a consciousness of the virtual community called up by the fleeting connection between the two men.

It is Gronniosaw's cosmopolitan experience, moreover, that allows this moment of complex sympathy with the young man. The description of his outward beauty recalls the ecstasy the author felt at the sight of his surroundings in Africa, and implies an ability to transfer the feelings and the skills acquired in one physical and cultural world to another. The moment conveys less a love of whiteness than a fusion of Gronniosaw's African aesthetic sensibility with a more cosmopolitan appraisal, independent, while still appreciative, of race. The white man remains distinctive as white but, in Gronniosaw's emotional world, becomes part of an affective community where both he and Gronniosaw belong as equals. Although the moment starts with individual sympathy, Gronniosaw tries to break through the imaginative limitations of liberal sympathy, and to imply a political vision that embraces both common humanity and racial difference. He and the white man belong to an interracial community, where they recognize each other in all their similarities and differences. The transnational and the transcultural echoes in the text are in direct contrast to the behavior of the captain, who expels the young man from the world of the ship on a national basis. In this fleeting moment of recognition, Gronniosaw does not so much subvert or transcend the world that surrounds him, as mobilize the different possibilities embedded in it. He has been affected by a culture of sensibility and of religious fervor, as well as by the republican world of the ships, and this multifaceted experience, combined with his exile from, and memories of, Africa, allows him to develop a special vision that emanates from this short moment of individual sympathy.[29]

Phillis Wheatley

In a famous passage from his *Notes on the State of Virginia* (1787) Thomas Jefferson uses as an argument for his biological racism the notion that blacks, by which he apparently means black men, "are more ardent after their female: but love seems with them to be more an eager desire, than a tender delicate mixture of sentiment and sensation" (139). When discussing blacks' inability to produce good art, he reiterates his point: "Their love is ardent, but it kindles the senses only, not the imagination. Religion indeed has produced a Phyllis Whately [sic]; but it could not produce a poet." Similarly, he seems to appreciate the letters of Ignatius Sancho, but "his imagination is wild and extravagant"; it "escapes incessantly from every restraint of reason and taste, and, in the course of its vagaries, leaves a tract of thought as incoherent and eccentric, as is the course of a meteor through the sky" (140). Imagination, like sentiment, needs to tread in the narrow path that to Jefferson defines the sensible, civilized mind. Sentiment and sensation, imagination and reason, need to find that delicate balance. As Peter Coviello puts it, "Jefferson's problem with blacks is not exactly that they cannot feel, but that they do not feel with the proper proportion, regulation, or intensity" (448). To Coviello, it is a sign of Jefferson's republicanism that he cannot envisage blacks remaining in the country after his prospective abolition of slavery: blacks' erratic sensibility proves that they do not possess the requisite virtue that is the mark of American citizenship. Interestingly for the purposes of this book, then, Jefferson uses the quality of feeling as a criterion for political belonging. He critiques trust in unconscious energy as evidence of an unsuitability for republican citizenship.

To Coviello, Phillis Wheatley's poetry does exhibit a republican sensibility. He shows how, in some passages of her poem "To the Right Honourable William, Earl of Dartmouth, His Majesty's Principal Secretary of State for North-America, &C.," "an intensity of feeling reads as an explicitly civic concern" (443). He focuses on the following segment:

> Should you, my lord, while you peruse my song,
> Wonder from whence my love of *Freedom* sprung,
> Whence flow these wishes for the common good,
> By feeling hearts alone best understood,
> I, young in life, by seeming cruel fate
> Was snatch'd from *Afric*'s fancy'd happy seat:
> What pangs excruciating must molest,
> What sorrows labour in my parent's breast?
> Steel'd was that soul and by no misery mov'd
> That from a father seiz'd his babe belov'd:
> Such, such my case. And can I then but pray
> Others may never feel tyrannic sway? (Mason 83)

According to Coviello, Wheatley here sends a message on "the very nature of civic virtue and virtuous citizenship" (445), through her reference to the "common good" and through her contrast between both her and her father's feelings of bereavement and the slaver's unfeeling acts, which make him unfit for the very citizenship he is enjoying. Republican virtue thus "requires a capacity for proper feeling" (446), and since Wheatley and her father, and by extension all blacks, display such capacity, Wheatley implies that their feelings prove their ability to be republican citizens. Even though they reach different conclusions, Wheatley and Jefferson, says Coviello, use a similar yardstick, in that "affect" is for both of them "a measure of citizenship" (448).

I would argue, though, that the quality of the affect in the poem is less republican than individualizing. The picture Wheatley paints of her capture focuses on one "parent's breast," her father's. Transporting herself back to that fateful moment, she imagines her father's grief in a display of Smithian sympathy with him. At the same time, she emphasizes that she herself used to live in an imaginary world, where her happiness was just "fancy'd," a product of her imagination. Feeling does not appear as a conduit toward virtuous citizenship but as a complex web of imaginary, individualized moments of sympathy. Though the poem can be read as springing from a desire for political independence, moreover, it could also express hope for repaired relations between a more lenient mother country and her colony. Indeed, Wheatley welcomes Dartmouth's "blissful sway" and "silken reins" (Mason 82).[30] In "America," a poem probably composed a few years earlier, in 1768, England appears as a loving mother bent on too much discipline until the child cannot stop weeping: "He weeps afresh to feel this Iron chain / Turn, O Brittania claim thy child again" (Mason 126). Here the focus on a familial link is made clearer. Wheatley's reference to the "common good" in the Dartmouth poem, then, is less the product of republicanism than of a wish for a harmonious union devoid of overly harsh discipline, as befits the relationship between mother and child. Although I will argue for a degree of republicanism in her work, Wheatley's use of affect in this particular poem is fundamentally liberal in the sense that it promotes the recognition of individualized interior connections.

Wheatley was steeped in the ideological currents of the time. According to Phillip M. Richards, "the cost of affirming Phillis Wheatley's adversary relationship with eighteenth-century Anglo-American culture is an evasion, or a repression, of the conventional way in which Wheatley assimilated the most central aspects of that culture's discourse" ("PW and Literary" 169). She could have developed her personal philosophy from any number of currents and events surrounding her. Growing up in the Wheatley family that had bought her in 1761, at the probable age of seven, Wheatley was taught to read and write, and was immersed in the culture of a middle-class Boston family on the eve of the Revolution. Thanks to these surroundings, she had access to any of the abolitionist pamphlets discussed earlier. James A. Levernier argues that she was "likely to have read John Woolman's 1762 *Considerations on Keeping Negroes: Part Second*" ("Style" 185); she was acquainted with Joseph Sewall, son of Samuel, and "it does not seem at all unlikely to assume that he would have drawn Wheatley's attention to his father's famous tract" (186). She may have known about "freedom suits," in which attorneys argued against slavery, and she may have known as well as about petitions by blacks, such as the ones discussed above, asking for the abolition of slavery. Baptized in 1771 and in constant contact with ministers, she also expressed a deep religious faith in her poems and letters. The Wheatley household, moreover, was open to the revolutionary ideas that swarmed in Boston at the time. And, of course, she knew the realities of racism and was familiar with the arguments brought to the defense of both slavery and the slave trade. More than any other eighteenth-century black writer, Wheatley was exposed to the complex political vocabulary of her time.

Republicanism was thus not unknown to her, and Coviello is not the only critic to argue for a connection between Wheatley's use of sentiment and republicanism. To Robert Kendrick, for example, her elegies "explore the performative, intersubjective activity of mourning as the ground for an ethics of contact" (44). One passage from "On the Death of the Rev. Dr. Sewell" illustrates this stance:

> "Sewell is dead." Swift-pinion'd Fame thus cry'd.
> "Is Sewell dead," my trembling tongue reply'd. (Mason 54)

To Kendrick, the poet here redirects attention from an anonymous public voice announcing the death of Sewell to a personal, embodied acknowledgment of it. She "transforms the role of public discourse" as defined by Michael Warner, in that she "questions the truth claims of the abstract public sphere and presents a call to bring the public mourning of Sewell back to the embodied subjects who create this sphere" (Kendrick 45). Kendrick's approach tallies with mine: Wheatley combines the abstraction needed to create a community with the embodiment and intersubjective recognition that allow her to reach beyond the limitations of liberalism. Wheatley "does not simply want abstract recognition . . . but equality as a matter of physical, lived contact with her audience" (Kendrick 47). Therefore, she "suggests that a re-evaluation of the emancipatory potential of the republic of letters is in order" (48). In the process, she leads the reader away from a Smithian model of interior sympathy toward a full recognition of the other person.[31]

One cannot deny, however, that Wheatley's gaze is often less horizontal than vertical, less bent on community and intersubjective recognition than on transcendence through a focus on the interior world, and this desire to move beyond the immediate and the concrete toward a form of religious sublime often colors her vision of race in the transatlantic world. Religious references to the spiritual realm invoke the liberal tendency to expect motivational energy to come from some source even more basic than individual imagination. Her few references to the Middle Passage suggest a transition from darkness to light, from ignorance to knowledge, from godlessness to conversion. "On Being Brought from Africa to America," which I quoted from earlier, starts as follows:

> 'Twas mercy brought me from my *Pagan* land,
> Taught my benighted soul to understand
> That there's a God, that there's a *Saviour* too:
> Once I redemption neither sought nor knew. (Mason 53)

She starts her poem "To the University of Cambridge, in New-England" with a similar idea:

> 'Twas not long since I left my native shore
> The land of errors, and *Egyptian* gloom:
> Father of mercy, 'twas thy gracious hand
> Brought me in safety from those dark abodes. (53)

Both passages convey a feeling of thankfulness for being lifted by God's "gracious hand" from her previous state toward a more ethereal state of religious conviction.

When she addresses the issue of community in her new American home, she invokes a shared belonging in a spiritual realm, not in the political life of the community. She expresses her thankfulness for being removed from a land of darkness, but the spiritual alternative has nothing to do with the Boston where she lives, or even with the new continent. As

Interiority, Aesthetics, and Antislavery Sentiment 57

she addresses the Harvard students with "intrinsic ardor," her first expression of enthusiasm pertains to higher regions:

> Students, to you 'tis giv'n to scan the heights
> Above, to traverse the ethereal space,
> And mark the systems of revolving worlds. (53)

The only space she seems eager to "traverse" is an "ethereal" one, which will take her away from the world below and toward different, "revolving worlds." In the end she admonishes the students, who have access to those worlds, to beware of sin's temptations:

> Ye blooming plants of human race devine,
> An *Ethiop* tells you 'tis your greatest foe;
> Its transient sweetness turns to endless pain,
> And in immense perdition sinks the soul. (52)

Her reference to herself as an "*Ethiop*" suggests an awareness of her low status, her racial difference, and the liberty she might be taking in addressing the students in this fashion. But rather than her difference, what ultimately matters here is that all of them belong to that "human race devine," and all of them are engaged in the common fight against the downward pull of temptation. The students should forget about her race and join her in trying to grow upward by turning inward.

Wheatley likes to present scenes of emotional exchange between religious interiorities. In "On the Death of the Rev. Mr. George Whitefield," she remembers:

> Thy sermons in unequall'd accents flow'd,
> And ev'ry bosom with devotion glow'd;
> Thou didst in strains of eloquence refin'd
> Inflame the heart, and captivate the mind. (55–56)

Whitefield managed to enter the hearts and minds of his audience, provoking elation while holding them captive. In these moments of intense emotional communion, he would exhort his audience to "take" Jesus, whether they were preachers, Americans, or Africans:

> "Wash'd in the fountain of redeeming blood,
> "You shall be sons, and kings, and priests to God." (56)

In the climax of his re-created sermon, Whitefield washes away racial difference, promising his listeners that their inner faith will elevate them toward a glorious station. Wherever they are born, all belong in those "native skies." In "On the Death of a Young Gentleman," the poet similarly begs for sustenance from above, after repeatedly asking what content to give her "sympathizing verse":

> Look, gracious Spirit, from thine heav'nly bow'r,
> And thy full joys into their bosoms pour. (59)

In "Thoughts on the Works of Providence," she even projects herself into a supraterrestrial perspective:

> Ador'd for ever be the God unseen,
> Which round the sun revolves this vast machine,
> Though to his eye its mass a point appears. (67)

Even if many of these images are common in neoclassicism and Puritan typology, their predominance in Wheatley's poetry points to a sensibility that found this form of mysticism of peculiar significance to a young black female slave.[32] The religious sublime, anchored in interiority, provides Wheatley with an emotional avenue toward freedom.

But if Wheatley's "central concern is always freedom" (Levernier, "Style" 175),[33] she occasionally displays a genuine struggle to express, through feeling, a desire for more than just freedom. With "On the Death of General Wooster," the reader might expect one of her traditional elegies, in which she focuses less on the life of the dead than on the tasks of the living, exhorting them to think with ecstasy about the glorious happiness now enjoyed by the departed. The last few lines do just that, but the main part of the poem exalts Wooster, who died during the Revolutionary War, and his role in the country's fight for independence. Here the poet offers a curious blend, freely mixing expressions of a desire for freedom with celebrations of strength and power. We first hear about

> His Country's Cause that ever fir'd his mind
> Where martial flames, and Christian virtues join'd. (Mason 171)

She wonders how she will "his warlike deeds proclaim":

> Thy grateful Country shall thy praise resound
> Tho' not with mortals' empty praise elate
> That vainest vapour to th' immortal State. (171)

She seems to struggle for the right form of admiration, aiming for the more ethereal realms she likes to inhabit, yet seemingly more taken with the image of a very real inner fire and combativeness. In a moment of sympathetic identification, she decides to let the dying man speak for himself, as he lies "inly serene," giving us a glimpse of a similar mixture of feelings. To the hero, it is for the "celestial prize" of freedom that "the Continent shines bright in arms." But the reason the Americans "combat on the feild of fame" is so that "social love and virtue" can remain. So he asks the "great power" to "lead *Columbia* thro' the toils of war," promising that a victory will "keep them ever virtuous, brave, and free." The language of freedom blends with that of virtue and of war, implying that the sacrifices are made not just for the sake of liberty but in order that "social love" can extend to the new republic. At this particular moment, Wheatley is searching for a vocabulary that can convey a vision of earthly caring, of concrete equality, more specific than ethereal appeals for a spiritual community.

The moment is fleeting, though. The conclusion of the hero's monologue expresses both the elating promise and the limitations of liberal feeling:

> But how, presumptuous shall we hope to find
> Divine acceptance with th' Almighty mind—
> While yet (o deed ungenerous!) they disgrace
> And hold in bondage Afric's blameless race?
> Let virtue reign—And thou accord our prayers
> Be victory our's, and generous freedom theirs. (171)

In this forceful condemnation of slavery, Wheatley uses the single most popular abolitionist argument of the time, creating a parallel between the colonies' fight for freedom and their own negation of that ideal in their treatment of blacks. Yet at the same time emancipation is presented as a "generous" gift made to compensate for a "deed ungenerous," implying a different kind of "freedom" than the one aimed for by the rebels. Indeed, the last line sees a clear division between what belongs to the colonists and what belongs to the Africans: here the elements of the mixture are separated out, power and victory assigned to whites, and a more vague, general freedom relegated to blacks. Possibly only an appeal to self-interest can boost white sympathy.

Still, Wheatley's rhetoric of republican sympathy keeps emerging. One signal of the presence of a republican sensibility is that she places repeated, if fleeting, emphasis on communication and dialogue. The fact that she was able to master new languages so quickly proves not just her talent but her curiosity about the larger world. In the few instances in which she refers to Africa in her letters, her immediate concern is communication. When John Thornton, a London merchant, suggested she might like to join an evangelizing mission, she answered with facetious skepticism: "Upon my arrival, how like a Barbarian Should I look to the Natives; I can promise that my tongue shall be quiet for a strong reason indeed being an utter stranger to the Language of Anamaboe. Now to be Serious, This undertaking appears too hazardous" (211). While her irony may, in its false self-denigration, reflect the prejudices of her time about Africans, it is clearly a warning that immediate reaction to appearance needs to be tempered by the rationality of language. Similarly, referring to Philip Quaque in a letter to Samuel Hopkins, she says she regrets hearing that his mission seems to be failing, and she suggests that "possibly, if Philip would introduce himself properly to them . . . he might be more Successful" (208). In passages like these, her sensitivity to the importance of conscious and deliberate communication and understanding evinces a desire to go beyond interiorized, Smithian sympathy.

Similarly, in the poem "Goliath of Gath," Wheatley reinterprets the story of David and Goliath by emphasizing communication and dialogue. She devotes quite some space to the intervention of a "radiant cherub" who warns Goliath of his impending doom, announcing that

> "Thee too a well-aim'd pebble shall destroy,
> "And thou shalt perish by a beardless boy. (64)

This prediction of his fate shifts the attention to the "how" rather than the "what" of the plot. When Goliath replies disparagingly "'Your words are lost on me'" (64), we receive confirmation that we are confronting a brutal force disdainful of the power of language. David is quite eloquent compared to Goliath, taunting him by announcing his coming victory, which will resonate so far that "'all the earth's inhabitants may know / That there's a God.'" As a consequence, Goliath's death appears less a result of the encounter itself than of the fact that he "heard and came" and was "deaf to the divine decree." By emphasizing the "terror" (65) his giant frame provokes, Wheatley also stresses his terrifying, possibly sublime effect. But while most of her poems present the sublime as a beatific feeling, what she emphasizes here is the importance of language and dialogue in dealing with horror, by implying that Goliath is vanquished because of his inability to communicate. Interestingly, then, she opposes the sublime to the power of language, especially in its beauty and eloquence, and encourages us to develop a feeling for community defined by language. She spurs us to expand our powers of sympathetic imagination to encompass difference through dialogue.

Besides the emphasis on communicative aspects of language, and contrary to Shields' assertion that she "shows practically no concern in her poetry for the aesthetic category of beautiful" (264), Wheatley at times leaves aside her pattern of interiority and sublimity to display a loving interest for the various shapes and forms of the world below, and I see in this aesthetic consciousness and this aesthetic feeling the subtle expression of a republican sensibility. Her two poems "A Hymn to Morning" and "A Hymn to Evening" subtly reveal this tendency by focusing on the beauty of exterior form. The hymn to the morning begins with an apparently traditional appeal to the muses, in which the poet asks them to "Assist my labours, and my strains refine" (73). The term "refine" is loaded, though, as it recalls another, now famous passage from "On Being Brought from Africa to America":

> Remember, *Christians*, *Negros*, black as *Cain*,
> May be refin'd, and join th' angelic train. (53)[34]

Here refinement seems to convey a superiority inherent in white Christian civilization, which, by asserting that blacks can attain it, she simultaneously implies they need in order to reach higher echelons than those they currently occupy. Placed in the new context, the refinement she needs from the muses takes on extra connotations, since she may hereby remind the reader of her difference, as if the morning required specific, culturally defined forms of praise. When she asserts that "Bright *Aurora* now demands my song" (73), the sense of urgency springs partly from an intimation that she needs to prove herself not just as a poet but as a black poet. The success or beauty of her poem becomes associated in the reader's mind with an acceptance of the poet as the same and yet different.

Consequently, these associations permeate the poem's strong emphasis on beauty. The poem turns into a description of her sympathetic identification with the concrete events of the morning, as the light turns brighter, a gentle wind blows, and "the feather'd race" wakes up:

> The bow'rs, the gales, the variegated skies
> In all their pleasures in my bosom rise.

Thanks to the "shady groves," which "shield your poet from the burning day," she manages to interiorize the colors and the harmonies she is witnessing. If she uses their "pleasures" as a means to feel her way toward what could turn into a sublime moment, the situation still remains thoroughly dependent on her aesthetic perception. Right then, though, the sun reaches higher and, as if bent on breaking this moment of intense pleasure, "His rising radiance drives the shades away." And so the poem ends rather abruptly:

> But Oh! I feel his fervid beams too strong,
> And scarce begun, concludes th' abortive song.

By illuminating the world, the sun cuts short her rejoicing, and aborts her sympathetic response to the beauty of her natural environment. Whereas she often equates the sun with spiritual warmth, here it acts as a negative force that puts an end to her moment of intense communion with nature. The masculinity evinced in the strong, "fervid beams" underlines her sense of frailty and physical inferiority, but also her desire to live in harmony with the elements below. This suggestive moment partly indicates an acceptance of her emotional limitations, in that the sun proves able abruptly to end the emotional transport that began the poem. But her creation, although aborted, still proves her power to enjoy the beauty of her surroundings.

As if she had disappeared during the day only to reappear at dusk, the hymn to the evening picks up right at the moment when "the sun forsook the eastern main," allowing her to experience another moment of aesthetic feeling. First the thunder conspires to efface all traces of the heat of the day, cleansing the air with its "Majestic grandeur." Then the west takes on a deep red hue. Full of religious feeling, the observers of this splendid evening can then repair to their beds:

> Fill'd with the praise of him who gives the light,
> And draws the sable curtains of the night,
> Let placid slumbers sooth each weary mind,
> At morn to wake more heav'nly, more refin'd. (74)

The word "refin'd" closes the loop, reminding readers once again that they are experiencing an emotional communion with a person who claims both similarity and difference. In the two poems, Wheatley expresses her openness to the world, even if she displays a simultaneous tendency to let this openness lead her to forms of retreat. Like Gronniosaw's in the first part of his narrative, her feeling originates in a quite sensual appreciation of light and sounds and colors, even as it leads to an interior enjoyment that makes her soar spiritually, that makes her "bosom rise." Through these two poems she tries to express a unique sensibility, one that brings readers into a spiritual realm but that also, through beauty, gives intimations of a concrete interracial community.

In her interest in beauty and the sublime, one could of course say that Wheatley inserts herself into eighteenth-century aesthetic discourses, but I argue that she gives the aesthetic a racial and political meaning. Whether or not she read Edmund Burke's *Philosophical Enquiry into the Origin of Our Ideas of the Sublime and Beautiful* (1757), her attention both to the beauty of concrete reality and to the ethereal implies that she wants to make a distinction between expressing a sublime feeling and focusing on what Burke sees as the pleasure caused by "the merely sensible qualities of things" (128), which he identifies in such qualities as smallness or smoothness. From a political perspective, one could say that Burke's definition of the beautiful as the perception of the "sensible qualities of things" describes the republican's pleasure at perceiving the self in the communal diversity of the world. And his definition of the sublime as the fear-inducing quality of the magnificent is compatible with the liberal's Smithian response at perceiving something so other that imagination can find nothing comparable in it with which to identify the self. While I do not argue that political ideology determines what we find beautiful or how we do it, I propose that the political and the aesthetic are elements of a cultural system that manages the interdependence of individual and communal interests. Wheatley shows an awareness that she must access this cultural system if she is to alter the way that Americans care about others.[35]

Some aspects of Wheatley's aesthetic sensibility, moreover, have a radically republican strategy of cosmopolitan or cross-cultural consciousness. Several poems from her 1773 collection convey this theme.[36] These poems find inspiration in a literary work or a work of art or both. Unlike her elegies, which address the departed, who were contemporaries, in their heavenly realm, some of these poems express sympathy for legendary characters who are brought down to earth and humanized by her verse. By putting herself between the original text, or work of art, and her audience, Wheatley acts as a translator of stories, and a participant in a community of readers. In this particular case, moreover, not only does her expression of feeling affect the feelings of other readers, but the scenes she evokes convey, more than any outcry for freedom could, a sense of a republican community. The self-consciousness implied in the theme of art, finally, shows that to her, artistic expression belongs to a realm of feeling that can help promote the political transformation made possible by cross-cultural transposition. That these poems appeared in the collection, published in London, and not in the Boston proposal may indicate that she anticipated different reactions from the London public, so that her participation in a transatlantic conversation shows how much her appeal to sentiment depends on the idea of cross-cultural contact.

By adding these poems to the British edition, of course, Wheatley participated in the commercial ethos of the imperial center.[37] Admittedly, she most likely had no hand in the steps taken by various persons to ensure the book's publication, from Susanna Wheatley, to Captain Robert Calef, who had the manuscript accepted for publication by Archibald Bell, to the Countess of Huntingdon, who accepted the dedication and even suggested that the book have "Phillis' picture in the frontispiece" (Mason 7). Wheatley's social position was marginal on both sides of the Atlantic. As Richards points out, Wheatley was a "doubly displaced writer," in that her "marginality as a black only complicated her culturally peripheral position as an American" ("PW, Americanization" 195). William H. Robinson suggests, commenting on an ad run in a Boston paper about the London publication, that it is Susanna who, "stung into resolve by Bostonian rejection" of the proposals, "may have run this advertisement-proposal notice in a pique of unchristian retaliation." She may even have been "excited by a rumored expectation of greater remuneration for a London-published edition" (24), a further indication of Phillis' entanglement in webs of exploitation. But a recourse to a British publisher might still have been seen by the American public as a sort of betrayal of Phillis' host country on her part, as a way of reaching directly for the top and bypassing the proper channels, of establishing a fresh and independent connection with the increasingly tyrannical and unacceptable mother country, even if the reason for doing so was that her call for subscriptions in Boston remained unsuccessful.[38]

Be that as it may, Wheatley's transnational, transatlantic consciousness, increased by this move to London, was also the source of her more radical moments. As Frank Shuffelton points out, there still existed "the potential for recapture of personal and social power within an imperial system" ("PW" 78). While Richards emphasizes Wheatley's provincial anxieties vis-à-vis Britain's "cultural and social power" (199), Shuffelton reminds us that "inclusion and expansion are sustaining principles of empire," since empire "legitimated itself by transforming dissimilar cultures, and thus always needed convertible and conversable subjects who could confirm its successes" (79). While the empire was anchored in inequality and oppression, it did create a model in its theory at least of a "commonwealth." As we will see in the following chapters, the presence of the

British Empire provided a number of antislavery arguments based less on the liberal notion that all people have a similar essence than on the awareness of belonging to a vast, possibly protective, entity. In this particular case, the atlanticism inherent in empire may have helped Wheatley's more radical moves. Unlike the interior logic of liberal nationalism, which thrives on a recognition of similarity and slips easily into an illiberal rejection of difference, Wheatley's occasional transnational feeling allowed her to bypass both her national marginality and her anxiety as an imperial subject, and to exploit the possibilities of international, communal feeling. These tendencies are to be seen in the poems that were not in the Boston proposal.

"To Maecenas" uses the theme of art and artistic beauty to convey a striking illustration of republican sympathy. Wheatley first pays tribute to her revered predecessor, Homer, whose *Iliad* she was well acquainted with through Alexander Pope's translation. Homer conveys situations with such art, she writes, that "A deep-felt horror thrills through all my veins." Here again, as in "Goliath," we have the presence and the experience of the sublime as terror. But once again the sublime is set off against passages in which Homer manages to elicit emotion in a different, more specific way:

> When great *Patroclus* courts *Achilles*' aid,
> The grateful tribute of my tears is paid;
> Prone on the shore he feels the pangs of love,
> And stern *Pelides* tend'rest passions move. (Mason 49)

By singling out the story of love and friendship between Patroclus and Achilles, Wheatley suddenly transports her readers into a world in which male love has an emotional expansiveness that carries the meanings of heroism, virtue, and the public good.[39] Her "tears" run down as a "tribute," as her compassion mixes with respect for such an all-encompassing ethos, and for the beauty of the art that conveys it. Here is the literary world she wants to emulate, one in which the beauty of friendship also conveys the ideological resonance of the republican concern to go beyond the individual self and to act in ways that benefit the whole community.

But she does not leave it at that: her vision is completed by an integration of race into that community. She wonders why the muses displayed such "partial grace" in giving "glory" to Terence, "one alone of *Afric's* sable race" (50). She does not acknowledge any other form of connection with Terence besides race; in fact, the stanza expresses something like indignation or impatience with what seems to evince racial prejudice on the part of the muses. Indeed, at the end of the poem, she establishes a clear line of descent between herself and Maecenas, by calling on him to shower her with his "paternal rays" (51), so that she asserts the reality of her mixed parentage. In several bold strokes, then, Wheatley presents herself both as a black poet and as one who carries the republican sensibility of the Greek world, in such a way that art becomes inextricably linked to that political vision, but with an added multiracial component. Once again, her racial consciousness helps her expand republicanism, in itself already an enlargement of the social horizon beyond the individual self, toward cross-cultural and cross-racial possibilities. No wonder she complains of a "grov'ling mind" (50), since in this exceptional poem a special sensibility struggles to be born, in which racial difference reconciles with a sense of republican equality in a moment of intense artistic emotion.

"Niobe" is even more strongly tied to the world of art, as it is an adaptation of both a literary model and a painting, and here again the sublime is present. Hoping to achieve more than a mere retelling of these myths, Wheatley invokes the muse to

> Inspire with glowing energy of thought,
> What *Wilson* painted, and what *Ovid* wrote. (98)

The poet plans to fuse in her imagination the feelings evoked by the two works of art, then to transform and transmit that inner "energy" through her own poem. Ovid's gruesome story of a mother losing her seven sons and her seven daughters, as he tells it in *Metamorphoses*, seems likely, once again, to evoke sublimity as horror. In Ovid's story, the sudden death of Niobe's seven sons and seven daughters seems meant to induce in the reader that particular feeling, in that the infinite magnitude of her loss remains almost beyond comprehension. To some extent, Wheatley conforms to this version of the sublime in the poem. Everything about Niobe seems to connote the sublime, from her "wide domain" and "potent reign" to her grandfather Atlas, "who with mighty pains / Th'ethereal axis on his neck sustains," and the other grandfather, who "on the throne on high / Rolls the loud-pealing thunder thro' the sky" (98).

Niobe evokes the sublime in other ways. True, as the story unfolds, Wheatley's Niobe grows into a more humanized figure than Ovid's. As Lucy K. Hayden points out, while Ovid's Niobe is "militant, aggressive, boastful, and provocative," Wheatley's is "more soft and tearful, more pathetic and conciliatory, more self-sacrificing and heroic" (443). Yet the new emphasis may be said to enhance the horror of the tale. Indeed, when the poet addresses Niobe: "thou had'st far the happier mother prov'd / If this fair offspring had been less belov'd," blaming her "love too vehement" (99), she shifts the emphasis from excessive pride, the motif in Ovid's tale, to excessive love, and creates a character not too far removed from Sethe in Toni Morrison's *Beloved*, whose love, as Paul D puts it, is "too thick." Niobe's feelings, like Sethe's, seem to belong to a world of infinite pain hardly comprehensible to the sedate reader.

But besides these sublime elements, Wheatley also gives pride of place to the beautiful by highlighting themes of art and physical beauty. While Ovid mentions Niobe's husband's "skill" (125) only in passing, assuming the reader's knowledge of his musical talent, Wheatley devotes a stanza to him, introducing him as the one who "divinely taught to sweep the sounding strings" (98). When she says of the children's charms that "no words could tell them, and no pencil paint," she self-reflexively reminds us both of Richard Wilson's painting, which has served as an inspiration for the poem, and of the description of the children's beauty she has just given, comparing them with the brightness of the dawn:

> From their bright eyes the living splendors play,
> Nor can beholders bear the flashing ray. (99)

Her references to Niobe keep emphasizing her physical beauty. Wheatley announces her story as that of a queen "all beautiful in woe" (98), and surpasses Ovid in her description of Niobe's stunning appearance at the altar of her rival. In an upsurge of her feeling for the shape of things, she focuses on bodily beauty, forcing us to imagine Niobe in other than the interior terms of her sublime pain. Here again, Wheatley partly diverges from her focus on interiority in order to force us to look at human bodies as they are caught in the ravages of passion and power, displaying a concreteness and a physicality that evoke the politics of embodiment elsewhere associated with republicanism.

Wheatley's literary production shows a deep complexity, partly because she stands at the crossroads of several intellectual and political strands in the late eighteenth century. She was uniquely positioned to develop a global consciousness, as a deeply religious black woman from Africa who lived in revolutionary New England, read British, Greek, and Roman authors as well as the Bible, and had the opportunity to travel to England. As Nandini Bhattacharya puts it, Wheatley's writings show "a curious blend of new world intertextuality and textual flight from the world which, taken together, stands for a unique new world expression of transnational identity: simultaneously embodied, localized, migratory, and virtual" (139). As we saw, her awareness of a British public may have guided her selections, or even her writing, of poetry. Her international, cross-cultural awareness allowed her to use various forms of feeling in order to convey an original political vision. Granted, the political strain of her poetry is mostly informed by the liberal rhetoric of the Revolution, and this in itself shows a desire to place the expression of sentiment under the emancipatory banner of individual freedom. But thanks to a wider cultural awareness, Wheatley occasionally gives us glimpses of a more radically egalitarian world, one in which dialogue, communication, and the exterior beauty of otherness are an integral part of the community's emotional world.

Wheatley's vision remained dynamic. Sometimes her love of freedom went together with a certain adherence to a sense of hierarchy she had obviously inherited from the ambient culture. In 1768, for example, she wrote with thankfulness about being brought from a "*Pagan* land," and told George III that "A monarch's smile can set his subjects free!" (53). She apparently situated herself in the middle of a hierarchy of nations and continents, as if applying to nations the notion of the chain of being, and then responded with spontaneous affect to smiles from above. Later, in 1774, after the death of her benefactor, Susanna Wheatley, she wrote John Thornton, who lived in England, that she wished he could "Supply her place, but this does not seem probable from the great distance of your residence." Here she emphasized her mistress's "friendship," as she did John Wheatley's "Paternal friendship" (210), and one perceives, as the feeling of friendship applies to Thornton as well as the Wheatleys, a possible shift in her cosmopolitan sensibility, a vision of transatlantic relations as less family-based and more equalized and communitarian.

That same year, her poem to a gentleman of the navy offered an amazingly romantic view of Africa, complete with "spring's luxuriant reign," "the various bower, the tuneful flowing stream," a "soil spontaneous," and "flowery births" (163). Though she shifts from one stereotype of Africa to another, the vision bursts open with a surprising suddenness, in a passage whose sheer enthusiasm suggests a moment of revelation about the richness of the continent, and the emphasis on beauty suggests a new openness to its possibilities. Here Africa does not signify darkness and paganism, but a world that needs to be discovered and communicated with. Apparently, Wheatley's ideological ground was shifting very quickly. As

Shuffelton argues, "the world she imagined in the proposed volume of 1779 was cosmopolitan, multiracial, and free" ("On Her Own" 188). More than anything else, it is her changing sensibility, especially her negotiation of interior delight with her feeling for the specific, concrete, beautiful shapes of things, that reveals her struggle with the political ideas of her time, and it is her cross-cultural handling of that conversation that shows her desire to push them toward more radical conclusions.

Interiority and White British Antislavery Writing

In his remarks on slavery, the British philosopher Francis Hutcheson, whose theory of benevolence I discuss in the introduction, defends a fundamental inner right to freedom. As he explains in *A System of Moral Philosophy* (1755), everyone possesses "a right to life," and "nature has implanted in each man a desire of his own happiness" (vol. 1, 293). Each person has a "natural right to exert his powers" for the purposes of "industry, labour, or amusements" (294), as well as a right "to acquire property" (298). Hutcheson calls this right "*natural liberty*," and "every man has a sense of this right." Indeed, "the sense of natural liberty is so strong, and the loss of it so deeply resented by human nature, that it would generally create more misery to deprive men of it because of their imprudence, than what is to be feared from their imprudent use of it." Depriving even "the weakest of mankind" of their liberty would produce "exquisite distress, and sink their souls into an abject sorrow" (294). People should enjoy their liberty as long as "no great publick interest requires some restriction of it." This right to liberty is suggested "by many generous affections, and by our *moral sense*" (295). Natural liberty seems very much dependent on feeling: one has it because one has "a sense of" it; one should not deprive others of it for fear they should fall into a deep "sorrow"; generosity ensures that this right will be guaranteed. As Wylie Sypher points out, "Hutcheson offers the charitable instinct in man as a guarantee of his liberty" (276).

But as in his theory of benevolence, in his view of liberty Hutcheson aims for a balance between interiority and exteriority, natural law and the common good, individual rights and the public interest. He often adds a restriction to his statements of natural rights, declaring, for example, that nobody can deprive others "of any of their natural rights, or innocent acquisitions, when no publick interest requires it" (299). In such statements, he leaves the door open for restrictions that are necessary for the public good. Because his theory is anchored in individual goodwill, this goodwill can be withdrawn as the demands of more general considerations require. To Hutcheson, the traditional, Aristotelian justification of slavery by nature or by conquest does not hold: no superiority, "natural or acquired, can give a perfect right to assume power over others, without their consent" (301).[40] But his stance on slavery is qualified. He finds it adequate to keep "idle vagrants" in slavery for life if they prove unable to take care of themselves and their families, implying that slavery can indeed plug the holes that a lack of benevolence leaves open, and can help "restrain sloth and idleness in the lower conditions." The same holds for those made "a publick burden" (vol. 2, 202) through intemperance. He does criticize the justification for slavery as compensation for saving persons from sure death in their own country; to him, "as soon as the value of their labours beyond their maintenance amounts to this sum, and the legal interest from the time it was advanced, they have a right to be free" (85). But his willingness to subordinate someone's liberty to the vagaries of contractarianism implies a notion of individual freedom as negotiable. As Roger Anstey points out, "this reasoning provides the bones of a possible justification of the Atlantic, and other, slave trades" (101).

Hutcheson's willingness to appeal to the public good signals a readiness to let it be a yardstick for social happiness instead of relying exclusively on interior, personal responsibility, and in this act of balance he is representative of a British attempt at equilibrium between liberal and republican tendencies. Interestingly, his willingness to compromise "natural liberty" also shows that keeping an eye on the public good could lead toward conservative, even proslavery stances. Hutcheson's works were widely read and taught in America.[41] But while liberty and the common good would polarize into liberalism and republicanism in revolutionary America, and into what Martin calls a "political dialectic" (11), Britain would keep the two more closely tied, and try to exploit their interaction. British antislavery discourse did contain many appeals to interiority through either religious feeling or the notion of natural rights, but Britain's very special form of Enlightenment usually kept this in balance with the demands of the common good. If this attitude sometimes led to a reinforcement of the social status quo, the large horizon covered by this social vision also made possible an escape from the claustrophobia of the individual, interior self. Granville Sharp, the famous British abolitionist, is a perfect example of this complex negotiation, and I will now turn to him.

Sharp played a role in the 1772 Somerset decision, and thereby associated himself, early in his abolitionist career, with the power of British constitutionalism. The decision prevented James Somerset from being sent as a slave to the West Indies. Despite caveats, it is considered a milestone in English law in that it sounded the death knell of slavery in England. Sharp was already known for his help and collaboration in that kind of legal case, and here he provided much legal counseling. An interesting aspect of the Somerset trial was the distinction drawn between American practice—Somerset was assumed to have sailed directly from Virginia to Britain with his master—and English law. Attorneys at the trial combined references to natural rights with assertions that the English Constitution did not condone slavery, that villeinage had disappeared from the island because discouraged by the courts, and that several legal decisions had made it clear that the air of England was too pure for slaves to breathe in.[42] In fact, the main questions were whether foreign laws should automatically be transferred to England, and whether a so-called contract of ownership could be trumped by natural law. According to most versions of his pronouncement, Lord Mansfield ruled that "slavery is so odious that nothing can be suffered to support it but positive law" (Wise 182), implying that unlike a marriage, a relationship of slavery imported from outside England could not be accepted if not explicitly condoned by the law. Lord Mansfield thus relied primarily on positive law. As Steven M. Wise concludes, "if English slavery was to exist, it would have to be legislated" (183). While Lord Mansfield was disregarding a number of previous decisions, and even if many found his decision shocking, he was arguing, not primarily from the principle of natural law, but from an adherence to the British Constitution.[43]

In his crusade against slavery and the slave trade, Sharp was undoubtedly moved by a desire to defend individual liberty, but he also used arguments that derive from considerations of social units. In his 1769 tract on the "Injustice and Dangerous Tendency of Tolerating Slavery," he argues that every person in England "is a bounden subject of the King, and thereby a part of his property, and entitled to his protection" (Hoare 41). Liberty here derives from belonging in a social entity headed by the king. Later tracts ground his argument primarily in an expansive notion of "law." In "The Just Limitation of Slavery" (1776), he applies himself to refuting those who use levitical laws about strangers to condone slavery, asserting that there is no "*authentic written commandment from God*" (*Tracts* 13) for the practice of slavery, and that "the *involuntary servitude* of *brethren* is entirely inconsistent with the Jewish Law" (16). To those who argue that Jesus Christ left national laws in place and did not preach universal freedom, inciting people only to behave righteously, Sharp answers that righteousness issues from the precepts of benevolence and brotherly love. And to those who argue that slaves in the West Indies are better treated than the poor at home, Sharp answers that the condition of the English poor is no excuse for the oppression of others. "When any of our own countrymen *at home* are miserable *poor*," he adds, "it is not always clear whether themselves, or others, are to be blamed" (36), whereas slavery is always a sign that the slave owner does not love his neighbor.[44] Sharp thought less in terms of natural liberty and free will for blacks, than in terms of an orderly and lawful society guided by a sort of Hutchesonian benevolence.[45]

His 1773 *Essay on Slavery* does emphasize the distinction between positive law and natural law, but then switches to an appeal to universal benevolence in order to enforce that natural law. He starts by arguing that "the Jewish Constitutions *were not 'strictly consistent'* with the *law of nature* in all points" (19), since they allowed, for example, divorce and remarriage, or a distinction between brothers and strangers. All these laws are "annulled or rather *superseded*, as it were, by the more perfect doctrines of *universal benevolence* taught by Christ himself" (23). Rather than establishing a binary opposition between positive and natural law, Sharp corrects himself, replacing the term "annulled" with "superseded" to imply a gradation between the different types of laws. Only benevolence can therefore have the power to override the iniquities endorsed and promoted by positive law. Sharp concludes that "the glorious system of the gospel destroys all *narrow, national partiality*" and "makes *us citizens of the world*" (28), a statement that might mark him out as a proponent of republican universal equality. But he adds that "more especially are we bound, as christians, to commiserate and assist to the utmost of our power all persons in *distress*, or *captivity*" (28). Sharp recognizes that natural law alone is imperfect and vulnerable against various forms of oppression, but his recourse is the law of the gospel, a doctrine of benevolence that, if not republican, springs from a concern for the welfare of the community.

The balancing act between individual freedom and the general welfare comes out even more forcefully in "The Law of Passive Obedience" (1776). According to the apostle Paul, slaves and servants are supposed to remain "*patient*," "*humble* and *submissive*" (*Tracts* 8), and Sharp accepts the injunction. He wants to address slaveholders specifically, who do not "act consistently with the christian profession" (12). That servants are enjoined to be submissive does not mean that "*tyrants* and *oppressors* have thereby obtained a legal *right*, under the gospel" (39), to own and mistreat them. More importantly, Sharp argues that if the individual Christian should "forgive all injuries, and pass over every affront offered to his *own person*," he should resist general injustice, so as to preserve "the *peace* and *happiness* of the community" (42). People should be motivated, not by "*private resentment*," but by a "zeal for *the public good*" (43). Fighting for just laws is not inconsistent with the law of passive obedience, since it pertains to the welfare of the community and the public good, rather than to the particular situation of an individual person. In "The Law of Liberty" (1776), Sharp similarly insists on a "conscientious regard to the *publick Good*" (*Tracts* 11), which derives from the principle of universal benevolence. He reminds his reader in the end that "the whole Community" (46) is involved in the issue of slavery. Sharp's argumentation shows the necessary alliance of a natural right to freedom with responsibility for the communal good and the demands of general social happiness. Benevolence helps the mixing of those elements. Sharp does not deny that individual distinctions are important, but he objects that the rules of specific relationships have displaced the rules of communalism. He is arguing that the Smithian requirement that sympathy be a product of personal interaction is being used to relieve people of communal responsibilities.

Ignatius Sancho's Balancing Act

Ignatius Sancho, the foremost black representative of eighteenth-century sensibility, both displayed and radicalized the balance between interiority and exteriority, feeling and duty, freedom and the common good, detected in British antislavery authors like Sharp. Sancho had been a slave in England for as long as he could remember. After working as a butler for the powerful Montagu family, he set up his own grocery store in Westminster. Thanks to this background, he came into contact with a good number of artists and literati. His sizable correspondence was published in 1782, two years after his death. On the face of it, Sancho adhered to traditional forms of benevolence, which British culture inherited from Scottish moral philosophy. Although we do not know whether he read the works of Francis Hutcheson or of Adam Smith, his letters reflect an intense devotion to the notions of generosity, charity, and good works. But where Hutcheson combined a republican concern for the common good and a liberal investment in self-interest, Sancho often radicalized each side of the equation, even as he tried to maintain the balance. He pushed the liberal commitment to the limit, regularly focusing on the personal, interior pleasures elicited by the sheer act of sympathy. At the same time, he displayed a transracial social consciousness: even though his self-deprecating statements, as well as his pity-inducing pronouncements on members of his race, seemed to express an accommodationist acceptance of the prevailing hierarchical social order, he did manage to smuggle in a leveling social vision. And the latter often seemed to spring forth from his profound attachment to the realm of the aesthetic. His particular concern with the world of artistic beauty, patronage, and gratitude evinced a political vision that radicalized notions of balance and exchange toward egalitarian, interracial, and transcultural possibilities.

Critical discussions of Sancho often mention the importance to him of Laurence Sterne's writings, emphasizing their common interest in the details of interior life, specifically the life of the emotions. Indeed, *A Sentimental Journey* (1768) shows how the language of sensibility became increasingly interiorized in the eighteenth century. Throughout the book Sterne's interest in his surroundings and in his fellow beings is subordinate to the interior riches they provide him with: the sentimental journey is first and foremost an inner journey, through which "a large volume of adventures may be grasped" and nothing should be missed that "he can *fairly* lay his hands on" (28). If the terms here reflect the discourse of acquisitiveness and self-interest, they more generally reveal the self-reflexivity of his perception. As Ann Jessie Van Sant puts it, Yorick, the protagonist, often "interiorizes external events," not unlike spiritual autobiographers, "for whom (as for Yorick) the external event is important not in itself, but as it figures in the internal landscape" (99). In an illustrative incident, a French officer eloquently defends mutual understanding and tolerance between nations: "The old French officer delivered this with an air of such candour and good sense, as coincided with my first favourable impressions of his character—I thought I loved the man; but fear I mistook the object—'twas my own way of thinking—the difference was, I could not have expressed it half so well" (Sterne 59–60). The interior journey comes upon narcissism, as Yorick hears in his interlocutor the brilliance of his own idea, and loves it. He admits that the man is more articulate than he is, but the qualities of the other man are not important to Yorick. The man's character is subordinated to Yorick's satisfaction with his own idea. Yorick forgoes any interrogation of his own feelings on the basis of communal consciousness. His faith in his own emotions makes him a Smithian individual.

Sterne thus seems to convey the political content of liberal sentiment. This dimension comes out in a well-known passage from *A Sentimental Journey* related to the issue of slavery in which, after envisaging the possibility of being thrown into the Bastille, Yorick hears a starling in a cage, crying to be let out. Vowing that "I never had my affections more tenderly awakened" (69), Yorick launches into an encomium to liberty. Back in his room, he tries to imagine the experience of imprisonment and slavery. But finding that the idea hovers at a distance, the picture remaining unclear through the "multitude of sad groups" he is trying to visualize, "I took a single captive, and having first shut him up in his dungeon, I then look'd through the twilight of his grated door to take his picture" (70). This individualizing move brings his imaginary experiment into the realm of Smithian sympathy. Finding himself incapable of envisioning the consequences of imprisonment for whole groups or communities, Yorick hopes that the one will stand for the many, and that his own personal sympathy will easily and magically be multiplied. As Markman Ellis points out, this scene shows how "sentimental scenarios" cannot represent "anything vast, unnumbered, terrible or threatening," but rather "work by being personalised, unique and discrete" (*Politics* 72). To Ellis, moreover, the focus on such an insignificant element as a little bird shows the "downwards momentum of the sentimental scenario" (73) in that, unlike the exultation and the gravitas involved in the sublime, the sentimental moment "leads nowhere: it is a closing off device, diffusing enquiry in bathos" (74).[46] Consequently, the sentimental offers a forum where the political is "managed and mystified" (98). Here we find the political downside I have associated with liberal, individualized, interiorized sympathy.[47]

But Sterne's prisoner scene cannot be reduced to a simple case of liberal sympathy either. After trying to imagine the captive's emaciated body, Yorick stops short: "But here my heart began to bleed—and I was forced to go on with another part of the portrait." Unable to concentrate on the captive's body, he diverts his attention to the ground, the walls, the chains, so that finally "I burst into tears" (Sterne 71). The tears are provoked, not just by his focus on the individual prisoner, but from examining his surroundings, his material circumstances, the context of his miserable life. This visual enlargement broadens the emotional span, forcing the reader to think in environmental terms. While such descriptions of a victim's surroundings were certainly common in sentimental works, the self-consciousness involved in the whole scene encourages a larger reflection on the uses of sentiment as related to social issues. Yorick is not actually witnessing this scene but picturing it in his mind's eye, after he "gave full scope" to his "imagination." The episode starts as a sort of exercise in philosophy in order to "figure to myself the miseries of confinement" (70). It follows up with a continued expansion of the social and emotional consciousness at work, in a movement that attempts to grasp the prisoner's individual suffering and his circumstances, with always, in the background, the knowledge of the existence of millions like him. No wonder Yorick "could not sustain the picture of confinement" that his "fancy had drawn," and "startled up" from his chair (71): the moment had slowly but surely been adding up to something more than mere liberal sympathy. It had pushed him toward a fleeting, but present, consciousness of an environment or a world that allows such confinement, and a consciousness of his own responsibility, not just for that particular man, but for the conditions that make such misery possible.[48]

It is this careful balancing act between an individual and a more expansive form of feeling that one also repeatedly finds in Sancho. In his letters, feeling and sensibility are the indicators, not only of a compassionate heart, but also of a concern for duty and the general interest. He reminds Jack Wingrave of the supremacy of religion, in that "every good affection, every sweet sensibility, every heart-felt joy — humanity, politeness, charity — all, all, are streams from that sacred spring" (26–27). He often provides his correspondents with lists of virtues that he thinks they should practice, such as "the right paths of humility, candour, temperance, benevolence" (44). He likes to expatiate on the inextricable connection of the head and the heart. He manages to negotiate the tricky ground between the importance of individual, virtuous acts and the determination of human life by bigger forces. On the one hand, he admires Bossuet's *Universal History* "beyond any thing I have long met with" (54), revealing his appreciation for a vision of history as informed by God's providence, and hence by a higher power than the sheer individual will of human beings.[49] But on the other, he says that "one ounce of practical religion is worth all that ever the Stoics wrote" (67), highlighting the impact of human feeling and passion on the here and now, and he praises Sterne's sermons for emphasizing "practical duties" (83). Sancho's letters are suffused both with punctual moments of sensibility and their practical applications, and with considerations of general duty and a wider world order.

Sancho did adhere to the conventions of benevolent liberal sympathy. He often praises small acts of charity inordinately, turning modest acts of giving into clichéd sentimental scenes. To Meheux, who has given a few worn-out clothes to a friend of Sancho's, he says he should have seen "the woe-worn object of thy charitable care—receive the noble donation of thy blest house!—the lip quivering, and the tongue refusing its office" (31–32), something he could not behold "without a tear" (32). Benevolence engenders gratitude, and he unashamedly admonishes friends to be thankful to their "noble and generous benefactors" (44). His notions of benevolence are even racially tinted. He thanks a correspondent for his "kindness to my poor black brethren—I flatter myself you will find them not ungrateful—they act commonly from their feelings:—I have observed a dog will love those who use him kindly" (45). Critics often see this trait as evidence of Sancho's adherence to the social and racial hierarchies of his time, and indeed, to some extent, his frequent dwelling on small charitable acts may indicate an avoidance of more systemic issues.

Through his letters, however, Sancho builds the image of a society that finds its balance through continuous forms of material and emotional exchange. He constantly comments on the mutual advantages of kindness to others, measuring the emotional benefits to both parties in giving and in receiving. In answer to Meheux, who has asked to correspond with him, he declares: "You do much more honor than I deserve, in wishing to correspond with me—the balance is entirely in your favor" (37). He often theatrically refuses to thank a do-gooder, averring that the act of giving afforded his correspondent more pleasure than the receiver felt in accepting the gift. He starts a letter so: "There is nothing in nature more vexatious than contributing to the uneasiness of those, whose partiality renders them anxious for our well-doing—the honest heart dilates with rapture when it can happily contribute pleasure to its friends" (64). The mutuality of feeling is so intricate that it dissolves the notions of giving and receiving, since the receiver of a friend's good acts and feelings shows tremendous generosity in trying to enhance the friend's pleasure. The self-reflexivity of such moments, the insistent highlighting of the infrastructure of giving and receiving, shows a tendency to think beyond the individual act toward more systematic forms of exchange. Benevolence does not just produce the occasion to shed a tear (although it does that too); it forms a building block in Sancho's wider vision of the common good.

His emphasis on, and his cultivation of, friendship underpins this vision. In a declamatory condemnation of "man," the first thing he deplores is the futility of trying "to form friendships, to make connexions" (28). Friendship is one of the pillars of his letters; to him it is "a plant of slow growth, and, like our English oak, spreads, is more majestically beautiful, and increases in shade, strength, and riches, as it increases in years" (30). Unlike enthusiasm, its rootedness in feeling does not preclude a balanced appreciation for its object: "Friendship founded upon right judgement takes the good and bad with the indulgence of blind love" (40). He reports with joy that "I have added to my felicity—or Fortune more properly has—three worthy friends" (52); he says somberly that "the parting of friends is a kind of temporary mourning" (56). Sancho's extensive circle of acquaintances and friends contributes to the sense that the personal and the communal mix in a perpetual round of exchange. His letters are always full of references to others, as if each letter constitutes an attempt to convey a sense of extended community of which he and his correspondent are the mere conduits.

His emphasis on exchange extends to an awareness of the forms of exploitation that sustain the social order. He tells Wingrave, a young white man who is in India, that "I do not wish you half a million—clogged with the tears and blood of the poor natives" (116). In a letter to Soubise, one of the few letters we have that he addressed to another black person, he exclaims: "Happy, happy lad! what a fortune is thine!—Look round upon the miserable fate of almost all of our unfortunate colour—superadded to ignorance,—see slavery, and the contempt of those very wretches who roll in affluence from our labours superadded to this woeful catalogue." While his aim is primarily to encourage Soubise to count his blessings, Sancho here does not use sentiment in his usual fashion, trying to instill pity in the beholder. Addressing a fellow black, he is attempting to awaken in him a level of consciousness by urging him, not to look at, but to "look round" and to "see." He urges him to see through a society where some steal the labor of others, and where property and "affluence" are distributed unevenly. "Some philosopher," he adds, "wished for a window in his breast" (46). As he recommends that Soubise reform and embrace virtue, he also implies that the society they live in could not stand such scrutiny, but that that is the ideal it should aspire to. He, in any case, sees through its systematic failures, and uses sentiment to try to induce a republican change in consciousness.[50]

But it is his special status as an intermediary between high and low, and between black and white, that gives his image of emotional exchange a radical edge.[51] Through his constant admonition and advice, Sancho creates a web of links that acquires a substance that signifies the thickness of communal life, a life that covers boundaries of race and class.[52] He starts a letter to Wingrave with some advice on how to lead a moral life; he finishes with references to two young men, the black man named Soubise and a white named C[harles] L[incoln], asking him to notice them, and to counsel them. If Wingrave does that, "I will regard it as a kindness to me" (28). Charity and benevolence become tools that help the actors move beyond the punctual exchanges inherent in the charitable act. The acts of giving and taking become rhizomic or even circular, and evoke a series of interracial horizontal entanglements that counter the vertical idea of the chain of being. Pointing out the racial implications of the chain of being, Helena Woodard underlines Sancho's "readaptation of sensibility as a seemingly custom-made philosophy for the debate on race and slavery," in that Sancho promotes "interracial bonding" (70) in the form of a "'chain of love'" (71). Indeed, Sancho writes that his vision of heaven is of a place where "we will mix . . . with all countries, colours, faiths," and "we will mingle with them, and try to untwist the vast chain of blessed Providence" (86). Even commerce constitutes for him a means "to unite mankind in the blessed chains of brotherly love—society—and mutual dependence" (131). The prominence of the theme of mixture and exchange, combined with Sancho's social and racial mobility, subtly undermines the British racial and social order, precisely by intensifying its ideology of balance through exchange that helped create that order in the first place.

It might seem ironic to characterize a poor, fat grocer and family man perpetually laid up by gout as mobile, but it is Sancho's perpetually moving point of view that makes his sensibility exceptional. Sancho assumes a variety of identities from letter to letter, and even though the whole correspondence builds up to a coherent personality, the facility with which he adapts tone and content to his correspondent is amazing. Keith A. Sandiford notes that Sancho had a "propensity to assume every posture from the solemn moralist to the frolicsome buffoon" (80). Similarly, Sancho displays a capacity to feel for people who are far apart on the social and racial scale, at one time supplicating in the name of "thousands of my brother Moors" (74) in his first letter to Sterne, and at another declaring of the Duchess of Kingston, in legal trouble because of bigamy, that "with all her wealth and titles, she is an object of pity" (70). He despises slavery, but he is equally disturbed by the impressment of seamen for the Royal Navy, enough to send a practical proposal to the *General Advertiser* on how to deal with the issue, so that "the honoured name of England may be rescued from the scandalous censure of man-stealing" (82). Another letter to the *Advertiser* makes a proposal to reduce the national debt "without oppressing the merchant, mechanic, or labouring husbandman" (113): the idea is to ask noble families to give up their family silver, "as a lasting testimony of their zeal for the public good" (114). It is this multifaceted generosity in his apportioning of compassion that makes his sentimental world exceptionally dynamic.

He deals with the uncertainties of his national identity with a similar blend of feelings. Sancho's letters do not convey the sense of a split identity. He speaks in passing of "our American grievances" (95) in a way that suggests an allegiance to the British interest. About the American Revolution, he hopes that "this cursed carnage of the human species may end—commerce revive—sweet social peace be extended throughout the globe—and the British empire be strongly knit in the never-ending bands of sacred friendship and brotherly love!" (106). While this passage might be construed as revealing the sort of global consciousness I will discuss in the next chapter, it shows a clear adherence to the idea of the British Empire. Yet in its exuberance it expresses a desire for transformation that, coming from Sancho's inclusive perspective, would not just be moral but also social and racial. It is Sancho's dynamic personality that allows him to bypass the schizophrenia of being a black in Britain. To Wingrave he says, "it is with reluctance, that I must observe your country's conduct has been uniformly wicked in the East—West-Indies—and even on the coast of Guinea," adding that it England is a country "which as a resident I love—and for its freedom—and for the many blessings I enjoy in it" (130). Yet when he hears of a naval encounter between the British and the French, he asserts that "we fought like Englishmen" (176). While he cannot identify himself as British, he conveys a sense of belonging and a possibility to envision a fuller integration based on the country's "conduct."

His artistic sensibility, I want to argue, contributes significantly to this radical tendency. Sancho stands out as an eighteenth-century Afro-Briton through his varied artistic interests, as a lover of literature, an apparently respected critic of theater and painting, the author of a now lost *Theory of Music*, and the composer of several musical pieces. But what is striking about the letters is his seemingly deliberate mixture of high and low culture, the overlaps between a delicate artistic sense and a down-to-earth epicurean enjoyment of the good life. A letter he writes from Scotland freely mixes references to architectural beauties, praise of "herrings in perfection" (39), comments on Rousseau's "Eloisa" and on David Garrick's comic opera *Cymon*, and the final comment that "we have fine weather—fine beef—fine ale—and fine ladies" (40). Apart from the liveliness and the flair for detail of the gifted letter writer, the letter exudes a special delight, even a sense of elation at its own cleverness. It is this self-conscious playfulness that the reader takes in and remembers, and that induces a blurring of aesthetic categories. Unlike Wheatley, Sancho does not keep his aesthetic worlds separate. On the contrary, his correspondence seems an extended attempt to transform the existing aesthetic hierarchy through mixture and exchange, and to stimulate a new vision of the world. His constant comments on the quality of his own and of others' letters reinforces the sense that everything becomes swept up in his aesthetic world. At one point he tells William Stevenson: "but what's all this to you?—nothing—it helps to fill up the sheet" (52). It is this surfeit, this filling of the sheet, that is transformative.[53]

While he emphasizes the interior qualities of the heart, one is never allowed to forget, reading Sancho, that people have bodies, and especially faces, and he invests as much feeling into watching them as into evaluating character. If interiority matters to him greatly, it competes with the sometimes sheer Rabelaisian enjoyment of physical existence. He is not afraid to refer to himself as "one huge mass of flesh" (166), or to describe an eventful evening in a crowded coach where a fat man "ventured his head out of the coach-door, and swore liberally—whilst his [arse] in direct line with poor S[tevenso]n's nose—entertained him with *sound* and sweetest of exhalations" (174). Faces fascinate him. He talks of "health smiling in the face" (25), of "joy sitting triumphant in his honest face" (26), of Mrs. Sancho wearing "a different face" (35), of someone's countenance "lit up with glee" (76). Meheux's brother George "has a pleasing, cheery phiz" (163), and "there is something in his face which will command attention and love" (166). If these remarks may simply reflect the popularity of physiognomy and the art of reading faces as signs, Sancho's descriptions also always convey the delight of watching a face for the sheer physical or aesthetic pleasure it creates.

These details may be seen as part of an observing nature—that of someone hungry, not just for feeling and friendship, but also for knowledge about what seems or looks new or different. He advises several young men to observe the society around them. To Soubise, who is in India, he says: "I wish to have your description of the fort and town of Madrass—country adjacent—people—manner of living—value of money—religion—laws—animals—fashions—taste, &c. &c." (149). His interest in the new includes an acceptance of different customs and beliefs. He condemns the anti-Catholic Gordon Riots, not just for the destruction of property they occasion, but also because "I am for an universal toleration" (220). This tolerant and anthropological streak contributes to the sense that his letters reflect the physiological and the racial medley of life.

Within this context, his frequent self-deprecating references to himself as a poor black, rather than comforting readers in their racist assumptions, forces them into an awareness of their difference even as they are in the process of exhanging letters, brought onto a common plane through the correspondence. Sancho forces the racial awareness of his body into his own leveling world. So when he asks: "for God's sake! what has a poor starving Negroe, with six children, to do with kings and heroes, and armies and politics?—aye, or poets and painters?—or artists—of any sort?" (107), he indirectly formulates the precise unusual appeal of his letters. But he goes even further. Recommending an African friend looking for a position, he describes his face as being "as dark as your humble [servant's]" (60), but ends by saying that "I like the rogue's looks, or a similarity of colour should not have induced me to recommend him" (60–61). By simultaneously raising and dismissing the issue of skin color, he brings up the notions of difference and similarity, signaling their importance but also undermining or demystifying their significance. Skin color becomes a marker to be reckoned with but also not to be reckoned with. Sancho plays with the signifier, asserting its presence but unmooring it from its associations. It is in these moments that race acquires a subtle republican dimension, since its invocation simultaneously dilutes the hierarchy it is supposed to evoke.

Sancho's sensitivity to male physical beauty and attractiveness also takes on political connotations when seen within this framework, as it suggests a full recognition of others and hence an equalizing move. Referring to Erasmus Middleton, a Methodist expelled from Oxford whom he hears preach while in Scotland, he emphasizes his "good strong voice" but also provides a portrait: "he is well-built—tall—genteel—a good eye—about twenty-five—a white hand, and a blazing ring" (42). He keeps reminding Meheux that his brother George is handsome. When he urges Meheux to "hold up the mirror to an effeminate gallimawfry" and to "rescue this once manly and martial people from the silken slavery of foreign luxury and debauchery" (48), he sounds downright republican. Sancho's aesthetics thus call up a world of masculine beauty, friendship, virtue, and valor, which is strongly reminiscent of civic humanism. Felicity A. Nussbaum argues that, at a time when black men were considered either noble or savage, and white masculinity "rested on imperialism, commerce, and trade" (57), Sancho (and Equiano) attempted to improvise a black masculinity not bound by stereotypes associated with either black or white men. Sancho "refuses to adopt an English masculinity based on commercial excess, or on foreign effeminacy, or even consistently as a man of feeling" (68). Unlike Gronniosaw, whose text carves out separate worlds whether based on interiority or on aesthetics, Sancho places his republican aesthetics within his racially, socially, and culturally constantly shifting discourse, exemplifying a radicalization of the British balancing act between freedom and the common good.

Chapter 2

Trade, Sailors, National Agency, and World Citizenship

Appeals to sentiment in antislavery texts of the late eighteenth and early nineteenth centuries reflected particular concepts of national and international identity, and these concepts in turn were strongly tied to political ideas. Liberalism and republicanism promote different emotional processes by which people create national identities, and these differences remain in the conceptualization of international or cosmopolitan identities. While liberal nationalism cultivates a normative image of the citizen, republicanism thinks of a nation in more horizontal, extensive terms, and these different tendencies shape attempts to conceive of international identities. A view that attempts to appeal to global feeling in the republican way can have more radical implications precisely because of this more collective mind-set.

While most of the black authors discussed in this book had a comparatively radical edge thanks to their international experience, the ones who appear in this chapter developed an emotional rhetoric that conveyed a more comprehensive theory of republican cosmopolitanism. The three black writers discussed here felt profoundly attached to a specific nation, yet they also developed a global identity as they moved from national, cultural, or racial attachment to the horizontal, communal form of "love" involved in republican world citizenship.[1] They acquired their international viewpoint thanks in part to their familiarity with issues of international trade, and with the culture of the ships that supported it. The African American Briton Hammon, and the Afro-British writers Quobna Ottobah Cugoano and Olaudah Equiano, all show that they were open to those influences.[2] While Hammon retains a certain adherence to the liberal individualism that suffused American culture, he also offers a peek into the special consciousness of a world citizen. Cugoano and Equiano can sound thoroughly British when they echo the British ideology of global commerce tempered by humanity, combining the freedom of trade with an eye on the common good. But at times they resist the imperialistic vision by insisting on a world made of equalized, intercultural, and interracial exchanges, thus radicalizing the balancing act performed by the British. As black writers in a white-dominated culture, Hammon, Cugoano, and Equiano demonstrate how sentiment could both express and radicalize the ideologies that surrounded them.

White Novelistic Sentiment, National and International

Because it provided a commentary on the political battles of the revolutionary period, the early American novel was intimately tied to a new sense of national agency, making it an important participant in the link between sentiment and national identity that is the subject of this chapter. As Cathy N. Davidson puts it, "a small body of Americans used the novel as a political and cultural forum, a means to express their own vision of a developing new nation" (*Revolution* 11). Even as most critics agree that the early American novel contributed to shaping the new national identity, however, its political valence is the subject of debate.[3] To Jeffrey Rubin-Dorsky, "the novelists themselves were too conservative in their relation to the state, too ambivalent about the location of legitimate authority, and too uncertain about where their loyalties ultimately lay to have become genuine 'cultural voices' and to have written powerful social critiques." They "remained wedded to the rhetoric of the Revolution, and thus were still intent upon educating an American readership to be good citizens of the Republic" (14). Rubin-Dorsky seems quite dismissive of republicanism, as he downplays its radical potential and highlights its defense of the status quo. Another critic follows Nancy Armstrong's lead in *Desire and Domestic Fiction* and suggests that "sentimental fiction is a catalyst for, not a symptom of, middle-class development" (Evans 41).[4]

Here the sentimental novel is seen as promoting antiaristocratic middle-class values, and as a genre through which a "new form of patriarchal authority depends on grounding male power in consent rather than coercion" (42). In this view, the novels promoted a discourse of self-governance, equating self-interest with a respect for the middle-class patriarchal order, thus imposing liberal ideas through an internalization of values.[5]

In this section I emphasize that, even as it held on to a fading republican vision, the early American novel of sentiment presented the liberal worldview as irresistibly seductive, and so conveyed the new energy involved in both individual and national agency.[6] In the moments when the early novel did hold on to the duties of republican citizenship, it downplayed individualism for the sake of the common good, emphasizing the awareness of one's duty, or holding out the promise of egalitarianism over against a growing competitive worldview. This political philosophy is present, in varying degrees, in all these novels. It is hard not to notice, though, that most of the characters who epitomize the republican ethic are represented as sententious, too good, too measured — as, in one word, boring. Most of the sympathy is reserved for the characters with liberal aspirations, as they are led astray by their passions, or are otherwise unable to control their fate and to act in their own self-interest. The novels seem to project a vision of republicanism as the fuzzy background against which flawed figures sharply profile themselves through their liberal desires, and grab the reader's attention and emotion.[7]

Novels whose main story line deals with seduction represent, and elicit feeling for, women as a way to display the new nation's political complexity, creating an undeniable link between sentiment and national identity. They usually depict as a background ideal a solidly republican wife, whose focus on the common good places her in a harmonious marriage based on sharply different roles allocated men and women for the sake of a stable republic.[8] The embattled protagonist is left to deal with the tragic consequences of a growing liberal individualism and of a "questioning of hierarchies within the family and outside it" (Kerber 485). These women are dealing with the limits of both republicanism, which can feel oppressive, and a seductive liberal ethos, which gives pride of place to individual freedom, even as this individualism implies a moral responsibility tailored to the needs of patriarchy through the relegation of women to the domestic sphere.[9] The novel encourages sympathy for a character who struggles with a constricting notion of the common good, but who is not yet able to locate her own interest in a supposedly free acceptance of a patriarchy built on her exercising moral virtue. Compassion plays a complex role, as readers are made to feel for a young woman whose behavior the novel has ostensibly been written to condemn. Compassion for the protagonist fills the gap left by the loss of the republican ethos and an inability to win the liberal game of freedom. But the game remains enticing.

Susanna Haswell Rowson's *Charlotte Temple* (1791) shows the irresistible enticements of liberal individualism. Montraville, Charlotte's seducer, is "eager and impetuous in the pursuit of a favorite object" (38). It is his impetuousness in the pursuit of his interest and his thoughtlessness as to consequences that make him dangerous, possibly as a warning to readers against the new rash vitality spreading through American society. Although the son of a gentleman, he, like his numerous siblings, has been raised to enter the professions so as to increase his fortunes and opportunities, in the words of his father, "on the basis of merit" (40). Montraville thus stands for an intermediary social class, enjoying the advantages of his birth,[10] but thrown into the individualist free-for-all of a growing capitalist economy. As his father reminds him, "your success in life depends entirely on yourself" (40). Unlike Montraville, Charlotte elicits sympathy because, confronted with his overwhelming, male energy, she finds herself weak and helpless, unable to display the aggressive concern for self-interest characteristic of the rising middle-class.[11] When the narrator implies that Charlotte does not have the "fortitude to resist the impulse of inclination when it runs counter to the precepts of religion and virtue" (29), she urges young women to follow moral principles, but she also acknowledges the existence of impulses, and attempts to teach young women to discriminate between good and bad ones.[12] In a society increasingly dependent on the satisfaction of individual desire and the pursuit of one's interests, women need to develop an ability to direct desires toward their proper goals, so as to contribute to the growth and the stability of the middle class. Charlotte lacks that ability, but the novel encourages the pursuit of that liberal goal for the new nation.

The big scene of compassion that closes the novel signifies an ultimate endorsement of the value of liberalism to the nation, even if some hesitation remains. Julia A. Stern sees it in positive terms, as the generalized commiserating with Charlotte's fate at the end enacts a "vision of a democratic community of compassion," which is part of the narrator's "egalitarian impulse" (68), especially since it is "powerful enough to cross the boundaries of class" (67). But compassion can also be the last recourse in a society more and more unhinged by class disparities, and it does not necessarily create a motivation to change the social conditions that led to the tragedy. When Rowson places in opposition the reactions to Charlotte's plight by two members of the working class—the farmer's wife, who expels her from the house, and the servant who takes her in—she implies that only individual generosity can make the difference between survival and downfall. Similarly, after Mrs. Beauchamp enters the servant's hovel, she sheds tears for Charlotte but can only feel "horror" at the sight of such poverty. The cross-class alliance forged by the spreading of Charlotte's tale does suggest the emergence of a community of compassion, but this community focuses its affect on one exceptional individual. Emotion here does not serve egalitarian ends: it shows an attempt by a community, one that has lost its republican ideals, to rally its members along the lines of individual, Smithian compassion. Still, this is presented as the new energy, and so it suggests that individualism is a main component of the new national identity.

The republican community plays a more important, though ultimately indecisive, role in Hannah Webster Foster's *Coquette* (1797). It is symbolized by Mrs. Richman's speech, in which she defends women's interest in politics as a normal consequence of their concern for the "common weal." At the end of her intervention, "the gentlemen applauded Mrs. Richman's sentiments as truly Roman; and what was more, they said, truly republican" (44), emphasizing her civic humanism and her communitarian spirit. Lucy Freeman reasons in similar terms, linking private behavior with the public good, as when she wishes that young women would adopt a behavior more conducive to the "public weal" (63). But the novel shows that liberalism is increasingly containing republican community within the family and, with it, the political aspirations of women.[13] Mrs. Richman seems aware of her new perspective when, after giving birth, she concedes that "all my happiness is centered within the limits of my own walls; and I grudge every moment that calls me from the pleasing scenes of domestic life." This process of increased privatization, and this acceptance of liberal motherhood, seem to render Mrs. Richman unable to attract the now depressed Eliza Wharton to her home. Just at the moment when Eliza needs the more communal support of friendship, Mrs. Richman expresses its diminished importance in her life: "Not that I am so selfish as to exclude my friends from my affection or society. I feel interested in their concerns, and enjoy their company. I must own, however, that conjugal and parental love are the main springs of my life" (97). The republican community is shrinking as Eliza reaches a crisis and stands "in need of the consoling power of friendship" (100).

Against this background, Eliza Wharton develops a liberal form of energy, and as in *Charlotte Temple*, our sympathy is directed toward a woman unable to channel her newfound desires toward individual morality and acceptance of the patriarchal order. When she tells Mrs. Richman to "let me then enjoy that freedom which I so highly prize," she expresses her awareness of a new frame of mind. "Had the Almighty spared life" (13) and kept her fiancé alive, she would have pursued the path her parents had laid out for her. She now interprets the divine intervention as a turning point, as a signal for her to embrace a new vision of herself and of society. She insists on keeping "the exercise of my free will" (29), and even conceives of marriage as a moment when she will "resign my freedom" (30), a moment she wants to put off. Both Mrs. Richman and Lucy react negatively to her use of the word "freedom," an indication that their worldviews are sharply diverging. Eliza's mother also reacts, but on slightly different grounds, arguing that "a dependent situation" is everybody's lot. Indeed, she continues, "are we not all links in the great chain of society, some more, some less important; but each upheld by others, throughout the confederated whole?" (41). The image of the chain, in spite of its egalitarian connotations, recalls the "great chain of beings," which was invoked to justify hierarchy as much as, even more than, to convey solidarity. Eliza wants to break out of the chain, though she knows that society finds ways to channel her liberal desires even as it stimulates them.

The gap that separates Eliza from her republican friends becomes tragically obvious when she and they have different interpretations of when sympathy is appropriate. After she has received a letter of rejection from Boyer, the minister, Eliza expresses her despair in a letter to Lucy. Her melodramatic outburst ("Oh my friend, I am undone!") highlights her feeling of "ruin," as well as her shame at giving him the "power" to make her suffer "all the pangs of slighted love" (105). In reply, Lucy makes fun of her appeal, playfully calling the elements of her "truly romantic letter" worthy of "a novel." To Lucy, Eliza has made a mistake, but she should recover her "strength of mind" and her "independence of soul" (107) and move on. "Date then, from this, a new era of your life" (108), she concludes. Lucy speaks from the superiority of her own beliefs, and decides that sympathy for Eliza would mean abiding by her worldview. To her, "sense, and sentiment" should make her "superior to every adverse occurrence." A life focused on civic virtue and the common good should subordinate the pain of an individual setback to the progress of reason. Indeed, she presents recent events as the logical conclusion to a former life of "fanciful folly" (107), and an opportunity finally to enter true republican adulthood. To Eliza, however, Boyer's rejection constitutes an indelible mark on her character, proof that she is incapable of playing the game of freedom, which has now become her sole measure of behavior. Her annoyance with his position of power in their relationship reveals that her demand for sympathy pertains not just to a broken heart but to a sudden sense of individual containment, a feeling that she belongs neither in the republican community nor in the competitive world of individual liberalism.

The last part of the novel shows the triumph of liberal sympathy, and a clearer path for the new nation. Just after Eliza has established a so-called friendship with the now married Sanford, her friend Julia expresses her anxiety that, in Eliza's behavior, "one extreme commonly succeeds another" (121). Julia's attempts to bring Eliza to Boston fail, as "sometimes she has been almost persuaded to a compliance with our united request; but soon has resolutely determined against it" (128). Eliza herself declares to Julia that "having incurred so much censure by the indulgence of a gay disposition, I am now trying what a recluse and solitary mode of life will produce" (135). She concludes: "I anticipate, and yet I dread your return; a paradox this" (135). Eliza's constant swaying anticipates the different forms of sympathy she receives as her end draws near. The republican friends express a mixture of affection, benevolence, and we-told-you-so moralizing. But they are upstaged by Eliza's mother, to whom Eliza directs all her thoughts and emotions before she escapes. Julia even finds herself "obliged to suppress my own emotions" (152) as she takes care of Mrs. Wharton. The predominance of the mother in the last part of the novel points to the subsequent development of the sentimental novel in the first half of the nineteenth century, where the biological maternal bond will override other forms of connection, reinforcing a liberal attachment to blood and similarity. Whereas Charlotte's end, and the reasons for her death, are symbolically publicized by the voice of the soldier who answers Montraville's question, the tombstone erected by Eliza's friend Lucy mentions her qualities virtues but decides to "throw a veil over her frailties" (169), signaling the official relegation of the issues to the private sphere, and the novel's final entry into the liberal realm.[14]

The politics of feeling not only played a major role in the early American novel's delineation of national character; it was also present in the representation of America's new identity on the international scene. Early American literature is often associated with the country's budding national identity, but the citizens of the young nation were very much concerned with its international status, especially in matters of commerce, and critics have only recently started to pay attention to what Gesa Mackenthun calls the "transnational and transoceanic vantage point" (343) of early American literature. I focus on two works related to the difficulties encountered at the time in the Mediterranean, where Americans were regularly abducted by so-called Barbary pirates: Rowson's play *Slaves in Algiers* (1794) and Royall Tyler's novel *The Algerine Captive* (1797). In both of these works, the appeal to liberal sentiment indirectly highlights the limitations of their international vision.

As in her novel *Charlotte Temple*, in *Slaves in Algiers* Rowson stages our two political philosophies in sentimental moments that stand out in this otherwise comic play. At the beginning of the play, Rebecca's pining for her enslaved son Augustus clearly associates him with the well-being of the republic. She exclaims: "Oh! my adored boy! must I no more behold his eyes beaming with youthful ardour, when I have told him, how his brave countrymen purchased their freedom with their blood." When she sees him, "my eyes o'erflow with tears" (11). Though feeling takes place on a personal level, it also implies that Augustus, as a son of the republic, possesses a devotion to its common good similar to the one he has inherited from his forefathers—as from his real father. The sentimental reunion at the end of the play has a different political meaning. Rebecca finds her long-lost husband Constant, as well as her daughter Olivia, and the now reunited family of four, together with others, are liberated from their slavery in Algiers. When they leave, a character declares that they are returning to their "native land, where liberty has established her court—where the warlike Eagle extends his glittering pinions in the sunshine of prosperity" (72). Freedom here applies specifically to the individuals of the liberated family. We know they return to America as individuals because "the warlike Eagle" specifically protects the pursuit of prosperity, connecting liberty with the free market of the individualist liberal ethic. It is this particular freedom that triumphs at the end of the play, once again proving the irresistible appeal exercised by the liberal worldview.

The play's international context not only serves, by contrast, to reinforce this national identity strongly anchored in liberalism, but it also functions as a vision of America's interaction with the world. And here Rowson offers the prospect, amazingly persistent until today, of a world remade in the image of liberal American freedom. Indeed, the play ends with Olivia's peroration: "Long, long, may that prosperity continue—may Freedom spread her benign influence thro' every nation, till the bright Eagle, united with the dove and olive-branch, waves high, the acknowledged standard of the world" (72). As Elizabeth Maddock Dillon argues, however, this freedom is predicated, as liberalism has in its practice already been shown to be, on racial purity. Dillon shows that none of the prospective interracial couplings in the play is realized. Using Nancy Armstrong's essay on daughters, which I referred to in chapter 1, she points out that Olivia is the daughter not of a "household," which encourages racial and cultural mixing, but of a racially pure, Anglo-American family. Rowson's vision of an Americanized world is "a disturbing vision of a racialized global geography" (*Slaves* 428). Since the main international concern of the United States was access to global trade routes, *Slaves in Algiers* sketches America's international role as a realization of liberal ideas, in which free trade combines with the philosophical and racial limitations that accompany liberalism.

In *The Algerine Captive* Royall Tyler seems more critical than Rowson about America's role in the world. The first volume ends with a striking change in tone when, after a series of entertaining, satirical segments about life in New England, the narrator tells about embarking as a doctor on a ship named *Sympathy*. The ship makes its way down the West African coast, and the captain starts bargaining for slaves. The protagonist then starts thinking about the victims of "this infamous, cruel commerce"; he imagines "the peaceful husbandman dragged from his native farm; the fond husband torn from the embraces of his beloved wife; the mother, from her babes; the tender child, from the arms of its parent," and he hates himself for participating in "this execrable traffic" (190). He gives heartrending descriptions of the treatment of the Africans, and ends up commiserating with "MY BRETHREN OF THE HUMAN RACE" (194). Like many other antislavery writers, then, Tyler anchors his criticism of slavery in a liberal appeal to sympathy, as he conjures up images of family separation and emphasizes the notion of a common humanity.[15] He uses this liberal appeal to criticize America's participation in what he sees as a despicable form of international commerce.

But the liberalism that drives his critique brings the narrator to conclusions regarding America's international role that are different from Rowson's. After recounting his liberation from slavery in North Africa, the narrator ends his narrative with an emotional appeal, praising "our excellent government, which I have learnt to adore" (240–41). He gives the following advice: "Let no foreign emissaries inflame us against one nation, by raking into the ashes of long extinguished enmity or delude us into the extravagant schemes of another, by recurring to fancied gratitude. Our first object is union among ourselves" (241). Unlike the vision of a world transformed by American liberty in Rowson's imperialistic gesture, the principle of liberty awakens in him an isolationist, exceptionalist reflex bent on reinforcing national identity at the expense of international engagement. The reader may well wonder what happens to his antislavery stance, now silenced, and the question is not answered. Tyler's racial principles may not be as clear as Rowson's, but one earlier passage is revealing. When he describes the language spoken in North Africa—"if language it could be called"—the narrator says it appeared "to be the shreds and clippings of all the tongues, dead and living, ever spoken since the creation" (67). He refers to it disdainfully as a "jargon" or a "medley of sounds" as opposed to "pure Arabic" (68). One can assume that there is only one step toward applying this logic of purity and mongrelization to aspects other than language, including race. In the end, the narrator's experiences in North Africa seem to make him recoil from an international point of view, and fall back on a nationalist rhetoric of union and similarity. Tyler's withdrawal forms an equally limiting counterpart to Rowson's invasive internationalism in the American international imaginary.

On the other side of the Atlantic, the novel of sentiment made an equally important contribution to the definition of national and international identity, but with different political implications.[16] With *Pamela* (1740) and *Clarissa* (1747–48), Samuel Richardson marked the resounding entrance of liberal individualism into the English novel, emphasizing its importance as a component of national identity. Concentrating on the shades and nuances of a character's psyche gave an individualistic push to the process of readers' identification.[17] In *Clarissa* the emphasis on "personal autonomy within a structure of family obligations and role expectations" (Fliegelman, *Prodigals* 29) signified a desire to forge one's destiny, over against established forms of patriarchal authority. This individualism had political ramifications, in that the woman in distress who elicits sympathy represents the aspirations of the middle class, as opposed to the aristocracy represented by the rake.[18] To Lynn Festa, the novel now acted as a "vehicle for fantasies of social mobility," turning into an "agent of social change" (82). Festa accounts for the "revolutionary labor" of *Pamela* through the theoretical appeal typical of liberalism: its "extension of humanity to one individual implies a synecdochal image of the whole," since "the minute particular contains the universal" (84). It works through a process where "sentimentality sought to create an acknowledgment of individual worth through recognition of the similitude of a particular individual; this recognition might then be imaginatively expanded to embrace *all* like individuals" (85).[19] In Richardson's novels, a liberal national identity is promoted through an appeal to feelings of similarity between individuals.

But if Richardson does represent the arrival of the fully subjective individual onto the novelistic scene, he also constantly defines this individual through his or her duties.[20] Unlike the French republicans, postrevolutionary Americans enthusiastically received the liberal dimension of Richardson's work, but as Jay Fliegelman points out, American editions of *Clarissa* suppressed its conflictual representation of authority and individual autonomy, turning the novel into "an unadulterated polemic against parental severity" (*Prodigals* 86). This reception fits the pattern that Fliegelman delineates, through which in America Lockean ideals of education, emphasizing noncoerciveness and voluntarism, increasingly replaced the traditional "fear of the rod." This "introjected voice" (33) of reason reflected the new liberal political ideals of the new American nation. Had the editions remained faithful to the original, or interpretations less one-sided, they would have conveyed Richardson's artful blend of liberalism and republicanism through feeling. To John Mullan, indeed, Richardson's language of feeling is meant to convey a system of values rather than a personal exploration. Just as with moral philosophy, it is the "description of forms of society" that is "the determining concern of the novel of sentiment" (Mullan 25). Richardson's novels consist less in an individual "psychological investigation" than in "moral didacticism" (68). The outward signs of sensibility do receive elaborate treatment in all his novels, which often emphasize the physical symptoms and the illnesses associated with an excess of feeling. But this excess is precisely brought under control, not so it can be "read" better, as in Adam Smith's theory of sympathy, but in a British fear of unbounded passion and "'enthusiasm'" (112). With Richardson sentiment reveals a republican mind that is suffused with liberal passion, but still in stoic control for the sake of the nation's common good.

The combination of liberalism and republicanism played a similarly important role in the sentimental shaping of British international identity. The notion of Englishness itself was made up of the many strands that composed the British Empire, both internal and external. Many British novels in the eighteenth century, from Daniel Defoe's *Robinson Crusoe* (1719) to Maria Edgeworth's *Belinda* (1801), convey both an enthusiasm for freedom and for the individual entrepreneurship made possible by the empire, and a vision of the common good that underlies the business of colonization. In *Belinda*, for example, freedom competes with responsibility and order in discussions of both England and the colonies. The Creole Augustus Vincent is characterized by almost uncontrollable passion, and Virginia's father, a planter in Jamaica, has been saved from a recent slave rebellion. The sentimental plot that links Belinda and Clarence Hervey implies the necessity of both British rule as a civilizing force, and patience and balance in the achievement of a free but well-ordered society. As we will see in the rest of this chapter, the balancing of liberal and republican ideas that marked the ideology of the British Empire would be taken up and expanded by black writers.

Global Trade and the Slave Trade

Probably the single most important factor in the development of an international identity in the eighteenth century was international trade, and that too was a highly political concept. In matters of trade, the opposition between liberal and republican ethics was not always clear-cut, though it is traceable. Trade is often associated with Lockean liberalism, in its emphasis on free contracts and exchange. But even civic humanists could not go against the commercial tide, and while they denounced the corruption that they saw as an inevitable result of commercialism, they knew they could not return to an exclusively agrarian world, so that as early as the turn of the seventeenth century they were looking for "a civic morality for market man" (Pocock, *Machiavellian* 432). They "conceded that trade and bullion had come into the world and irrevocably modified the social character of land" (447). Even Thomas Jefferson, often seen as a representative of the republican viewpoint and as a defender of the independent "yeoman farmer," was a strong promoter of international trade, activated by European demand for American grain. According to Joyce Appleby, Jefferson was not an agrarian romantic: his vision was "both democratic and capitalistic, agrarian and commercial" (267).[21] He opposed heavy taxes so as to increase economic freedom, and in this he displayed a fundamentally liberal creed, a belief in "the limitation of formal authority in deference to individual freedom" (274). The issue was not whether to engage in commercial activities but in what form, and with what kinds of regulations.

The different attitudes to trade that existed on each side of the Atlantic meant different ways of tackling the issue of the slave trade. As David Armitage shows, the British attitude to trade reflected a peculiar balance of liberalism and republicanism that had characterized British politics throughout the century.[22] The British had a long history of mercantilism and government intervention in matters of trade, and British abolitionists presented the elimination of the slave trade as one of the government's roles in the promotion of the common good. They showed that blind faith in the Smithian "invisible hand" could lead to horrible oppression and suffering, and that republican appeals to the common good could still inflect, and even trump, liberal approaches to trade. As part of this concern for the common good, abolitionists favored promoting an increase in exchange of nonhuman commodities with the Africans. Because this increase would help to spread wealth and civilization in the process, abolition would lead to an expansion of imperial power. Arguments for the abolition of the slave trade thus combined governmental market intrusion with a backhanded boosting of a liberal commercial policy that served national and imperialistic interests.[23] In America, on the other hand, the debate was rather about the internal workings of liberalism. Americans showed an enthusiasm for free trade.[24] They tended to couch their opposition to the slave trade in the liberal language of natural rights. The debate came to pit blacks' natural right to freedom against freedom of contract for slave traders.

American discussions of the slave trade showed the fragility of the concept of freedom when faced with other interests or beliefs. Individual freedom had much to battle against, and if it triumphed, it is because the American states perceived that the abolition of the slave trade did not fundamentally go against their interests. During the Revolution, the American colonies considered the possibility of abolishing the trade, but only as part of their desire to sever themselves from commerce with the mother country. They soon forgot about it, and the Articles of Confederation did not mention the trade.[25] Discussions about the slave trade during the 1787 Constitutional Convention showed that ideals of freedom and individual integrity were powerless against the interests of slaveholders, who used the same arguments as a threat to the formation of the Union.[26] Even Northern representatives argued thus, evincing the general sentiment that freedom to trade naturally overruled the bestowal of freedom on all persons. Roger Sherman of Connecticut, for example, "declared his personal disapproval of slavery but refused to condemn it in other parts of the nation" (qtd. in Finkelman 214). When, as part of the final compromise, the Constitution barred Congress from prohibiting the trade for the next twenty years, James Madison commented that "twenty years will produce all the mischief that can be apprehended from the liberty to import slaves" (qtd. in Finkelman 218). It was clear to him that "liberty" was being prostituted. The relativity of the concept comes out when we realize that the South accepted the power of Congress to regulate commerce once the issue of the slave trade was out of the way.

The American abolition of the trade twenty years later is less surprising than one might think in view of these discussions. Already during the Constitutional Convention, none of the states was actively importing slaves. In fact, one needs to keep in mind that North America was, by comparison, never a big importer of Africans. Estimates show that "over the entire history of the Atlantic slave trade, North America received no more than 6 per cent of the Africans imported into the New World" (D. Davis, *Age of Revolution* 58). The South had also won a victory when, for all practical purposes, it obtained the extension of slavery into the newly acquired Louisiana Territory in 1803 — in contrast to the British handling of captured islands such as Trinidad and Dutch Guiana, which were left out of the slave trade. So when in his annual Message to Congress in December 1806 President Jefferson condemned those "violations of human rights which have been so long continued on the unoffending inhabitants of Africa" (qtd. in Thomas 551), he was aware that his urging to put an end to the slave trade did not fundamentally oppose the interests of the Southern states. The argument of "human rights" could now prevail relatively unimpeded. The fact that the debate in Congress focused on questions of enforcement rather than of principle also suggests the awareness that smuggling would spread widely, as it did.

British abolitionists did use the theme of freedom, but mostly placed the debate within a wider concern for global civilization. British debates displayed an interesting evolution when the importance of "civilizing savages" became an antislavery rather than a proslavery argument. A major proslavery argument had insisted that the slave trade removed Africans from the clutches of a barbarian and pagan culture, and gave them the so-called benefits of Western civilization and religion. Many antislavery writers tried to show that a humane trade based on nonhuman commodities would achieve that purpose more efficiently and to the benefit of all involved, strengthening rather than weakening British and African interests alike. Of course, this means that abolitionism partly relied on the ideologies of capitalism, imperialism, and cultural superiority. But to some extent these ideologies did encourage an international give-and-take between equal participants. The future abolitionists envisioned was not only one of neoliberal globalization and unfettered enterprise, but also one in which commerce carried values of mutual recognition and respect. David Brion Davis points out that, during the independence struggles of Latin America, the rising bourgeoisie of those countries looked with admiration to Britain's "civilized liberalism" (*Age of Revolution* 71), a complex idea that combined trade, capitalism, and moral value. Though it made abolition appear as "an act of free will" (71) on the part of nations that went along, Britain's international suppression of the trade showed, ironically, the emancipatory potential of imperialistic coercion.[27] If "both self-interest and ideology" (83) motivated these moves, they had the power to reinforce each other in a way they did not when the American North left the South to its own devices.[28]

White abolitionist texts about the slave trade used sentiment in a way that reflected these various imbrications of liberalism and republicanism on each side of the Atlantic.[29] In the British approach—which is also that of a few early American authors—sentiment appears at the juncture where freedom (notably freedom of contract) needs to be restricted in its application because it leads to human exploitation. Sentiment guides the reader toward a desire to suppress freedom of contract so as to achieve a common good, which often consists in the spread of culture from the imperial center. In those texts, there is always a balance between maintaining individual freedom and bestowing the benefits of civilization. In most American texts, on the other hand, feeling is directed more sharply and more exclusively toward the individual. It overwhelms the reader with a sense of individual sympathy, obscuring the restrictive components of a feeling enlisted for the sake of the common good. Here individual connection matters, rather than an overall sense of a society taking it upon itself to restrict particular aspects of its liberal credo. The forms taken by sentiment in texts about the slave trade thus reflect an important difference between American and British approaches, or between the negative freedom symbolized by the 1790 debate in the U.S. House of Representatives, which considered a clause "*denying* its authority to legislate" (D. Davis,

Age of Revolution 133) about the treatment of slaves, and the British series of measures that imposed norms on its colonies.

In *Considerations on Slavery* (1767) the American Nathaniel Appleton reaches for sentiment at the moment he hits on liberalism's internal contradiction between freedom of trade and the human right to freedom. Appleton first sets up a contrast between a free Briton and a slave, resorting to strikingly Lockean terms to emphasize the contradiction in the Briton's right to enjoy the products of his labor and the slave's lack of that right. A slave, moreover, "can't marry, because marriage is founded on promise, and slaves can promise nothing" (Appleton 129), an interesting illustration of what Thomas L. Haskell considers one of the premises of capitalism.[30] Appleton clearly uses the tools of liberalism to launch his critique. But he also finds himself condemning the particular forms of trade and capital accumulation that result from the slave trade. "It is well known," he says, "we have been above a century past crouding our luxuries upon the Africans"; as a consequence, "they were tempted to sell their brethren, to purchase our intoxicating liquors and childish toys; thus we imposed upon their weakness, and encouraged their barbarity." In its dealings with the Africans, Appleton suggests, free trade has been carried too far. Appleton then suddenly reaches for sentiment, describing heartwrenching scenes of family separation, and exclaiming dramatically: "Oh! methinks I hear their screeches, rending the very Heavens, when these horrid scenes take place!" (130). When he confronts the exploitation engendered by liberal ideology, Appleton cannot respond otherwise than by impassioned appeals to feeling that somewhat avoid a resolution of the contradiction between individual freedom and freedom of contract. Feeling is used to convey the looming realization that liberalism needs to be supplemented, reined in, or supplanted, but its motivational energy comes from sympathy at the level of the individual and the family.

The abolitionist writings of the Quakers are representative of the difference between American and British responses to slavery and the slave trade. In Pennsylvania, where they had a tradition of social leadership, and where they took pains to continue their adherence to a number of causes as a form of participation in the Revolution so as to ward off possible accusations of loyalism, the Quakers based their appeals on natural rights and the Declaration of Independence.[31] In Britain, on the other hand, Quakers tended to collaborate with Parliament and government officials, evincing a more pragmatic concept of abolition, one that combined natural right with considerations of what was best for the empire.

The distinction may also reflect the differences between American and British feeling about race. As Davis points out, the American Quakers "understood the extent and depth of racial prejudice" (*Age of Revolution* 225), and even as they focused on the practical insertion of free blacks in society, they knew that an appeal to natural rights would fit into the revolutionary liberal viewpoint. British Quakers lived at some distance from the conditions they were addressing, and, like other British abolitionists, they sought to integrate blacks into the common good of the empire.

The American Quaker Anthony Benezet stands out, in that his stances sound generally more British, and his most profound impact was on British abolitionists.[32] His outraged annotations to a 1772 proslavery text by Reverend Thomas Thompson are a good illustration of a close but evolving relationship between liberty and the common good. Thompson first brings up the common good in order to defend slavery. "The subject will grow more serious upon our hands," Thompson announces, "when we consider the buying and selling negroes, not as a clandestine or piratical business, but as an open, public trade; encouraged and promoted by acts of parliament. For so, if being contrary to religion, it must be deemed a national sin" (11). Of freedom, he acknowledges that "by the law of nature, all persons are free. But absolute freedom is incompatible with civil establishments. Every man's liberty is restricted by national laws, and natural priviledge does rightly yield to legal constitutions, which are designed and enacted for the public weal" (23). To Thompson, the public nature of the trade, as well as its contribution to the "public weal," should trump any scruples one might have about the cruelty involved. But he links this point to a strict reliance on legal status, arguing that "it is alledged that the setting to sale human creatures is violating the natural distinction of the species, and levelling men with beasts. But to this it may be answered, that every person is treated as a human being, who is treated according to his lawful state and condition. The buying a slave is taking him as what he is; and the sale does but signify, that his owner is willing to part with, and another has a mind to have him. Here then is no violation of humanity; and the property in such individual is transferable, like all other property" (29). Thompson typifies the mixture of implied contractarianism and concern for the common good that had justified slavery for many years.

In his annotations to Thompson's pamphlet, Benezet makes it clear that moral feeling should inform political ideology. He notes that the trade is "certainly a national sin!" ("Unpublished Notes" 218), implying that the nation, like a person, has a moral responsibility.[33] His reaction to Thompson's theory of freedom shows that, unlike Thompson, he is willing to put limits to contractarianism on the basis of a higher principle or good: "Absolute freedom is not incompatible with civil establishments: because absolute freedom can only consist in restraining Evil Doers by just & equitable Laws, that the Weak & Poor, may be as free as the Rich & Strong, for all men ought to be absolutely free to do good according to their ability; & if they are not free to do evil, it is not to be accounted a restraint upon liberty; but a restraint only upon Tyranny; so that the author has manifestly confounded the one term for the other" (220). He allows for the value of freedom, but only when qualified as "absolute" freedom. "Absolute" can connote the unrestricted behavior of freedom in its simplest sense, but for Christians the "absolute" is the divine reality of moral purity, which is consistent with his insistence that only moral behaviors express absolute freedom. Benezet strengthens this moral connotation of "absolute freedom" by replacing it with the word "liberty" and its connotation of the free citizen ennobled by moral restraint. He then foregrounds that moral limits serve the common good, by placing "liberty" in opposition to the brutal selfishness of "Tyranny." Benezet displays a desire to merge liberalism and republicanism in his take on the motivational power of the word "freedom" in early America. His equation of simple freedom with tyranny and his insistence that "Evil Doers" must be restrained for the good of "all men" show a profound respect for the notion of freedom, but mixes fear of an excess of such freedom with an emotional appeal to a republican communal identification.[34]

The idea of freedom as a mixture of individual freedom and a higher good is, in a slightly different form, at the heart of his famous 1771 pamphlet, *Some Historical Account of Guinea*. Here we find a book-length promotion of trade, not just as an appurtenance of freedom, but as a factor in the spreading of the common good throughout Africa. In this, Benezet amplifies the notion of *doux commerce* that had emerged in the course of the eighteenth century. His depiction of the African West Coast as a land of paradisiacal fertility, and his primitivist account of the inhabitants, set the stage for the argument that "it was the unwarrantable lust of gain, which first stimulated the Portugueze, and afterwards other Europeans, to engage in this horrid traffic." The natives were "an inoffensive people, who, when civilly used, traded amicably with the Europeans" (Benezet, *Guinea* 50). One feels here the sense of a missed opportunity to use this openness of the natives in more benevolent ways, and to spread both civilization and Christianity to a people who would benefit from the superiority of European culture. Abolishing the slave trade would "give them a better sense of the true use of the blessings of life," and this process "would produce the same effect upon them, which it had on the inhabitants of Europe, formerly as savage and barbarous as the natives of Africa" (58). This view may be seen as announcing the double-edged use of the common good in the imperialistic mindframe, as it urges an intrusion on immoral trading activities in the name of superior values. In any case, it shows both a promotion of a commercial mind-set and a willingness to restrain capitalism for the sake of a moral social order.

Benezet's use of sympathy underpins this approach. He devotes the middle section of the book to depictions of hardships, cruel treatment, torture, and death. While he aims at shaking his audience emotionally, urging the reader to "bring the matter home to thy own heart" (102), the real point is that this suffering is inefficient and wasteful. He does recreate scenes of family separation, asking about the family members: "what sympathy, what commiseration, do they meet with?" (107), in a way that Keith A. Sandiford calls "a classic of antislavery sentimentalism" (50). But Benezet also embeds his criticism of cruel treatment within an argument for the ultimate material and moral benefits of freedom. In an early footnote, he quotes approvingly from William Robertson's *History of Charles the 5th*, in which the author describes the effects of the abolition of servitude in England, where "'new prospects opened, and new incitements to ingenuity and enterprise presented themselves, to those who were emancipated.'" People were prodded to useful economic activity by "'the expectation of bettering their fortunes, as well as that of raising themselves to a more honorouble position'" (57). Toward the end of the book, Benezet reminds us that "it is a fondness for wealth, for authority, or honour, which prompts most men in their endeavours to excell" (112), and Africans will not be able to participate in this endeavor, or to even have the motivation to do so, as long as they are treated like brutes. Benezet channels the reader's sympathy toward acceptance of a world based on individual enterprise, so that imperceptibly the notion of common good slides toward a legitimation of capitalism. In Benezet's antislavery feeling, we see a very British use of the role of the common good, in its mix of morality, commercialism, and paternalism.

The direction of his thinking is confirmed by one appendix, which consists of selections from Malachy Postlethwayt's *Universal Dictionary of Trade and Commerce*. Here the famous political economist places the abolition of the slave trade within a clearly delineated philosophy of commerce. He asks whether Africans, "notwithstanding their colour, are not capable of being civilized," the way other "primitive inhabitants" have been. Indeed, might not these people, "by proper management in the Europeans, become as wise, as industrious, as ingenious, and as humane, as the people of any other country has done?" (qtd. in Benezet, *Guinea* 122). It might be wiser for Europeans "to endeavour to cultivate a friendly, humane, and civilized commerce with those people, into the very center of their extended country" (123). Hasn't commerce "proved the great means of civilizing all nations, even the most savage and brutal" (124)? Postlethwayt's discourse of humanity, combined with the ideology of civilization, buttresses Benezet's argument. Together, Benezet and Postlethwayt reveal the British attempt to combine notions of freedom and the common good in order both to abolish immoral forms of trade, and to promote a commerce that will increase imperial wealth and power.

Thomas Clarkson, on whom Benezet's book had a tremendous impact, continued in that line of thinking. The indefatigable British abolitionist starts *An Essay On the Impolicy of the African Slave Trade* (1788) by establishing the "commercial spirit of the Africans," so that "much higher advantages might be derived in another line of trade" (Clarkson 4) than the slave trade. He then brings up two propositions: first, "that the Africans, by proper encouragement, can be brought into habits of labour," and second, "that free labour can be made the medium, through which the productions of their country may be collected, or brought to maturity and use" (5). Indeed, the traffic in natural goods rather than people would be much more beneficial to the nation. Clarkson then proceeds to explain in great detail how Africa can contribute to the growth of a global market in commodities bought and sold at lower prices, through its woods, drugs, peppers, spices, tobacco, rice, indigo, and even cotton. After referring to Postlethwayt, he summarizes his argument by stating that "they would afford an inexhaustible mine of wealth to our dyers and artificers in wood; that they would enable us to break the monopoly of the Dutch; would repay us for the loss of America; be the cheapest market for all sorts of raw materials for our manufacturers; and abound with other national advantages" (22). Notwithstanding the strength of his pleas for individual sympathy, it was by appealing to a larger notion of the common good, in the form of increased global commerce, higher standards of living, and inexhaustible sources of goods and employment, that Clarkson hoped to sensitize and convince his audience. Free trade could not be totally free, but this lack of freedom was meant to encourage a morally defensible and ultimately more beneficial form of exchange.

While these kinds of arguments may be conceived of as fundamentally liberal, their global vision bespeaks a desire to establish forms of freedom that were not just "negative." Admittedly, many of these abolitionist writers may have been influenced by Adam Smith, who in his *Wealth of Nations* (1776) defended the organization of society around free labor as more stimulating of individual enterprise and hence as more productive of wealth. This argument was already in use in the American colonies. In his 1773 *Brief Considerations on Slavery*, for example, William Dillwyn argued that enslaved persons have no personal motivation to promote the peace and prosperity of the country that enslaves them. He opposed the slave to the servant who, because he can look forward to independence and freedom, feels involved in "promoting the prosperity of his country" and hence has "beneficial effects" on "our lands and produce" (273). But many of the British arguments recognize that some contracts should be invalidated because a society based on global exchanges can impose norms that positively advance the public good. The logic that justified imperialism simultaneously granted a government the powers that could offset some unwanted consequences of liberal individualism. When Granville Sharp brought up the point that blacks too were the king's subjects and hence under his protection, he was expressing this very belief.

Sailors, Democracy, and World Citizenship

The other major international hub in the eighteenth and early nineteenth centuries was the ship, the world of sailors. Sailors were an important part of the global capitalist network, and yet when looked at politically, they formed an essential component of what Peter Linebaugh and Marcus Rediker have called the "many-headed hydra" symbolic of oppositional and revolutionary forces in the seventeenth, eighteenth, and early nineteenth centuries. To these authors, sailors represent a vital spirit of democracy and freedom, but also of communal engagement, which manifested itself as early as 1609 on the island of Bermuda, where the *Sea-Venture* was shipwrecked and where sailors rebelled against the authority of their leaders, organizing mutinies and even a maroon society. When in *The Tempest*, which was based on the story of that shipwreck, Shakespeare imagines that Trinculo and Stephano form an alliance with Caliban, he is hinting at a possible interracial solidarity between members of oppressed classes, brought together by the exigencies of the sea. The two Europeans represent a working class deprived of its livelihood through the phenomenon of the enclosures, and Caliban typifies the colonized native, but together they nurture similar grievances, and face regimes of terror. Linebaugh and Rediker argue that the exploration and colonization of the Atlantic engendered situations, such as a shipwreck and the formation of a community on an island, that helped foster a revolutionary consciousness outside national boundaries. In Britain, this consciousness took on various shapes and forms, ranging from the Putney Debates and the Levellers to the active proletarian spirit two centuries later, which to the established order were embodied in the threatening monstrosity of the hydra. The sailors keep recurring as important figures at the heart of a number of democratic and revolutionary movements.

One could say that the world of white sailors enacted a complex combination of liberal and republican influences. Sailors often writhed under what they experienced as an oppressive system. Linebaugh and Rediker use the term "hydrarchy" to refer to both the discipline imposed from above and the sailors' own culture developed from below, a double meaning that highlights the complex ideological influences that suffused the sailors' world. The ship was "both an engine of capitalism in the wake of the bourgeois revolution in England and a setting of resistance" (Linebaugh and Rediker 144). Indeed, if the ships were becoming an essential component in the fast-developing capitalist order, an order in which the sailors participated, the workers on those ships had various forms of oppression to contend with. Because of the notoriously harsh discipline and low wages, sailors "mutinied, deserted, rioted, and altogether resisted naval service" (150). The involuntary recruitment by press gangs also represented a form of slavery to many sailors, who tried to resist it. This culture of resistance went together with the forging of solidarity. The sailors' world was "proletarian and oppositional" (154), a breeding ground for progressive and liberatory ideas.

The internationalism of the sea promoted this special brand of radical thought. Because captains in need of a workforce often recruited independently from skill, ethnicity, or nationality, the ship became, "if not the breeding ground of rebels, at least a meeting place where various traditions were jammed together in a forcing house of internationalism" (151).[35] The world of the sailors survived through cooperation that broke the barriers of ethnic and national identity. Because of the limited space on a ship, its crew formed a microcosm where equal participation in work, survival, and rebellion fostered a sentiment of equal belonging. Being a member of this "motley crew" meant, by extension, being a citizen of the world, in the real sense of belonging to an inclusive, international, egalitarian community. This concept of global citizenship was new. The 1659 parliamentary debate on slavery, for example, revealed its racial roots, defining whites as English and Englishness as a "global citizenship that protected its owners against violence" (134). By contrast, in *Two Dialogues on the Man-Trade* (1760), J. Philmore emphasized that blacks and whites are "members of one and the same great society, spread over the face of the whole earth." Indeed, "if I see an Englishman in distress, I pity him, and think myself obliged to relieve him, if I can, more as being a man, than as being born in the same country, or as being a member of the same civil society as myself, more as a citizen in the world, than as a citizen of England" (9). Philmore's statement emphasizes more than a mere human bond: the whole world forms a "civil society" of which blacks and whites are equal members or citizens. Further on, he defends the slaves' right to "repel that force with force" (54), condoning resistance and rebellion. Since his text is partly based on accounts he has received "from the mouths of some sailors" (14), we see a link between their culture and Philmore's notion of true, interracial global citizenship.[36]

Black sailors grasped fully the import of this cosmopolitan egalitarianism. As W. Jeffrey Bolster points out, many early black autobiographers who had also been sailors presented themselves as "citizens of the world" (37). Black American sailors dealt directly with the pragmatic notion of citizenship, since in 1796, in response to British impressment of American seamen, Congress issued Seamen's Protection Certificates intended for American citizens, among which, if free, black sailors were included. Citizenship became a concept not so much to be attained as to be extended, both in its content and in its reach. Enslaved seamen inevitably came into contact with these free blacks and with the egalitarian maritime world, even if most of them did coastal work.[37] Both free and enslaved black seamen were thus thoroughly familiar with the sailors' culture of solidarity, resistance, and rebellion. That was the case in the North especially, where many blacks were concentrated in maritime towns. All blacks were aware of the advantages offered by a life at sea, including wages, worldliness, and forms of respect and cooperation unlike any found on the mainland. For a black man, "ships provided a workplace where his color might be less a determinant of his daily life and duties than elsewhere" (75). Indeed, "skill mattered more than race" (80) in the determination of the hierarchy on the ship. Black seamen lived in constant contact with whites, and shared labor, various concerns, and cultural practices with them, especially when brought together in the forecastle. In many ways, white sailors saw themselves as slaves in a ruthless system, and this feeling sharpened their sympathy with the plight of blacks.

The maritime Atlantic world was not devoid of racism, however, and the white sailors' democratic vision did not always extend to an acceptance of multiracial equality and citizenship. According to Bolster, "many white seamen simply did not like blacks" (93). Black sailors, as a result, often combined their cosmopolitanism with a sense of a racially based community that announced future forms of black nationalism and black internationalism. The status of the blacks aboard ship was often limited because of their race. Many of them were cooks, stewards, or musicians. This discrimination often heightened their awareness of racial politics, at a time when racial discourses were crystallizing on both sides of the Atlantic. It also contributed to the creation of an African consciousness, as men originally from different African regions and tribes were lumped together in the same category. This gave them an identity that was both black and international, unlike that of slaves isolated on mainland plantations. Interestingly, the incipient black nationalism of black sailors differed from the kind of nationalism that aimed for middle-class respectability and acceptance by the wider community.[38] Bolster emphasizes that "the values inculcated by maritime work rarely promoted the responsibility and respectability so important to free black society in its formative stages" (159), and that sea work maritime culture was "stigmatized by the taint of immorality" (160). The black sailors' type of social and political mobility engendered a freer form of racial consciousness, relatively independent from middle-class values, and hence more open to radical influences.

In spite of these gestures toward black nationalism, black sailors were ideally placed to develop a multifaceted, diasporic identity, appreciative of global cultures and not limited by a racially exclusive concept of community. Their position led them to acquire a unique sense of the possibilities of multiracial, world citizenship. They found themselves in a world of constant exchange, and cooperated with both blacks and whites on many levels, including collective work, and strikes and mutinies. Some mutinies may even have resulted from ideological motivations rather than from specific grievances, indicating a possible awareness of more radical political ideas. As Bolster points out, the Atlantic world saw "currents of black people in motion carrying and exchanging ideas, information, and style," contributing to "the evolution of diasporic consciousness and blacks' cultural hybridity" (21). Their identity was therefore extremely shifting and mobile. They "combined and recombined their various identities (racial, regional, gender, class, occupational) in different ways" (35). While still partly defined by their race and nationality, they were international citizens par excellence.

Literary and dramatic representations of sailors did not reflect this potential radicalism; in fact, they revealed an elasticity that points to a certain discomfort with what was often experienced as alien in the appearances and the lives of sailors. The most common image of the sailor was of a rough, rambunctious personage, fond of women and booze but also loyal to his country. As such, the image of the sailor helped enhance the mythology that Britain was destined "to achieve military and commercial glory as a maritime nation" (Quilley 81). Geoff Quilley emphasizes that artistic and cultural representations of the sailor partly contributed to a unified national identity. On the other hand, the supposedly inherent masculinity of the type also made way for more feminized and sentimentalized versions. These images not only expressed homoeroticism but also conferred on images of sailors the ability to promote a different sensibility, and hence a different politics. According to Gillian Russell, "if the heroicization of the tar represented a legitimation of plebeian patriotism, to characterize the sailor as a creature of feeling rather than intellect, like a woman, was one way of ensuring that the legitimation would not go too far" (103). Sentimental moments could function as a fulcrum toward a different political vision.

Briton Hammon

The straightforward, adventurous tale of Briton Hammon, published in Boston in 1760, and the first African American prose text to be published in North America, contains a climactic moment that, in its appeal to individual sympathy, anticipates forms of liberal sentiment found in many later slave narratives. With the permission of his master, General Winslow, Hammon had left Massachusetts on a ship to Jamaica in 1747, shipwrecked off the coast of Florida, spent several years as the captive of an

Indian tribe, escaped, but was then taken prisoner in Cuba. In the following passage, Hammon has been serving the governor of Cuba for several years. When he is discovered by the captain of a ship on which he is trying to escape, and the captain orders him and his friends to be taken back to shore, Hammon switches to a supplicatory mode: "I entreated the Captain to let me, in particular, tarry on board, begging, and crying to him, to commiserate my unhappy Condition" (23). This moment is different in tone from the rest of the narrative. In his previous descriptions of his peregrinations, Hammon has adopted a matter-of-fact attitude that, in spite of his various captivities, has made him sound cool and in control, his eyes always open for the next possibility of escape. Now he has been spotted by the captain through some inexplicable imprudence: after the ship started sailing, "I thought myself safe, and so made my Appearance upon Deck" (22–23). His only recourse at this point seems to be an appeal to the captain's humanity.

The moment anticipates liberal appeals not only through its reliance on individual sympathy but also, as was the case in texts discussed in the previous chapter, through its simultaneous staging and suppression of the racial body. Hammon's decision to appear on deck is significant in a narrative so much dependent on acts of seeing and being seen. When stranded off the coast of Florida and paddling ashore, for example, Hammon and his crewmates had "espy'd a Number of Canoes, which we at first took to be Rocks" (21), and which turned out to be sixty Indians. They paddled back to the ship, and the Indians "order'd us round to the Starboard, and as we were passing round the Bow, we saw the whole Number of Indians, advancing forward and loading their Guns" (23). When the Indians saw Hammon jump out, they went after him and caught him. In these scenes, readers are forced clearly to visualize the characters, and are picturing what they know from the narrative's title is a black man, but his race remains absent from the text of the whole tale itself. When he is spotted on the ship and addresses the captain, though, Hammon seems to make an indirect reference to his race, requesting compassion for himself "in particular" compared with the other stowaways, and pointing to his "unhappy Condition." The euphemism reveals the workings of the liberal sentimental moment: racial appearance is the origin of both oppression and sympathetic identification, but the discourse of sympathy needs to suppress it in order to appeal to humanitarian feeling.

Against this liberal sentimental politics of the body, however, a different, republican strain marks descriptions of other sentimental moments, and shows the validity of Bolster's point that "Hammon, his black shipmates, and those with whom they conversed were citizens of the world" (9). A feeling of egalitarian brotherhood particularly suffuses the passage where Hammon lists the individual names and origins of the sailors who would be killed during the Indian assault. Some come from Plymouth, another from Cape Cod, others are "Strangers," and one of them is a "Molatto." This one moment when race is made explicit in the text becomes swept up in what Robert Desrochers, Jr., calls "egalitarian undercurrents" ("'Surprizing'" 155), the same way the "strangers" are.[39] The person of mixed race can be identified by that trait because it does not need suppression: it does not mark him for oppression but simply constitutes his most distinctive visual characteristic. Race is present, and becomes part of the republican feel of the community on the ship. The whole passage overflows with strong feeling about this massacre of "the whole of the People" (Hammon 21), so that the sympathizing reader is made to feel for a small republican world that would otherwise threaten the social order were it extended to the mainland. This scene conveys political thoughts at odds with those of the scene discussed before, and shows Hammon's radical leaning, in spite of a clear simultaneous adherence to liberal sympathy.

The narrative, moreover, contains a wider international feeling that, while also marked by some liberal sympathy, constitutes an even sharper radicalization, all the more striking compared with the forms of sentiment found in white-authored texts at the time. Again, the liberal element is present, and announces the nineteenth-century slave narrative. The moment of Hammon's reunion with his "master," General Winslow, anticipates later sentimental reunion scenes, except that in this case, of course, the reunion takes place with the white master.[40] Hammon has heard that a General Winslow is present on board, "and in a few Days Time the Truth was joyfully verify'd by a happy Sight of his Person, which so overcome me, that I could not speak to him for some Time" (24). The narrative obviously presents itself as a story of return, with clear allusions to the prodigal son. General Winslow represents the father, the equivalent of the family, including the national family, to which Hammon feels he belongs, as is confirmed by the ship's lieutenant when he refuses to deliver "any Englishman under English Colours" (23) in response to the Spaniards' demand to have him back. When Winslow, equally glad to see Hammon, tells him that he is "like one arose from the Dead" (24), Winslow sees him as a Lazarus, simultaneously reducing the international space Hammon has just navigated to a subterranean realm of the dead. Hammon has risen back to the English nation, situated at the apex of the world of the living, and this international hierarchy underpins the moment of sentimental reunion between them.

But while Hammon seems to agree with this nationalist reading, the story we have just read does not. It presents a number of episodes of captivity and escape, striking in their parallelism. Each time, the captivity is mitigated. The Indians end up being "better to me then my Fears"; they "soon unbound me, but set a Guard over me every Night" (22). In Cuba, he is employed by the governor, and in the end "I had my Liberty to walk about the City, and do Work for my self." In spite of this relative freedom, when a ship comes in, he has "nothing now to do, but to seek an Opportunity how I should make my Escape" (23). One is left to wonder, in spite of all the elements of closure, whether the ending does not hook back up to the beginning, with Hammon again feeling the desire to escape that may have motivated him to leave in the first place. The return would then echo the other captivities described in the narrative. Desrochers convincingly speculates that "the preface and postscript offer instances in which we can see the handiwork of an editor who took it upon himself to attach appropriately pious introductory and closing remarks" ("'Surprizing'" 57). If that is the case, the celebration of Hammon's return "to my own Native Land" in the last paragraph, which can be attributed to the white editor, contrasts sharply with the import of the previous paragraph, which is probably Hammon's own conclusion. There he expresses the desire to "retain a grateful Remembrance, as long as I live in the World" (24). Instead of burying his experiences in praise of his nation and his God, he seems to wish to keep those memories alive and present, as a contribution to his awareness of himself as a global citizen. As a concluding statement, this belonging in "the World" seems to triumph over the moments of liberal sentiment that appear in other parts of the narrative, sending the reader out with a wider international consciousness filled with republican longings.

Quobna Ottobah Cugoano

A British attitude to trade partly comes through in Quobna Ottobah Cugoano's *Thoughts and Sentiments on the Evil of Slavery* (1787), but it underpins a unique global sensibility derived from a Black Atlantic outlook.

Cugoano was not a sailor, but he did have a transatlantic experience, as he was snatched from Africa at an early age, transported to the West Indies, and then brought to England in 1772. Working as a servant in the home of the painters Richard and Maria Cosway, he soon acquired literacy and a substantial knowledge of British literature and culture. He also developed a friendship with Olaudah Equiano, who was himself profoundly acquainted with both the British and the international maritime world, and his radicalism carries whiffs of that culture's multiracial cosmopolitanism. In his indictment of the slave trade, Cugoano uses much of the typical rhetoric, calling it "iniquitous traffic" (9) and referring to its practitioners as "those who must eventually resign their own claim to any degree of sensibility and humanity, for that of barbarians and ruffians" (10). Much later in the essay he points to the advantages, to all involved, of free and humane trade with the Africans. A voracious reader, especially as concerns slavery and the slave trade, Cugoano was possibly influenced by some of the white writers discussed above. In any case, his approach reflects that mixture of belief in a balance of freedom and the common good that characterized British writings on trade at the time. But Cugoano was also most probably influenced by his discussions with Equiano, whose text will be discussed in the next section. He uses feeling in his ideologically complex text in ways that support the political infrastructure of this trade theory, but as we will see, his international, Black Atlantic consciousness, and its focus on a world citizenship, lend it a more radical bent.

Like most writers at the time, Cugoano uses the language of the liberal Enlightenment in order to attack the violations of natural rights and liberties perpetrated through the slave trade and slavery, and he presents these principles with a great deal of feeling, never forgetting to emphasize the immense human suffering involved. He opens his essay by praising abolitionist writers who "have endeavoured to restore to their fellow-creatures the common rights of nature," a most important assistance to "the unfortunate Black People" (9) who have been deprived of them. The whole essay is partly an attempt to convince its readers of the breach to "every idea of justice, equity, reason and humanity" (10) that these practices represent. When he thinks of his time in Grenada, "the grievous thoughts which I then felt, still pant in my heart" (15); and he knows that, today still, many "are suffering in all the extreme bitterness of grief and woe, that no language can describe" (16). The captains are "unfeeling monsters," and the parting of families leads to the most horrendous scenes: "Here daughters are clinging to their mothers, and mothers to their daughters, bedewing each others naked breasts with tears" (74).[41] A strong appeal to liberal sympathy suffuses the whole text.

At the same time, Cugoano does not see contracts, which are the staple of a liberal world, as necessarily always valid. To him, there is a difference between slavery and "voluntary service" (35), since the latter involves consent of the person offering his or her services, while slavery consists in sheer theft and robbery. Taking away someone's liberty is "the worst kind of robbery" (11), he says. Cugoano thus places the notion of natural rights within a clear mercantilist context, insisting that his grievances are not just about fundamental humanity but also about the lack of validity of any kind of contract that would involve the selling of a human being. He makes his way through these ideas, ending up asserting that some principles trump the freedom to make contracts. To those who argue that the Africans themselves are contributing to the trade by capturing and selling their own people, he answers that "if there were no buyers there would be no sellers" (16). Some items should thus be forbidden entry into the market. The mere existence of buyers and sellers willing to exchange particular items that happen to be human beings does not justify the practice. Similarly, African slave catchers may be "a set of as great villains as any in the world," but they have been "greatly corrupted, and even viciated by their intercourse with the Europeans," and they would be horrified if they knew what treatment awaits the persons they sell. They are "beguiled" and "deceived" (26) by the Europeans, so that even if those contracts are apparently made voluntarily, nothing can excuse the games of seduction that take place behind them. Only such deviousness can explain why African men would sell their wives and children, since "nothing can be more opposite to every thing they hold dear and valuable" (27). Along the same lines as many of the British writers we have discussed, Cugoano thus appeals to a higher good that trumps the ideology of free trade.[42]

His feeling about British imperialism, and imperialism in general, is similarly ambivalent. On the one hand, his essay is an outright attack on the workings of empire. He uses emotional outbursts partly to convey his outrage, an attitude that makes Cugoano one of the most strident anti-imperialist and anticolonialist writers of his time. Going in detail into the colonization of the American continent, based on his reading of William Robertson's *History of America* (1777), he warns that "no man of sensibility and feeling can read the history without pity and resentment." He talks about the "infernal conduct" of Columbus' "Spanish competitors," about their "base perfidy and bloody treachery" at Hispaniola, about the fate of Montezuma at the hands of "the treacherous Cortes," about the "base treacherous bastard Pizarra [Pizarro] at the head of the Spanish banditti of miscreant depredators" (62) and their treatment of the Peruvian monarch Atahualpa. He then describes the treachery and the carnage that followed, and concludes that "the history of those dreadfully perfidious methods of forming settlements, and acquiring riches and territory, would make humanity tremble, and even recoil, at the enjoyment of such acquisitions and become reverted into rage and indignation at such horrible injustice and barbarous cruelty" (65). Relying on William Bollan's *Britannia Libera* (1772), he similarly condemns the "great devastations" (68) committed by the British in their imperialistic adventures in Africa, America, and Asia. His global awareness, nourished by his extensive reading, allows him to cast a critical eye at the power abuses taking place on the major continents, and to develop a unique multicultural perspective that allows him unconditionally to sympathize with the colonized.

At the same time, Cugoano manages to convey a certain love and admiration of Britain. He is thankful, for example, that he learned to read and write, activities "which soon became my recreation, pleasure, and delight" (17). With these words suggestive of love he announces his deep emotional entanglement with the country he lives in, the country responsible for both his education and the enslavement of millions of Africans. Considering the emotional discourse he also holds about many oppressed people around the world and through history, it is clear that Cugoano tries to represent the complexity of feeling that accompanies his political ideology. He loves some aspects of Britain, even though on an emotional level he does not belong to one country, or one continent, or one race. He bemoans that the slave traders contribute to the "universal depravity of one of the finest constitutions in the world" (70), and declares that "law and liberty, justice and equity" are "the proper foundations of the British government" (76). Indeed, Britons "ought to be considered as the most learned and civilized people in the world" (86), if it were not for slavery. Cugoano evinces a certain patriotism that he takes pains to nourish side by side with his global vision, and he hopes that this love will be transformative.

Part of this love comes through in the belief that Britain could use its imperialistic enterprise for more beneficent ends, that it can combine its mercantile objectives with its ability to spread the common good. He asks the "most respectful and generous people of Great Britain" to make the good decisions, and to "extend their power and influence to do good afar" (96). This can be done through humane commerce, and indeed Cugoano adheres to the notion of *doux commerce*. With the abolition of the slave trade, "there might be a very considerable and profitable trade carried on with the Africans." The Britons should realize that this "might be made greatly to their own advantage, as well as they might have the happiness of being useful to promoting the prosperity and felicity of others" (100). He warns that the wickedness of an empire based on slavery leads to national debt, which "stops ingenuity and improvements" and "clogs all the wheels of commerce" (69). A commonwealth based instead on free workers would be an advantage to all, since it would procure "the happiness and good of doing justice to others," even as it would "bring in an immense revenue to government." Like Adam Smith, he believes that freedom brings overall material benefits, since independent persons "would improve the most barren situations, and make the most of that which is fruitful," and their labor "would soon yield to any government, many greater advantages than any thing that slavery can produce" (92). Cugoano believes in the benefits of an imperialism that spreads its liberal values — and its Christian religion — globally. In this, he shows his adherence to the British model, which intricately combines and balances ideas of freedom and of the common good. He hopes his readers will enter his emotional world by extending their own love of the common good, and of empire, toward an acceptance of abolition in the name of that empire.

Still, his longing for the presence of a true, egalitarian global feeling — unlike one shaped by the workings of empire — often predominates. Cugoano rarely thinks in nationalistic terms. Both his historical and his geographic reaches encompass the history of the globe. In order to refute the common explanation for the exploitation of Africans, he treats his readers to an excursus on the geographical dispersion of the sons of Ham, covering the Middle East, Africa, and even England. To those who try to defend slavery in one place by pointing to worse cruelties in another, he answers that we need to jettison this kind of national approach that derives some pride from limited comparisons. "An equal degree of enormity found in one place," he warns, "cannot justify crimes of as great or greater enormity committed in another." The various cruelties committed "on different parts of the globe, may not be all equally alike bad," but only a global consciousness and global feeling can bypass the petty considerations that keep the great European powers busy, and help foster values that function on a universal level. In casting his "cry of justice" far and wide, he also counters the voices that manipulate global feeling to serve the status quo. He ridicules slave owners who are "like the monstrous crocodile weeping over their prey with fine concessions (while gorging their own rapacious appetite) to hope for universal freedom taking place over the globe" (21). Aware of the possibly weak impact of global arguments, like the one made by slave owners who can only offer vague sympathy for individual victims while knowing that they will be unable to achieve freedom individually, Cugoano offers a horizontal look at the slaves inhabiting the world, at their different fates, and at their equal right not only to individual dignity but to participation in the world community as citizens. Only a far-reaching, all-encompassing look can unite all those personal struggles.

He even projects, and invests his emotions in, a future of international cooperation, in which the nations of the world would exert their influence on each other to promote the greater good. If a nation observes another committing unjust acts, it cannot consider itself innocent "unless it remonstrates against that wickedness of the other nation, and makes use of every effort in its power to help the oppressed, and to rescue the innocent." It is unlikely that Cugoano developed a precise scheme for his idea of international collaboration, but here he seems to be arguing for humanitarian intervention and an international standard of justice. There is a "universal rule of duty" (87) to do good, and it applies to nations as well as people. Indeed, it is the only valid reason for war, unlike the ones that are "about the purposes of envying one another concerning any different advantages of commerce, or for enlarging their territories and dominions, or for the end of getting riches by their conquest" (88). He directs the blame mostly at Britain, which in spite of its high degree of civilization has done nothing to combat the slave trade, but his gaze is global. He seems to envision a community of nations spurring each other to establish universal goals of justice and equal citizenship. Implying that general statements about universal, individual freedom are not enough, he directs his look horizontally at nations and communities, and at their international interaction. No wonder he feels compelled to ask for "universal emancipation of slaves, and the enfranchisement of all the Black People employed in the culture of the Colonies" (91), since to him it is a natural component of his program of international balance, exchange, and justice.

This global vision of balance and exchange, moreover, is infused with radical feelings. Cugoano's international, multiracial sensibility particularly savors any upset of entrenched hierarchies, and many of his more sarcastic comments convey his glee at imagining an exchange of social roles and positions. In his criticism of James Tobin, a West Indian planter and author of *Cursory Remarks upon the Reverend Mr. Ramsay's Essay* (1785), he mocks Tobin, who "finds fault with a plan for punishing robbers, thieves and vagabonds." Probably aware of what this law would mean for slave traders, Tobin points out it would be "'an event which would undoubtedly furnish a new and pleasant compartment to that well known and most delectable print, call'd, *The world turn'd up side down*, in which the cook is roasted by the pig, the man saddled by the horse.'" Tobin is referring to popular images at the time that represent an absurd world out of sync with the natural order. Cugoano jumps on this comparison: "If he means that the complicated banditties of pirates, thieves, robbers, oppressors and enslavers of men, are those cooks and men that would be roasted and saddled, it certainly would be no unpleasant sight to see them well roasted, saddled and bridled too; and no matter by whom, whether he terms them pigs, horses or asses." He then goes on to make fun of Tobin's "monkeyish comparison." Cugoano obviously enjoys the carnivalesque element in this passage, in its transposition of hierarchies and its animalistic imagery, and makes the reader share his joy. Even if carnival has often been analyzed as only a temporary transgression that ultimately might confirm the social order, by fudging categories Cugoano underlines the unpredictability of social change. Within the context of his global consciousness, he implies that revolutionary change can help anybody, independently from "external complexion" (19).

He uses a similar strategy of reversal when he tries to undermine color prejudice, bringing the reader into his own emotional world. He first points out how "discouraging" (11) it is for someone to be the brunt of racial prejudice, which he summarizes as follows: "'That an African is not entitled to any competent degree of knowledge, or capable of imbibing any sentiments of probity; and that nature designed him for some inferior link in the chain, fitted only to be a slave'" (11–12). Interestingly, in his own personal formulation of these preconceived ideas, he emphasizes notions of "degree" or of links in a chain, or of level of openness to the environment through "imbibing," preparing his reader for a possible reversal of roles. He then switches the spotlight to the slaveholders, and argues that "if such men can boast of greater degrees of knowledge, than any African is entitled to, I shall let them enjoy all the advantages of it unenvied, as I fear it consists only in greater share of infidelity, and that of a blacker kind than only skin deep" (12). Here again we find the sarcastic tone, and an anticipation of a world upside down, where whites find themselves at the bottom of the chain through their excess of negative knowledge. There is a certain playfulness in Cugoano's approach, a delight in this turning of the tables. But what he seems to savor the most is his ultimate watering down and confusion of the criteria that created the hierarchy in the first place. His upsets are not simply carnivalesque: they aim at undermining some of the major categories that held sway at the time, and at revolutionizing the way roles are distributed in the Atlantic, and indeed around the world.[43]

Once he has prepared the reader emotionally for any blurring of categories, he uses the strategy to reach fundamentally disruptive conclusions. Addressing the proslavery argument that many English and Irish poor are worse off than West Indian slaves, he responds that "bad as it is, the poorest in England would not change their situation for that of slaves" (19). Not content with this comparison, he adds that even if the free poor were worse off, the problems would remain. Indeed, he asks self-reflexively, "what would the comparison amount to?" It would actually "cry aloud for some redress" on both sides of the Atlantic. Unlike many white abolitionists who were accused by their opponents (and have been repeatedly since then by historians) of downplaying proletarian exploitation at home,[44] Cugoano turns his argument around, managing to encompass several oppressed groups while maintaining essential distinctions between freedom and slavery. His model of international citizenship allows him to make this grand, sweeping gesture without losing any of his specificity and punch. He goes even further, and takes this opportunity to make a statement on general policy, presenting it as a "great duty" to "order and establish such policy, and in such a wise manner, that every thing should be so managed, as to be conducive to the moral, temporal and eternal welfare of every individual from the lowest degree to the highest; and the consequence of this would be, the harmony, happiness and good prosperity of the whole community" (20). One would be hard-pressed to find such an all-encompassing statement among his contemporaries, such a concern for both individual and community, and the conditions that promote their welfare, in the context of a global, interracial, multicultural ideology.

The picture of a world turned upside down informs his sensibility to the extent that he seems open to rebellion and revolution. In his discussion of appropriate laws and punishments in a civilized society, he abides by the notion of retaliation. But he adds that "when the punishers went beyond the bounds of a just retaliation, and fell into the same crimes as the oppressors," then "the consequence is plain, that an impending overthrow must still fall upon them likewise." In his wide historical and geographical span, the overturning of the social order seems a common and conceivable way of dealing with oppression: "History affords us many examples of severe retaliations, revolutions and dreadful overthrows; and of many crying under the heavy load of subjection and oppression, seeking for deliverance." In this still general statement, he establishes a pattern of revolution that crosses borders and centuries. He continues: "And methinks I hear now, many of my countrymen, in complexion, crying and groaning under the heavy yoke of slavery and bondage, and praying to be delivered" (60). Here is the end product of his radicalization of exchange and reversal of roles, informed by his global and interracial perspective. Emotionally, he identifies with the ones he calls "my countrymen, in complexion," a strange expression that conveys both the desire for equal citizenship and the rejection of national boundaries. Obviously, his approval of revolution is also ideological.

Cugoano's emotional world, then, reveals both a radicalization of the British notion of balance and exchange, through his emphasis on global, interracial citizenship, and a continued adherence to a certain form of empire. Cugoano's religious sensibility reflects this complexity. His text is often read as a jeremiad. The jeremiad could be seen as the vision of ultimate balance and exchange, the sinners finally receiving their due at the hand of their god. But Cugoano's religious vision of exchange is less radical and mobile than his political one. Unlike the egalitarian outlook in his vision of humanity, he accepts the existence of an unquestionable moral hierarchy with Protestant Christianity at the top. When he mentions Gronniosaw's struggle with poverty in England, he declares that in spite of that struggle, "he would not have given his faith in the Christian religion, in exchange for all the kingdoms of Africa" (23), so that his religious belief trumps any other form of solidarity. Christianity is part of Cugoano's global vision, as he refers to "the Universal Father and Sovereign of Mankind," and mentions Christianity's duty to extend "universal philanthropy" (24). But it cannot be overthrown. An enslaver cannot also be a Christian—he can only "be called by its opposite, the Antichrist" (67). The Spaniards' colonization of the Peruvians might have been acceptable had they used the power of ideology rather than that of the sword: "Had the Peruvians been visited by men of honesty, knowledge, and enlightened understanding . . . they might have been induced to embrace the doctrines and faith of Christianity, and to abandon their errors of superstition and idolatry" (65). To Cugoano, religious indoctrination is part of the common good. The "hydra-headed kingdom" (67) here does not refer to political radicalism but to the work of Satan, and to the two apostasies, Islam and Catholicism. The citizen of the world may be of any color or social status but needs to be a Christian, and the right kind too.

That Cugoano adhered to major thought currents of the end of the eighteenth century is without doubt and should not be surprising, but his feeling for world citizenship lends those ideas the radical bent of equality. Roxann Wheeler states that *"Thoughts and Sentiments* is remarkable for its peculiar mix of a range of conservative and radical positions to persuade readers against slavery and the slave trade" (34). We have seen that Cugoano's complex position vis-à-vis empire, and his hierarchical view of civilization in economic and religious terms, mark him out as conservative. She also argues that his conservatism shows when, as she explained earlier, "Cugoano's position harks back to anti-empire discourse that claimed that the lure of luxury topples nations, that pursuit of unregulated commerce is suspicious" (27). This republican streak, though, which focuses on the dangers of unbridled commercial and economic freedom, reveals Cugoano's faith in the strength of republican principles in combination with the erratic possibilities of freedom. Anthony Bogues argues that Cugoano radicalizes the notion of liberty, giving it "a new set of meanings" (43). In my analysis, this "new set" involves the notion of the common good applied universally. The emotional infrastructure of Cugoano's text reveals his desire to move beyond liberal sympathy toward the sort of principled love that would possess enough power to lead to the abolition of slavery and the slave trade, and universal equality.

Olaudah Equiano's Diaspora

There is also something very British about Olaudah Equiano, the author of the most famous eighteenth-century slave narrative, even as he deploys a special form of cosmopolitanism that fulfills the promise of the branding of his texts as "Black Atlantic." In some ways, Equiano's vision of global trade does not much differ from the tenets of British imperialism and market capitalism, which emphasize the exploitation of natural resources throughout both the formal and the informal empire. Even his arguments against the slave trade conform to widely accepted notions of *doux commerce* at the end of the eighteenth century, according to which commercial relations need to be put in the service of humanizing and civilizing goals that usually imply an imposition of Western values. At the same time, in the representation of his relationship to Africa especially, Equiano seeks to establish more equalized and less exploitative forms of international relations. Using the political ideologies present in the culture that surrounded him, in the form of liberalism and republicanism, he extends them into a radical form of cosmopolitanism. Particularly in his depiction of his African childhood—including the possibility that he invented an African past—and in the way he describes his participation in the Sierra Leone settlement project, do I see a desire to create this new paradigm. The skillful appeal to feeling in both these sections of the narrative plays an important role in promoting this political agenda.

That the *Narrative* reveals the personality of a capitalist merchant and evinces a belief in the benefits of international free trade has been pointed out, and has led to a few sound thrashings, by several critics. One of them refers to Equiano's "problematic mercantilism," which "placed him squarely within the dehumanizing ideology of capitalism's driving slave market" (Hinds 636). Even as he threw himself into the capitalist game that directly led to his achievement of freedom and independence, the argument goes, Equiano was perpetuating a mode of exchange that had produced his own enslavement in the first place. Indeed, as Houston A. Baker, Jr., was among the first to point out, the narrative "can be ideologically considered as a work whose protagonist masters the rudiments of economics that condition his very life" (*Blues* 33). In his insightful discussion, Joseph Fichtelberg uses Marxist vocabulary to show Equiano's "ideological appropriation of capitalism" (472), marked by a shift from an African society that functions on the basis of intrinsic value to a system where all persons and things are related through the power of exchange value. The intense marketing of his book after 1789 shows a man perfectly in control of the movements, the networking, and the activities demanded by commercial exchange.[45]

But Equiano's unique black internationalism—born of his travels through the Atlantic and the Mediterranean from Africa to the West Indies to the American continent to, among others, England, Canada, Spain, Turkey, the Arctic, and South America—was anchored in his African diasporic identity, and is reflected in his representation of Africa in the *Narrative*. Equiano has become somewhat of a controversial figure partly because of the uncertainties concerning his real place of birth. The archival work that suggests he was born in South Carolina raises questions of authenticity, but it also allows us to reflect more fully on the significance of the African section of his autobiography. The section signals its importance by being strongly and explicitly linked to the language of sentiment, yet it represents more than a repository of some vague, romanticized roots. I argue that because sentiment has a political meaning in this text, the African section allows Equiano subtly to develop his sophisticated concept of internationalism. Inspired by a combination of liberalism and republicanism, as well as by the egalitarian world of the ships he knew so well, Equiano keeps presenting ideals of interracial and international communities based on exchange and negotiation in a nonimperialistic context. He uses the model of exchange he has learned from his mercantile dealings, but insists on egalitarianism when he transfers it to the politics of the cosmopolitan world he inhabits. In this, he represents an original voice in the eighteenth century, and gives a new meaning to the experience of diaspora. That is why his description of Africa, and the proposals he makes for its future after abolition, have a slightly different ring compared with those given by others around him.

The meaning Equiano gives diaspora is sophisticated. Because the concept of diaspora implies a dispersion away from an ancestral homeland, it has traditionally carried connotations of loss, and of a movement away from an original purity or fullness. Even though contemporary theory has warned of a reductionist danger in such readings, they remain appealing. In his narrative Equiano handles life in the diaspora with such subtlety, or maybe with such ambivalence, that critics have swung between emphasizing his re-creation of Africa as an Edenic point of origin from which he subsequently "fell," and highlighting his near-total assimilation to his British identity. These critical swings reflect a dynamism at the heart of the narrative, as Equiano presents himself as a man in search of an identity, and for whom his diaspora constitutes a constant negotiation with the outside world. Africa becomes an essential tool in the elaboration of this diasporic condition because it is part of the movement of reinvention that drives the protagonist. It is precisely because he presents Africa—rather than, say, South Carolina—as his place of origin that Equiano can include it in his evolution toward his identity as citizen of the world, and toward his view of internationalism as relational. Equiano is not a colonialist in blackface. He tries to redefine diaspora as a construction, as a constant redefinition, rather than as a clear movement away from a point and a longing for a return back to that point.

That Equiano displays British political impulses is undeniable, and as pointed out above, this comes out particularly in his attitude toward trade, which partly informs his prescriptions for the future of Africa. As Tanya Caldwell puts it, Equiano "reveals the thoroughly European nature of his mind most convincingly when he proposes strengthening the system of which he is part by offering up Africa to the forces of British trade" (265). Like Benezet's, his recommendations for the abolition of the slave trade are paired with the prospects of mutual benefits humane free trade could bring to both Britain and Africa. Indeed, "a commercial intercourse with Africa opens an inexhaustible source of wealth to the manufacturing interests of Great Britain" (Equiano 234), and in return the Africans would receive the benefits of civilization, as they "would insensibly adopt the British fashions, manners, customs, &c" (233). The typical combination of freedom and the common good gives Equiano enthusiasm for the measures the government might take, expecting much from the "gentlemen in power," in that "these are designs consonant to the elevation of their rank, and the dignity of their stations." In this view, it is precisely the representatives' status well above the vagaries of local representation that gives them the independence and the ethical grounding to work solely for the wider common good of the nation, and even of the world. When "connected with views of empire and dominion," these benevolent acts could bring "substantial greatness" (232) to Britain. To Equiano, then, abolition is intricately linked to the imperialistic enterprise, the spread of British civilization, and the attendant industrial and commercial development. Abolition would turn out to be "an universal good" (234).[46]

This approach tallies with his own liberal belief in the power of self-interest to promote material well-being, though, in a typically British fashion, that type of freedom is often inscribed within notions of the common good. His attitude on trade, like that of many who favored that theory, partly reflects the views of Adam Smith. Much of his antislavery and antiracist discourse revolves around the ways slaves and blacks in general are regularly taken advantage of in commercial transactions. The "cabinet of horrors" section of his narrative, in which he describes various forms of tortures endured by slaves, concludes with considerations of the better profit that can be had by good treatment. Many slave owners, he points out, have found out that "benevolence was their true interest" (105).

At the same time, one can say that, apart from the slave trade, Equiano sees that self-interest as working best within the structure of the British Empire. The solutions he proposes "strengthen the infrastructure of traditional British institutions by allowing political and economic progress within those institutions" (Caldwell 267). One finds in Equiano's politics the yearning for a balance of republicanism and liberalism we have identified as typical of the British eighteenth century.

But he has other political models, particularly the seafaring community. Although his status on ships changed as he rose from seaman to able seaman to steward to traveling slave owner, his accounts often reflect the egalitarian solidarity that was predominant in the sailors' culture. During his first voyage on a ship, he is befriended by a young white man named Richard Baker, and they develop the kind of male camaraderie typical of a republican world. They become "inseparable," and go through "many sufferings together." Indeed, "we have many nights lain in each other's bosoms when we were in great distress." His entry into this interracial, homosocial relationship shapes his almost simultaneous entry into the world of transatlantic slavery. He is now conscious of himself as a slave, and he even knows that Baker has "many slaves of his own" (Equiano 65), so very early on he becomes aware of the exceptionally versatile character of the political life aboard ships. Similarly, aboard the *Roebuck* later on, he enjoys life with "a number of boys . . . for we were always together" (70). When Michael Henry Pascal unexpectedly decides to put him on a ship bound for the West Indies, the boat's crew express their solidarity, and they later come to Portsmouth to try and save him, though in vain. Although Equiano also reports examples of cruelty and prejudice among sailors, the narrative shows the tremendous impact his maritime experience had on his political self. Obviously it contributes significantly to the development of his international consciousness, not simply because of his travels but also through his contacts aboard ships. In one anecdote, he recounts sailing with a man who had fought on the French side during one of the French navy's engagements with the British, and who told him "our ships had done considerable mischief that day" (81). This sailor's polyvalence signals all sailors' relative independence from any national allegiance.

Considering this varied social and political experience, it is thus interesting to inquire what political views are served by the early African section. Its veracity has been questioned by a number of scholars. Internal evidence has always perplexed Africanist scholars because of several inconsistencies. Even though it would make sense to locate Equiano's native area in the Ika Ibo region west of the Niger River, several customs he refers to, such as the scarification of chiefs or the retrieval of oil from the sap of oil palms rather than from raffia palms, do not occur in that area.[47] It has always been obvious that Equiano relied on a variety of travel accounts to fluff up what could only have been sketchy memories. As S. E. Ogude points out, Equiano may have been inspired by "the body of legends about Africa that naturally developed among the African slaves" (31). External evidence has raised more questions. Vincent Carretta has unearthed archival material suggesting that Equiano may have been born and raised in South Carolina. The parish register of St. Margaret's Church, Westminster, where Equiano was first baptized on February 9, 1759, records him as "'Gustavus Vassa a Black born in Carolina 12 years old.'" The muster book of the ship *Racehorse*, which sought a northwest passage through the Arctic Ocean in 1773, identifies a "'Gustavus Weston'" as "an able seaman, aged twenty-eight, and born in South Carolina" (Carretta, "Questioning" 232). As Carretta speculates, Equiano certainly had rhetorical and financial reasons for altering the story of his early life. An African birth gave him an "authenticity" that was "fundamental to the effectiveness of the autobiography as a petition against the Atlantic slave trade" (228). Rather like the twentieth-century *Roots* phenomenon, also, African origins added a decidedly exotic and commercial appeal to the book, all the more since the account did not in any significant way depart from the noble-savage depictions of Africa predominant throughout the century.[48]

An African youth also allowed Equiano to represent his life as a trajectory from innocence to experience, and to highlight the self-made aspect of his character. His account of his abduction and subsequent events presents him in a state of constant surprise and wonder, and although some scenes forcefully convey his fear and horror, he also often winks at Western readers, colluding with them to smile at his ignorance and naïveté. In these cases, looking back at his former uncivilized self allows him indirectly to create a sense of cultural belonging with his audience. If Equiano was born a slave in South Carolina, relinquishing this part of his life also meant effacing his ties to the nation that had recently become independent from Britain, and placing his Western education completely in a British context. Indeed, in the United States the narrative never achieved the popularity it did in other countries. Even as it increased his exotic appeal, then, the African section created a special connection with his audience, and emphasized their ideological ties. Equiano could afford to present this alien culture as his, since by the time he was writing, he had remade himself as an independent, respectable British subject. The African connection may also have helped reassert his standing after his unfortunate experience with the Sierra Leone emigration project. Of course, his description of Africa is also obviously meant to counter images of Africa as savage and barbaric. As Ogude puts it, "to judge by his own account, Equiano's Africa is a veritable paradise" (40). But his emphasis on cleanliness, humanity, morality, and physical beauty reveals a degree of romanticization that can only help his personal story of development and achievement.

The African section also represents a particular political model, so that the sentimental coloring of Equiano's supposedly African past raises the question of its political meaning, and is thus deeply implicated in the controversy over its authenticity. Adam Potkay asserts that, for many critics, "the question of Equiano's origins or real identity will not matter at all" because what matters is "its role in the cultural archive, its fusion at a more or less critical juncture of several available, interrelated discourses or historical 'languages'—those of race, evangelicalism, abolitionism, travel, and political economy" (603–4). While it is indeed impossible at this point to determine with any certainty the veracity of Equiano's African narrative, the question matters somewhat more than Potkay surmises because, if contrived, it reveals a deliberate political strategy. The archival work performed on Equiano's early life can thus help uncover the extent to which that section of the *Narrative* is a political gesture. More specifically, I argue that the insertion of an African section, and its prominent dramatization of sentiment, allow Equiano to develop a highly sophisticated theory of diaspora and internationalism, with the notion of world citizenship anchored in a negotiation between communities and political models. Equiano's possible invention of an African birth matters in that it shows that the section is more than what Potkay calls "a rhetorical performance of considerable skill" (604). It shows Equiano at work constructing a diasporic black identity defined by much more than the vagaries of transportation and enslavement.

One important emotional strain of the African part of the *Narrative* is the familial one. Equiano emphasizes his attachment to his mother, and his description of his encounter with his sister during his trip to the coast after his kidnapping stands in for the feelings occasioned by the violent tearing apart of African families because of the slave trade. One evening as he arrives at a house, he is surprised to see "my dear sister," who "gave a loud shriek, and ran into my arms" (Equiano 51). For some time they "clung to each other in mutual embraces, unable to do any thing but weep." They are allowed to sleep together, with a man lying between them, "while she and I held one another by the hands across his breast all night." In the morning they are again separated, and Equiano describes his anxiety and pain, climaxing with a pathetic address: "Yes, thou dear partner of all my childish sports! thou sharer of my joys and sorrows! happy should I have ever esteemed myself to encounter every misery for you, and to procure your freedom by the sacrifice of my own" (51). This episode allows Equiano to convey unconditional familial love, and to make readers sympathize with the pain of their separation, as well as of their enslavement. With this scene he inserts the narrative within the liberal abolitionist discourse, which criticizes slavery by emphasizing the breaking up of families and the negation of natural rights. Later on, he implores Europeans to "melt the pride of their superiority into sympathy for the wants and miseries of their sable brethren," and to look upon the world with "benevolence" (45). He thus seems to use the African section as a conduit for common, liberal sentimental appeals.[49]

But there is another political strain at work in the African section, underlined less by a liberal form of sympathy than by a feeling of solidarity. Indeed, Equiano represents a society organized around clearly republican principles. It is built on a communitarian ethic, according to which "every one contributes to the common stock" (37–38); the "tillage is exercised in a large plain or common," and "all the neighbours resort thither in a body" (38). Equiano also likes to emphasize its simplicity, noting that "as our manners are simple, our luxuries are few" (34), and that "as yet the natives are unacquainted with those refinements in cookery which debauch the taste" (35). For the defense of the village, "all are taught the use of the weapons," so that "our whole district is a kind of militia" (39). By listing these characteristics, Equiano must have known he was pushing many republican buttons, as he depicted the sort of political organization that was at the time already looked back on with nostalgia as the embodiment of a preliberal state not "feminized" by commerce and excessive refinements, but that was still holding on to the national political imaginary. Even his emphasis on physical beauty and absence of "deformity" (38) evokes the harmonious proportions of classical beauty. Equiano is doing much more here than participating in the myth of the noble savage; he is presenting his African community as the result of a carefully thought out political choice that partly puts it on a par with some of the best ideals that Western political culture had produced.

By presenting his native community as partaking of both the liberal and the republican ethos, and by making his reader sympathize with both political allegiances, Equiano implies that African lifestyles, as well as African social and political organization—and here the village certainly stands for a certain vision of Africa as a whole—constitute a model that can absorb novelty, even as it has its own undeniable virtues. After all, English society at the time was dealing with similar political choices, as its increasing liberalization found itself in constant conflict with residual republican values. He wants to counter images of Africa either as barbaric and politically chaotic, or as noble and untainted, and he wants to show that there is room there for the introduction of Western things and ideas.[50] So he presents a viable political alternative to his audience, even as, at the opposite end of the book, he envisions a possible transformation of that order through commerce. It is this tension between political visions that shows him at pains to develop a complex form of internationalism. The tension produced by the section, and by the book as a whole, reproduces the kind of political tension between liberal and republican views that informed the eighteenth century. Africa becomes part of the national dialogue, and finds itself on an equal footing.

Critics have pointed out that Equiano relied heavily on travel accounts, and indeed many passages do not differ much from other sources of information available at the time. There are elements of the "noble savage," as Equiano follows a long tradition of writing about Africans as naturally happy and simple, and living in a consistently fertile environment. Much of this emphasis he derives, as he acknowledges in a note, from Benezet's *Historical Account of Guinea*. Benezet himself compiled several travel accounts, and he selected for inclusion passages that emphasize the Africans' "innocent simplicity" (Benezet, *Guinea* 2), their frugal way of life, and the lushness of the environment. For example, he quotes from Michel Adanson's *Voyage au Sénégal* (which he read in the English translation), who keeps emphasizing fertility and diversity of fauna and flora.[51] Several passages in Equiano's account seem frankly borrowed from Adanson. For example, his description of "palm wine" (Equiano 35), of its initial sweetness and its propensity to sour quickly, seems lifted from Adanson's discussion (Adanson 98–100). It would be possible to view Equiano's African section as a sort of collage, albeit put together by a personalized voice.

Yet even if all his information was borrowed, his selection and his emphases confirm a unique construction of African society as politically deliberate, and on the cusp between liberalism and republicanism. Most commentators on Africa did not lend the objects of their observation this kind of political sophistication. Many aspects of the noble-savage mystique, for example, such as simplicity and a spartan life, evoke republican ideals, but most writers on Africa avoided this kind of rapprochement. Equiano plays it up, carefully weaving communitarian and militia-like ideals into his descriptions. His emphasis on physical beauty may have been influenced by Michel Adanson's *Voyage au Sénégal*: "On peut dire que les nègres du Sénégal sont les plus beaux hommes de la Nigritie. Leur taille est pour l'ordinaire au-dessus de la médiocre, bien prise et sans défaut. Il est inouï qu'on en voie de boîteux, de bossus, de noués, à moins que ce ne soit par accident" (38–40).[52] But as pointed out earlier, it also fits within the republican ethos. Similarly, his description of village huts is strongly reminiscent of Adanson, who also details their mode of construction (Adanson 38) and mentions cow dung as a building material.[53] But Equiano is careful to add in conclusion that "the whole neighbourhood afford their unanimous assistance in building them" (36), blending an image of domestic intimacy with one of communal solidarity. Conversely, he infuses descriptions of traditional, even scripted activities with a sense of openness. The dances follow a prescribed pattern, for example, but they also represent something, and "as the subject is generally founded on some recent event, it is therefore ever new" (34). Here is a society that, in spite of its traditional, republican foundation, is also energetic and open to innovation.

His account of his kidnapping is particularly revealing, in that it conveys the political theme through an appeal to the reader's sympathy. Equiano first declares that he was "the greatest favourite with my mother," emphasizing the familial bond. But this connection is bound up with the nature of his community, as he adds that he was "trained up from my earliest years in the arts of agriculture and war: my daily exercise was shooting and throwing javelins; and my mother adorned me with emblems, after the manner of our greatest warriors" (46). From an early age, domestic life and the feelings that spring from it are deeply bound up with the military responsibility typical of republican citizenship. A first attempt at kidnapping the village children fails because he gives the alarm from the top of a tree, and the "rogue" is surrounded by the children, who move in as a team and "entangled him with cords." They are not as lucky the second time, as Equiano and his sister are stolen when they are "left to mind the house" (47), fending for themselves in a domestic space left vulnerable by an absent community. The text elicits the reader's sympathy for the loss of a son (and a daughter), as well as for the loss of a member of a tightly knit community based on republican ideals. Sentiment here confirms political sophistication.[54]

Equiano also inserts Africa within a dynamic international network. He constantly stresses a parallel between the African society he grew up in and the ancient Jews, linking his ancestors' arrival in Africa with a particular form of biblical diaspora. Equiano and his audience were of course aware of the proslavery myth that circulated at the time, purportedly accounting for the existence of black skin. In *Thoughts and Sentiments*, Cugoano takes pains to refute it. First, he asserts, nothing in the Bible indicates that the mark of Cain "consisted in a black skin," and Cain's posterity was "destroyed in the universal deluge." Further according to the Bible, he says, the whole present world population is descended from Noah's three sons. But the curse that supposedly fell on the descendants of Ham as a punishment for his conduct, he continues, actually affected only "the families of the descendants of his youngest son, Canaan" (31). The Canaanites settled in an area in the west of Asia, and because of their "abominable wickedness and idolatry" (32) were either destroyed or reduced to subjection. But, Cugoano continues, Ham's other sons did not fall under the curse; they "dispersed and settled on the different parts of the earth" and became "very formidable nations." Some crossed over to the African continent, reached Ethiopia, and "dispersed themselves throughout all the southern and interior parts of Africa" (33). The climate alone induced the darkening of their skin. Equiano was quite possibly aware of Cugoano's line of defense.[55] The Jewish parallels in Equiano' narrative manage to place the Africans within a continuity or a dynamic movement of populations radiating from elsewhere. Rather than a static notion of roots, the village where he was born and grew up represents a spot on the globe that is susceptible to arrival and departure, and is inevitably part of that century's increasingly globalized travel and change.

That Equiano sees political models as fluctuating rather than set and hierarchical shows at other moments in the narrative. Even when he seems absorbed by the ideology that surrounds him, he establishes a direct or indirect dialogue with other political forms. Probably his first major sign of assimilation is the enthusiasm he displays in his description of his part in the Seven Years' War. He first emphasizes various moments of surprise, fear, and ignorance, but then comes a turning point. "I ceased to feel those apprehensions and alarms," he recalls, and even began to "long for an engagement" (70). As the French become the mysterious enemy to be attacked and pursued, Equiano rises above the conflict. In her analysis of the various cultural functions performed by the African sections, Murphy points out how the "warrior ethos provided yet another parallel to European culture" (564). While he has indeed emphasized his training in "the arts of agriculture and war" (Equiano 46), his most emotional moment happens during the capture of Louisbourg. "To my very great joy," he says, "I had now more liberty of indulging myself, and I went often on shore." What matters more than the issue of the conflict is his own freedom to wander about and observe. He particularly admires the "most beautiful procession on the water I ever saw," which together with the official ornaments, formed "a most grand and magnificent spectacle" (74). Rather than becoming absorbed in the events, he signals his ability to take some distance and admire the "spectacle" of war, retaining an observer's independence of movement and thought. His African identity as a warrior is mixed with his individual enjoyment of these events as a "spectacle." Equiano's international experience leads to both an involvement in the scene and an awareness of other forms of consciousness and sensibility. The dialogue taking place inside him typifies a politically multifaceted person, working for inclusiveness and dynamism.

That such an international perspective requires complex forms of negotiations comes out symbolically and forcefully in an episode that takes place about three years later, during the British assault on Belle-Isle. Equiano launches that section with a formula borrowed from adventure tales: "we sailed once more in quest of fame," and "I longed to engage in new adventures, and to see fresh wonders" (85). A few pages earlier he quoted from the *Iliad*, reminding us once again of the republican world he, according to the narrative, originally comes from. Moved by his "curiosity" (88), he goes to the English battery that is assaulting the French citadel, where he "had an opportunity of completely gratifying myself in seeing the whole operation." But very soon he is caught in the cross fire, "running a very great risk, both from the English shells that burst while I was there, but likewise from those of the French." He ends up lost "between the English and the French centinels." After an English sergeant reprimands him, he manages to get away on "a French horse belonging to some islanders" (89), until he finally finds himself "at liberty" (90) and goes back to the ship. While the episode makes an entertaining contribution to the picaresque content of the narrative, as well as to the theme of a watchful providence, it also nicely presents Equiano as caught between national conflicts, and longing for his own "liberty" independent from them. Once again his "curiosity" indicates a belief in the interesting superiority of these cultures, a superiority he asserted a few pages earlier, where he presents Westerners as "men superior to us," so that "I had the stronger desire to resemble them; to imbibe their spirit" (78). But we are allowed to forget neither the admirable Homeric bent of his African society nor his own desire to negotiate a distance—and fast—from these cultures he is slowly imbibing.

Equiano's adventures during his period of enslavement in the West Indies start out with a similar emphasis on the need for negotiation in cross-racial and cross-cultural encounters. After he decides to "commence merchant" (116), he embarks on a trip to Santa Cruz; aboard is an older black man who "had brought his little all for a venture, which consisted of six bits worth of limes and oranges in a bag." Equiano also plans to sell his twelve bits' worth of fruit, "separate in two bags" (117). But as soon as the two would-be fruit sellers arrive onshore, they are harassed by two white men who steal their bags and go into a house. Equiano and his companion follow them, begging for the bags and trying to give the two men a sense of the value the fruits have for them. They try to seek redress from a commanding officer, who throws them out. "Still," Equiano says, "we persevered." Going back to the house, he and his companion "begged and besought" the white men "again and again for our fruits." Finally, the men agree to return Equiano's two bags but refuse to give back the other one. When Equiano and his companion come out, the old man starts crying, which, Equiano says, "so moved me with pity for him, that I gave him nearly one third of my fruits" (118). The transactions involved here reveal several aspects of Equiano's political position. By presenting as the result of pity what one could consider a simple act of fairness toward the older black man—after all, Equiano seems vaguely aware that a fair deal involves returning to the man a third of what they were able to recover—he acknowledges a sentimental, and possibly racial, connection with him. At the same time, the perseverance they display in negotiating the return of the bags points to an insistence on their rights. Even if they end up losing one bag, the resolution affirms Equiano's political links in his solidarity, if partial, with his shipmate, and his commitment to dealing with whites as a person due the respect of a citizen. In one stroke, he shows his multiple forms of political allegiance, and the way he can navigate between them.

This episode is also one of the few in which Equiano uses uncharacteristically strong emotional language, equating it with other events for which he used such language, such as the forced separation from his sister. Seeing the white men leave with the bags puts him in a state of "the greatest confusion and despair." Reflecting on what he and his mate could be losing, he calls the situation "an insupportable misfortune!" (117). The event puts him "in the agony of distress and indignation" (118). Earlier in the narrative, the language of sentiment revealed the political consciousness of the African section, and it does the same here, linking the memory of Equiano's past with his fast-developing internationalism. The episode constitutes one of the fits and starts in his political evolution. Moments like this one in the narrative help bring a corrective to the notion that Equiano becomes a merchant simply bent on promoting neoliberal ideals for the glory and wealth of Britain. The presence of the African section in the narrative does not just present Africa as a virgin land to be deflowered for Britain's benefits. The section plays an important role in the narrative of Equiano's growth as a citizen of the world who envisions the world in its multiple facets and needs.

The Sierra Leone Project

Equiano's specific brand of cosmopolitanism is most clear in his involvement with the Sierra Leone resettlement project, especially in the dispute that led to his dismissal as the government's commissary for it. The project started out early in 1786 as a charitable action organized by the Committee for the Relief of the Black Poor, a committee of gentlemen and merchants eager to help—and to rid the streets of—the East Indian as well as the African poor who were desperately trying to eke out a living in the heart of London. The government became involved in the project because it felt a moral obligation toward the many blacks who had fought on the British side during the American Revolution, and who had come to England at the end of the conflict.[56] The committee offered Equiano the position of commissary, which means he was in charge of acquiring and distributing supplies for the emigrants.[57] At first he expressed his skepticism, but he was prevailed upon to consent. The period between then and his dismissal in March 1787 is open to historians' speculations. As the ships that would carry the emigrants and their supplies were anchored at Spithead, waiting to load, Equiano got into a dispute with the financial agent Joseph Irwin, former clerk and friend of the original, now deceased, initiator of the project, Henry Smeathman. Equiano accused Irwin of embezzlement. "I could not silently suffer government to be thus cheated," he says, "and my countrymen plundered and oppressed, and even left destitute of the necessaries for almost their existence" (228). His ultimate dismissal seems to indicate that Equiano himself had not fulfilled his duties properly, but the rhetoric used by all the parties that commented on the conflict points to deeper issues, including the political and racial nature of this international enterprise.

Even if the scheme was undoubtedly an expression of white philanthropy, like any black emigration project it pointed to the rough outlines of a racially separatist ideology. The emigrant group was in fact interracial,[58] but it seems that to most white minds it symbolized a racial other. In his *Short Sketch of Regulations*, his plan for the political organization of the new colony, Granville Sharp refers to "the community of free African settlers" (3) as a matter of course. At the start of the project, Henry Smeathman, a white biologist who had spent several years on the western coast of Africa, had approached the committee with a plan for a settlement. In his subsequent formal request to the Treasury, he "expressed a desire to remove the 'burthen' of the blacks from the public 'for ever' by 'putting them in a condition of repaying this Country the expense' of their support." After the Treasury promised help with the funding, the committee "ordered the printing of a handbill that announced magisterially to the blacks that 'no Place' was 'so fit and proper' for their settlement 'as the Grain Coast of Africa, where the Necessaries of life may be supplied by the force of Industry and moderate labour, and life rendered very comfortable" (M. Norton 408). In his *Plan of a Settlement to Be Made near Sierra Leone*, Smeathman addressed the needs of blacks specifically, referring to "many black persons, and people of Colour" (qtd. in Carretta, *Equiano* 222). Considering the expense incurred by the government for the whole enterprise—including a certain amount per settler, transportation costs, the hiring of doctors and schoolmasters, the furnishing of supplies for several months, the providing of military assistance, and administrative costs—one is struck by a willingness on the part of the government to give so much financial help abroad to people who would otherwise have been left destitute at home.[59]

Interestingly, the blacks themselves showed a strong reluctance about the whole project, and Equiano stands out among them.[60] When they considered emigration, they originally envisaged places like Nova Scotia, where black loyalists had already settled, or the Bahamas. As Carretta points out, there was no "back to Africa" ideology at work here, since "the vast majority of the black loyalists had never been to Africa, and their sense of 'home' was in the Americas" (221). Jonas Hanway, the chairman of the committee, was confronted with this reluctance head-on when the settlers insisted on "a written guarantee of their freedom." At first shocked that the settlers doubted the benevolent intentions of the government, he eventually had to give in, and "drew up a formal agreement" (M. Norton 409). The settlers knew they were defined first and foremost racially, and their fears of being sent to a coast that was a center of slave-trading activity were well founded. Equiano himself mentions that the main reason for his initial reticence were "some difficulties on the account of the slave-dealers, as I would certainly oppose their traffic in the human species by every means in my power." Here, though, Equiano signals his unique position as a westernized African who would wield a certain amount of power. Rather than expressing fear at the very real possibility of kidnapping and asking for formal agreements regarding his freedom, he predicts conflicts between himself and all participants in the slave trade, which, as was well known, included Europeans and Africans. Even though he applauds the initiative of sending blacks to "their native quarter" (226), he situates himself in a no-man's-land and defines himself through his egalitarian values rather than through racial or national identity. All in their own way, then, Equiano and the settlers resisted white attempts to box them in.

In a decade when Equiano would increasingly identify himself as an African, his attitude toward the enterprise may project a black-identified identity. Indeed, the language used by his critics suggests a typical white fear of black power. In a letter that contributed to Equiano's dismissal, the commander of the *Nautilus*, Thomas Boulden Thompson, refers to him as "turbulent and discontented, taking every means to actuate the minds of the Blacks to discord"; Thompson is convinced that "unless some means are taken to quell his spirit of sedition, it will be fatal to the peace of the settlement and dangerous to those intrusted with the guiding [of] it" (qtd. in Carretta, Equiano 229). Moreover, in a letter to Cugoano published in the *Public Advertiser* on April 4, 1787, Equiano complains that the villains "now mean to serve (or use) the blacks the same as they do in the West Indies." Another letter published in the same paper two days later, and probably penned by Cugoano, asserts that in their petitions and statements, the blacks say "they are much wronged, injured, and oppressed natives of Africa," who "under various pretenses and different manners, have been dragged away from London, and carried captives to Plymouth" (qtd. in Carretta, *Equiano* 230). They fear they do not have "any prospect of happiness to themselves, or any hope of future advantage to Great-Britain," and that "the design of some in sending them away, is only to get rid of them at all events" (231). The sources of confrontation between Equiano and the project's backers seem to have involved much more than a conflict about supplies, or even about competence.

But the language of sentiment in Equiano's rendering of the whole episode carefully parses out the degrees and forms of emotional involvement. On the one hand, Equiano creates solidarity with the future settlers by calling them "these wretched people" (228), and by listing the various ways in which they are being maltreated. Here he makes a clear link with slaves, in the name of whom he adopts a similar tone in the rest of the narrative. The fact that Cugoano publicly participates in the debate adds a layer of emotional rhetoric to the creation of this solidarity. On the other hand, Equiano is also careful to underline his allegiance to the government, and the fact that he took his role as commissary very seriously — "perhaps too seriously," says Carretta (*Equiano* 228). Equiano states: "I could not silently suffer government to be thus cheated, and my countrymen plundered and oppressed, and even left destitute of the necessaries for almost their existence" (qtd. in Carretta 228). Eliciting from his readers some form of sympathy for the government, Equiano places his sentimental rhetoric in the service of a political entity that he obviously feels is partly responsible for the common good of the prospective "free" settlement. Even as he emphasizes the black nationalist dimensions of the project, he also shows his openness and his flexibility when it comes to the political and economic infrastructure of this social experiment.

Keeping in mind the significance of Africa to Equiano, as well as his original reluctance to be part of the Sierra Leone project, it is thus possible to infer his deep feeling about the enterprise, and the way it fits into his internationalism. It is not quite certain what made Equiano change his mind about taking the job. The settlement was supposed to be free. If, as seems likely, he rejoiced about implementing his ideas on commerce and Christianization, Equiano may have seen in the project a unique opportunity to create a democratic settlement that would have combined aspects of his beloved Britain with the politically republican elements of Africa he would put forward in the narrative. He may have tried to impress on the emigrants the importance of keeping their independence, and of developing a political structure that would stand its ground amidst the nations of the world. This may have been all the more necessary in that Sierra Leone was a site onto which various people projected their political and economic utopian brainchildren, from Sharp's communistic system based on frankpledge to Henry Trafford's "re-transplantation" scheme.[61] Far from suggesting a black nationalist framework, I speculate that Equiano may have seen in the project a way to implement his identity as a citizen of the world, by creating a settlement open to difference, open to trade, and at the same time inspired by the best political models around the globe, whether liberal or republican. From this perspective, the inclusion of an African section at the beginning of the narrative, and its association with sentiment, implies that this is the model for which he has a real affinity, including the plans he had for its future. Devoid of national allegiance, his cosmopolitan vision sees communities as part of a global network without being dependent on it or exploited by it. It may be this desire for independence that irked several of his white colleagues.[62]

Equiano's ultimate statement on national identity is couched in emotional terms. After describing his supposedly African origin, he states his hope not to have imposed on his reader's patience by dwelling on scenes from the past that marked him for life. For, he continues, "whether the love of one's country be real or imaginary, or a lesson of reason, or an instinct of nature, I still look back with pleasure on the first scenes of my life, though that pleasure has been for the most part mingled with sorrow" (46). In this bold statement on national identity, Equiano implies that national attachment is impossible to explain, and that its existence owes little to any essential attributes the beloved country may have. Love for one's country is a construction, susceptible to the forces of other constructions. By hinting at the pliability of his emotional attachment to Africa, he may also undermine similar feelings harbored by his readers for their own nations, opening up some space for other political allegiances. It is a lukewarm statement, but by laying bare and questioning the infrastructure of national feeling, it destabilizes his audience, and encourages new forms of international feeling. Here is an African who, though he states his love for his roots, simultaneously questions the psychological basis for such love. In his mixture of pleasure and sorrow, he hints at a diasporic consciousness that goes beyond a bland, touristic internationalism toward a reflection on the very notion of diaspora. While crossing borders can sometimes reinforce the nationalist meaning of such borders, it helped Equiano to envision a world of citizens with more universal attachments.

Chapter 3

Brotherhood, Radicalism, and Antislavery

The notion of brotherhood constitutes one specific cranny of the history of emotion in general, and it plays an important role in the literature of sentiment, as well as in antislavery literature. Its familial metaphor places it in a politically marginal space between interiority and exteriority, liberalism and republicanism, conservatism and radicalism, ready to swing one way or the other depending on the philosophy that it supports.[1] In the seventeenth- and eighteenth-century literature of sentiment and sensibility, brotherhood and homosocial friendship often acted as signposts for a republican worldview. But there were differences in its handling by American and British writers, especially in the late eighteenth and early nineteenth centuries, after the advent of the French Revolution and the upsurge of radicalism and other forms of Jacobin thought in which brotherhood played a role. In this chapter, which focuses on that particular time period, we will see that differences also played out in the way black antislavery writers used the notion of brotherhood on each side of the Atlantic. While John Marrant and Prince Hall adapted the ideology of fraternity inherent in Freemasonry in order to push it in both liberal and black nationalist directions, Robert Wedderburn radicalized the British balance of freedom and the common good, and developed a highly original intellectual mix of abolitionism and communism. In each case the appeal to emotion in general, and to notions of brotherhood in particular, reveals a political infrastructure. The transatlantic comparison also shows a radical surplus in British texts.

The Politics of White Literary Brotherhood

In some late-seventeenth-century British texts, sentiment already showed political tensions between a republican, public ethos expressed through the theme of brotherhood and homosocial friendship, and the rise of liberal interiority.[2] Indeed, before sensibility and sympathy became associated with women and melodrama, they appeared in texts that often linked sentiment with masculinity and issues of the state—what Julie Ellison calls the "long pre-eminence of masculine tenderheartedness" (19). A number of British late-seventeenth- and early-eighteenth-century plays about ancient Rome display a decidedly republican sensibility, where interior connections are less important than the common good achieved through the shared state interest, civic virtue, or male bonding. In that perspective, self-interest matters less than feelings nurtured outside a personal or familial context. Love and friendship, often between men, are inextricably linked to the well-being and survival of the republic. Yet at the same time, the republican creed suffers from its roots in homogeneity, or is already under the pressure of an emphasis on private, individual relationships that locate the source of essential interests within interiority or the private sphere. In typically British fashion, the use of sentiment in these texts shows an attempt to achieve a balance between those two political ideas.

In *Lucius Junius Brutus* (1680) by Nathaniel Lee, the major voices point toward a republican sensibility, but one can also hear different, more liberal murmurings coming through. Titus, a sensitive young man guilty of conspiracy against his father Brutus, is sacrificed for the sake of preserving the integrity of the new republic. The rape of Lucrece by Tarquin's son at the beginning of the play conjures up a similar, profoundly republican moment, in which Lucrece publicly commits suicide and her body is carried in full view by the Romans who swear revenge. Although they cry at first, Brutus reminds them that tears do not help their cause: "There's not a common harlot in the shambles / But for a drachma shall outweep you all" (Lee 1.428–29). The control of feeling through stoicism indicates the priorities of a republican sensibility. The last scene of the play, in which

Brutus condemns his son Titus to death, can be said to echo this earlier one in its endorsement of sacrifice for the sake of the purity of the republic. To Ellison, however, "what we remember is the recurring cost of republican law, not reinstated distinctions between public and private" (32). The son's tragic fate is the "price paid by the republican family for its own appetite for impersonality." Indeed, "Lee makes sensibility fundamental both to legitimizing and to criticizing postmonarchical forms of power" (36). Brutus preserves the republic through the death of his son, but his entourage's negative reaction suggests a less stoic community deeply committed to personal, familial links. Republican feeling achieves an official victory, but is already subtly undermined by more liberal leanings.

Republicanism is shown to be both strong and struggling as it tries to integrate liberal elements. Brutus early adopts a republican logic of similarity, when he asks Titus not to consummate his marriage to Teraminta because she is Tarquin's, or the enemy's, daughter—in Titus' words, a request that "Rome, ere yet she can be well, / Must purge and cast, purge all th'infected humors" (Lee 2.445–46). In the end, he destroys Titus' body because of its alien alliance against the body of the state; he must destroy it in order to "settle the loose liberty of Rome" (4.514). One should not "call it shameful, / That thus shall fix the glory of the world" (554–55). Family or blood bonds, which will increasingly function as links in an otherwise frighteningly pluralistic nation, here recede before the common good, but Brutus' vision of his republic is still grounded in the homogeneity typical of classic republicanism. Titus, on the other hand, represents a more complex position. He loves and marries Teraminta, the alien element, yet finds himself unable to make love to her because of his promise to his father. Interestingly, his quick disengagement from the conspiracy, which he had signed on to under pressure from her, is explained, not through allegiance to his father, but through apocalyptic visions of Rome under destruction. Titus thus represents an attempt at a blending between a republican and a liberal sensibility, where private sentiment merges with visions of the good of the republic, even if the two remain in tension. His inconstant sensibility, what Ellison calls his "incontinent theatricality" (32) because of its display of various bodily fluids, points further, in its difficult negotiation of body and abstraction, same and alien, private and public good, to a search for a more comprehensive, less divided vision.

In Thomas Otway's *Venice Preserved* (1682), sensibility seems to play more starkly antithetical roles, swaying between heterosexual love, which takes place at the personal, private level, and a homosocial bonding with deeply political ramifications. The play predominantly shows "a conspiratorial masculine subculture that is laden with affect" (Ellison 41). Caught between his love for his wife Belvidera, who leads him to betrayal, and his allegiance to his friend Pierre, his co-conspirator against Venice, Jaffeir represents a fundamental dilemma between heterosexual passion and homosocial love. When Belvidera tells him that he will be remembered as a hero who saved his nation, he replies he will live on as the man who broke "The sacred bonds of oaths and holier friendship, / In fond compassion to a woman's tears" (Otway 4.1.15–16). When she draws graphic and sentimental images of bereaved mothers, "Their naked mangled breasts besmeared with blood" (55), he turns into "a tame lamb" (87) unsuccessfully trying to smother his feelings of guilt at betraying "My truth, my virtue, constancy and friends" (75). Ultimately it is at Pierre's feet that he grovels in despair, before in a final scene, which cannot but echo Romeo and Juliet's death scene, he declares his love to Pierre, who breaks down in tears, then stabs him before stabbing himself. That the play ends with Belvidera's loss of sanity and her death does not undermine the theme of a male solidarity born from a combination of love and political idealism. Whoever Otway's specific historical targets were, the play carries a republican sensibility, in which male friendship transforms itself into a public bodily ritual that is also a political statement.

Addison's *Cato* (1713) similarly associates sensibility with republicanism. Cato is the hero of the play; his valor, rectitude, and stoicism constitute its republican core. The good characters that surround him seem to bathe in this light, having inherited their republican principles either by blood or by mimesis. When we meet his daughter Marcia, she refrains from showing Juba, the young African prince obviously in love with her, any signs of affection. When her friend Lucia gently chides her for her sternness, Marcia affirms she cannot think of love when her father's life is threatened by Caesar. Juba's own virtue is highlighted in the first scene, when Cato's son Portius tells Marcus, his brother, how Juba "breaks the fierceness of his native temper / To copy out our Father's bright example" (Addison 1.1.81–82). Portius uses the example of Juba to exhort his brother to control his passion for Lucia: "Put forth thy utmost strength, work every nerve, / And call up all thy father in thy soul" (63–64). Marcus and Portius may be said to represent the republican homosocial center of the play, tied as they are by blood and friendship. Marcus makes the distinction clear in a later scene: "Nature first pointed out my *Portius* to me, / And early taught me, by her secret force, / To love thy person, e'er I knew thy merit; / 'Till, what was instinct, grew up into friendship" (3.1.3–6). The play, then, seems to encourage republican values, which culminate in Cato's actions at the end. He first expresses satisfaction at hearing of his son's death while fighting the enemy: "Thanks to the Gods! my boy has done his duty" (4.4.70), then waxes pathetic when speaking of Rome, eliciting more admiration from Juba: "Behold that upright man! Rome fills his eyes / With tears, that flow'd not o'er his own dead son" (96–97). After Cato commits suicide in the last scene, Lucius announces that his body will be taken publicly to Caesar, as a source of protection but also as a symbol of his famed virtue.

The fact that the play ends with the announcement of two weddings, however, as the dying Cato expresses his wishes about Portius and Lucia as well as Juba and Marcia, signals the presence of a less stern sensibility. As Laura Brown puts it, Cato "is a public hero, and yet the center of a domestic intrigue." Consequently, he "reflects contemporary concerns with the validity of Stoical ideals," hence representing "the first major effort of a sentimental age to incorporate the Stoic hero into an anti-Stoic sensibility" (156). The intrusion of marriage as a major plot element implies a new, liberal emphasis, in that it presents the future of the nation as more bent on domestic and private acts in order to solve social and political problems. As Lisa Freeman puts it, the combination of Cato's fall with a comic, domestic ending implies that "the kind of heroism embodied by Cato no longer obtained either as a realistic expectation or as a desirable model in the context of eighteenth-century culture" (466). While Cato obviously remains a site of admirable glory, Addison suggests that his ethos is no longer exclusive. That the new ethos was far from established, though, is clear from the negative critical reaction to the love scenes.[3] In this perspective, the homosocial affection and bonding between Cato and Juba may hint at evolving or mixed political ideas.

The tensions visible in these Roman plays, in which private attachments are played up against republican brotherhood, herald the conflict between individualism and the common good that marked the eighteenth century on both sides of the Atlantic, but the political ferment at the turn of the century took a different direction on each side. While, as we will see, brotherhood became a password for liberal humanitarianism, by the end of the eighteenth century and the early decades of the nineteenth century it was also used by radical writers to promote more subversive political views. Radicalism was fueled from different sides by the American Revolution, the French Revolution and the growth of Jacobin ideologies, the revolution in Saint-Domingue, and the publication of various radical works, such as those of Thomas Paine. But ironically, the democratization of America, and the taming of the Revolution through the Constitution, did not spur the same kind of radicalism that developed in Britain at the time, where if anything the government became more oppressive. These differences manifested themselves in the culture of sentiment. More specifically, the depiction of brotherhood and of homosocial relationships had different political implications in British and American texts. In the rest of this section, I take a brief look at two writers eminently representative of this theme and its variations, William Godwin in Britain and Charles Brockden Brown in America.

Godwin's treatise *Enquiry concerning Political Justice* (1793) stands out as the British radical statement of the 1790s. From our perspective, in this treatise Godwin may be said to attempt a merging of radical notions of the public good with radical notions of the individual. While his political views have been called libertarian or even anarchistic, Godwin is also engaged in a search for the greatest good of society. Political morality, he states, ought to be "determined by a consideration of the greatest general good" (*Enquiry* 67). The main principle underlying good governance is that "nothing shall be done in the name of the community, which is not conducive to the welfare of the whole" (68). His famous example is the dilemma that consists in choosing, in case of a fire, between saving François Fénelon, the famous French writer, and saving his valet. Because Fénelon benefits the public good more than the valet, his life is worth more and he should be saved. Godwin goes further, arguing that, had the valet been "my brother, my father or my benefactor," this should have made no difference in his decision. Not my individual connection to the victim, but my assessment of his "importance to the general weal" (71), should guide my decision. In this philosophy, brotherhood, in the sense of familial connection, is trumped by a more expansive notion of brotherhood, that of a social connection for the welfare of all. At the same time, though, Godwin believed that the entity originally designed to promote that welfare, government, had become corrupt and oppressive. It was up to the individual to promote that disinterested benevolence Godwin aspired to, and his social project leaves humans with a great degree of independence. Godwin was not a precursor of socialism. His peculiar theory, though, shows the result of a radical balance of the needs of individualism and the common good, and his notion of brotherhood in particular reflects that balance.

One could say that Godwin applied his political principles in his novel *Things as They Are; or, The Adventures of Caleb Williams* (1794), to the extent that the male double at the heart of the book, the pursuer and the pursued, reflects what Pamela Clemit calls the "destabilization of hierarchical values" (57). Caleb's trajectory represents a slow and painful liberation of the servant from the power of the master, the painful birth of a full-fledged individual. Yet, at the same time, the obsessional relationship between the two men emphasizes a sort of codependence, as each of the two lives is fundamentally defined by the other. From the beginning, indeed, Caleb states that "there was a magnetical sympathy" (Godwin, *Caleb Williams* 117) between him and Falkland, and this attraction between two very different men suggests both a drive toward the breakdown of hierarchy and an ineradicable mutuality. Caleb early declares that he cannot become an informer on his patron because "'my soul yearns for his welfare'" (143), and he remains driven by these feelings. The revised ending of the novel, which has surprised some critics, perfectly conveys Godwin's double goal. In his generosity, Caleb shows his moral independence and disinterestedness. At the same time, as Falkland's emotional reaction shows when he falls into Caleb's arms, Caleb is reinforcing the bond with the man who has been after him for so long. The homosocial theme in *Caleb Williams* reaches a radical climax in this unexpected melting of its liberal and republican dimensions.

Charles Brockden Brown's novels reveal much about the American attitude toward brotherhood and radicalism, in that the liberal and republican tendencies remain in opposition rather than in dialogue with each other. The novels often stage a confrontation between different kinds of sympathy, none of which seems to contain the germs of individual or social happiness. To an interior, Smithian form of sympathy, which often deteriorates into narcissism, madness, or religious fanaticism, Brown often opposes a republican sympathy, based on a full recognition of the other, but which carries its own threats in the form of a contagion or a loss of the self. As in sentimental novels, such a contrast contains resonances about the possibilities and the dangers faced by the new nation, though by representing their acute consequences, Brown shows a more radical political consciousness. A few decades ago, Larzer Ziff expressed admiration for the "extraordinary manner in which Brown employs sentiment against itself" (51), as he raises the reader's sentimental expectations only to crush them and provoke an insight into the complexity of human psychology. While I agree that Brown complicates the strategies of sentimental literature, I also see in this complication a reflection of his search for political relevance. Unlike seduction novels, his novels focus less on a pursuit of agency and freedom than on the susceptibility of perception to emotional predispositions, but as in the sentimental novel, these predispositions have political implications, and reveal conflicts between particular worldviews.[4]

In *Wieland* (1798), Brown opposes the dangers of obsessive interiority to the perils of a republican consciousness clothed in the language of brotherhood. Wieland has a liberal sensibility, with a focus on the individual interior life. Clara, his sister and the narrator, points to his religious propensities and his melancholy, as shown in his approach to texts, which he reads only to discover "confirmations of his faith" (C. Brown, *Wieland* 28).[5] The focus on interior life is carried to terrible extremes when he kills his family at the order of imaginary voices, which penetrate him through a sort of "irradiation" (190). Though he temporarily interprets his act as going "beyond the reach of selfishness" (195), the gruesome murder testifies to the perverse consequences of an enclosed self, to a notion of virtue deformed beyond any form of personal morality, and to a "degeneracy" (196) that befalls that kind of sensibility. The liberal focus on individual interiority leads to disastrous consequences. Carwin represents a force from the outside, and a republican worldview.[6] His abhorrent behavior throughout the novel can be interpreted generously, in that his invasiveness testifies to an insatiable curiosity about others, and his ventriloquism turns him into a symbol of a whole community. As we learn from his memoirs, *Memoirs of Carwin the Biloquist*, he carries memories of his mentor, Ludloe, whose principles, like those of his probable model William Godwin, sound radically republican. Ludloe's notion of benevolence fits this image. "Generosity had been expunged from his catalogue as having no meaning or a vicious one" (304), as to him it should result, not from a moment of intense sympathy between two persons, but from a higher principle unrelated to personality. Ludloe represents the yearning for "absolute equality" (306) and the rejection of "the absurd and unequal distribution of power and property" (315). It is within this political context that homosocial friendship plays a role.

The clash between familial and republican brotherhood comes to a head, as the young people live in a closed circle whose apparent harmony will not prevent its self-destruction. As they live in a microcosm, meeting daily at the temple, where "the social affections were accustomed to expand, and the tear of delicious sympathy to be shed" (26), this constant sympathetic exchange ends in tragedy.[7] At the root of this violence lies the fact that, underneath conflicting personalities and divergent political visions, the members of this community seem bound, not by rational communication, but by more intense, interior attraction. This merging and melting together suggests the danger of liberal sympathy.[8] As the plot develops, characters take on characteristics from others. Pleyel abandons his usual good cheer and rational approach as he lets himself be deceived by Carwin's voices and builds an improbably amoral picture of Clara. Clara herself increasingly doubts her rational capacities. In the final confrontation with her brother, she says, "my state was little different from that of my brother. I entered, as it were, into his thought. My heart was visited and rent by his pangs" (263). In this moment of ultimate sympathy, she merges with a being whose actions constitute the horror at the heart of the novel. The incestuous motif in *Wieland* warns about a new nation apparently committed to heterogeneity, but in reality prone to the dangerous seduction of similarity.[9] As in *The Power of Sympathy*, incestuous sympathy wreaks havoc. While Carwin's intrusion contributes to the tragedy by accelerating the destructive process, the blame falls less on the worldview he represents than on the weaknesses inherent in a community based on familial sympathy.[10] Still, possible republican brotherhood competes with real brotherhood, and gets dissolved in the destructive familial network.

In *Ormond*, liberal individualism and liberal sympathy, represented by Constantia Dudley, are opposed to republican characters such as Ormond. In her strength and her self-reliance, Constantia announces the independent young women who will populate nineteenth-century "woman's fiction." When she turns down Balfour's marriage proposal because, among other reasons, she is now "at least mistress of the product of her own labour" (Brown, *Ormond* 103), she highlights her adherence to Lockean values. She thinks of marriage as a consensual contract, resulting from "the conformity and concurrence of intentions and wishes" (164). She displays compassion and benevolence to individuals around her. As a representative of a radical republican vision, on the other hand, Ormond has much in common with Carwin. His "political projects" imply a link with the Bavarian Illuminati,[11] a sect whose existence became legendary, and whose supposed radicalism inspired much paranoia in the decade Brown was writing these novels. Ormond is led by principle rather than by individual need. To him, "the principles of the social machine must be rectified," since "efforts designed to ameliorate the condition of an individual were sure of answering a contrary purpose." Benevolence and sympathy on a small scale cannot lead to beneficent results. Man was "part of a machine," and "contiguousness to other parts—that is, to other men—was all that was necessary to render him a powerful concurrent" (127). Once again, republican idealism, as much as it is associated with "notions of equality" (129), and with a notion of "contiguousness" that fits in with the horizontal, communal strain we have been associating with that worldview, finds itself associated with a character both fascinating and despicable.

In this novel, the positive potential of homosocial relationships sees itself undermined by liberal sympathy. Constantia rejoices at the prospect of meeting Martinette because various similitudes between them seem to indicate she has found "a companion fitted to partake in all her sympathies" (188). But like Ormond, Martinette turns out to represent "large experience," and is associated with revolution and political upheaval. Her enthusiasm for military prowess springs from a love of liberty but also from "the contagion of example" (206), a feeling that implies an awareness of that different kind of bonding. By contrast, her individual mode of friendship shows no "traces of sympathy" (191). As those qualities become increasingly clear to her, Constantia develops "antipathy" (207) for her companion, and that relationship fizzles. The major friendship at the heart of the novel is that between Constantia and Sophia, "a being like herself" (188). The fact alone that Sophia narrates the story shows her liberal credentials, since she manipulates the story in that direction. Sophia's remarks about Europe and America also sound decidedly Hartzian, as she notes that "in the former, things tended to extremes, whereas, in the latter, all things tended to the same level" (230). But while their love functions as a symbol of strength and social harmony, it also threatens through its excess. In the first indirect reference to Sophia—to herself, thus—the narrator describes the effect of her miniature portrait on Constantia: "Its power over her sensations was similar to that possessed by a beautiful Madonna over the heart of a juvenile enthusiast" (96). Their reunion is characterized by "intoxication" and "inebriation" (241). Here again, the perils of liberal sympathy hover over a relationship between two persons very close to each other, undermining the possibilities it simultaneously opens up.

Edgar Huntly feels quite different from the previous novels, in that it explores the possibilities of homosocial sympathy, and hence of brotherhood, more systematically. Still grieving from the death of his friend Waldegrave, Huntly wanders one late evening toward the place of his murder. There he observes, thanks to the moonlight, "the shape of a man, tall and robust." He keeps observing the stranger: "Something like flannel was wrapped round his waist and covered his lower limbs. The rest of his frame was naked" (Brown, *Edgar Huntly* 7). Huntly wonders about this strange presence and, upon seeing the man grieving, "every sentiment, at length, yielded to my sympathy" (7–8). As he leaves the spot, as if in a trance, the stranger "came so near as almost to brush my arm" (9). The next day, Huntly decides to follow this man, Clithero, into the wilderness. Elizabeth Maddock Dillon remarks about Huntly's instantaneous interest in Clithero, as well as about Huntly's trust in a stranger who, later in the novel, comes to claim some money, that his responses hinge "upon the sympathetic and quite physical identification or *equality* he feels with another male body." Because these relationships prove much more engrossing than his relationship to his fiancée, Huntly displays a pattern "of abandoning the heterosexual marriage narrative in favor of masculine sympathy" (Dillon, *Gender* 165). As in *The Story of Quashi*, which I discussed earlier in the introduction, homosocial bonding is at the core of what constitutes sympathy in *Edgar Huntly*.

This form of sympathy embodies the possibilities of political radicalism. To Dillon, what explains the attraction Huntly feels for Clithero is "a pleasurable identification of male bodies with one another that is less sexual than political and that makes visible a form of liberal sociality dissociated from more stable and rigidly biologized accounts of bodies produced in and through narratives of sentimental marriage" (166). The physical nature of the attraction shows that Huntly has a desire "to produce himself as embodied," by achieving "physical equality" (167) with Clithero, and that he experiences embodiment as a rebirth rather than a regression. This desire is "a republican one." Here Dillon uses a concept of radical republicanism that is close to the one I use in this book, rather than the more common assessments of republicanism as "predicated upon *disembodied* forms of virtue and reason" (169). Against Michael Warner's view of *Edgar Huntly* as liberal rather than republican, Dillon offers a view of the novel as not only republican but radically so, in that the protagonist "seeks to fashion a republican body of his own through a mimetic identification with other male bodies," a form of politics that is "more Jacobin than Harringtonian, that is, they resemble the politics of the French Revolution rather than those of Britain's Country party in the seventeenth century." This vision is predicated on *"fraternity and equality"* (176). The "radical republican nature of his search" partly comes out in his identification with Clithero, himself, as an Irishman, associated at the time with revolutionary ideas. Huntly seeks a *"republican embodiment or a bodily equality"* (177) with his fellow men. Ultimately, he represents a threatening cosmopolitanism that divests American identity of its national and racial privileges.

The nature of this radical republicanism is reflected in the complex role played by body and mind, outside and inside, in Huntly's sympathetic relation to the world. Dillon freely mixes terms like "identification," "equality," and "similarity" (178). One scene in particular, where Huntly wakes up with this hair entangled in the matted blood of an Indian he has killed, gives an image of "dissolving boundaries" (178) between men of different races. When later on he is shot at by a group of white men who mistake him for an Indian, the distinction between white and nonwhite, says Dillon, has apparently disappeared. While Huntly indeed seems to take on the characteristics of the men he pursues and the world he inhabits, he distinguishes himself through his constant attempts to understand difference, to enter into the mind of Clithero even as he observes his appearance and behavior. When seemingly lost in tortuous conjectures, he often decides to initiate a direct communication with the object of his thoughts, either by confessing about his inspection of a box, by calling to Clithero across a ravine, or by comforting him. This last requires Huntly "to sit by him in silence, to moisten his hands with tears, to sigh in unison, to offer him the spectacle of sympathy" (Brown 110). In this description Huntly remarkably avoids the language of interiority typical of liberal sympathy, evoking a moment of total acceptance even as it keeps the other mysterious. His wanderings are often described as labyrinthine, but they often have to do with inside and outside, or inner and outer edges and surfaces. In that, he resembles Clithero, who describes a normal state as one in which "I could disengage myself at pleasure, and could pass, without difficulty, from attention to the world within, to the contemplation of that without" (74). These behaviors reflect a complexity of sympathetic apprehension, a full engagement with a community of others, a feeling of complex fraternity.

That the novel leaves the fate of Huntly dangling, however, indicates Brown's discomfort with the political implications of these behaviors. In the end, Huntly is "left abandoned, on a path leading nowhere, without social recognition or voice, misguided by his own republican desires" (Dillon 183). But liberal sympathy does not come out as a triumphant counterpart either. In the course of the novel, it has brought destruction to many characters. The tragedy of Clithero has its roots in his understanding of Mrs. Lorimer's connection to her brother, whom he has just killed: "'A fatal sympathy will seize her. She will shrink, and swoon, and perish, at the news!'" (Brown 78). Huntly has no admiration for that form of sympathy: "Exempt as this lady was from almost every defect, she was indebted for her ruin to absurd opinions of the sacredness of consanguinity" (126). Mrs. Lorimer's miscarriage at the end of the novel, while an indirect reproach of Huntly's actions throughout the novel, also intimates a dire future for the representatives of a liberal worldview. In a moment of philosophic reflection, Huntly acknowledges the impossibility of true, complete sympathy, in that "every man who suffers is unavoidably shackled by the errors which he censures in his neighbour, and his efforts to relieve himself are as fruitless as those with which he attempted the relief of others." His subsequent decision simply to offer Clithero some food hints at forms of solidarity not exclusively predicated on the interior connections so prized by the advocates of liberal sympathy, and at a worldview that, if not necessarily endorsed by the novel, is not downplayed either. Indeed, Huntly continues, the "magic of sympathy . . . might work a gradual and secret revolution" (115)—a significant wording, even if it applies here only to Clithero's state of mind.

While Brown investigated its radical possibilities, however, brotherhood in America often developed conservative overtones. It is well known, for example, that Leslie Fiedler considered homosocial relations in American literature, especially of the interracial kind, a sentimental, even childish, perversion of the mature, British heterosexual plot. They were also questionable from a racial point of view. Quite often, the black man (or the Indian man) was a mere darker version, a darker reflection of the white man. Similarly, David Greven points out that antebellum homosociality did not necessarily have the "transgressive" dimension that contemporary critics have taken to celebrating in their "fraternalist fantasies" (84); to him, fraternity had aspects that were "normalizing and compulsory" (100).[12] As we will see in this chapter, black writers managed to recuperate the theme of brotherhood and fraternal friendship in order to convey a political desire for equality. With black writers too, though, the sense of equality fostered by brotherhood served different sorts of political allegiance, some more radical than others.

Brotherhood and American Antislavery

The division in the political landscape of Charles Brockden Brown's novels reveals a hesitancy with radical ideas that contrasts with the definite appeal these ideas had for the black community in the new United States—as well as for some white pockets in the culture—although in that community also, brotherhood and homosocial friendship acquired different political valences depending on the political context. By the end of the eighteenth century, brotherhood had become a salient element of the humanitarianism present in antislavery appeals on both sides of the Atlantic. But the radicalism of the period took on specific forms with some African American thinkers and leaders, some of whom carved out a new space for republicanism. Black nationalism made its entry into the discourse of the black community at the end of the eighteenth century, in the form of black benevolent and mutual improvement societies, some of which advocated emigration to Africa.[13] The notion of brotherhood often found itself at the core of those societies' appeals. When the Newport African Union Society was attempting to rally its Providence counterpart for an emigration scheme, for example, it "invited the blacks of Providence to help them 'unite our brethren . . . as one Mans family' by joining in a 'Union Society'" (Miller, *Search* 13). Calling others one's "brethren" had different possible implications, some more radical than others. In this case, brotherhood belonged less to the realm of liberal, familial interiority than to the desire to create an independent community founded on equality. The fact that this community was conceived as racially circumscribed, though, placed this homosocial rhetoric in a unique niche. The racial politics of this niche would be a source of wavering for the black Freemasons discussed in this chapter, as they would struggle to ally brotherhood with a budding black republicanism.

Fraternity has a complex history in the United States, whose tail end is our current association of the word with the mindless conformism of Greek university associations. The concept's cross-cultural ubiquitousness should warn us about idealizing its radical potential. While the notion of fraternity seems to imply egalitarianism, its connection with an ideology of the family allows it to retain more restrictive, even hierarchical, connotations. The emotion fraternity conveys can also dissolve into a vague, noncommittal feeling of universal connection since, as Wilson Carey McWilliams puts it, "it is possible to love everyone equally only if one loves nothing in particular" (48). Fraternity has been the symbol for radical change in certain cultures,[14] but in the United States, where the ideal of fraternity has suffused less the political discourse than sites marginal to politics, such as communitarian, mutual aid, and religious groups, it seems that the viability of the concept has precisely been tied to its inability to enter the political stage. John Winthrop's enticing vision of "brotherly affection" (225) as the basis for the survival of the community, and hence as a political principle anchored in sharing, still depends on a notion of similarity: "Each discerns, by the work of the spirit, his own image and resemblance in another, and therefore cannot but love him as he loves himself" (221). More than a century later, Cotton Mather's "zeal to defend the traditional ideal of Christian fraternity led him to abandon the political" (McWilliams 159), and Jonathan Edwards "all but eliminates the political and communitarian aspect of Puritanism" (169). With the Enlightenment, brotherhood starts acquiring a biological or racial tinge.[15] Friendship becomes "a diffuse fellow-feeling, based not on deep bonds but on the suppression of anything that might divide" (182).[16]

The American Quaker John Woolman stands out as an exception. Indeed, his antislavery stance makes a surprisingly radical use of the concept of brotherhood. *Some Considerations on the Keeping of Negroes* (1754) starts with remarks that at first seem to have no connection at all with the topic at hand, but which ultimately support this philosophy. Woolman presents "*Natural Affection*" as "that which inferior Creatures have." Creatures will love best "that which is a Part of Self," so that "*Natural Affection* appears to be a branch of *Self-love*." In this unexpected opening, Woolman undermines the notion of blood ties, highlighting its grounding in visions of similarity in the way they inevitably point back to the self. Fortunately, he says, God provides a way to escape this solipsism, by prodding us, as Christ did, to ask the question: "*Who is my mother, and who are my brethren?*" God makes it clear that "the earthly Ties of Relationship, are comparatively, inconsiderable." Kinship is determined by whether one "shall do the will of my Father which is in Heaven." Hence love operates "on principles unalterable and in themselves perfect" (Woolman 335). Woolman starts an essay against slavery with an undermining of strict notions of blood and family.

This extension of notions of the family to anybody belonging to the human race might ring a bell to those of us familiar with abolitionist propaganda, yet Woolman's position belongs to a different realm. The most famous image associated with the abolitionist movement is a medallion produced by Josiah Wedgwood (the author of the original design remains unknown)[17] representing a kneeling black man, naked except for manacles and chains, and surrounded, almost like a halo, by an inscription that reads: "Am I Not a Man and a Brother?" The original seal was ordered by the committee of the 1787 London meeting of the Society for Effecting the Abolition of the Slave Trade, led by Quakers, and it would be easy to draw a direct line between Woolman's preface and the medallion. But the medallion, which became popular and fashionable, projected an image of submission and supplication that "came to crystallize and enshrine the idea of pathetic, docile subservience and black inferiority" (Honour 64), an image little applicable to Woolman's writings. The medallion's appeal to brotherhood functions differently than Woolman's appeal. The Quaker divests brotherhood of its blood connotations and hooks it up to higher, impersonal principles; the medallion, on the contrary, incites its viewers to think of all humans as real brothers because of an inner link similar to the ties of family. While the latter appeals to the interiority of liberal sympathy, slipping easily from supposed brotherhood to actual submission, Woolman envisions a larger community of people linked by a higher good.

Woolman does make appeals to the "natural Right of Freedom" (341) and to feelings of brotherhood, but he places these ideas within a less sentimental framework of justice and respect. It is his search for higher principles, that makes him sound as if he is trying to break out of what have come to be seen as the liberal pieties of sympathy. For the 1762 reprinting of the essay, he intended to replace his invocation of the golden rule with the enjoining to "'love the Lord our God with all our hearts, and our neighbours as ourselves'" (336), probably a better expression of his encouragement to focus on the other. He tries to strike a balance between an appeal to sameness and an urge to accept difference when he says of blacks that "they are now amongst us, and those of our Nation the cause of their being here" (341). Even as he separates "us" from "them," unlike Joseph Sewall, who was discussed in chapter 1, he also intimates the necessity of cohabitation and possibly future integration. Toward the end of the essay, he refers to men, "both Apostles and others," who "have really come to the Unity of the Spirit and the Fellowship of the Saints"; in them, "there still appears the like Disposition, and in them the Desire of the real Happiness of Mankind, has outbalanced the Desire of Ease, Liberty, and many times Life itself." In what sounds like an eerie anticipatory subversion of the Declaration of Independence, Woolman intimates that the precious goals of individual life and liberty may not measure up to the active pursuit of happiness, which to him entails, not an individual pursuit of self-interest, but "the Wisdom from above, agreeable with Justice, Equity, and Mercy" (346). This distinction shows that, to him, unity with suffering was "not only trans-personal but profoundly social" (Stewart 269). His sympathy is entangled with his egalitarianism, and his original notion of brotherhood symbolizes this political stance.[18]

This elasticity of the concept of brotherhood highlights its ability to shield both radical and conservative values. In her thought-provoking book on "national manhood," Dana D. Nelson argues that the manufacturing of the ideology of fraternal national manhood for white men, between the 1780s and the 1850s, helped produce an imaginary homogeneity and a feeling of solidarity that worked both to veil and keep in place the competitive individualism of the emerging capitalist economy. Indeed, the "process of identifying with national manhood blocks white men from being able efficiently to identify socioeconomic inequality as structural rather than individual failure"; furthermore, it prevents them affectively from developing "more heterogeneous democratic identifications and energies" (Nelson ix). Fraternity is projected into the white men's imaginary, while at the same time its potential radical consequences are never realized. In fact, brotherhood sees itself thwarted in various ways, whether in Benjamin Rush's advice on the education of boys, where the development of real emotional ties between boys must be prevented at all costs — it seems an "actual *threat*" (Nelson 13) to national manhood — or in adult fraternal orders, where the hierarchical structure belies its purported egalitarianism and "the rituals became so long that they left little time for men to enjoy friendship or even casual association" (184). According to Nelson, then, brotherhood remains an unattained ideal, floating in the white male national imaginary but never actualized, except in fleeting nostalgic remembrances of dead men. Not the concept of brotherhood itself, but the nation's inability, or unwillingness, to actualize the concept's potential, defused the various democratic energies flaring up at the time. It may be that the concept had reached its limits.[19]

Brotherhood could be the signal of a focus on the common good, or of a more communitarian, even communistic vision, but it is hard to find traces of that use in the young American nation. Alfred F. Young's two collections of essays on American radicalism show that the revolutionary era witnessed many manifestations of radicalism from below — from artisans, laborers, and farmers. Sean Wilentz argues that one can see traces of a budding class consciousness among craft workers, as they became confronted with the rise of wage labor in a growing capitalist system. Many craft societies popped up at the time, guildlike organizations where fraternity carried more than a vague humanitarian appeal to brotherhood, signifying similar economic interests and a shared vision of society. While most did not deal in wage negotiations and emphasized moral reform, and others were drinking fraternities, reading groups, or gangs, some journeymen's associations played the role of trade unions and organized strikes.[20] However, most of these groups were motivated either by a desire for more political power or by a fear of losing their independence or their private property.[21] Eric Foner points out that the artisans' concept of private property differed from the merchants', in that artisans specifically conceived of property as the result of labor rather than as a path to the accumulation of wealth. Still, their republican focus on virtue and the common good was combined with a liberal emphasis on natural rights, so that "there was a recurrent tension between the sense of mutuality and community, whether confined to a specific craft or extended to all artisans, and the strong tendency toward individualism and self-improvement" (Foner, *Tom Paine* 40). The ideal of individual liberty as trumping any notion of brotherhood thus remained a strong component of the most radical elements in American culture.

That such a tension suffused the black community should not be surprising, and here too one can see the political slipperiness of the notion of brotherhood. Many activist blacks were caught between the liberal individualist discourse of abolition, the black republicanism of black benevolent and fraternal societies, and possibly the more radical socioeconomic egalitarian discourse of the American working class. As Foner shows in his essay, albeit about the antebellum period, there was no love lost between labor and the abolitionists.[22] While certainly not radical, though, most benevolent black societies offered a bridge between sheer individualism and thorough social change, by providing a social context in which brotherhood meant a limited form of redistribution within the group. Their major features were "sickness and disability benefits, pensions for deceased members' families, burial insurance, funeral direction, cemetery plots, credit unions, charity, education, moral guidance, and discussion forums" (R. Harris 614). When it came to slavery, black abolitionists also used brotherhood as a connection between themselves and slaves all over the nation. The resolution of a meeting about the issue of colonization held in Philadelphia in 1817, for example, asserts that, by leaving, free blacks "would be turning their backs on the slave, 'our brethren by the ties of consanguinity, suffering, and wrong'" (Quarles 16). While "consanguinity" forms one component of the connection they feel with slaves, the added components foster the sense of a republican brotherhood held by a commitment to the common good of the group. In this case, the term "brethren" refers to people who are racially similar, but the resolution also makes clear that they are bound above all by a similar oppression. It seems as if this homosocial tie could be easily expanded.[23]

John Marrant

John Marrant's notion of brotherhood is caught in the turmoil of its liberal and republican implications. His political sensibility shows an interesting evolution from religious individualism to the budding republicanism of black Freemasonry, and his notion of brotherhood can be placed within this evolution. This development can be partly attributed to his transatlantic voyages and persona. Marrant was born in New York City in 1755, then moved to Florida, Georgia, and South Carolina. After several years in the Royal Navy, he was ordained a Methodist minister in England and published his *Narrative* there in 1785. He spent some time in Nova Scotia as a minister, then in Boston, and finally returned to England, where he published his *Journal* in 1790. He died the next year. In his writings Marrant makes few references to slavery, except for his fourth edition of the *Narrative*, as well as a few mentions of slavery in his sermons. But those references signal a philosophy in movement.

Marrant's world of feeling was filled with religious faith, and as with Phillis Wheatley, this sensibility partly led to a focus on interiority. Marrant published the *Narrative* the year he was ordained in Bath by the Huntingdonian Connexion, a Methodist sect endowed by Selina Hastings, Countess of Huntingdon, also famous as the person to whom Wheatley's collection of poems and Gronniosaw's narrative were dedicated. The year he was ordained, Marrant left England and sailed to Nova Scotia, where a community of black loyalists had settled, hoping for land and economic independence. Once there, he established a church and a school in Birchtown, and also worked in the area as an itinerant preacher. He stayed there for a few years, and after a sojourn of several months in Boston, he sailed back to England, where he published his *Journal*, which records his experiences in Canada and Massachusetts, and died in April

1791. Unlike the Wesleyan Methodists, who were Arminian, the Huntingdonians believed in predestination. Joanna Brooks shows how Marrant's Calvinism easily integrated what she presents as an essential trope of early African American literature, the motif of Lazarus. Based on John 11, in which Lazarus is raised from the dead by Jesus, this motif informs black texts with images of suffering and death followed by symbols of resurrection and regeneration.[24] The images fit a black experience marked by suffering and loss, and by attempts to deal with that loss that are grounded in religious and biblical feeling. Marrant's *Journal* was such an attempt: it emphasizes an ideology of conversion, salvation, and new birth.

But the *Journal* also shows a more communal dimension. Brooks highlights in Marrant what at the time may have seemed an old-fashioned idea, the notion of a covenant between God and the black community.[25] According to Brooks, in Birchtown Marrant "promulgated a powerful black Atlantic theology specific to the community's needs and experiences." Part of this theology "restored the abandoned Calvinist concept of the covenant community as a site of regeneration, and Marrant redeveloped this covenant theology for the black Atlantic. God had gathered Birchtown to advance the liberation and redemption of all black people, he preached" (Brooks, *American Lazarus* 89). To John Saillant, moreover, "Marrant articulated a vision of a holy black African community, a Zion united under God in a covenant of grace" ("Wipe Away" 1), and he "preached that God was forming a black covenanted community, purified in tribulations by the atoning blood of the Lamb and ordained to sail away from suffering and trials in an exodus to Africa. There, Marrant preached, this pure, covenanted black community would build a holy black paradise" (8). His writings are "an extended commentary on religious faith and blackness" (23). These critics highlight Marrant's less individualistic use of religion, as he puts the notion of covenant in a black nationalist framework informed by his transatlantic experience.

Saillant emphasizes that his reading functions at an intertextual or exegetic level, and indeed a general reader armed with this interpretation may experience puzzlement when perusing the *Narrative* and the *Journal*. The *Journal* contains very few references to race, except when Marrant notes that he preached to mixed audiences. In "Explaining Syncreticism," Saillant also argues that Marrant introduces Africanist elements in his theology by identifying death with a return to Africa: "Marrant's message was that since the souls of the black dead flow across the Atlantic to an ancestral homeland, blacks should make the journey in life" (28). Nowhere in Marrant's writings is this idea explicitly stated. Angelo Costanzo sees Marrant in the *Journal* as a Saint Paul figure, "converting the sinners and unbelievers, and sacrificing his life for his fellow men and women" (103). The question of the extent to which the Nova Scotians had developed a "return to Africa" ideology remains open. James W. St. G. Walker recounts how Thomas Peters, representative of the black Nova Scotians, arrived in London seeking help and bearing a petition asking for land, and adding that "'some Part of the said Black People are earnestly desirous of obtaining their due Allotment of Land and remaining in America but others are ready and willing to go wherever the Wisdom of Government may think proper to provide for them as free Subjects of the British Empire'" (95). Since by chance the recently formed Sierra Leone Company needed immigrants when Peters was residing in London, Walker suggests that the petition "was re-written in England" and that "the 'British Empire' paragraph could have been added at that time" at the suggestion of the company (114). The African consciousness may thus have developed at a later date than assumed by the critic.

It is the case, though, that blacks in Nova Scotia formed a "distinct and separate community" (64), and that both their religious denominations and their schools fostered the "image of themselves as a select group uncontaminated by the sins of the white world" (79). In his enlightening article, Cedrick May points out Marrant's frustration with the Huntingdonian Connexion's lack of financial support for his mission in Nova Scotia, and with its "indifference to the new congregations forming his ministry" (561). This attitude must have reinforced the sense of solidarity the black community already felt after subsequent betrayals by America and Britain. Whether bound by the notion of a special covenant or not, the Nova Scotia black community formed a unique site of black solidarity.

During his stay in Boston, Marrant came into contact with members of the New Divinity as well as with black Freemasons, and he was probably further influenced by both. New Divinity adherents emphasized the ultimate benevolence and glory of God; they expressed themselves strongly against slavery and the slave trade, yet also envisioned the existence of this sin as an opportunity for God to manifest goodness and power, in this case by allowing slavery to bring Christianity to Africa. As Mark Valeri shows, New Divinity adepts, though Calvinist, had relinquished the notion of covenant and "sought to reconcile the Calvinist doctrine of Providence to the conception of natural law regnant in British moral philosophy"; they "asserted that Providence ruled through a moral law" (743). In "A Dialogue on Slavery" (1776), for example, Samuel Hopkins tightly mixes the language of benevolence and charity with that of justice and natural rights. He appeals to notions of both "justice and benevolence," positing that abolition will "greatly promote the happiness of those oppressed strangers and the best interest of the public" (398). He emphasizes a situation that elicits "a mixture of grief, pity, indignation, and horror" while also pointing to the fact that Africans have "never forfeited their liberty or given anyone a right to enslave and sell them" (404). He ends by reiterating "regard to justice, humanity, and mercy" (426). Combining theology with the liberal ideas of the day, New Divinity adherents also displayed the racial separatist tendencies observed in many liberal texts. Hopkins encouraged emigration of black Americans to Africa, and helped educate John Quamine and Bristol Yamma for that purpose.[26] Emigration did appeal to some blacks, and the black Freemasons initially endorsed similar schemes, but through an ideology of brotherhood rather than one of benevolence.

In contrast with these complex influences, the earlier *Narrative* seems more bent on emphasizing interior, individualized emotion. While in the *Journal* emotion mostly punctuates moments of sudden reception to the spirit and expressions of a desire to be saved, usually accompanied by shouting and crying, the *Narrative* encourages a distinction between feeling and sensibility, associating the latter with more material concerns, and the former with inner emotion. Made prisoner by an Indian tribe, Marrant starts crying when the King interrogates him, and he cries when he sees the elaborate preparations for the horrible torture they plan to inflict on him; he also cries when he comes home after several months of absence and realizes his family considers him dead, and when they are unable to recognize him. The tears seem to indicate a form of emotion connected to linguistic or face-to-face communication, or more generally to the realm of the body. As in many spiritual autobiographies, Marrant reserves the language of powerful feeling for moments of deep interior connection, such as his own as well as others' conversions. After he disrupts a meeting held by George Whitefield, he is struck to the ground with the power of his words, "every word I heard from the minister was like a parcel of swords thrust in to me" (51), heralding the beginning of a violent opening up of his interior world. He spends three days lying sick, but when a minister sent by Whitefield works on him, "near the close of his prayer, the Lord was pleased to set my soul at perfect liberty, and being filled with joy I began to praise the Lord immediately; my sorrows were turned into peace, and joy, and love" (52–53). This episode sets the pattern for later acts of conversion. After all arguments have failed, for example, the king of the Cherokees is magically "awakened" during prayer and "a great change took place among the people" (64). Later, when the king rides into Charleston with General Clinton, he tells Marrant that the daughter "was very happy, and sometimes longed to get out of the body" (72). Similarly, when he comes back to his family, Marrant warns his readers, keeping his eye on the prevalence of spiritual matters, that "the following particulars, relating to the manner in which I was made known to my family, are less interesting." He only recounts them because he knows that "perhaps, some readers would not forgive their omission" (66). Indeed, the account makes much mention of tears, and brings on the comment that "this was an affecting scene!" (67), as if he (or his amanuensis) knew that the passage will appeal to the melodramatic penchant of the reader's sensibility. By contrast, the only member of his family who immediately recognizes him is his young sister, in the sort of immediate emotional knowledge easily attributed to children, and quite different from the overall pathos of the scene, again pointing to a hierarchy of feeling in the text.[27]

The fact that inner emotional connection appears at the top of this hierarchy has political implications. The narrative remains closer to the first American captivity narratives, which Roy Harvey Pearce describes as "simple, direct religious documents" (2), such as that of Mary Rowlandson, as opposed to later ones more bent on thrill and sensibility. Karen A. Weyler points out that, while in the white captivity narrative, sensibility "appears as a marker to distinguish the civilized nature of the white captives from the barbarity of their captors," thus "re-affirming the white writers' racial difference," Britton Hammon and Marrant "create for their subjects identities marked not by race, but by piety" (43). While much can be made of the fact that, apparently acculturated, he adopts the Indian dress and speaks the Cherokee language,[28] Marrant obviously retains the main and overwhelming component of his identity, his Christianity. As Michelle Burnham puts it, "Marrant's narrative never demonizes the Indians; in fact, the Cherokees' conversion unites them with their captive-turned minister in a Christian community" (125). The more material aspects of their exchange are made subservient to an interior, spiritual connection. Precisely because of Marrant's "transcultural mobility," "his ability, including the ability of his body, to move between cultural categories" (129), his body becomes an interchangeable envelope for a stable inner core, in a case of liberal sympathy we have found in other texts. Marrant can be seen as a colonizer. As Burnham points out, the Cherokee conversion "subordinates the national difference between captive and captor to a common Christianity that colonizes the Cherokee nation within English imperial interests" (127). Once again the supposed neutrality of the language of interiority carries special interests, as liberal emotion is made to serve imperialism.

Yet contrary to William L. Andrews' statement that "Marrant's racial identity in this work is almost totally subsumed under his generic identity as Christian pilgrim" (45), Marrant's emphasis on interiority does not quite diminish the importance of emotional ties to his racial community. At first his separation from his family to go wander in the wilderness allows him to move closer to his god. But after staying with the Indians for several months,[29] "I now and then found, that my affections to my family and country were not dead; they were sometimes very sensibly felt, and at last strengthened into an invincible desire of returning home" (65). His account of his reunion with his family, which he had presented as uninteresting, climaxes when he is finally recognized, and so "the dead was brought to life again; thus the lost was found" (67). Combining the motif of Lazarus and that of the prodigal son, the episode turns out very interesting after all, thanks to Marrant's symbolic resurrection. Although he had initially mentioned his affection for "my family and country," the reunion takes place at a very local level, as he is "made known to all the family and acquaintances" (67). In his description of his stay with the Indians, Marrant had not really presented himself as a member of their community" he "was treated like a prince" (64) and remained in the king's palace. Now he rejoices about being surrounded by a well-defined community to which he knows he belongs. The emotion associated with his return to a community of the same complements, and contrasts with, the more individualized forms of emotion he had been emphasizing until now.

A similar hankering suffuses a description of his attempt to Christianize a community of slaves on a South Carolina plantation where he temporarily worked as a free carpenter.[30] In this moving story, Marrant elicits sympathy for a group of people obviously longing for some spiritual nourishment, and suffering horribly violent treatment in order to get it. As he sits in prayer and singing hymns, "the little negro children would often come round the door with their pretty wishful looks," indicating what is to him a natural desire for knowledge and religion. Children and parents start learning, and "I soon had my society increased to about thirty persons." At those times "the Lord was pleased often to refresh us with a sense of his love and presence amongst us" (68). When the mistress finds out about this religious instruction, she persuades her husband to put an end to it. In a gory scene the master and several associates flog all the members of the group. When the master later tells Marrant that Marrant "should make them so wise that he [the master] should not be able to keep them in subjection," Marrant asks him "whether he [the master] did not think they had Souls to be saved?" (69). Marrant then decides to leave, after he "encouraged the poor creatures to call upon God as well as they could." Later on he hears that they "continued their meetings though in such imminent danger" by meeting at midnight in different parts of the woods. After the mistress' death, "her husband gave them liberty to meet together as before, and used sometimes to attend with them" (70). The addition of this incident to the fourth edition transforms Marrant's life story, essentially a conversion narrative, into a different text, one that forges a parallel between his own personal struggle and this small community of slaves. Here liberation is coupled with an image of resistance and solidarity, and of a community that even occasionally includes the white outsider.[31]

Taken together with the other moments of feeling discussed above, this episode gains more significance, reflecting the racial complexity characteristic of all Marrant's writings, one that makes Benilde Montgomery characterize him as "an emerging, polyethnic American identity" (105). The emotion elicited by the anecdote encompasses both the saving of the slaves' souls and their incipient creation of a resistant community. It points toward both the sublime of spiritual salvation and the republican goal of solidarity and brotherhood. While not liberal in the sense of being based on an ideology of freedom, and while not fully republican in the sense of demanding recognition and equality, it carves out a special space for black-identified unity. This unity is not necessarily racially closed off, though, as attested to by the white man's participation in their rituals, and by the second episode Marrant adds to the fourth edition. In it he tells the story of Mary Scott, a young girl he knows after he is back in Charleston, and of her "remarkable conversion" (*Narrative* 70). Mary predicts her own death, and on that fateful day, in a scene that anticipates the death of Little Eva in *Uncle Tom's Cabin*, she passes away describing visions of heavenly glory. Because it is impossible to determine whether Mary is black or white, the episode adds an aura of racial uncertainty or racial integration to the previous one. This racial fuzziness remains until the end, when Marrant looks forward to sailing to Nova Scotia so that "the black nations may be made white in the blood of the Lamb" (73–74). Like Wheatley, he cannot totally relinquish the Christian color symbolism indicative of Western racism, yet at the same time he sees his evangelizing enterprise as a sort of spiritual racial uplift. More than the other Black Atlantic writers, Marrant uses emotion to express a search for a political vision that shows sharp swings between liberal and republican approaches.

As part of this political complexity, Marrant seems aware that brotherhood can be shrunk or expanded. The fact that he writes these episodes from London suggests that his transatlantic experience has sharpened his sense of belonging in a community linked by a strict sense of brotherhood. Indeed, after the Revolution he lived seemingly happily in London for three years, but gradually he developed "a feeling concern for the salvation of my countrymen: I carried them constantly in the arms of prayer and faith to the throne of grace, and had continual sorrow in my heart for my brethren, for my kinsmen, according to the flesh" (73). Even though he is here referencing the Bible (Romans 9: 2–3), the fraternal feeling sounds racial in its suggestion of biological ties. Indeed, that is when he forms the project to join his brother in Nova Scotia. When he ends the *Narrative* by quoting from Revelation, though, he "points the way to a transcendent world to which he has been journeying, and he hopes now that readers of his spiritual life will also undertake that arduous but worthwhile pilgrimage" (Costanzo 102). In all these episodes, Marrant seems to go through periods of detachment from, and reattachment to, his family and brotherly community, as if to indicate a fluctuation, maybe even a conflict, between his spiritual and his more earthly emotional bonds. This fluctuation inevitably affects his sense of who his "brothers" are.

Prince Hall and Black Freemasonry

The mixture of republican and liberal feeling through the role of brotherhood reaches its most interesting form of complexity in a number of speeches delivered to the Boston African Lodge of Freemasons in the last decade of the eighteenth century, the first by Marrant, the other two by Prince Hall, master and later grand master of the lodge. Here sentiment wavers between liberal sympathy and the most extensive struggle with republican feeling seen to date in a black text, especially between its racial and its nonracial tendencies. The black Masons found themselves at the confluence of several identities, as African Americans, as Christians, and as Masons, and each identity pushed them in different political directions. By manipulating stories of transhistorical and transnational connection, Marrant and Hall call up a notion of brotherhood that wavers between forms of black nationalism and more expansive ideas of solidarity. At the same time, they maintain an emotional appeal that is predominantly middle-class in its aspirations, thereby placing fraternal feeling within bounds of social respectability, and tying it to the pieties of liberal individual achievement.

Marrant's June 24, 1789, sermon displays these sometimes conflicting allegiances. A June 4, 1789, report mentions that Marrant was admitted as a member of the lodge and made its chaplain. The lodge itself had come together about a year after Prince Hall and fourteen other black men were made Masons by an Irish army lodge in 1775, and it had received its official charter from the London Grand Lodge in April 1787.[32] Most probably Marrant received assistance from Hall in drafting the text of the sermon, and Hall himself obviously found some inspiration in the 1723 *Book of Constitutions*, cowritten by James Anderson and Jean Théophile Desaguliers.[33] The most striking leitmotif in the text, the notion of brotherly love, provides a good entry into its politics of feeling. The sermon ostensibly offers a reflection on Romans 12:10: "*Be kindly affected one to another, with brotherly love, in honour preferring one another*" (78). Throughout the text, the quotation shrinks and expands in meaning, at times referring to love for the black community, for the network of Freemasons, or for humanity, offering the reader an amazing sample of an identity struggle between the local and the universal that was intensifying at the end of the eighteenth century.

While the sermon often ostensibly addresses a general audience, the mere fact that Marrant is addressing an African lodge gives the text an undercurrent of black solidarity, which regularly comes to the surface in specific references to Africans and Ethiopians. As he begins to explicate the biblical passage, Marrant points out that "we ought to apply the gifts we have received to the advantage of our brethren, those of us especially who are called to any office in the church, by discharging it with zeal and integrity and benevolence" (*Sermon Preached* 78). By first putting an emphasis on the particular responsibility of some people among a supposedly undefined but obviously racially focused "us," Marrant forces his audience to think of brotherly love in terms of a community whose members need to "prefer one another." "Benevolence," he continues, "does yet further oblige christians to love and bless those who hate them and injure them," confirming that he is addressing a very specific group, made of people who perpetually suffer hate and injury.

Yet he sums up his introduction with the following admonition: "These and many other duties are required of us as christians, every one of which are like so many links of a chain, which when joined together make one complete member of Christ; this we profess to believe as Christians and as Masons" (79). The mixing of metaphors reveals the tension at the heart of his appeal. On the one hand, his listeners constitute a "member" of Christ, a reference to the apostle Paul's statement that "we, being many, are one body in Christ, and every one members one of another" (Romans 12:5). Yet Paul also says that "we have many members in one body" and that "all members have not the same office" (Romans 12:4), a passage that can easily justify the status quo. Over against this image Marrant uses the metaphor of the chain, one that can convey suffering and slavery but that can also suggest a more egalitarian notion of humans as equal links of a chain. The chain links the Mason's black-identified brotherly love with the wider Christian profession of love, leaving the interpretation open to universal love or black republican solidarity.

The body of the sermon follows a similar pattern. Marrant establishes the "anciency of Masonry" (79) by referring to builders in the Bible, starting with the entity he refers to as God, the great architect. He presents man, God's creation, as "a world within himself": "In him is the spiritual and immaterial nature of God, the reasonableness of Angels, the sensative power of brutes, the vegetative life of plants, and the virtue of all the elements he holds converse with in both worlds." In a magisterial mixture of religious and scientific language, Marrant presents human beings as microcosms that reflect the harmonious order of the universe. Rather than appealing to notions of freedom and humanity, he gives an image of a tight system imposed from above that cannot be tampered with. It is then easy for him to accuse "these God-provoking wretches" who "despise their fellow men, as tho' they were not of the same species with themselves" (80). Similarly, in his description of the four rivers of Eden, he emphasizes the river Gihon, which "compasseth the whole land of Ethiopia." Therefore, he asks about all those nations, who will "dare to despise or tyrannize over their lives or liberties, or incroach on their lands, or to inslave their bodies?" (81). In both cases the universal reach of his vision narrows down to, and underscores, his criticism of the mistreatment and the enslavement of blacks.

On the other hand, when he refers to Cain, he initially foregrounds the racial connection, asking why "our modern Cains call us Africans the sons of Cain," referring to one of the myths circulating at the time to justify the enslavement of blacks. Even so, he shows his readiness to "admit it if you please," only then to place Cain in a tradition of universal knowledge. His father Adam, when inhabiting Eden, "was to employ his mind as well as exercise his body; here he was to contemplate and study God's works; here he was to enjoy God, himself and the whole world." So Cain, if black, becomes the representative of "architecture, arts and sciences," carrying the flame of civilization and transmitting its light to the rest of humanity.

The notion of brotherly love once again undergoes a shift in focus when Marrant describes the transmission of Masonic knowledge after those first generations. Pointing out that "in whatsoever nation or kingdom in the whole world where Masonry abounds most, there hath been and still are the most peaceable subjects, cheerfully conforming to the laws of that country in which they reside" (82), he advises that "we should not only live happily ourselves, but be likewise mutually assisting to each other." The focus seems nationalistic. Indeed, he adds, "it is not only good and beneficial in a time of peace, in a nation of kingdom, but in a time of war, for that brotherly love that cements us together by the bonds of friendship, no wars or tumults can separate."

But the scope of brotherly love expands again, as he uses the example of Benhadad in Kings 20, whom king Ahab immediately recognized as a "brother": "behold the brotherly love of a Mason!" From here on, that feeling was transmitted like a gene through generations, and the special knowledge crossed national and linguistic boundaries and expanded, "notwithstanding the confusion of languages, which gave rise to Masons['] faculty and universal practice of conversing without speaking, and of knowing each other by signs and tokens" (84). This form of immediate, almost mystical recognition must have appealed to Marrant, whose *Narrative*, as we have seen, contained several examples of it. Similarly, the masons who worked in King Solomon's building projects "were partitioned into certain Lodges, although they were of different nations and different colours, yet were they in perfect harmony among themselves, and strongly cemented in brotherly love and friendship" (86). And so "these are the laudable bonds that unite Free Masons together in one indissoluble fraternity"; "this it is to be kindly affectioned to one another, with brotherly love, in honour preferring one another" (87). What originally sounded like a racial appeal has now turned into a transnational vision. Its universalism, though, is undermined by the exclusiveness of membership, so that while the audience should "remember your obligations you are under to the great God, and to the whole family of mankind in the world," they should also "remember you are under a double obligation to the brethren of the craft of all nations on the face of the earth" (88). Brotherly love proves a relative concept, to be divided into multiple obligations. The move toward republicanism is significant, since Masons "are not ashamed of the meanest of their brethren," even of Africans, "though at present many of them in slavery" (89), even as it remains within the constraints of a politics of sameness.

The two sermons by Prince Hall display a similar wavering between those various sentiments, identities, and political ideas, but one can perceive in that struggle a gradual evolution toward a more frankly republican vision. Hall encourages the placing of the three speeches (his two and Marrant's) in a series by opening each of his own speeches with a reference to the previous one in the series. He starts his 1792 *Charge* by stating that Marrant built the "foundation" and that he will offer the "superstructure" (192). Contrary to Marrant, though, he starts by taking up the theme of "universal love and friendship" (Marrant, *Sermon Preached* 90) that Marrant had reiterated at the end of his sermon; Hall asserts that "love and benevolence" are due "to all the whole family of mankind," "of what color or nation they may, yea even our enemies, much more a brother Mason." While echoing Marrant's gradations in obligation, the emphasis here is on universality, on having to "love a man for the sake of the image of God which is on him" (Hall, *Charge Delivered 1792* 192). Just as in Marrant's depiction of human beings as small replicas of the outside world, Hall bases his humanism less on a liberal emotional exchange than on a third-party or overarching order, which leaves it less dependent on the vagaries of human feeling and more firmly anchored in a sort of universal law. Later he will remind his audience that a Mason needs to attend meetings, "for masonry is of a progressive nature, and must be attended to if ever he intends to be a good Mason" (193–94). This strikingly anti-essentialist statement complements his earlier universal stance, by emphasizing that Masonry does not consist in some pre-existing, inherent quality but is open to all willing to accept its demands. In a few clear strokes, Hall establishes a strong universal vision at the beginning of his sermon.

This strong opening, however, is counterbalanced by an equally bold insistence on racial feeling in the rest of the speech. When picking examples of benevolence from the Bible, he chooses the black man Ebedmelech who saved Jeremiah in Jeremiah 38, or the Good Samaritan, who showed compassion even though "at that time they were looked upon as unworthy to eat, drink or trade with their fellow-men" (193). Yet his examples of benevolence reveal a specific philosophy: "Good advice may be sometimes better than feeding his body, helping him to some lawful employment, better than giving him money; so defending his case and standing by him when wrongfully accused, may be better than cloathing him; better to save a brother's house when on fire, than to give him one" (194). In an early variation on the well-known foreign-aid motto that it is better to teach how to fish than to distribute food, Hall takes pains to underline that benevolence comes in many forms, and that long-term establishment of independence for the sufferer should take precedence over the immediate satisfaction of a charitable impulse. His references to blacks in the rest of the speech highlight both their uniqueness and their equal right to citizenship. His examples of forefathers include Tertullian, "born in Carthage in Africa," who "defended the Christians against their heathen false accusations" (194). He bemoans the fact that black children are deprived of education, referring to a commonly used passage from the Bible: "*Aethiopia shall stretch forth her hands unto me*" (196). And he points out that blacks defended the Republic during the Revolutionary war, when "they marched shoulder to shoulder, brother soldier and brother soldier, to the field of battle" (197). In this budding political philosophy, blacks are both unique and part of the republican body. The discourse of liberal benevolence is slowly shifting toward one of deserved equality as citizens and as blacks.

This philosophy crystallizes in the 1797 *Charge*. When Hall announces that "I shall now attempt to shew you, that it is our duty to sympathise with our fellow men," he is also announcing that he will offer his own definition of sympathy in the black Freemasonry. Even though he stresses that sympathy "is not to be confined to parties or colours," he starts his reflection with "our friends and brethren," the enslaved. He first paints a picture, by then familiar in abolitionist literature, of people "dragg'd from their native country" and "from their dear friends and connections, with weeping eyes and aching hearts," drawing on the human drama of forced separation. Interestingly, though, he refers to the whole process as the application of an "iron hand of tyranny and oppression" (*Charge De-*

livered 1797 200), revealing terms in connection with slavery, in that they imply the flaunting of pre-existing rights of citizenship, rather than the usual focus on basic human rights. He makes the emphasis clearer when, referring to black resistance, he continues by saying that "if I mistake not, it now begins to dawn in some of the West-India islands" (200–201). This indirect reference to Saint-Domingue, and from there to the ideals of the French Revolution, moves the sentiment elicited earlier toward a more radical statement of freedom and equality.

The rest of the speech buttresses this approach. When he takes up Saint-Domingue again later, Hall describes the tortures suffered before the revolt and praises heaven that now the whites "confess that God hath no respect of persons, and therefore receive them as friends and treat them as brothers." The concept of brotherhood has definitely been expanded here, compared with its uses in Marrant's speech. Hall concludes the paragraph with this ringing statement: "Thus doth Ethiopia begin to stretch forth her hand, from a sink of slavery to freedom and equality" (204). "Freedom" finds itself combined with "equality," a rare pairing in abolitionist texts. Earlier in the speech, Hall had already announced that "there is not an independent mortal on earth; but dependent one upon the other, from the king to the beggar" (201). Marrant's chain links can now be seen to have anticipated this notion of mutual dependency and universal connection, pointing forward to an egalitarian vision that reduces the distance between the king and the beggar.

At the same time, though, Prince Hall's Freemasonry shows a willingness to embrace the possible limitations of the metaphor of brotherhood. Certainly, the history of Freemasonry confirms a tendency to cross the boundaries of social class, yet it does not necessarily show a commitment to equality. Developed in early modern Europe as associations of craftsmen, lodges in Britain expanded in the seventeenth century to include gentlemen and men without any connection to the building trades. According to Mary Ann Clawson, such a class mixture was made possible thanks to a general interest in magic and esoteric knowledge, as well as a long-standing collaboration between scientists and artisans. Scientists in particular needed skilled workers because "the understanding of material processes that had been accumulated in the practice of various crafts constituted a massive source of knowledge for scientists who wanted to learn about the physical world" (Clawson 62). This collaboration implied a fostering of commerce, manufacture, and exploration, and thus of the tenets of a fast-developing capitalist society. The latitudinarianism that informed the Grand Lodge, formed in 1717 out of four already existing lodges, promoted the "acceptance of an emerging market society" (68), including its foregrounding of proprietorship and its belief in individual mobility, even as it tried to "moderate the excesses" (72) of budding capitalism with expressions of solidarity, such as mutual aid and the valuing of manual labor. Indeed, says Clawson, "it was precisely the contradictory character of its message that gave Freemasonry its appeal as it entered the nineteenth century" (83).

While historians disagree on the extent to which fraternal orders in the United States contributed to the development of a class consciousness, Clawson suggests that, unlike fraternal affiliation in Europe, where workers quickly became organized in homogeneous groups defending workers' rights, "American workers' continued affiliation with cross-class fraternal orders was consistent with a generally less developed conception of themselves as a separate and oppositional class" (106). It seems that the concept of brotherhood underlying the cross-class appeal of the order might actually have impeded the egalitarian process, not because its ideal was not achieved, but because as a concept it may actually have prevented the desire for more radical forms of distribution. In other words, it may have functioned more as a liberal than as a republican concept.

In his history of American Freemasonry from 1730 to 1840, Steven C. Bullock keeps emphasizing one major aspect of the fraternity: its contradictory combination of inclusiveness and exclusivity. It united men of various socioeconomic, political, and religious backgrounds, creating an expanded, cosmopolitan family tied by enlightened ideals and virtuous behavior. The cross-class mixing improved in the course of the century, after the rise and success of Ancient Masonry added a significant contingent of artisans to the gentlemen, merchants, and professionals who had formed the previous, now moribund Modern branch. But the ideal of universal love preserved its attachment to the goals of gentility and refinement, aspects that artisans on the rise wished to identify with. Masonry came to mirror the ambivalence of "a post Revolutionary society in which nearly all forms of distinction remained suspect but many sought high social status" (Bullock 108). Specifically, it could not "fully resolve the tension between general regard and individual attachment" (192) as it tried to negotiate between its commitment to universal love and its encouragement of preference in social and professional relations. It could try to justify such favoritism by responding that "particular loyalty only increased universal benevolence" (193), but it became obvious to many

Americans that this sort of loyalty loaded the dice in favor of particular persons, and that it impaired rather than promoted the public good, a supposed main value of Freemasonry. It now seemed as if "brotherly ties operated much like the older, more particular loyalties of family, sect, nationality, and neighborhood" (218). The ideal of brotherhood, as it worked on the sidelines of politics, could not transcend its partial roots in the realm of the particular. The history of Freemasonry in America thus attests to the shifting meaning of brotherhood, a malleability that should warn us about its political uses.

The ideal represented by fraternal Freemasonry was bound to attract African American men at the end of the eighteenth century. It combined vague promises of universal egalitarianism with a masculinity anchored in independence and the nobility of manual labor. As Maurice O. Wallace points out, the artisan "personified values of muscular labor, capitalist productivity, economic independence, and masculine self-sufficiency in direct response to the social and economic imperatives of early modern proprietorial culture" (64). Many black men were craftsmen, and found in the order a philosophical link between their professions and the liberal ideology spreading throughout the new nation. They also found a source of identity formation in "the symbolic application of architectural principles to the construction of male subjects as edifices." Freemasonry promised "the interior adjustment of the fractured life of black manhood to the promise of cohesiveness represented by buildings" (67). In other words, the order promoted the individualism sorely lacking at the heart of African American experience, promising an "interior" construction that would allow better participation in a society that demanded self-sufficiency and personal responsibility.

Both Wallace and Nelson emphasize the importance of self-discipline and self-regimentation to the ideal of national manhood generally, and to the masculine ideal promoted by the Freemasons more specifically. The notion of self-control connected the black members to the world of the white middle class. According to William A. Muraskin, from the very beginning Prince Hall Freemasonry "has served as one of the bulwarks of the black middle class," and it "has worked to separate its members, both socially and psychologically, from the black masses" (26).[34] He shows that the list of strict requirements for adherence to the order conforms to profoundly bourgeois ideals. At the same time, the common experience of racism helped maintain a link with blacks of lower status. Loretta J. Williams emphasizes that "from the start of black Freemasonry, members were involved in community uplift" (41), and that it might even have been "the catalyst for societal reform" (114). So what we have seen as the contradictory message of Freemasonry seems to apply to black Freemasonry as well, in that the notion of brotherhood was necessary to inject the order with a degree of egalitarianism, but proved insufficient for a more radical questioning of the surrounding capitalist order.

Prince Hall's political career reflects this conceptual complexity. Most of what we know about Prince Hall is contained in texts—letters, petitions, and sermons—he has left behind, and those testify to a thorough familiarity with the language of the Enlightenment, in both its contractual and its affective dimensions. A January 13, 1777, petition to the Council and the House of Representatives of Massachusetts, signed by him and seven other men,[35] first states the "Natural and Unaliable Right" to freedom, which "they have Never forfeited by any Compact or agreement whatever"; indeed, they were "Unjustly Dragged by the hand of cruel Power from their Derest friends and sum of them Even torn from the Embraces of their tender Parents." It emphasizes both the "violation of Laws of Nature and off Nations," and "all the tender feelings of humanity." The readers of the petition should know that "A Live of Slavery Like that of your petioners Deprived of Every social privilege of Every thing Requisit to Render Life Tolable is far worse then Nonexistence"—a possible echo of Patrick Henry's famous revolutionary outburst delivered less than two years earlier. The connection with the Revolution is made explicit when the petitioners assert that "Every Principle from which Amarica has Acted in the Cours of their unhappy Dificultes with Great Briton Pleads Stronger than A thousand arguments in favours of your petioners" (Aptheker 10). This petition displays an intelligent—if misspelled—and well-informed mastery of the liberal language of the law, combined with an appeal to familial sympathy.

In 1787, Hall put his signature to two petitions of seemingly contradictory intent. A January 4, 1787, petition, signed by seventy-three men, pleads for assistance for emigration to Africa. It starts with a sober assessment of race relations in America, acknowledging that, even though slavery has received a blow in Massachusetts thanks to its new constitution, the human-rights motivations behind the measure cannot prevent that "we yet find ourselves in many respects in very disagreeable disadvantageous circumstances; most of which must attend us so long as we and our children live in America" (Wesley 66). Unable to find the civic equality they feel entitled to, the petitioners long to "live among our equals" in Africa with "our brethren there." In a rare indication that they are using the vocabulary of brotherhood in a republican way, they further explain that "they who are disposed to go and settle there shall form themselves into a civil society, united by a political constitution" (68). If brotherhood here connotes racial similarity, it also foregrounds a principled adherence to equal citizenship at the core of its political values. Hall was the leader behind an October 17, 1787, petition addressed to the State Legislature, which requests equal rights to education, arguing that "as we are willing to pay our equal part of these burdens, we are of the humble opinion that we have the right to enjoy the privileges of free men." Here again we can hear the revolutionary motto of "no taxation without representation," as well as a hint at a long list of grievances, since "we beg leave to mention one out of many." Interestingly, although Hall would school black children in his own home, the petition does not specify the racial organization of the education he expects. He just points out that black children "receive no benefit from the free schools in the town of Boston, which we think is a great grievance, as by woful experience we now feel the want of a common education" (Aptheker 19). While the goal of African migration now seems swept aside, the question remains open whether Hall merely flaunts the human right to education, and whether he aims to push for cross-racial equality.

That Hall resorted to a pragmatic use of the political concepts that surrounded him at the time, making the idea of brotherhood run the gamut from liberal universal feeling to more radical republican equality, comes through in the complexity of the three sermons to the African Lodge discussed above. Most striking is the way in which the three texts combine the operative and the speculative components of Freemasonry. By the time Hall was writing, Masonry had become exclusively speculative in its emphasis, dwelling on abstract concepts and symbols rather than on concrete elements of the building crafts. The three charges, though, put much emphasis on examples of actual building and construction. About the creation of man, "Seneca says, that man is not a work huddled over in haste, and done without fore-thinking and great consideration, for man is the greatest and most stupendous work of God" (Marrant, *Sermon Preached* 79). Adam in the garden was supposed to "contemplate and study God's works." He must have taught his sons "the art of Masonry," since "bad as Cain was, yet God took not from him his faculty of studying architecture, arts and sciences," and "his sons also were endued with the same spirit." God gave Noah "a compleat plan of the ark and sets him to work" (82). God "hath from generation to generation inspired men with wisdom, and planned out and given directions how they should build, and with what materials" (83).

There is much description of the dispersion of masons and the propagation of their knowledge by the descendants of Noah, all the way down to Moses and Joshua, who "raised the curious tabernacle or tent," God having given Moses "an exact pattern of it" and "inspired Bezaleel with knowledge to do all manner of cunning workmanship for it." The Sidonians are praised for their "skill in working of metals, in hewing of timber and stone; in a word, for their perfect knowledge of what was solid in architecture" (85). Solomon requested Hiram, king of Tyre, to "send him a man that was cunning, to work in gold and in silver, and in brass, iron, purple, crimson and in blue." Marrant gives a precise account of the thousands of skilled workers involved in building the temple, concluding that they were "in perfect harmony among themselves, and strongly cemented in brotherly love and friendship" (86). These are the "laudable bonds that unite Free Masons together in one indissoluble fraternity" (87). Although this sort of genealogical excursus was part of standard Masonic lore, the sheer amount of space devoted to it, and the elaborate emphasis on craftsmanship, manual labor, and the solidarity that emanates from such collaboration, not only indicate what must have made Freemasonry so attractive to black men at the time, most of whom belonged to the working class (Hall himself was a leather dresser); they also infuse that "indissoluble fraternity" with a spirit of artisan republicanism.

Artisan republicanism, the term used by Sean Wilentz to refer to New York artisans' ethic during the Revolution and in the first decades of the nineteenth century, subtly informs the three texts discussed here, and helps to supply the potentially vague, sentimental, or contradictory vocabulary of brotherhood with more radical possibilities. Wilentz shows how the traditional workshop, threatened by the developing financial and merchant interests, involved a supposedly harmonious collaboration between masters, journeymen, and apprentices, in which hierarchy stood in the service of the transmission of knowledge and skill. Although artisans certainly respected private property and valued independence and initiative, the importance of collaboration and of the "common good" of the group had a definite republican inspiration. As some enterprising masters started expanding and hiring semiskilled and cheap labor, lower-class masters and journeymen developed forms of resistance, such as demonstrations and strikes, that made them into a visible, emerging working class, even as they infused their republicanism with democratic ideals. "Artisan republicanism," Wilentz sums up, "provided the journeymen a kind of moral ledger with which to judge their masters and defend themselves" (100). While wages and tariffs were the main issues fought over, the proud exhibiting of insignias and symbols of the crafts at various occasions, many of them borrowed from European guilds founded in the Middle Ages, suggests a deeper general concern among journeymen about a "dilution of skill" (33), a slow disintegration of a body of knowledge accumulated over centuries, as well as a concern to promote the idea of craftsmanship as "a collective sense of public service." In this context, the expression of "'mutual sympathy'" and of "'the strongest feelings of the heart'" (91) carries a republican content.

The fact that Marrant's sermon displays a similar pride in the crafts and their origins could be explained away as the necessary "foundation" that makes Hall's own "superstructure" (192) possible or, more simply, as pointed out earlier, as the feeding of common Masonic fare. But Hall himself continues in the same spirit, albeit in less obvious terms, and in ways that apply more specifically to African Americans. After starting his 1792 speech with a few examples of "love and benevolence to all the whole family of mankind" (*Charge Delivered 1792* 192), examples which also assert "humanitarian principles over property rights" (Brooks, *American Lazarus* [138]), he mentions "some of our fore-fathers, for our imitation" (*Charge Delivered 1792* 194). The examples he brings up, though, have less to do with love than with fidelity, loyalty, and the defense of minorities. Tertullian, an African, defended the Christians against their critics. Cyprian is singled out for his "fidelity to his profession." The next example, "out of hundreds," is Augustine, who treasured the following words: "He that doth love an absent Friend to jeer / May hence depart, no room is for him here" (195). Finally Fulgentius decided to "let my care and employment be among the humble and poor servants of Christ." When he follows up immediately with his criticism of the lack of educational opportunities for blacks in Boston, and his hope that, as in Philadelphia, the city may soon see "a School for the blacks" (196), Hall has managed to place the topic of black education within the long tradition of ancestors' devotion to their faith and to others and, although they were not Masons, to give it republican overtones of solidarity, whether through the display of loyalty or through the precious and democratic sharing of knowledge. Indeed, he then proceeds to describe the dispersion of Masonic knowledge that took place after the siege of Jerusalem, down to the Knights of Malta, again making the point that those orders accepted Africans. Hall clearly puts his internationalism in the service of black republicanism.

In his second speech, which, as we have seen, is more overtly devoted to slavery and racial discrimination, Hall pursues and expands the theme of exchanging knowledge, referring to Jethro, "an Ethiopean" (*Charge Delivered 1797* 201) and instructor of Moses, who "understood geometry as well as laws" (202); to the Ethiopian Eunuch, who did not think it "beneath him to take a poor servant of the Lord by the hand" (203) while Philip "did not think himself too good to receive the hand, and ride in a chariot with a black man in the face of day" (202); and to the Queen of Sheba, with whom Solomon deigned to converse "on points of masonry (for if ever there was a female mason in the world she was one)" (203). In what feels like a climactic moment in the speech, Hall comforts his audience: "Although you are deprived of the means of education; yet you are not deprived of the means of meditation; by which I mean thinking, hearing and weighing matters, men, and things in your own mind, and making that judgment of them as you think reasonable to satisfy your minds and give an answer to those who may ask you a question. This nature hath furnished you with, without letter learning" (204). Many can repeat parts of a sermon just by listening to it; many "of our brethren that follow the seas can foretell a storm some days before it comes" (204–5), and this "without any other means than observation and consideration"; the same people "without a telescope or other apparatus have through a smoak'd glass observed the eclipse of the sun." Although these statements run the risk of verging on primitivism, with their emphasis on untaught, unlettered knowledge and with Hall's conclusion that "God can out of mouth of babes and Africans shew forth his glory" (205), they also emphasize intellectual independence and the fact that the group possesses the resources necessary for its own survival.

Overall, then, just as the arm-and-hammer emblem or the various mottoes in artisan pageants symbolized much more than mere tradition, Hall transforms the Masonic theme of esoteric knowledge into an instrument for propagating an idea of equality more specific than that invoked by the liberal notion of brotherhood. The theme of slavery, and the sympathy he tries to elicit from his listeners, become irrevocably tied to a republican outlook virtually absent from contemporary abolitionism and, more specifically, to a black republicanism that anticipates the black nationalist forms that would develop in the nineteenth century.

Brotherhood and English Radicalism

Brotherhood as a component of radicalism played a slightly more important role in England than in the United States in the late eighteenth and early nineteenth centuries, and this dimension is to be found in some of the antislavery discourse circulating at the time. Whether radicalism influenced antislavery or vice versa remains an open question. James Walvin has argued that "the experience and rhetoric of the antislavery cause were infused into other early nineteenth-century working class agitation" (343). For example, he points to the flooding of Parliament with petitions just after the creation of the Abolition Society in 1787, a tactic that "was to remain a dominant feature of radical working class politics until the 1840s" (344). In 1792 the London Corresponding Society was set up by Thomas Hardy, who was a strong proponent of abolition. Other critics tend to underline the dissensions between abolitionists and radicals. Patricia Hollis argues that abolitionists, especially after the French Revolution, were wary of associations with radicals, and that on their part radicals saw abolitionism as contributing to an undermining of their own cause. Whatever the relationship and degree of mutual influence, brotherhood occasionally acquired a more radical meaning within both movements.

There were important differences between British and American radicalism. In their introduction to *The Origins of Anglo-American Radicalism*, a collection of essays by British and American scholars, Margaret Jacob and James Jacob find that, "in contrast to the considerable emphasis laid upon the force of political ideas in most of the English papers, the American essays are much more attentive to social and religious behavior" (6). The American essays show that, in America, order "was maintained through close attention to prescribed forms of public conduct. Every social act therefore conveyed a political message" (7). This emphasis on social act rather than on political ideas can point to the existence of an underlying liberal consensus in America that did not hold the same kind of appeal in Britain. A manifestation of resistance would reveal a desire less for a dramatic reversal of the social and the political order than for the complete realization of liberal ideals. In his essay for the collection, for example, Alfred F. Young tackles the thorny issue of the extent to which English plebeian culture was retained after it crossed the ocean. He argues that when American artisans organized major parades in 1788 in celebration of the Constitution, they acknowledged that the document met their needs by giving them democratic rights, and by giving the central government the power to influence the economy in their favor. Quoting from E. P. Thompson, the famous historian of the British working class, who argues that English plebeian culture "'bred riots, but not rebellions; direct actions but not democratic organizations,'" he concludes that "in America, plebeian culture seems to have carried people farther" (Jacob and Jacob 206). But the nature of this "farther" is debatable. While the American working class adhered to the principles of liberal democracy, the English proletariat would develop more radical movements inspired by notions of redistribution and socialism.

Indeed, the parameter of freedom took on an exclusivity in the United States that it did not have in England. In her essay for the same collection, Joyce Appleby points out how, in England, "the political stability established by the consolidation of Whig power led to the reassertion of government control over economic life." Of course, "the ambit of individual freedom continued to expand for entrepreneurs in England, but less was published about an inexorable dynamic towards a world of free trade. Capitalism had been joined to statism" (Jacob and Jacob 278). This was in keeping with a civic humanism that had been part of Whig ideology throughout the century. Even their notion of freedom was different: "To be sure, the English opposition party cherished liberty, but it was the liberty of constitutional rights not the bourgeois liberty of careers open to talent" (279). The country party was thus conservative to the extent that "man's nature made authority the necessary companion of liberty" (279). At the same time, though, it is this particular balance that allowed British radicals to develop their radicalism "farther," I would argue, than the American ones. In America, even the Jacobins and the Jeffersonians discussed by Richard J. Twomey "did not question the socio-economic premises of private property, 'possessive individualism,' and 'market society'" (9–10). They focused above all on democracy and libertarianism, and their internationalism was part of the transatlantic liberal Enlightenment. If one should not underestimate the degree to which they publicized the notion of the sovereignty of the people, their democratic egalitarianism formed a variation on the notion of freedom that had already been at the heart of the Revolution. They were not prolabor.[36] Twomey sees this brand of Jacobinism as fundamentally belonging to the "transatlantic humanitarian impulse" (99) of the time.

On the other hand, those were heady times for English radicalism, in spite of continuous government repression. Many radical figures crossed ideological boundaries and skipped from one organization to another, running the gamut from reformism to revolutionary radicalism. Many groups mixed members of the working class and the middle class, who occasionally found a progressive common ground. The Association Movement, started under the influence of the ideals of the American Revolution, demanded a democratization, though still limited, of the government and of the election process. Because of an economic downturn, especially after the beginning of the war in 1793, order was frequently disturbed by food riots and other demonstrations. Not just the French Revolution but also the publication of Thomas Paine's *Rights of Man* a few years later increased revolutionary fervor, (both of) which in turn provoked repression. Some skilled workers started to organize unions, and many met in political clubs and tavern fraternities. The London Corresponding Society (LCS), "usually seen as the first working-class political organization" (Wright 37) though it included quite a few members from the middle class, was founded in 1792 in order to campaign for parliamentary reform and the extension of the right to vote. When it was dissolved in 1799, its members found other outlets for their ideas. According to D. G. Wright, many radicals and Jacobins did not really tackle the problem of "economic inequality" (38) and were afraid of being seen as Levellers. Many of them concentrated on political reform, and even avoided the social and economic reforms recommended by Paine. But all adhered to at least the liberal notion of better political representation, and many hoped that these reforms would lead to a more egalitarian spreading of the common good.

Radicalism, of course, formed only one corner of English political culture at the time.[37] White abolitionists, for one, were not political radicals. William Wilberforce proved a conservative on many social and political issues. David Brion Davis has famously linked the growth of the abolitionist movement to a downplaying of proletarian exploitation in England. That makes the politics of Afro-British abolitionists even more interesting. Equiano was no radical, but he was a member of the LCS; he was also well acquainted with Thomas Hardy, and wrote his narrative while staying at Hardy's house. Only in England, then, could such a figure have emerged as Robert Wedderburn, who combined freedom, brotherhood, and radicalism in a unique way.

Robert Wedderburn

Brotherhood had a special meaning to Robert Wedderburn, a Jamaican mulatto who emigrated to England around 1778. Unlike Sancho, Equiano, and Cugoano, Wedderburn joined a London underworld marked by poverty and legal marginality. Coming under the influence of political radicalism, especially in the form of Thomas Spence's theories, Wedderburn developed an extremely original blend of ideas, which combined communist notions of land redistribution with a strong abolitionist and revolutionary fervor. His transatlantic consciousness allowed him to offer the image of an interracial brotherhood based on freedom, the abolition of private property, and the achievement of equality for all. One could say that Wedderburn represents a climax in the ideological arc traced by this book, in that his cross-cultural, international consciousness helped him radicalize the very radicalism that inspired him. It is in his emotional appeals that this political stance comes through most forcefully.

Wedderburn's life story reflects the international, cross-racial, and cross-cultural mobility characteristic of the Black Atlantic writers we have been dealing with. He was born free in Jamaica in 1762, the son of an African-born slave woman and of James Wedderburn, a Kingston doctor and sugar plantation owner. As a teenager he left the island to become a sailor in the British navy, seeing action against French and Spanish fleets, and he may have re-enlisted in the mid-1790s, thus becoming well acquainted with the culture of sailors depicted in chapter 2. After being discharged in London, he probably hung out in the rookeries around St. Giles, where most poor blacks congregated, and lived in a legal gray zone. He may have participated in the Gordon Riots, which Sancho had referred to disapprovingly in his letters. He then became a journeyman tailor, and was probably registered in the book of trades, which gives him an important link to the world of skilled artisans and their love of independence. But competition from the semiskilled forced him to find other ways to make ends meet. In 1786 he underwent a conversion to Methodism and, at one point, became a licensed dissenting minister. In 1812 he met Thomas Spence, a proponent of radical agrarianism who spread his ideas in the London underworld through meetings at taverns. When Spence died in 1814, Thomas Evans founded the Society of Spencean Philanthropists, in which Wedderburn became an active member and even a leader after Evans' arrest in 1817. Wedderburn also spread his abolitionist and revolutionary ideas through a chapel he opened in Hopkins Street in Soho. In 1822 he was charged with blasphemy, was convicted, and then spent two years in Dorchester Prison. He landed again in prison in 1831. His later whereabouts and time of death are unknown.[38]

Spence represents an extreme radicalization of the British balance of freedom and the common good. Born in Newcastle, he started spreading ideas of shared property in his early twenties. After relocating to London in 1792, he spent the rest of his life trying to publicize his "Plan," constantly distributing tracts and pamphlets. As G. I. Gallop points out in the introduction to an edition of his works, Spence quoted people such as James Harrington, Milton, Locke, Sidney, Fletcher, Trenchard, Swift, Price. Gallop comments: "It is worth noticing with Caroline Robbins that 'the exponent of a new egalitarianism looked not to levelling tracts, but to the great Whig canon for support.' By taking the natural rights doctrine literally and infusing it with social and communitarian content Spence took the 'Real Whig' tradition into the world of socialism" (Spence 16). Of course, the Real Whig tradition already had a double focus on the common good and natural rights, so that Spence can be said to have thoroughly radicalized their positions in order to take them into the world of freedom, egalitarianism, and common ownership. Although Spence's plan was not widely popular, a Spencean Society was formed in 1807 to debate his ideas. Thomas Evans, who had been a secretary in the LCS and a member of the United Englishmen, another radical group, became a major figure in the defense of Spence's ideas. Spence, says Gallop, "despised the *political* radicals and social and economic *reformers*" (Spence 18). That Wedderburn became an adherent of his theories thus says much about the intensity of his own radicalism.

When Wedderburn spoke of brotherhood, he was a world away from the middle-class aspirations of Prince Hall and the African American Freemasons. Although he did become part of the fraternity of artisans for a while, since his name was registered in the book of trades, Iain McCalman reminds us in his introduction to Wedderburn's writings that if the late-eighteenth-century London artisans shared values such as pride in their craft and their independence, this pride did not "carry its later connotations of moral respectability." Wedderburn's culture, writes McCalman, was one of "workshop pilfering, promiscuous sexuality and drunken conviviality" (McCalman 8). Moreover, Wedderburn's world was clearly multiethnic and multiracial. In his 1817 short-lived journal, *The Axe Laid to the Root*, he displays Spence's radical combination of Jacobin thought with agrarian radicalism. What makes him unique, however, is what could be called his double relevance, in that his references to slaves in Jamaica can easily apply to the English workers, and vice versa. Of course, Equiano had already made a step in that direction, through his association with the London Corresponding Society, but he died before the association radicalized itself. Like other Black Atlantic writers before him, Wedderburn gleaned elements from the surrounding ideology and combined them with his own interracial, transatlantic consciousness, in order to blend several worlds together and to create a more radical worldview. The appeal to emotion in general, and to brotherhood in particular, served a uniquely radical, interracial view of community, where freedom and the common good form the most explosive mix, the most radical balance, we have witnessed until now.

Like Spence, Wedderburn firmly anchored his political philosophy in liberal ideals of freedom and the rights of man. He starts the first issue of *The Axe Laid to the Root* by charging "all potentates, governors, and governments of every description with felony, who does wickedly violate the sacred rights of man." He demands, "in the name of God, in the name of natural justice, and in the name of humanity, that all slaves be set free," and he closes his first essay by declaring that "I am a West-Indian, a lover of liberty, and would dishonour human nature if I did not shew myself a friend to the liberty of others" (Wedderburn 83). He thus proves himself particularly adept at manipulating the liberal language of the Enlightenment. During his trial for blasphemy in 1820, Wedderburn reads a text whose thesis is "*Religious Liberty* and the *Universal Right of Conscience*" (133). The text is peppered with references to such Enlightenment eminences as Voltaire and indirectly Paine, whom Wedderburn describes as "a very shrewd and acute writer of modern times" (134). Part of Wedderburn's radicalism thus springs from the defense of freedom and natural rights, and a respect for their most radical defenders.

In *The Horrors of Slavery* (1824), though, written when he was over sixty, Wedderburn subtly conveys an ideology that criticizes the notion of individualism. From the beginning, he makes clear that "not to my own misconduct is to be attributed my misfortunes, but to the inhumanity of a MAN, whom I am compelled to call by the name of FATHER" (44). Looking back on his life, Wedderburn probably sees a few shady areas, such as his hard times in the London underworld when he sometimes had to resort to illegal tricks to make ends meet. But he is firm in his environmentalist point of view, emphasizing the systemic circumstances that lead to crime rather than the moral makeup of the individual. When his half brother accuses his mother of "a violent and rebellious temper," Wedderburn similarly asks the reader "whether she had not some reason for her conduct" (47). He criticizes his father's attitude along the same lines. A doctor, his father was "physicing the poor blacks, where those that were cured, he had the credit for, and for those he killed, the fault was laid to their own obstinacy" (46). Wedderburn shows the whimsical use of individualism made by the oppressor, and hence the danger of such an ideology. This wariness toward the politics of individualism reflects his lifelong struggle to inculcate much more than just liberal values.

His advice to the slaves in *The Axe Laid to the Root* already smacks of a less individualistic approach to political rights, one that emphasizes brotherhood and solidarity in action. He urges the oppressed to use no violence, and to avoid the bloodstained kind of revolution that happened in Saint-Domingue. His advice may sound original: it is to "pretend to sleep one hour beyond the appointed time of your rising to labour; let the appointed day be twelve months before it takes place; let it be talked of in your market place, and on the roads" (81). This display of solidarity and organized action, he predicts, will "strike terror to your oppressors" (81). Only through this "union among you" can the oppressed attain their full liberty. By recommending what amounts to a general strike, Wedderburn links the fight for liberty to working-class tactics that call for a different kind of solidarity, one that induces the class consciousness of organized labor. Freedom is here definitely linked to other forms of social and political ideals. Indeed, by discouraging the oppressed from using petitions, which he finds "degrading," he underlines his rejection of typically liberal tools like the ones used on the other side of the Atlantic.

Wedderburn thus puts his emotionality in the double service of abolition and agrarian socialism. In a climactic moment, he addresses his general audience in a melodramatic outburst typical of abolitionist rhetoric: "Oh, ye christians, you are convinced of the crime of stealing human beings," which he ends with an address to "Oh, ye Africans." Between these two moments of pathos, he almost glibly makes a passing reference to himself as "the deluded Spencean," which allows him to start the next paragraph thus: "Dear countrymen and relatives, it is natural to expect you will enquire what is meant by a deluded Spencean." The link is made. By inserting his Spenceanism into an otherwise rather clichéd abolitionist appeal to sentiment, Wedderburn creates an indissoluble connection between the ideal of freedom and the theory of land redistribution, and he gives it the emotional power inherent in sentimental rhetoric.

To Wedderburn, land and wealth are at the heart of all social and political conflict. He keeps emphasizing the link between the oppression of slaves in the British colonies and the exploitation of the working poor in England. In this address (published in *The Axe Laid to the Root*), he informs the Jamaican slaves that, in England, "thousands of families are now in a starving state . . . whilst the landholders, in fact, are surrounded with every necessary of life." The European poor are even more destitute, since they have lost the land they used to possess in common; the slaves, he points out, should "mind and keep possession of the land" (82). He then explains his agrarianism in more detail: "When you are exorted to hold the land, and never give it up to your oppressors, you are not told to hold it as private property, but as tenants at will to the sovereignty of the people" (83). The people should act as renters of the land, which remains the property of the whole community, and hence never becomes private. Underlying this philosophy is the belief that "the earth cannot be justly the private property of individuals, because it was never manufactured by man." It is a profound injustice that some few should have all the power over big pieces of land that would if held in common, ensure the subsistence of the majority of the population. Because of the particular rhetorical organization of his speech, and his constant parallels between Jamaica and England, Wedderburn implies that this common renting should break racial boundaries. In fact, one should "preach Spenceanism at all times, and in all countries." By imparting a strong international and interracial character to his theory, Wedderburn anticipates the radical left-wing theories that would develop in the course of the century.

Wedderburn makes it clear that his theory goes well beyond liberal appeals to democracy, and so does his concept of brotherhood. "To have a parliament, and every man to vote, is just and right; a nation without it, may be charged with ignorance and cowardice," he asserts. In the next issue of *The Axe Laid to the Root,* he will point out that "every thing should be settled by votes throughout the nation" (90). But, he continues, "without an equal share in the soil, no government can be pure" (84). When we describe Wedderburn as a "radical," then, we need to emphasize that he stands to the left of the forms of Paineite and Jacobin radicalism focused on freedom and democracy. While he always maintains the importance of those goals, he also always presents them within the context of a philosophy bent on keeping alive a sense of a shared common good.

In a letter he writes to a supposed Miss Campbell, a Maroon in Jamaica who has decided to free her slaves, he launches into a melodramatic appeal against the inhumanity of slavery, in the form of a conversation between Miss Campbell and her slaves. Rather than relying on "Wedderburn, the Spencean," she reminds them of "the Christians of old," who "attempted this happy mode of living in fellowship or brotherhood" (99) until an official church was established and those original ideals were trampled. Brotherhood becomes integrated into the communist ideal, as represented by both the early Christians and Wedderburn the Spencean, showing its ability as a concept to range from fundamental humanism to the most radical social and political theories.

Once again Wedderburn clearly draws a parallel between the Jamaican slaves and the oppressed in England, incorporating his ideal of brotherhood into his assessment of class warfare. In another issue of *The Axe Laid to the Root*, the supposed Miss Campbell, who calls him "brother," declares that "I was quite surprised to find that the good people of England were so much against the Spenceans." Indeed, "I thought the Blacks were the only objects of slavery and oppression." But, she adds, "it is true what Solomon said, the rich hates the poor, no matter what colour" (106). She then mentions a member of Parliament who "holds a great deal of land as private property" and "receives a great deal of interest money, which is the same as wages from slaves, with this difference—a slave has a house for nothing, and pays no wages when he is sick" (107). At the risk of fudging his message by dragging in an argument made by proslavery advocates, namely that slaves have it much better than the English poor, Wedderburn shows that his allegiance is not solely determined by his West Indian identity. As an internationalist, his left-wing politics include a brotherhood determined by class and oppression, rather than by race and national identity.

Indeed, his social analysis also emphasizes the ways in which the powers that be try to prevent the creation of this international feeling of brotherhood. In her last letter, Miss Campbell notes that the governor has ordered a meeting of the assembly to discuss her decision to free her slaves. Her report on the discussion, whose contents she could not have known "were it not for the young man who keeps my company" (108), suspiciously sounds like an invention from Wedderburn, who uses it to satirize the officials and introduce his social critique. A certain Mr. Macpherson suggests that she be declared a lunatic, and advises the House "to send immediately to England for a million of gags, one million yards of chain, one million iron collars, and to send to Scotland for one hundred thousand starving Scotchmen to manage the slaves." And "unless our petition is attended to, I will recommend a revolt." Indeed, "there is no danger to be apprehended from any European power, for their strength is scarcely sufficient to keep their starving subjects in obedience to their will" (109). Once again, Wedderburn draws a clear parallel between the two forms of oppression, and hints at the way the officials try to use desperate poor whites to lord it over the slaves, in order to prevent any kind of interracial solidarity. Macpherson recommends the importation of servants from England, who "are dying for want," so they will "strengthen your hands against the Blacks" (110). He is also careful to recommend stamping out the Spencean doctrine, as he is doubtless aware that it would undermine the racial as well as the social hierarchy that underpins the colonial system.

A few years later, Wedderburn was reported by government spies as advocating revolution. A meeting at his Hopkins Street Chapel discussed the issue "whether it be right for the People of England to assassinate their rulers" (Wedderburn 116). The informer recommends making an example of Wedderburn and others, who "avow their object to be nothing short of the assassination of their Rulers & the overthrow of the Government" (117). At another, October 1819 meeting, Wedderburn urges his followers to avenge the Peterloo Massacre that took place in Manchester that August, "declaring with a vehement voice that the Revolution had already began in blood there and that it must now also end in blood here" (118). Another meeting brings up the question of "Which of the two Parties are likely to be victorious, the Rich or the Poor in the event of Universal War" (120). Obviously Wedderburn was transforming his agrarian brotherhood into a much more explosive concept, and had reached the limits of radicalism.

Wedderburn's religious beliefs supported rather than hampered his radicalism. During this era of many radical movements, Methodism often branched out in all directions, such as antinomianism, religious rationalism, millenarianism. Because it placed grace and personal conversion at the heart of its spiritual appeal, Methodism promoted the sort of interiority and liberal individualism discussed in chapter 1. That dimension in and of itself already made it suspicious to the establishment. Yet, at the same time, it could lead to more radical conclusions when paired with a desire to transform the social order. Methodism, because of its strong popular appeal and the important role played by the sense of togetherness fostered among participants, added a strong social element to its creed of personal redemption. In more radical hands, it could lead to millenarian tendencies. Millenarianism provided a strong link with the radical political movements of the time, through its emphasis on a vision of overall social change. As McCalman puts it, "eschatological utterances had a way of becoming socially and politically seditious in the mouths of poor and alienated men" (*Radical* 61). Those radical, self-appointed prophets provided their eager audiences with visions of social and political revolutions even as they strengthened their sense of inner faith.

In a short, apparently innocuous piece titled *Truth Self-Supported; or A Refutation of Certain Doctrinal Errors Generally Adopted in the Christian Church*, published around 1802, Wedderburn shows indications that his Methodist beliefs contain more radical seeds, and that his idea of brotherhood has come to color what is at heart an individual form of religious conviction. The opening quotation, from I Corinthians 1:27–28, sets the tone: "GOD hath chosen the foolish things of the world, to confound the wise; and God hath chosen the weak things of the world, to confound the things that are mighty; and base things of the world, and things which are despised hath God chosen, &c." (Wedderburn 65). The quote admonishes readers to view Wedderburn's beliefs in the light of this initial statement, which presents the image of a world upside down, of an overturned sense of order and hierarchy. Indeed, to McCalman, this quote evokes "the spiritual levelling of Gerrard Winstanley and other plebeian sectaries of old" (*Radical* 58). This possible link to the Diggers and their advocating of agrarian communism during the English Civil War shows that Wedderburn's religious belief went hand in hand with his political commitment.

Wedderburn does emphasize in *Truth Self-Supported* the profound role played by individualism in the process of his conversion. One day, after spending several years "amongst a set of abandoned reprobates," he heard a Wesleyan preacher, and was struck with a strong conviction of personal sin. The message he retained from the preacher was that "every man, conscious of the enormity of sin, and willing to turn from the evil of his ways, and accept of the mercy offered in the Gospel, the Lord would abundantly pardon." Wedderburn accepted this teaching and soon found himself in a state of grace. But he then fell under the influence of "erroneous preachers" (Wedderburn 66) who "denied him the privilege of examining their doctrines." Adopting the discriminating attitude typical of the Enlightenment, though, Wedderburn decided that "they could not all be in the right," and resolved to admit of no doctrine "but what he perceived in his own judgment was clearly and evidently contained in the holy scriptures." Confident in having chosen his own path, he was "not in the least alarmed by the threatenings of the preachers" (67), finding in his own chosen method the right way to attain truth. His certainty here even smacks of antinomianism, as he asserts that God had "removed him by HIS power from a legal state of mind" into "a deliverance from the power or authority of the law" (67). According to McCalman, Wedderburn did not push this antinomian element in the following years. But the sense of independence from the prevailing moral law expressed here hints at the libertarian and possibly anarchic possibilities inherent in the individualistic approach of Wesleyan Methodism.

But Wedderburn's visions of the future carry elements of the radical brotherhood that underlies his political stance. He looks forward to a time when believers will be reunited in the Father's house, "A joint Heir and Brother with Christ" (Wedderburn 69). Yet this will only happen after the dreaded process presided over by Christ, since "however he is rejected and despised, there is a day coming, when his friends and his enemies will know — the one with pleasure, the other by woeful experience, that he is possessed with power, by authority of the Father, to condemn the one, and reward the other, and appoint to each their portion" (68). In light of the introductory quotation in his *Truth Self-Supported*, Wedderburn encourages his readers to think of this moment of retribution as also a moment of redistribution, or of complete reversal of the current social hierarchy. His millenarianism becomes automatically imbued with a touch of prophetic radicalism, with which he would become associated for the rest of his life. Peter Linebaugh and Marcus Rediker emphasize that Wedderburn's religious philosophy was anchored in the idea of jubilee, which according to the Bible happened every fifty years. During jubilee the Hebrews restored land to its original owners and freed slaves, and thus it symbolizes not just liberation but also land redistribution. Through his notion of jubilee, Wedderburn aimed at "synthesizing radical Christianity and Painite republicanism, combining both with a proletarian abolitionism" (290). Jubilee was also an important aspect of African American Christianity and abolitionism. In Wedderburn, then, we find the most dense and explosive combination of radical ideas that a transatlantic consciousness could strive for. While integrating the liberal discourse of freedom found in Paine, he put it in a radical balance with a left-wing notion of common good, in a combination that gave the idea of "brotherhood" its most far-reaching political potential.

Chapter 4

Blood, Bodies, and the Antebellum Slave Narrative

The first half of the nineteenth century saw a significant development in the discourse on slavery, especially in the United States, as a major shift occurred toward the representation of bodily pain. As Elizabeth B. Clark points out, in antebellum America "the story of the suffering slave . . . began to play a crucial role in an unfolding language of individual rights." The increased representation of physical pain was linked to a deepening culture of sentiment and compassion, but also to the growing notion that "to be free of physical coercion and deliberately inflicted pain was an essential human right" (Clark 463). In America especially, sympathy received a new kick start, partly thanks to a period of evangelical revival, and a revitalization of the abolitionist movement after William Lloyd Garrison arrived on the scene in the early 1830s. Two important works marked this new trend: Lydia Maria Child's *Appeal in Favor of That Class of Americans Called Africans* (1833) and Theodore Weld's collection *American Slavery as It Is* (1839). While this new emphasis may have contributed to an increased sensationalism in the discourse on slavery, the individual sympathy it aimed at eliciting was supposed to offer the right conduit toward an abolitionist stance based on humanity and natural rights. At the same time, the narratives appealed to other pillars of liberal society, such as the desire for "freedom, love, family" (Clark

470). The path was broken for the tremendous success of *Uncle Tom's Cabin*. Liberal sympathy had finally arrived.

The fact that most of these texts attempted to create moments of Smithian, liberal sympathy while at the same time focusing on bodily pain introduced a difficulty peculiar to the logic of liberalism. We have repeatedly seen throughout this book that liberal sympathy fostered a movement toward interiority, an (often unsuccessful) attempt to turn a blind eye to the politics of the body. The liberal focus on individual freedom and human rights, and its simultaneous attempt to neutralize the corporeal realm, left it with little ideological equipment when it came time to submerge the public with shocking images of physical suffering. The public's low tolerance for racial difference impelled a number of strategies on the part of black and white authors bent on eliciting liberal emotion, most of which were designed to downplay representations of the racial body even as the body itself tended to become objectified. In her investigation of several sentimental antislavery stories, Karen Sánchez-Eppler uncovers their tendency to combine the "effort to depict goodness in black" with "the obliteration of blackness" (31). One good example is Harriet Beecher Stowe's description of Dred in her 1856 book, in which, Sánchez-Eppler points out, he appears as "a magnificent, herculean, and imperial gladiator" (28). Here the downplaying of blackness makes it easier for Nina Gordon to "read" him, and the power of physiognomy helps the book's liberal paradigm, in its confidence that the sign represented by the body can be a truthful mirror of its interior qualities. Black authors found themselves adopting similar strategies for predominantly white audiences. In black texts, though, as this chapter will show, one does find some attempts to induce a full recognition of bodily others, in passages that aimed at drawing readers emotionally into a more republican worldview.[1]

It is thus predominantly in its appeal to sentiment through representations of blood and the body, and by extension of the family, that the nineteenth-century slave narrative conveyed its political ideas. Bodies in pain are ubiquitous in the slave narrative, yet they reveal their political content only through their particular emphases and their narrative context. The liberal impulse often entailed a suppression of race and an objectification of the body, even as the retreat into interiority fostered definitions of the individual self through blood, which now carried a metaphorical rather than a physical meaning. More republican, community-oriented visions, on the other hand, did attempt representations of bodies even though, as the authors were probably fully aware, those bodies would be experienced as alien by most readers. The contrast between a retreat away from the racial body and an attempt at full recognition forms the emotional core of many nineteenth-century slave narratives, and reveals their political leanings. The language of individualism and of contract is an inevitable indicator of a liberal worldview, and that of equality and citizenship bespeaks republican ideals; and it was by appealing to sympathy for mistreated and tortured bodies that black authors made these political views sink in.

Here also, the African American and the Afro-British texts display significant differences, even as both radicalized ambient ideologies. Their narrators reflect some of the ideological leanings they were exposed to. At the same time they were travelers, and they possessed a transnational or transcultural experience that gave them added political insight, thus continuing a Black Atlantic pattern. The American texts, though, show a decreased international consciousness, which is replaced by a vision of the United States as bisected by the Mason and Dixon line. According to Russ Castronovo, John Latrobe sees the line, in his 1855 *History of Mason and Dixon's Line*, less as an instance of national division than as, on the contrary, a way to promote a sense of common national destiny. This division can thus indirectly boost nationalism at the expense of an international consciousness. Still, the authors of the slave narratives show an ability to move between different cultural and political worlds, and to develop more incisive political visions than many of their white counterparts. In *The History of Mary Prince*, on the other hand, published in London in 1831, the British author (Mary Prince herself) has a deep awareness of place and of changing political context, and even though all the spaces she inhabits are technically British, her movements between islands and across the Atlantic impart a cross-national and slightly more radical consciousness to her text that is absent from the American texts published at the time.

These differences inform these authors' political stances. *The History of Mary Prince* shows a certain love of political balance we have encountered in many British texts, even as it uses it to present a view of a different social order. The American slave narrative first displayed a continued split between liberal and republican tendencies, before it exploded into full-scale liberalism in the 1850s. According to Charles Nichols, the slave narrative before 1831 adopted "a less sentimental and propagandistic tone" (553) than in the following decades. Indeed, these texts from the first decades of the nineteenth century may be said to describe a race after full-scale liberalism, dependent less on an explicit appeal to sympathy than on a display of the qualities necessary for the individual to become self-reliant and to participate freely in the American economic system. Yet emotions are present; they remain mostly hidden inside the deep core of a self that devotes its energies to fighting for its place in the system. It all happens as if the gradual relinquishing of the republican worldview left an initial emotional blank, keeping the emotions implicit as the more and more predominant ideology fell into place. When emotions became more explicit in the few decades before the Civil War, the slave narrative would plunge into this deep emotional substrate and bring out a discourse of interiority that gave a sophisticated shape to the liberal worldview. Still, until then, and even up until the 1840s, black authors found it hard to relinquish republicanism altogether. This chapter explores this transitional period.

White Liberal Sentiment

In the first half of the nineteenth century, the American novel of sentiment displayed a clearer, though not total, allegiance to liberalism. Of course, the period was not ideologically monolithic. But the predominance of the liberal worldview, made even more popular by the Jacksonian era, is undeniable. It manifested itself in the individualism of the heroines who populated what Nina Baym has called "woman's fiction," as well as in the public sentiments that accompanied the humanitarian impulse present in the literature of reform. Still, the desire to attain a republican form of community and citizenship had not died down, and kept manifesting itself in various forms and at various moments. Ann Douglas makes a distinction between two generations of women writers: the first one, including authors such as Catharine Esther Beecher and Catharine Maria Sedgwick born before 1810, focused more clearly on social appeal; the second one, which includes writers like Harriet Beecher Stowe, "defined themselves more entirely in literary terms" (86) and were less directly under the influence of theological language. This second generation, which more often represents what we commonly understand by "sentimental novel" as a mass-marketed product written by and for women, and advocating the power of feminine influence and motherly love as a mainspring of social change, remains out of the bounds of this book. I focus on mostly transitional decades in which liberal and republican discourses can still be seen to compete, even if it is already clear that the former has won. The sentimental novels that appeared during this period reflect this complex political configuration.[2]

Two ideal representatives of this transitional political discourse are the novels *Hobomok* (1824), by Lydia Maria Child, and *Hope Leslie* (1827), by Catharine Maria Sedgwick. Both are historical romances that look back on the Puritans as representatives of a strict republican order, against which individual benevolence and the power of sentiment bespeak a more attractive, liberal ethos. In *Covenant and Republic* Philip Gould demonstrates the extent to which these two novelists engaged early national anxieties on the changing nature of republicanism. More specifically, Gould presents the novels as "self-conscious recodifications of republican language" (102), in that they undermine and revise republican ideas such as virtue, citizenship, manhood, womanhood, and marriage. Focusing on appeals to sentiment and sympathy in the novels confirms these findings, but shifts the emphasis to the ways in which individualized, interiorized forms of communication reveal a clear liberal worldview. Like Gould, though, I also see a certain ambivalence lingering in these texts, since neither Child nor Sedgwick seems to feel comfortable with a total relinquishing of older communitarian values.

Both novels present not just the Puritan republican ethos but also the Indian one as an oppressive devotion to the common good at the expense of the individual, so that even as they rewrite history in order to include a Native American point of view, they also safely place both worldviews in a time now left behind. In the society where Hope Leslie lives, "though human affections were permitted, they were to be in manifest subservience to religious devotion" (Sedgwick 138), and "self-denying virtue" (135) means not only a religious commitment but an adherence to the republican principles underlying the Puritan ethic. Indeed, when Mr. Fletcher asks Everell to forgo any thought of marrying Hope because this act might appear mercenary to the rest of the community, he argues that "'our individual wishes must be surrendered to the public good'" (161), a proposition directly contradicted by the sympathy for Everell that the narrator is eliciting from the reader. Governor Winthrop echoes this idea later in the novel when he again admonishes Everell that "'private feelings must yield to the public good'" (234). Similarly, Mononotto tries to rally the tribes of New England by appealing to "sacrifice to the general good" (195). In *Hobomok*, Mary's father is an antagonist in that he tries to enforce his own vision of the general good, without any consideration for the personal feelings or inclinations of others.

This worldview is contrasted with that of individuals who display an ability to feel deeply, and to be driven by their profound sympathy for other individuals, a capacity that is connected to a desire for liberty and independence. In *Hope Leslie*, Everell shows an "instinctive sympathy" (Sedgwick 26) for Magawisca. Hope Leslie's courageous actions are driven by her individual feelings for the people she gives succor to, since she "took counsel only from her own heart" (120), and she is quick to shed "tears of sympathy" (139) with friends. At the same time, she is the character who is constantly reproached with allowing herself too much liberty. In a conversation with Digby, she ventures that she may have been "'too headstrong in my own way.'" When he replies, "'why this having our own way, is what every body likes; it's the privilege we came to this wilderness world for'" (225), he is already rewriting the Puritan history with an eye to the future—the future in which Sedgwick will be writing this novel—placing the Puritans at the origin of a teleological line that leads to the current liberal worldview. Sentiment thus serves the novelist's liberal agenda, and Leslie, through both her independence and her ability to sympathize, represents America. In *Hobomok*, Mary fulfills similar objectives as a character, through both her independence and her need for communion, or exchange of "sympathies of taste" (Child 91).

This liberal sensitivity is associated with an attachment to the private sphere, to the wholeness of the family, and in a more general and abstract way to the privileging of interiority. When Magawisca gives Everell her own version of Puritan history, describing the destruction of her loved ones by the English, Sedgwick invites the reader to build an equivalence of feeling, since both societies are equally hurt in their familial and tribal relationships. It is the personal and the familial that connects them. In *Hobomok*, as Carolyn L. Karcher shows in her introduction, the power of sentiment and of feminine influence guides the plot. It is also the feminine element that advocates more openness and tolerance in religious matters, advocating a religion of the heart. They are opposed to the men with more doctrinaire attitudes. When Governor Endicott, for example, referring to sects like the Quakers, declares that "there is much appertaining to error implied in the doctrine of inward outpouring" (Child 39), Child points to a republican dislike of such interior empowerment at the expense of outside authority, and implicitly criticizes it. Feeling and interiority go hand in hand in the liberal viewpoint.

The emphasis on liberal feeling often implies that the republican ethos is devoid of any feeling at all, and hence cannot be a solid basis for a truly civilized society. In a letter to her husband, Mrs. Fletcher reminds him that "'if I have fallen far short in duty, the measure of my love has been full'" (Sedgwick 35), implying that the emotional dimension of their bond matters more than any other. When the neighbors visit Mr. Fletcher in his grief after his family has been murdered, the narrator presents them as "spectators of suffering" (72) unable to truly communicate with him emotionally. As they try to interpret his appearance, "all these many coloured feelings fell on Mr. Fletcher like light on a black surface—producing no change—meeting no return" (71–72). Unlike its subordinate role in Smithian sympathy, here stoicism makes an exchange between interiorities impossible. When Mr. Pynchon suggests to Fletcher that he should say something, "'that you counted the cost before you undertook to build the Lord's building in the wilderness'" (72), the emphasis on the common good at the expense of personal suffering sounds callous and reprehensible.

Child even implies that a devotion to republican principles is ultimately anchored in personal feeling. In a moment of honest self-examination, Mary's father wonders whether he did not "mistake the voice of selfishness for the voice of God." He tries to convince himself that "earthly motives had nothing to do with his hatred of Episcopacy." Before hearing of Charles' death, he had looked forward to realizing his wife's deathbed wish and "making a sacrifice to the peace of her only child." The current tragic news deprives him of this opportunity for "atonement" (Child 119). In this psychologically complex moment, Child forces her character to face his possible unconscious motivations, and makes his concern for the religious common good dependent on his personal feelings and failings. The fact that in the end the father enters the community of the sentimental family, by pardoning his daughter and welcoming her and her husband back, shows the trajectory from stoic republicanism toward liberal feeling as both beneficent and inexorable.

Yet in the end, through a variety of elements, the novels do evoke some nostalgia for a world gone by, in which asceticism, a sense of duty, and the commitment to a communal enterprise prevailed.[3] Through characters like John Gardiner and Mrs. Grafton, both novelists criticize the love of luxury and of adornments, evincing a typically republican fear of the dangers of corruption and degradation through indulgence. In *Hope Leslie*, Magawisca's description of the attack on the fort suggests an irretrievable world that balanced profound familial attachment with heroism and devotion to the common good. Of her brother, for example, she says that "'his limbs were like a bending reed, and his heart beat like a woman's'" (Sedgwick 50–51), thus combining aspects of both philosophies.[4] After she finishes her tale, Everell expresses "his sympathy and admiration of her heroic and suffering people" (54), in a moment of emotional appreciation for a society now irrevocably destroyed. In *Hobomok*, Hobomok's final gestures, which give the novel a bittersweet ending, convey a certain nostalgia for multicultural possibilities that will never materialize. Although he and Mary are shunned by the community, Sally's visits, as well as hints at a budding love between their children, seems the promise of further racial mixing and a possible acceptance of a truly plural, republican society. By leaving and allowing Mary and Charles to reunite, Hobomok returns the plot to similarity, and as a good liberal citizen, he even takes care of the necessary legal procedures. His expulsion from the social circle could anticipate a similar expulsion of nonwhites at the end of *Uncle Tom's Cabin*, but while the latter novel celebrates the African Americans' emigration, the former elicits the reader's sympathy for Hobomok's disappearance, and hence for the lost social and political possibilities he represents.

The British sentimental novel that emerged in the first decades of the nineteenth century showed that devotion to an autonomous self had made equal headway on that side of the Atlantic, yet in a pattern we have seen repeatedly throughout this book, this liberalism often merged with other ideas of social order. As Gary Kelly points out, the typical novel of the time addressed "the gentrification of the professional classes and the professionalization of the gentry" (19), and the novel of sentiment in particular explored "the collision of the rights of individuals and the duties demanded by social convention" (44–45). On the one hand, there was a "cult of individualism" (43) that benefited from the growth of a Romantic culture. On the other, the self was very much bounded by moral, social, and political matters. The gothic novels of Fanny Burney, as focused as they were on the subjectivity of the heroine, also showed that "subjectivity is everywhere to be dominated by reason and self-discipline" (52). Similarly Maria Edgeworth, even more than Burney, and in anticipation of Jane Austen, was "suspicious of subjectivity" (79). She "dramatized the triumph of reason and self-discipline over both social folly and individual self-excess" (79). Any focus on the self brought an almost automatic fear of its excesses and its transgressions. However much liberalism exploded in the literary field, just as it did in the social and political field, it always remained, more than in the United States, a source of wariness and suspicion.

The Race for a Liberal Self in the Slave Narrative

In his *Life*, published in 1825, the first book-length American slave narrative, William Grimes aims at eliciting sympathy for the sufferings he has endured both as a slave and as a free man in the North, but his own emotional world often seems closed off and out of reach, full of what William L. Andrews calls "psychic wounds" (*To Tell* 81). "To him who has feeling," Grimes states in the preface, "the condition of a slave, under any possible circumstances, is painful and unfortunate, and will excite the sympathy of all who have any" (186). Grimes shows he knows the vocabulary of sympathy, even though he also manages to convey his doubt, twice in this short sentence, that such a feeling is a universal attribute. Throughout the narrative, he occasionally reminds the reader that the enslaved have normal feelings, such as "hopes," "gratitude" (192), or the feelings "excited by the influence of female attractions" (193), yet he seems to assume and accept that, to his reader, he will remain an alien conundrum.[5] After he describes his first whipping, he appeals to his reader's compassion in a traditional way, showing himself "without friends" and "torn from the arms of my mother." He then asserts that the knowledge of her grief, "together with my suffering, is sufficient to convince my readers, that any boy of my age would endeavor to find, and also improve an opportunity to clear themselves from the house of bondage." Coming after his cool appraisal that "the crime was sufficiently deserving the punishment" (190), this appeal to the reader sounds less like an invitation to enter his emotional life than like an objective statement justifying his eventual flight. Overall, of course, the cruelties he describes mostly speak for themselves. The overseers, for example, "have an unlimited control over the slaves on the plantation, and exercise their authority in the most tyranical manner" (191).[6] The reader cannot but shudder at the gothic depictions of this erratic violence. But when, after another cruel flogging, Grimes asserts that "it seems as though I should not forget this flogging when I die: it grieved my soul beyond the power of time to cure," assuring the reader that "I should not have been alive now if I had remained a slave" (194), he hints at a profound form of despair that he knows his comfortable readers can hardly fathom.

The emotion Grimes mobilizes through the narrative as a whole does not rely either on republican brotherhood or on an interior connection; in its alienating effect, it entices the reader to enter a world much closer to that of Thomas Hobbes. Hobbes' political philosophy is grounded in a vision of human beings as caught in perpetual motion, whose "small beginning . . . within the body of man" (34) consist in desires or aversions. Humans tend to consider good that which they desire, and evil that which they hate. As a consequence, they will expend all their energies toward the satisfaction of these personal desires. Because we all follow this selfish pattern, we enter into competition with one another, displaying "a perpetual and restless desire of power after power"; indeed, a man cannot stick to a moderate desire for power, "because he cannot assure the power and means to live well, which he hath present, without the acquisition of more" (66). If left unregulated the process is bound to produce lawlessness, to prevent the development of a civilized and safe society, and to lead to a life "solitary, poor, nasty, brutish, and short" (84). So for the sake of self-preservation, and of "getting themselves out from that miserable condition of war" (111), humans need to erect a sovereign power that will keep those passions in check. According to C. B. Macpherson, when describing the state of war Hobbes is performing "a logical abstraction drawn from the behaviour of men in civilized society," uncovering "the 'natural' proclivities of men by looking just below the surface of contemporary society" (26). Yet in an apparent contradiction, Macpherson also argues that Hobbes' state of war pertains to actual seventeenth-century English "possessive market society," a model of society in which the ability to sell one's labor allows the transfer of power from wage earners to employers, and which, unlike the "customary or status society" and the "simple market society," "permits and requires the continual invasion of every man by every other" (42). Even if we allow that the possessive market model comes closest to the state of war as Hobbes envisioned it, it seems plausible that scratching the surface of the other two models would uncover a similar pattern.

In his description of his life both as a slave and as a free man, Grimes seems to imply such a continuity. Slave society displays all the characteristics of a violent "status society." But the system itself allows for such treatment because "the disposition to tyrannize over those under us, is universal" (Grimes 198). Slave society seems to constitute the last stage, when Hobbesian passions for power are allowed to develop unchecked. It combines the elements of an oppressive system with the remains of the state of war, forming not just a world of violence and oppression but one without solidarity, in which relationships reflect self-interest, the need for survival, and the power negotiations entailed. From early on in his career as a slave, Grimes learns that most people around him, black or white, are out to manipulate and take advantage of him: the servant Patty adds medicine to the coffee Grimes prepares for the household in order to have him punished and, he explains, to "compel me to go on the plantation, and have one of her children in my place" (189); slaves betray him when he tries to run away; masters and overseers are unbearably cruel and violent. But once in a while Grimes can remind a master he saved his life, blackmail an overseer who buys stolen goods from slaves, or feign sickness to make a master believe his value is decreasing.

The occasional language of sympathy cannot compete with the predominance of this worldview. When Grimes addresses the separation of families and exclaims dramatically: "Oh! my poor mother!" (195), he cannot efface his earlier remark that, as a slave, "I have been so hungry for meat that I could have eat my mother" (194). The struggle for individual survival receives a Darwinian emphasis much stronger than in later narratives. The Hobbesian streak also comes clearly to the surface in his account of his life in the North, in a society that displays many aspects of Macpherson's possessive individualism. There everybody seems out to get him, manipulate him, cheat him. His individualism is not the "individualism triumphant" (Andrews, *To Tell* 78) of the antebellum slave narrative, but the loneliness of the outsider.

Against this Hobbesian background, though, Grimes skillfully attempts to invest his reader's sympathy in episodes that show him avid and ready to participate in free exchange and consensual legal contracts, emphasizing his willingness and aptitude as a liberal subject. He once knowingly acts against his own interest, when even after he has been warned by a soothsayer he still agrees to be bought by a man from Georgia who will turn out a tyrant. But the passage describing the transaction is replete with the seductive discourse of consent, indirectly justifying why Grimes cannot resist: his master "asked me if I wanted to go with that gentleman" and he refuses, but "after a great deal of coaxing and flattering, I finally consented to go," so that the gentleman tells the master "that I had consented to go" and the master "said he would not force me to go, but if I was willing he would consent to it" (199). Grimes also usually has some input in the negotiations and manipulations involved in his passing from one master to another, showing that he is ready for a society based on such transactions. Loss of trust seems extremely painful for him, as when one master believes he made fun of a doctor with a drawing of a duck that says "quack," or another one thinks he stole a bottle of wine.

Blood, Bodies, and the Antebellum Slave Narrative 201

Immediately after the quack episode, he tells of an evening when he drove the horse carriage still sleepy from a nap, and managed not to let his mistress notice: "I did not know where I was, where I had been, nor where I was a going. I knew no more where I was than if I had been blindfolded" (207). While the anecdote could be seen as an example of a slave's manipulation of the mistress to avoid punishment, it turns out a pertinent comment from a man who has tried to play by the rules of trust and honesty, and is at a loss to understand how or why those rules continuously break down.

Grimes' representation of his travails in the North conveys a similar message. When a free man in Connecticut, his most aggrieved statement is that "it is very mean and cruel, to drive a man out of town because he is suspected of some crime, or breach of law. If he is guilty, punish him, but not set him adrift on suspicion, or from mere tyranny, because his poverty exposes him to it" (230). Grimes has shown himself ready to participate in the entrepreneurial game, and to use the law to defend himself, as his tendency to sue enemies attests. But playing by the rules in this society is just not enough. As he says, "it has been my fortune most always to be suspected by the good, and to be cheated and abused by the vicious." The reader is meant to sympathize with this constant victim of American "rascability" (226).

Against this emotional and ideological background, Grimes' narrative handling of his body is conspicuous. Indeed, his liberal mind-set shows in the way he handles race, or rather does not handle it. It takes him a while to reveal that he looks white and actually can pass, and when he does, it sounds like a desultory comment, as he innerly rejoices that his master doesn't know that "the guard never attempted to meddle with me, they always took me to be a *white man*" (213). His subsequent examples of passing seem meant for comic relief rather than as a reflection on the absurdities of American racial categories. As Andrews points out, Grimes "pictures himself almost as much a class as a caste victim in this country," a portrayal that "was a risky step" since "the preponderant ideology of the antislavery movement did not favor studying the slave in the light of class oppression" (*To Tell* 78). But his class analysis is mostly limited to a desire to exercise his individual rights, and his handling of race stands out by the suppression of it. In typical liberal fashion, Grimes tries to stay at equal distance from the two bugaboos.

At the same time, he shows a definite interest in notions of blood. Although he asserts that the subject of his white father leaves him "with indifference," he devotes the whole first section of the narrative to him and his grandfather, instead of to his master or his situation as a slave, and presents his father as "a wild sort of man," possibly "a very brave man." Though this wildness comes across as "insanity," Grimes feels the need to establish the biological connection. He wonders about the fact that his father "suffered his blood to run in the veins of a slave" (187), and later in the narrative he asserts that "I had too much sense and feeling to be a slave: too much of the blood of my father, whose spirit feared nothing" (198). Though this notion of blood does not sound particularly racial, it shows a desire to define oneself through one's deep-seated, inner ties, in a way that demarcates him from others. Indeed, while Grimes ends his narrative with an indictment of slavery, he allows for the possibility that some slaves, "who have kind masters, are perhaps as happy as the generality of mankind" since "they are not aware that their condition can be better" (231). Behind his assertion that slavery goes against any natural human feeling lies a mind-set that possibly accepts fundamental differences between the rebellious and the contented, the winners and the losers. If not necessarily determined by race, these differences may have some deep biological roots. As we saw particularly in chapter 1, the liberal turn toward interiority sometimes leads toward an anchoring of emotion and sympathy in blood and biology. In that respect, and in his other liberal attributes, Grimes represents the ideal transition toward the nineteenth-century American slave narrative.

The contractual mindframe we have seen in Grimes' 1825 narrative already suffused the repressed sensibility of Venture Smith, whose *Narrative*, published in 1798, also illustrates this transitional period. Although he obviously despises the whole system of slavery, Smith seems at pains also to present it as a form of contract that gives him certain rights. He initially shows "many proofs of my faithfulness and honesty," concluding that "my behavior had as yet been sumissive and obedient." With this conclusion, by subtly implying that it is the master who has as yet given him no cause to rebel, he establishes himself as a man with his own notions of fairness and balance of powers.[7] These notions are soon put to the test as Smith mockingly describes his master's son, "big with authority," who "very arrogantly" (12) orders him to perform a task. When Smith defends himself, his "upstart master" turns into a crybaby and runs to his mother. Calming down, Smith "voluntarily caused myself to be bound" (13). The episode is striking in the self-evident, self-assured way in which Smith offers resistance, and sticks to the agreement "that my master had given me so much to perform that day, and that I must faithfully complete it in that time" (12). The power of the agreement is to him stronger than any amount of psychological or physical force applied to him, and it controls the strength and the direction of his emotions.

Smith's contractualism goes hand in hand with his individualism. By having himself "voluntarily" bound, he asserts a degree of control over the situation. At a later time, when he is handcuffed and his master threatens to send him away and he answers: "'I crossed the waters to come here and I am willing to cross them to return'" (16), he makes it clear that he conceives of himself as an autonomous being. This comment is not about returning to one's roots, or colonization, or solidarity, but about an individual's determination to remain unattached, in geographic or ideological terms, and, ironically, tied only to his own freedom of movement. And to Smith, this freedom symbolizes his economic autonomy. Indeed, even though after gaining his freedom Smith buys considerable amounts of land, and is allowed to remain on Long Island even after a law is passed expelling all blacks, his eager participation in the capitalist system makes him a fitting representative of the freewheeling, independent individual defined first and foremost by commercial exchange. The fact that he evaluates the loss of his son and his daughter in monetary terms signals that the discourse of emotion has given way to the language of money and commerce.

Just like Grimes, though, Smith runs into the limits of liberal exchange in a society dominated by racial discrimination, as well as by overall dishonesty, and offers more emotional moments of insight. According to David Kazanjian, the end of the eighteenth and the beginning of the nineteenth centuries saw the "emergence of a mutually constitutive relationship" between "hierarchically codified racial and national identities" and the "formal, abstract equality characteristic of modern capitalism." Smith's narrative reflects this mutual articulation. Whether or not one agrees with Kazanjian's slippage from a capitalism "influenced in this 'most fundamental way' by racism and nationalism" toward one that "depends upon" (151) them, Smith's narrative certainly shows how racism intruded on his ability to conduct free commercial exchange. As with Grimes, his most fervent outburst occurs when he runs up costs after the laws are bent against him; he is unfairly made to pay for a loss of molasses: "Such a proceeding . . . would in my native country have been branded as a crime equal to highway robbery. But Captain Hart was a *white gentleman*, and I a *poor African*, therefore it was *all right, and good enough for the black dog.*" At the same time, Smith also bemoans "the injustice of knaves," "the cruelty and oppression of false-hearted friends," and "the perfidy of my own countrymen" (24). These remarks clearly anticipate the Hobbesian climate that suffuses Grimes' narrative, similarly watering down the racial critique and exposing less a system of racial exploitation than one of unlimited acquisitiveness. But Smith clearly fits in comfortably with that system, and criticizes those who prevent it from running smoothly.

Yet in contrast with Grimes, Smith still retains a representation of race that shows remnants of republican egalitarianism. From the beginning Smith draws attention to his body, informing us that he "descended from a very large, tall and stout race of beings, much larger than the generality of people in other parts of the globe, being commonly considerable above six feet in height, and every way well proportioned" (4). Throughout the narrative he reminds us of his extraordinary physical endowments, emphasizing the amount of work he performs, or some unusual feat, as when he "took upon my knees a tierce of salt containing seven bushels, and carried it two or three rods" (14), or when, assaulted by two white men, he "immediately turned them both under me, laid one of them across the other, and stamped them both with my feet what I would" (15), or when he carried a black man on his shoulders for two miles and back. At one point he summarizes his activities by calling them his "singular and wonderful labors" (20), as if to help build the legendary figure that he actually became.[8] One anecdote contains a peculiar detail. One day he hears a quarrel between his mistress and his wife; when he comes in and tries to intervene, the mistress attempts to beat him with her horse whip, but "while she was glutting her fury with it, I reached out my great black hand, raised it up and received the blows of the whip on it which were designed for my head" (15). Whatever the reason Smith felt the need to specify that his big hand was "black," the very gratuitousness of the word, the unnecessariness of the information, indirectly adds a racial dimension to the bodily references that pepper the whole narrative. Even as he tries to present himself as a liberal subject participating in a capitalist system, Smith seems to want us to keep constant an awareness of his blackness.[9] Toward the end of the narrative, he points out that, at fortysix years old, he "had already redeemed from slavery, myself, my wife and three children, besides three negro men" (22). While in the course of his narrative he had not made clear his motivations for buying those black men, here he implies that he did it out of a concern and a solidarity similar to those he feels for members of his family. Overall, then, Smith plants a number of clues for his readers, indicating that in spite of his bottom-line "commercial mentality" (Desrochers, "Not Fade" 51), he also desires intersubjective acknowledgment as a black, as a member of a particular culture with particular roots.

Pointing toward, and eliciting emotion for, the racial body can thus have the kind of political import that we have seen in other black texts. Grimes ends his narrative dramatically by stating that, if his skin had no scars, he would ask in his will that it "be taken off and made into parchment, and then bind the constitution of glorious happy *and free* America" (232). This final picture seems like a desperate appeal, similar to Smith's self-descriptions, to make his skin visible, as it contains, but also remains separate from, the core of American ideals. Ultimately, though, it is the gruesomeness of the picture, even as Grimes acknowledges its impossibility, that says much about the plight of blacks in America. Yet, in an ironic twist, the reader knows that this skin that would be used as parchment is white. All its connections with blood and vessels having disappeared, what will be left of his body will be fundamentally indistinguishable from what will be left of the white reader's. Grimes forces the reader to look at that skin, and to gain an insight into its symbolic complexities, even as the morbidity of the image induces a simultaneous movement of identification and rejection. Just as the reader is forced to look at Smith's herculean black hand, he or she is made to acknowledge Grimes' skin as both the same and different. Both moments induce notions of autonomy and independence, one through resistance and the other through a reference to the Constitution, but it is a liberal message that also carries all the emotion of a demand for a full look at, and recognition of, the other's body. In narratives that tend to suppress emotion, these peaks of feeling carry much political weight, and show a desire to break out of the limits of liberalism.

The repression of feeling is made most explicit in the narrative of Charles Ball, *Slavery in the United States* (1836), at least as a stated intention. In the preface Isaac Fisher, his amanuensis, declares about Ball that "many of his opinions have been cautiously omitted, or carefully suppressed, as being of no value to the reader; and his sentiments upon the subject of slavery, have not been embodied in this work" (Ball 264). According to William Andrews, this decision turns the narrative into a compendium of "*assertives*," a term he borrows from John Searle to designate speech acts that make words "signify, conform to, or 'fit the world'" (*To Tell* 83), and hence limit them in the attempt to change the world. In this perspective, the use of "*expressives*," which are "designed to express one's psychological state with respect to the propositional content of a given utterance," and which will be used in later narratives, can better "subvert the conventions of speech action and reader response that defined and legitimized the early slave narrative in the 1830s" (85). This distinction seems to imply that the ability to express one's thoughts and sentiments automatically makes a text more subversive. But Ball's narrative contains a complexity that dilutes this sort of binary distinction. This complexity is partly due to the issue of authorship, since the text makes it impossible to distinguish Fisher's from Ball's contributions. The first publisher of the narrative alleged that Fisher told him that "'many of the anecdotes in the book illustrative of southern society, were not obtained from Ball, but from other and creditable sources'" (Andrews, *To Tell* 84). The mitigated position about slavery expressed in the text, for example, could reflect the mixed sentiments of either of the two contributors. But, more important, the supposed avoidance of expressive speech acts leaves open the realm of interpretation. This situation does make the text less sentimental, but not necessarily less apt at eliciting the reader's sympathy. The fact that the narrator remains for the most part an observer does not make some of his observations less painful, and hence less moving. The repression of unexpressed feeling, just as its expression, can shape readers' responses in radically different ways depending on what is being expressed or repressed.

While, as Andrews rightly points out, the lack of expressives typical of "ontological distanciation" hinders the development of a textual black subjectivity, these early nineteenth-century texts aim at the construction of a liberal self through other means. The reader is certainly made to feel in Ball's narrative, but those feelings are constantly channeled through one basic value: self-interest. Through its encyclopedic descriptions of the cultivation of tobacco, cotton, corn, and indigo, the text gives a unique account, for a slave narrative, of the interest that drives slave owners. When the narrator, who shows some taste for the gothic genre, describes the country he passes through during the long march south, he deplores, less the institution of slavery, than the lack of wisdom in adopting a system that leads to the depletion of the soil, and overall desolation. Slavery is criticized, but this criticism makes a strong link with the fact that slavery leads to "the general poverty and weakness of the slave-holding states" (Ball 281). The country "had originally been highly fertile and productive," and then the plantation owners "supplied themselves with slaves from Africa" and "cleared large plantations of many thousand acres," but "regardless of their true interest, they valued their lands less than their slaves, exhausted the kindly soil by unremitting crops of tobacco, declined in their circumstances, and finally grew poor." Consequently, "Virginia had become poor by the folly and wickedness of slavery, and dearly has she paid for the anguish and sufferings she has inflicted upon our injured, degraded, and fallen race" (280). It is hard here to disentangle the humanitarian from the calculating argument. Ball's condemnation keeps pairing "slavery and tobacco" (283), "*idleness and tyranny*" (284). In fact, he is convinced that if cultivation had been done more wisely, "the condition of the coloured people would not be, by any means, a comparatively unhappy one" (283).

The condemnation of the misguided search for wealth and opulence rests on an even more deeply embedded ideology at the core of the text, the Northern work ethic. In the passage just quoted, the narrator deplores that "industry, enterprise, and ambition, have fled from these abodes" (282), and ridicules so-called gentlemen averse to dirtying their hands, and young women "engaged in reading silly books" instead of "attending to the dairy, or manufacturing cloth" (283). He will set himself up as a contrast, relying on that "honest and honourable industry" (283) he praises, during his own career as a slave. He gives a precise account of his various initiatives to improve his lot, from growing a vegetable garden to hunting and fishing, as well as working on Sundays for wages. Interestingly, he describes a system that indirectly acknowledges the slave's ability to sell his or her labor. When slaves work on Sundays, "their employers never flog them," and "never give them abusive language": "I worked faithfully, because I knew that if I did not, I could not expect payment; and those who hired me, knew that if I did not work well, they need not employ me" (341). Other slaves spend their precious free time manufacturing various objects, selling them, then using the money for necessities. Indeed, "a considerable traffic is carried on between the shop-keepers and slaves." Ball also makes an arrangement with the family he has been assigned to live with, that "I would bring all my earnings into the family stock, provided I might be treated as one of its members, and be allowed a portion of the proceeds of their patch or garden." The proposition is agreed to, and "from this time we constituted one community" (343). Because of these possibilities for initiative, however limited, the slaves do not live "in a condition of the most perfect equality" among themselves;

reflecting the inequalities of a system based on individual enterprise, "there was in fact a very great difference in the manner of living, in the several families" (379). This sort of information forms the backbone of Ball's description of his life as a slave. Indeed, he points out later, the reader cannot possibly form a true picture of "all the minute particulars of the life of a slave on a cotton plantation," of "the system of parsimonious economy, that the slave is obliged to exercise and maintain in his little household" (379). By investing his reader's sympathy into those details, which literally constitute a surplus in the narrative, the narrator, as in the two previously discussed narratives, indirectly builds an image of African Americans as particularly apt for survival in the budding liberal, capitalist system.

Abstract Bodies

In two texts published in 1838, by Moses Roper and James Williams, which focus on survival in a system based on sadism and torture, the matter-of-fact descriptions of brutality are meant to shock the reader into a recognition of the horror at the heart of the institution of slavery. Just as in the narratives just discussed, these texts depend less on a description of the narrator's thoughts and feelings than on an indirect tangling with the reader's emotions. Andrews underlines Williams' "emotional restraint," his "reticence about personal feelings and judgments" (*To Tell* 89), and the fact that he avoids "revealing the horrors within the psyche" such as "outrage, vengefulness, bitterness"; he also notes Roper's "dispassionate tone and an undeviating attention to the plain facts of the matter" (90). The lack of a "'center of feeling or consciousness'"—an expression Andrews borrows from Charles T. Davis—even makes Roper's "an alienating text" (92). Indeed, Roper's narrative practically consists in a succession of escapes from Mr. Gooch, followed by capture and violent punishment. Williams mostly focuses on his time as a slave driver on a cotton plantation in Alabama, where the overseer Huckstep freely gives vent to his drunken rages. While once again the adherence to the assertive mode prevents the construction of a full-fledged self, these narratives raise the question of unencumbered voyeurism as an emotional strategy. A reflective narrator would allow the reader to penetrate his or her emotional world, creating the possibility for a moment of Smithian sympathy or of intersubjective recognition. The bourgeois narrators discussed above use a limited degree of emotion, as well as the absence or presence of bodies, to welcome the reader into their ideological world. But Roper and Williams limit themselves to the representation of brutalized bodies, forcing the reader to witness what Ball had called "horrible spectacles" (424), and to see black bodies turned into objects. And yet the depiction of horrible violence is a mainstay of all slave narratives, and cannot by itself determine a reader's reaction. Once again, it is the ideological context that helps give meaning to the horror the reader is bound to feel.

There are a few moments of sentimental reflection in Roper's narrative, and they occur in connection with his family. When at the end of the narrative he rejoices about his newfound freedom, he remarks that "my feelings of happiness at having escaped from cruel bondage, are not unmixed with sorrow of a very touching kind." Indeed, "*'the land of the Free'*" still contains the mother, the brothers, and the sisters of Moses Roper, not enjoying liberty, not the possessors of like feelings with me" (Roper 519). The importance of this communion of feeling between Roper and his family informs a moving scene in the middle of the narrative, in which he comes home after one escape and reunites with his family, "amidst the ardent interchange of caresses and tears of joy" (501). Andrews points out that the various references made in this passage to the reunion of Joseph with his brothers and father in Genesis become a means of "forcing the reader to recognize himself in a role analogous to that of the false brothers in the biblical story" (*To Tell* 95), hence provoking a moment of self-understanding. Seen in this perspective, the narrative turns into a plea to consider all humans, and certainly all Americans, as "of one blood," and hence as all deserving of liberty. Roper's final and rather shocking reflection that "I am unwilling to speak in any but respectful terms of the land of my birth," though supposedly based on the fact that "I love her institutions in the free states" (519), makes an obvious connection between his birth or biological origin and the nation he feels he belongs to. Indeed, he emphasizes his "blood" many times throughout the narrative since, except for his curly hair, he looks white. He tells us twice about his ancestry, informing us that his mother is partly white and his father white. In fact, he starts the narrative with a scene readers of slave narratives are familiar with, in which the mistress of the plantation plans to murder his mother after inquiring about the color of the child and finding out that Roper is "very white" (493). As he grows older, traders and slave owners find him a hard sell because of his color, and a doctor who buys him "soon sent me to his cotton plantation, that I might be burnt darker by

210   SLAVERY AND SENTIMENT

the sun" (494). During his escape, he passes as a white indentured servant, eliciting sympathy with his personal story and his professed desire to be reunited with his family. The sentimental emphasis on family, then, links up with an image of America as a country that is no more than a big family united by blood.

This desire to emphasize an inner, biological connection seems to impact Roper's unsentimental representation of bodies, as if even in his obligatory account of physical maltreatment he wished to downplay the victims' physicality. Roper seems aware of his audience's inability to detach the "brothers" they might peek at, in the passage just discussed, from their racialized exterior. Ultimately, he seems to abide by the same standards. In spite of his exploitation of his whiteness, he, like Grimes earlier, offers no reflection on the aberrations of race in America. He accepts the idea that he is lying about his racial status, and even apologizes for it in a footnote, acknowledging that he "now saw the wicked part I had taken in using so much deception in making my escape" (517). While his sober descriptions of numerous acts of torture do provoke an emotional response in the reader, their matter-of-factness tends to objectify the bodies depicted, turning them into undifferentiated receptacles of violence. This method reaches a climax in a famous passage, in which Roper uses a diagram to describe one particular form of torture, which he describes as follows:

> This is a machine used for packing and pressing cotton. By it he hung me up by the hands at letter a, a horse moving round the screw e, and carrying it up and down, and pressing the block c into the box d, into which the cotton is put. At this time he hung me up for a quarter of an hour. I was carried up ten feet from the ground, when Mr. Gooch asked me if I was tired. He then let me rest for five minutes, then carried me round again, after which he let me down and put me into the box d, and shut me down in it for about ten minutes. (506)

Roper's body becomes part of a scientific experiment, a technological feat; his account emphasizes the material workings of torture rather than the inner response of the person tortured. That he seems to want to provoke interest in Gooch's methods rather than in his own self becomes clear when he concludes that, in the end, Gooch "hardly knew what to do with me" since "the whole stock of his cruelties seemed to be exhausted" (506). In his combined attempt to shock the reader into horror while preventing a consciousness of the racialized body, Roper runs the risk of keeping the reader at a distance, which the few moments of family feeling in the rest of the narrative cannot possibly counteract. As Charles T. Davis points out, "these atrocities are not placed in a context that has meaning or that demands from us great sympathy" (89). Roper runs head-on into the liberal conundrum, in which the rhetoric of personhood has no corporeal strategy, and the strategy he chooses produces neither sympathy nor intersubjective recognition — just abstract bodies.

James Williams' narrative adopts a similar logic.[10] Williams establishes a clear liberal framework when he begins with an account of his brother, who "on one occasion preached a sermon from a text, showing that all are of one blood" (26), in the process running the risk of heavy punishment. From the beginning, then, the reader is made aware of the narrator's stance, and knows that it informs his reaction to all subsequent events. Hence the significance of an incident where Williams' master, George Larrimore, asks him, in front of a group of white men assembled in Richmond for the Convention of 1829 to amend the state constitution, "if I wished to be free and go back to my own country." Williams' reaction is worth millions: "I looked at him with surprise, and inquired what country." This calm statement of surprise and puzzlement, which I read as masterly false naïveté, neatly captures the gulf between the whites' racial outlook and Williams' own American one. When Larrimore answers, with a laugh that might evince his own uneasiness, "'Africa, to be sure,'" Williams "told him that was not my country — that I was born in Virginia" (30). Williams clearly aims at creating a bond with the reader through a double appeal to personhood and nationhood. Once he begins his account of his life as a slave driver on an Alabama plantation, however, the narrative quickly devolves, like Roper's, into a succession of horrible scenes, provoked by the pathologically violent white overseer, in which bodies similarly turn into objects of torture. Racial considerations only lead to even more violence, as when the overseer tells Williams, after he has only pretended to whip a slave, that "the only reason I did not whip her was that she was a white woman, and I did not like to cut up her delicate skin" (65). As with Roper, once we enter the chamber of horrors the narrative becomes more episodic, turning into a list of cruelties with very little emotional context.

More than in Roper's narrative, we feel the narrator's gradual emotional detachment from his own experience. In spite of his display of some measure of solidarity with the slaves whom he is being coerced into bullying and whipping, Williams occupies a no-man's-land in the cotton plantation hierarchy, forced to live with an overseer he hates and who tries to "separate me in feeling and interest as widely as possible from my suffering brethren and sisters" (48). Some of the slaves he drives are actually his relations, and he "used to call them my cousins," but the overseer "forbid my doing so, and told me if I acknowledged relationship with any of the bands [sic] I should be flogged for it" (49). Williams does express admiration for Big Harry, who has kept "a high and proud spirit" (53); indeed, he points out, "on almost every plantation at the South you may find one or more individuals whose look and air show that they have preserved their self-respect as *men;* that with them the power of the tyrant ends with the coercion of the body—that the soul is free, and the inner man retaining the original uprightness of the image of God" (53–54). Here is the almost unattainable ideal, the one that Big Harry will die for, displaying a form of courage and belief in his own humanity that links him to the brother mentioned at the beginning of the narrative.

Williams himself, by contrast, struggles for survival, both physical and emotional. Unlike Roper, who is captured after his first successful escape because his family has prevailed upon him to stay, persuading him "to go into the woods in the daytime, and at night come home and sleep there" (Roper 501), Williams escapes straight to the free states: "I longed to visit my wife and children in Powhatan County, but the dread of being discovered prevented me from attempting it" (Williams 96). While he acknowledges the "sympathy and kindness" he has received from abolitionists, he ends the narrative wishing the slaves themselves "could know that thousands in the free states are praying and striving for their deliverance"; then, "how would the glad tidings be whispered from cabin to cabin, and how would the slave-mother, as she watches over her infant, bless God, on her knees, for the hope that this child of her day of sorrow might never realize, in stripes, and toil, and grief unspeakable, what it is to be a slave!" (99). With this bleak, emotional ending, Williams emphasizes that there is yet no real sympathetic connection between benevolent abolitionists in the North and enslaved people in the South. Contrary to Roper's optimism, the editor of Williams' narrative reminds readers in a postscript that slavery "pervades the whole land" (Williams 101). Abstraction threatens to erase one's consciousness of bodies and minds, and he hopes that the text will awaken "in the hearts of all who read it a sympathy for the oppressed which shall manifest itself in immediate, active, self-sacrificing exertions for their deliverance" (xxii–xxiii), and that it will "prevent the avowed and associated friends of the slave from giving such an undue importance to their own trials and grievances, as to forget in a great measure the sorrows of the slave" (xxiii). Ironically, the narrative he introduces carries some of that remoteness, showing how easily liberal sympathy can slip into abstraction or self-absorption.

The 1840s

The liberal individualist streak of the slave narrative is usually seen as culminating with the achievements of the 1840s, in the incredibly popular narratives of Frederick Douglass, Lewis and Milton Clarke, William Wells Brown, Josiah Henson, Henry Bibb, Henry Box Brown, James W. C. Pennington. Andrews shows how these fugitive narrators "infused into their writing a quality that the dictated Afro-American narratives of earlier decades rarely communicated—a sense of an individual authorial personality, the sound of a distinctive authorizing voice" (*To Tell* 98–99). He attributes this new turn to the role played by abolitionism, which encouraged the cult of the fugitive hero, as well as the attempt to produce a radical conversion in the white reading public. Moreover, many of these narrators had enjoyed extensive rhetorical practice on the abolitionist lecturing circuit, and were hence better prepared to tackle the writing of their life stories. Indeed, the "degree of egocentrism in black autobiography of the 1840s, when compared to the self-effacement instanced in so much of the genre before that decade, could not have appeared or have met with such public sympathy without the support and sanction of the antislavery movement" (100). In terms of its form, then, of "the crucial property and quality *of* a text" (104), the slave narrative links up with the "preoccupation with selfhood and identity" (102) typical of the Romantic literature popular at the time. No wonder, Andrews writes, Theodore Parker thought that "all the original romance of Americans is in them" (98).

Yet I would argue that, from a political and ideological point of view, the 1840s constitute more of a transitional decade for many commentators on slavery. Politically and economically, the decade witnessed a few swings. Although it came in the wake of a Jacksonian reign that celebrated rugged individualism, it also opened with a general depression, created by the 1837 Panic, whose effects rippled well into the middle of the decade. The quick succession of William Henry Harrison, John Tyler, and James K. Polk as presidents, as well as the divisions within the two main parties, helped maintain a sense of a lack of consensus on such weighty issues as the sale of western lands, the use of tariffs, or the annexation of Texas. Against this background, and because it follows directly on the split between the Garrisonians and their opponents in 1840, the decade reverberates with deep divisions concerning the relationship of abolitionism to politics. While the newly founded American and Foreign Anti-Slavery Society favored an approach that focused on politics and the law, the Garrisonians stuck to their strategy of moral revolution. Though the latter could come across as proponents of the politics of interiority as I have described them in this book,[11] they aimed to use moral reform, not for a piecemeal change of society, but for a thorough transformation of the social order. So, as Aileen Kraditor puts it, they "could not, without distorting the nature of the problem, have dealt with it otherwise than as largely a moral problem." Indeed, "they always accompanied their demand for abolition with the demand for equal rights for the Negro and the ending of racial prejudice" (Kraditor 22). In this revision of the racial order, in this readiness to appeal to sympathy for the goal of equality within difference, the Garrisonians partly displayed a republican sensibility that left its mark on a few major antislavery texts of the 1840s.

Lewis and Milton Clarke do not display this kind of solidarity, but their 1846 *Narratives* keep reminding the reader that, whatever inner continuity a person might possess, his or her fate is constantly and ubiquitously determined by the body, and particularly by skin color. Reader sympathy is invested in the ups and downs of their situations, depending on how they fit in the racial hierarchy. Lewis starts with a sharp attack against whiteness, presenting "the Algerines of Kentucky" as barbarians, even among themselves, since "slaveholders have not arrived at that degree of civilization that enables them to live in tolerable peace, though united by the nearest family ties" (609); the woman who will own him for several years resembles nothing more than a wild animal. Displaying a common reaction, she "seemed to hate and abuse me all the more, because I had some of the blood of her father in my veins" (613). Once, "in a burning hot day, she *made me take off every rag of clothes, go out into the garden*, and pick herbs for hours, in order to *burn* me black" (614). The complexities of Lewis' racial background come out in a richly ironic episode, when he stops at a tavern in Cincinnati as he is running away. People hear he is a Kentuckian, and want to know whether he is a slaveholder. Not only is he running a risk by passing, but he also needs to be careful as a white man, since he may be dealing with abolitionists and anti-abolitionists alike: "I at length satisfied them, by assuring them that

I was not, nor my father before me, any slaveholder at all; but, lest their suspicions should be excited in another direction, I added, my grandfather was a slaveholder" (621). Because readers know that he is fooling his audience while at the same time strictly telling the truth, this cunning moment invites them to ponder the American absurdities surrounding race and skin color. An episode with similar implications, reported by the Liberty Press, takes place when his brother Cyrus tries to vote and the judge says he cannot, because he is a colored man. Since the judge is very dark skinned, Cyrus points out that "we are both colored men; and all we differ is, that you have not the handsome wavy curl; you raise *Goat's wool*, and I come, as you see, a little nearer *Saxony*" (632). Cyrus is finally allowed to vote. Milton's narrative ends with a rebounding account of his trial as a fugitive, together with claims that he is a white man, and funny quid pro quos on the basis that people think he is white. As he concludes about a racist who has just asked him if he has seen the "nigger" he is looking for, Milton says that "his philanthropy was graduated, like many others, upon nothing more substantial than color" (651). The Clarkes' narratives probably constitute the first sustained ironic attempt to keep skin color a major motif while demonstrating its ridiculous intricacies.

The sense of control that emanates from the Clarkes' masterly use of irony is counterbalanced by what could be called the politics of fear. Many narrators, of course, created suspense while recounting their stories of hairbreadth escapes, but the Clarkes seem to pay particular notice to their states of fear and anxiety, in ways that emphasize gut reactions based on skin color. Lewis describes slaves who are thinking of running away: "No tongue can tell the doubt, the perplexities, the anxiety which a slave feels, when making up his mind upon this subject." If he manages to get away, "all the white part of mankind, that he has ever seen, are enemies to him and all his kindred. How can he venture where none but white faces shall greet him?" As a consequence, "a horror of great darkness comes upon him" (619). This instinctive fear of a prospective sea of hateful white faces underlines how deeply his unconscious life is bound up with race. When Lewis attempts his own escape, he runs into a minister who seems suspicious and delays him, but who seems to base some of his trust on Lewis' skin color. Clarke concludes: "I sometimes wonder that a slave, so ignorant, so timid, as he is, *ever* makes the attempt to get his freedom. '*Without* are *foes, within* are *fears*'" (620). This is more than an attempt to make the reader sympathize with the slave's feeling; Clarke forces us to envision the mind-and-body situation of the slave, the conditions within and without.

The interaction between the two sides comes out later in a rather humorous scene when, in order to avoid recognition, he buys "a pair of double-eyed green spectacles": "When I got them on, they blind-folded *me*, if they did not others. Everything seemed right up in my eyes. Some people buy spectacles to see out of; I bought mine to keep from being seen." He can become invisible only at the cost of his own perception, and the bizarre, almost expressionist image called up by the spectacles stresses once more the zaniness of his situation. But in case we forget, he reminds us very quickly that he hardly slept that night: "All was confusion, dreams, anxiety, and trembling" (621). Even after he arrives in Canada, apprehensions and uncertainty prevail: "My hands, my feet, were now my own. But what to do with them, was the next question. A strange sky was over me, a new earth under me, strange voices all around; even the animals were such as I had never seen." Although he plays some of this anxiety for laughs, as when he feels sure that a redcoat is after him, the way Olaudah Equiano had done in order to underline his naïveté at the sight of snow or technology, Clarke manages to convey that he feels "entirely alone" (623), and that this loneliness takes much away from the enjoyment of his newfound liberty. He needs a community, that very dimension which, as he has made us understand, often prevents slaves from trying to run away in the first place. While freedom comes across as a major theme in the narrative, the continued emphasis on fear and anxiety, the willingness to acknowledge the fact that freedom is indeed scary for someone enslaved since birth, takes readers' gaze away from the individual focus on liberty and forces them to keep their focus on more systemic issues.

Henry Bibb's 1849 narrative is often associated with a focus on the family. It indeed draws much of its emotional power from Bibb's ceaseless efforts to be reunited with his wife, which from the very beginning he places within the context of liberal human rights: "I believed then, as I believe now, that every man has a right to wages for his labor; a right to his own wife and children; a right to liberty and the pursuit of happiness; and a right to worship God according to the dictates of his own conscience" (15). In fact, his individualism goes so far as to underpin his argument that slavery deprives slaves of the opportunity to fend for themselves, since "unlike other men, he is denied the consolation of struggling against external difficulties, such as destroy the life, liberty, and happiness of himself and family" (15–16). A person enslaved is denied the chance to participate in the American Darwinian game, "is not allowed to struggle," "is not allowed to help himself" (16).

Very early in the narrative Bibb makes it clear that relations between men and women are a part of this individual struggle. After a scene of sentimental longing for liberty, in which he describes himself pining away on the banks of the Ohio River, in a passage reminiscent of Douglass' address to the sailboats on the Chesapeake Bay, unlike Douglass he then directs his attention to the subject of "young women" (20). Here the liberal language of contract takes over. After he meets Malinda and they acknowledge a "union of feeling" (22), they enter a "conditional contract of matrimony" (23) that lasts a year before the actual marriage. The rest of the narrative consists in Bibb's escape north, and in his repeated returns down south in order to free his family, and climaxes with a heartrending scene when Bibb comes back to his wife's owner in an attempt to buy her. As soon as Malinda sees him, she "came rushing to me through the crowd, throwing her arms about my neck exclaiming in the most sympathetic tones, 'Oh! my dear husband! I never expected to see you again!' The poor woman was bathed with tears of sorrow and grief." Unfortunately, "such appeals made no impression on the unfeeling Deacon's heart" (73). In a scene that clearly anticipates *Uncle Tom's Cabin*, Bibb associates family with humanist sentimental and tearful appeals.

Yet unlike the love that climaxes in a happy, tearful family reunion toward the end of Stowe's novel, the heterosexual love at the heart of the emotional climax in Bibb's narrative is directly impacted by the social system. In a highly original move Bibb's narrative invests an important part of its affective capital in a mature love story between a black man and a black woman, but this love story has no happy ending precisely because it is so deeply embedded in the institution of slavery. Love is not a pure, stable, untainted feeling here—it suffers from its social environment and, as such, it is pitched against the achievement of freedom. As he is mulling over running away as a young man, and after he "had determined to carry out the great idea which is so universally and practically acknowledged among all the civilized nations of the earth, that I would be free or die," Bibb "suffered myself to be turned aside by the fascinating charms of a female" (21). Similarly, the time taken celebrating their union "should have been spent in running away to Canada, for our liberty. But freedom was little thought of by us, for several months after marriage" (25). By apparently setting up heterosexual love and the love of freedom against each other, Bibb turns liberty into a superior principle that trumps the particulars of personal attachment. Indeed, he calls his decision to run away "one of the most self-denying acts of my whole life" (27), implying that love of freedom occupies a different realm from that of his most natural human feelings. Furthermore, when he later hears that Malinda is living with a white man, his rationalization of it by invoking her circumstances as a victim of slavery does not totally cover up his implicit feeling of betrayal. He even muses that "it is also reasonable to suppose that there might have been some kind of attachment formed by living together in this way for years" (92). At this point when he allows himself to explore the unthinkable, Bibb projects himself into her life, uses his power of sympathy to try to understand her emotional state, while at the same time speaking from the superior standpoint of achieved freedom. In this complex moment, he manages to create a form of sympathy different from the simple interior exchange, one that cannot function without an awareness of race, gender, and oppression, and a recognition of their subtle workings.

In fact, as a narrator Bibb creates the image of a world where sympathy and intersubjective recognition are possible across race and class. This form of recognition entails not a suppression of race but an acceptance of it. The point is made clear when, even as he is using his light skin to avoid detection and reach freedom, Bibb denounces the fact that "the Anglo-Saxon race" (28) has "almost entirely robbed me of my dark complexion" (29). Here race pride trumps the enjoyment of tricking white folks. But racial identification does not necessarily mean solidarity in this narrative. Bibb is once betrayed by two black men, and he later asserts that "domestic slaves are often found to be traitors to their own people" (69). Throughout his adventures, he at times receives help and sympathy from white men. As he is being taken back to slavery, for example, his kidnappers, "seeing that I was much dissatisfied, commenced talking to me, by saying that I must not be cast down" (37). After he escapes, he is aware that his wife is being watched "by white and by colored persons" (43). When he is jailed after another betrayal, the prison appears a vision of hell for both blacks and whites; his fellow inmates "professed sympathy for me" (50) when he tells his tale, and his wife's distress "struck a sympathetic chord through all the prison among the prisoners" (51). Similarly, the Southern sportsmen who buy him "expressed much sympathy for me in my bereavement" (72), and Bibb could see "the sympathetic tear-drop, stealing its way down the cheek of the profligate and the blackleg" (73); indeed, they "felt sorry for me" (74). The sheer accumulation of those moments, most of them in homosocial contexts such as a boat, a prison, a company of sportsmen, endows these exchanges with a republican feeling that will long remain with readers, maybe even longer than Bibb's panegyrics to freedom.

In his 1849 narrative James W. C. Pennington shows a similar effort to elicit feeling for communities, groups, and systems, instead of for the individual. In the preface already, he insists that slaves and masters are prisoners of a system; because the system is anchored in the "chattel principle," "the relation between master and slave is even as delicate as a skein of silk: it is liable to be entangled at any moment" (108). Similarly, after a suspenseful and rather entertaining account of how he escaped from a group of white men on his way north, instead of celebrating his wily victory he concludes: "The history of that day has never ceased to inspire me with a deeper hatred of slavery; I never recur to it but with the most intense horror at a system which can put a man not only in peril of liberty, limb, and life itself, but which may even send him in haste to the bar of God with a lie upon his lips" (128). This sense of higher principles he owes allegiance to comes across from the beginning of the narrative, in which he emphasizes the importance of an enslaved person's social and communal identity. He laments the fact that the slave child "is thrown into the world without a social circle to flee to for hope, shelter, comfort, or instruction" (114). The family turns out to play all those roles when it can. When one day the master assaults Pennington's father with a cowhide, Pennington highlights the social consequences, giving them the looks of a family feud: the "act created an open rupture between the master's and Pennington's family—each member felt the deep insult that had been inflicted upon our head; the spirit of the whole family was roused." When he subsequently declares that "in my mind and spirit, I never was a *Slave* after it," the echo from Douglass' narrative also captures the fact that, rather than being a moment of individual triumph, his realization is grounded in his belonging to a family and a community.

Moreover, Pennington is a blacksmith with "a high degree of mechanical pride" (117), whose collaboration with other skilled workers plunged him into a male professional community, and he may have inherited some republican principles from that environment. Ultimately, his social identity shapes him as a narrator. As he points out, "the reader will observe that I have not said much about my master's cruel treatment; I have aimed rather to shew the cruelties incident to the system" (118). Whether or not Pennington's structural emphasis was inspired by an awareness of his

British audience, and although the second part of his narrative takes a more conservative approach by focusing on the need for free blacks to elevate themselves, this original distancing from the individual puts him in a different tradition from the one that would celebrate individual sympathy throughout the next decade.

Mary Prince's Cosmopolitan Body

Mary Prince, a West Indian, displays the more harmonious mixture of freedom and the common good that has been the hallmark of the British texts discussed in this book. But she represents yet another political ground compared to the radical ideologies discussed in chapter 3, and to the notion of world citizenship developed by Equiano. Like Robert Wedderburn's, Mary Prince's trajectory takes her from the Caribbean to England, but the consequences for her politics are less radical. Unlike Equiano, also, she does not develop a form of cosmopolitanism that aims at expanding equal opportunities in various places around the globe. Her cosmopolitanism is grounded in a very strong sense of individual, local origin. Like the African American narratives just discussed, Prince's *History* shows an attraction toward liberalism and its notions of freedom, promise, and contract. It departs from them, however, through her attempt to give liberalism a fuller, more positive substance, to bypass its racial limitations, or to combine it with glimpses of the common good. It is in moments of appeals to the reader's sympathy, and especially through representations of the body, that those ideas come through.

Mary Prince's narrative certainly has a cosmopolitan bent, especially when placed next to the African American slave narratives written at the time. Ifeoma Kiddoe Nwankwo terms her outlook a "'cosmopolitan consciousness'" in order to convey "the coexistence of an interest in, knowledge of, and engagement with the world at large with the embrace of a racially based notion of community" (162). This cosmopolitanism differs from the current notion of "a detachment from a singular local place in favor of an embrace of all places, of the world." Indeed, a cosmopolitan consciousness does not "necessarily depend on a detachment from home." What Nwankwo means by "home" is the West Indian home provided Prince by her husband and the black community, and it is the case that throughout the narrative Prince shows a consciousness of her belonging to a particular community. She "clearly values a conception of group identity based on race and condition" (Nwankwo 164). Her description of her condition as a slave includes many references to her comrades in suffering. As she concludes after yet another story of maltreatment, "in telling my own sorrows, I cannot pass by those of my fellow-slaves—for when I think of my own griefs, I remember theirs" (Prince 75). Her description of Hetty's fate early in the narrative conveys this feeling. Hetty was "my fellow slave" (67), and "all the slaves said that death was a good thing for poor Hetty" (67). She thus displays a sense of solidarity partly based on race. To Nwankwo, this is part of Prince's cosmopolitanism, as distinct from the desire simply to be "a citizen of the world" (163). This way, Mary Prince makes an original contribution to the cosmopolitan ethos of the early nineteenth century.

Prince does indeed work with a deeply embedded sense of home, but the most strikingly emotional moment in her *History* is associated with the completeness of what comes across as the original family. She reserves the language of sentiment, which remains conspicuously absent from much of the narrative, for her depiction of an almost paradisiacal youth, when she was surrounded by her own family as well as by the white family that owned her. Unaware of her status as a slave, she nurtured a deep affection for her mistress, and imagined herself part of the family. The day she had to leave and work for Mrs. Pruden, who lived about five miles away, is marked by many tears. When after a while her mistress dies, she is "told suddenly of her death, and my grief was so great that, forgetting I had the baby in my arms, I ran away directly to my poor mistress' house; but reached it only in time to see the corpse carried out." Prince the narrator renders the pathos of that day: "Oh, that was a day of sorrow—a heavy day! All the slaves cried. My mother cried and lamented her sore; and I (foolish creature!) vainly entreated them to bring my dear mistress back to life" (59). In a narrative that focuses resolutely on bodies, and especially on excruciating bodily pain, Prince can only express her profound sorrow through a desire to bring her mistress' body back to life, even as she is holding a baby's body in her arms. As she is caught between two white bodies, which she deeply feels for and which also represent the beginning and the end of life, the moment might represent her entrapment in a white world, but because of its emotional impact, it also conveys the sense of an origin in a recognizably interracial family. It is an origin that will slowly recede as she gets older, but the weight given it in the narrative by the presence of sentiment conveys its meaningfulness as a vague memory of interracial bliss never again to be attained.

In keeping with this interracial dimension, the descriptions of pain throughout the narrative show a combination of plainly humanist sentiment with an awareness of race. Prince's descriptions of bodily suffering show an attempt on her part to find a middle ground between erasure and representation of race, the sign of her desire simultaneously to convey the fullness of personhood and the intensity and dehumanization of corporeal violence. In an episode not unlike Douglass' introduction into the world of slavery when he watches his aunt Hester being whipped, Prince lets us into the unbearable cruelty of her new masters by describing the treatment of other slaves. In a first harrowing scene, she sees the master go down into the kitchen one evening, a cowhide in his hand; a few minutes later, she hears "the cracking of the thong, and the house rang to the shrieks of poor Hetty." She comments that "this was a sad beginning for me." Not seeing what happens, yet hearing Hetty implore the master to have mercy on her, she "sat upon my blanket, trembling with terror" (65), a scene that is bound to provoke a strong emotional reaction in the reader, who can sense Hetty's full humanity as much as her violent treatment, as well as sympathize with the young Mary. This episode makes the following scenes of Hetty's torture and death all the more unbearable. Because Prince has managed to convey a certain sense of Hetty as a person and as a subject, the description of her physical trials does not objectify her. The Hetty episode shows a narrator able to make us care for Hetty as a person, as a black, as a woman, as a battered body.

Even as she displays this combination of individualism and a feeling for members of her community, there is a sense in which Prince's ideology bears the mark of the predominant liberalism of her age. Her story is one of increased resistance, and of a gradual movement toward, and longing for, individual freedom. After an episode in which she tells us that Justice Dyett ruled she was in the right in a dispute, a moment whose importance she marks by saying that "this was about two or three years after I came to Antigua," she reports her first gesture of resistance, when she finally tells her mistress "that she ought not to use me so" (80). From then on, Mr. Wood starts a strange round of manipulations: he tells her to go look for an owner, and when she finds one, he refuses to sell her, and beats her for her impudence. Just as did Equiano, she learns the game of negotiation, and the way whites often load the dice. But this also helps her make some money, as she "took in washing, and sold coffee and yams and other provisions to the captains of ships." Indeed, "I did not sit still during the absence of my owners; for I wanted, by all honest means, to earn money to buy my freedom" (81). Her sense of freedom seems to increase as she converts to Christianity, and decides to get married. She finally asks her owners to let her buy her freedom. Her narrative seems to follow an arc similar to that of nineteenth-century American slave narratives.[12]

Her liberalism, though, is idiosyncratic. When her mistress asks her "who had put freedom into my head," she answers: "'To be free is very sweet'" (85). This is a singular answer indeed. Prince is not using the language of natural rights but that of pleasure. This is a strategic moment in a slave narrative, when the slave appeals to the owner's and the reader's emotion in order to justify her desire for freedom, and Prince decides to talk of "sweetness," which denotes well-being and quality of life. More than the just life, Prince wants the good life. Freedom has not functioned as a main theme throughout the narrative, but rather the desire for fair treatment and good working conditions. What she remembers from Turk's Island, for example, is the violence, but especially the "work — work — work!" (73), an outcry that is echoed at the end of the narrative, when she says that slaves will "work — work — work, night and day, sick or well, till we are quite done up." What she and her fellow slaves want, in words that anticipate the language of unionized labor, is "proper treatment, and proper wages" (94). Mary Prince bypasses the language of natural rights to enter the realm of workers' rights and proletarianism, and her use of emotion reflects that shift. This is a clear signal that, to her, liberalism needs to be supplemented.

Like her liberalism, Prince's cosmopolitanism may at first seem unsophisticated. While it is true that she makes several passages from one island to another, and that this movement helps her develop a cosmopolitan consciousness, this hardly contributes to a sense of herself in the world. After she speaks of Turk's Island as a "horrible place," she adds: "The people in England, I am sure, have never found out what is carried on there" (74). Through this statement, she shows an awareness of the role of distance in the prevention of knowledge, and hence the prevention of sympathy—an awareness that, as I noted in the introduction to this book, Bruce Robbins considers the only realistic starting point for a cosmopolitan outlook and a building of global feeling. When her owners tell her they are going to England, Prince allows that she "was willing to come to England: I thought that by going there I should probably get cured of my rheumatism" (86). Though she mentions just afterward, as a sort of afterthought, that she also hoped her master would free her there, she presents England as simply a different place, which has hardly any value to her except as a cure for a bodily ailment. While we cannot possibly know the truth of the statement—according to John A. Wood, her master, he "brought her from Antigua at her own request and entreaty" (96)—she avoids presenting a consciousness of special links between different parts of the world, and in this case between different parts of the empire. England comes across as merely the next stop on her life's itinerary, and at the most as a possible source of physical well-being. One can hardly call this outlook a cosmopolitan one.

But her cosmopolitanism is more subtle, in that it shows an awareness of a transatlantic common good, or some indication of the existence of a community within the empire. In Bermuda, her master starts beating her when she tries to save his daughter from his blows, and she says: "'Sir, this is not Turk's Island.'" She confirms her point by concluding that "he wanted to treat me the same in Bermuda as he had done in Turk's Island" (77). With this explanation she is obviously trying the enlist the reader's indignation at the idea, and in the process to instill her geography of West Indian pain. This geography seems built on an invisible hierarchy, descending from a high point of humanity down to extremes of mistreatment. It is hard not to imagine that Prince is thinking in terms of the British Empire, and of how its common good spreads out from its center but runs thin at its edges. She is enticing the reader also to think in those terms, and since most readers of her narrative will be English, this looks like a strategy meant to make them expand their emotional imagination all the way across the Atlantic, even as it impresses them with the awareness that they are members of that community and responsible for its well-being. Of course, she will do this explicitly also, by appealing directly to their sympathy. But this episode shows the subtle way in which she conveys a political ideology, one that contains a republican form of cosmopolitanism, through scenes of emotional appeal.

Prince's cosmopolitanism is not primary, but it is never far behind. Her deepest desire when in England is to return home. Her hesitancy to leave her masters when in London shows a complex form of attachment. Understandably, she is reluctant to go out into an unknown world where most blacks occupy lowly positions or are reduced to begging. She also resents the fact that her owners are throwing her out after her years of working for them "like a horse" (88), and we are made to feel her sense of entitlement for the labor she has performed throughout the years. But her owners also represent where she comes from, and after she leaves them, even though she is now comfortable with the Pringle family, she hates being "separated from my dear husband, and away from my own country and all old friends and connections" (92). Prince's sense of community is local, not global. The feeling she elicits in her readers through her narrative, and especially through her special blending of subjecthood and victimhood in her depiction of bodies, is meant primarily to awaken their sense of freedom. Not just any freedom: as we saw, she endows her liberalism with a full array of qualities. Her final call for freedom, for example, harps on the notion of happiness: "how can slaves be happy" (93), she asks, when they are treated like beasts and their families are separated? In other words, the enslaved do not just want to be free; they also want the appurtenances of happiness, among which are the pleasures of community. In Prince's notion of local, individual freedom, the transatlantic common good is only a few steps away.

Chapter 5

The Case of Frederick Douglass

Frederick Douglass' 1845 *Narrative* shows some influence of his schooling in republicanism, from his familiarity with *The Columbian Orator* to his close collaboration with the Garrisonians in the years between his escape from Baltimore in 1838 and the moment he sat down to write it in 1844. It is true that, as William Andrews points out in Searlian terms, Douglass uses the "expressive" mode of speech extensively, letting the reader know "how to *feel*" (*To Tell* 103) about events. But precisely "how" he wants readers to feel is a complex question, not easily subsumed under a narrative of increased individualism. Indeed, it seems that his closeness to his experience as a slave in these early fugitive years allowed him to display a unique ideological mix, inspired both by his own history and by his gradual acquaintance with abolitionist ideas. Eric Sundquist praises Douglass' second autobiography, *My Bondage and My Freedom*, published in 1855, over the first, pointing out the "definite limitations" of the *Narrative* "as a revelation of his identity and his thought" (88), calling it "something of a memorized lecture performance transferred to paper," in contrast with the "more sophisticated 'American' identity" he constructs in the second. *My Bondage and My Freedom* reveals an attachment to the founding fathers and to the ideals of the American Revolution, an "entry into America's revolutionary tradition of liberal individualism" (89), and an "embrace of the principles of autonomy, property, and equal rights" (89–90). So in addition to what he sees as a stylistic improvement, an area in which he differs from several critics,[1] Sundquist positively assesses Douglass' attainment of the liberal ideal. While I agree that the 1855 autobiography enters the realm of liberalism with more self-assurance, I would argue that this step does not make the *Narrative* less interesting, let alone less radical, in its political thought.

In the few speeches from his early years that have remained extant, Douglass took a unique approach meant to awaken his audience's sympathy while at the same time maintaining a certain distance from it. As John Blassingame argues, Douglass later presented "a contradictory and sometimes misleading picture" of the restrictions placed on him as a lecturer. In *My Bondage and My Freedom*, Douglass explains that he chafed under his white colleagues' admonitions to keep his tale factual and simple: "It did not entirely satisfy me to *narrate* wrongs; I felt like *denouncing* them" (220). But, says Blassingame, Douglass "denounced wrongs at the very beginning of his lecturing career" (lii); he seemed quite familiar with many issues at the heart of abolitionism, such as freedom of speech or the right of petition, and broached them freely. In fact, the passage just cited, in which Douglass criticizes his abolitionist friends, lacks logical coherence. He first describes the abolitionists' efforts to convince him to speak plainly: "'Better have a *little* of the plantation manner of speech than not'" (220), he was told. The passage establishes paternalistic treatment. When he starts the next paragraph by stating that "at last the apprehended trouble came" (221), the reader feels sure he is about to explain why he broke from the group. But here he goes on to describe how audiences started to doubt he had ever been a slave. The logical slip blurs the distinction between racist audiences and his abolitionist collaborators, shattering the dream that "for a time I was made to forget that my skin was dark and my hair crisped" (219).[2] In spite of this stated hope, though, reading his early speeches gives a sense of a budding black orator, eager to elicit audience sympathy yet also ready to remind them of the world that separated them. It seems as if Douglass started his speaking career with a strong urge to assert his blackness and his difference, and to try and force the audience to do its emotional work within that premise.

Most striking in Douglass' emotional approach in his early speeches is his creation of a gulf between himself (and, through him, the slave community) and his audience. The abolitionists know a lot about slavery, he says in his first fully recorded speech, given in Lynn, Massachusetts, in

October 1841, but they "cannot speak as I can from *experience*" (*Frederick Douglass Papers* [hereafter *FDP*] vol. 1, 3); his audience "cannot feel the slave's misery" (5) endured from the separation of families. His listeners also underestimate the extent of the slaves' knowledge of their condition, not realizing that "a large portion of the slaves *know* that they have a right to their liberty." Douglass unveils the existence of a homegrown reverence for liberty, and of a revolutionary tradition that seems to have developed independently from all outside influence. Unlike the suggestion of a common heritage in his later allusions to the founding fathers and the American Revolution, Douglass here asserts a separate worldview, one that, even if based on concepts like liberty and revolution, seems to have arisen from a specifically black experience, and from a communal sense or recognition of a right to freedom. When in a November 1841 speech he praises abolitionist petitions because, through the grapevine, they help "hold the slave in check" (8), he builds an image of two different worlds, the abolitionist one slowly imposing itself on the black one. Douglass often emphasizes racial division in his early speeches, in repeated references to the "hard hands" (3) of slaves as opposed to the "delicate white hands" (3–4) of slave owners whenever he satirizes Southern sermons, or in his extensive focus on Northern segregation. In his still hesitant and not yet well-oiled addresses, he mixes appeals to humanity with reminders of a racial difference that is plain for all to see. While this attitude will soon become subsumed under a smoother, more coherent form of liberal humanism, Douglass' early emphasis on difference reminds us that his later appeals to liberal sympathy could have turned into a more embodied form of egalitarianism.

It is this egalitarian attitude that makes the *Narrative* distinctive, as several of its most affecting emotional moments are suffused with the republican ethos. Its first violent scene, the whipping of Aunt Hester, which Douglass introduces as "a most terrible spectacle," almost seems borrowed from Roper, as the distanciation turns Hester into a brutalized body. But Douglass is so "terrified and horror-stricken at the sight" (*Narrative* 15) that he hides in a closet; at this moment, as a narrator, he is moving away from the Roper type of narrative, yet not without first hooking up with his predecessor, and impressing on the reader this haunting image of torture. His discussion of the slave songs at the end of the following chapter indirectly presents his own model for a different kind of sympathy, one that moves beyond an abstract body and is not reducible to a mere interior connection. He first alleges that as a young slave, he could not understand "the deep meaning of those rude and apparently incoherent songs," drawing a contrast between then, when he stood "within the circle," and now, when he identifies with "those without." Through this strategy, Douglass forces the reader to think in terms of surface and depth, exterior and interior, before he himself enacts the process of sympathy as, while he is thinking about the songs, "an expression of feeling has already found its way down my cheek." He urges readers to go to a plantation, listen to the songs, and "analyze the sounds," so as to "be impressed with the soul-killing effects of slavery" (19). Rejecting the simple pattern of interior identification, Douglass manages to present the slaves' culture, just as he does their notion of revolution in his speeches, as an independent unit with its own rules, one where cultural actors do not resort to a Smithian adjustment to the sympathizer. Any effort to understand it will require an analysis of the whole, a multifaceted appreciation, an emotional identification within difference.

The two salient moments of sympathetic identification in the *Narrative*, one about intellectual resistance through literacy, the other about physical resistance, have a similar political complexity. In a famous scene, Douglass' desire to learn how to read is fired up when he overhears Hugh Auld tell his wife it would spoil him as a slave, and he understands "the white man's power to enslave the black man" (29), thus clearly associating his literacy with his identity as a black man. His learning process bathes in a republican atmosphere, as he acknowledges the help he received from a community of white boys, as well as the important role played by *The Columbian Orator*. As Granville Ganter explains, Caleb Bingham's *Columbian Orator*, an anthology of oratory published in 1797 and used widely in American secondary schools in the next decades, promoted a notion of virtue typical of the republican view, which "held virtue to be a disinterested civic duty," as distinguished from liberal virtue, which pertained more specifically to "codes of conduct" (465). Suffused with Bingham's congregationalism, "the *Orator*'s stoical and communitarian New Light Calvinism was boldly critical of the self-interested aspect of economic individualism" (466). Bingham obviously aimed at keeping republican radicalism alive. For example, he added an epilogue to Addison's *Cato*—a play that, as we saw in chapter 3, straddles the divide between republican and liberal sensibility—which "unites the words of oratory with the deeds of revolution," thus contributing to a "radical appropriation of the play" (467). Douglass' mere mention of the *Orator* in his *Narrative* was bound to stir republican feelings in the reader.

When studying the *Orator*, Douglass was famously inspired by the dialogue between master and slave, in which the slave wins his freedom through his own argumentation. Bingham had developed a fondness for dialogue during his years at Dartmouth College, where educational dialogue was greatly encouraged, together with "a bias toward public-spirited conclusions" (Ganter 473), and Douglass proves an ideal student of this republican message. Assessing the importance of the documents contained in the *Orator*, Douglass concludes that "they gave tongue to interesting thoughts of my own soul, which had frequently flashed through my mind, and died away for want of utterance" (*Narrative* 33). In this important statement, he declares the pre-existence of the *Orator*'s ethos in his own mind, uncovering his acquisition of literacy as a process of correspondence between his interior life and the book. Unlike Gronniosaw, though, who felt rejected by the talking book but later discovered a correspondence between his spiritual longings as an African child and the religious teachings of the white man, Douglass finds a link between his inner life and a republican book that acknowledges his existence as a black man and a slave. In the dialogue, although he makes a basic appeal to his natural right to freedom, the slave also forces the master to consider his whole self as separate, to conceive of him "body and soul," to "look at these limbs" before he considers his "spirit"; he rewards the master for his emancipation by enlightening him about the state of mind of the slaves, his "implacable foes" (211), full of "resentment" and "ferocity" (212), always ready to rebel. Contrary to Houston A. Baker, Jr., who critiques Douglass' acquisition of literacy as his buying into the dominant system, Douglass says that *The Columbian Orator* "talks" to him as "a human, black identity" (38), in a linguistic alternative to the literacy of liberal individualism.

The *Narrative* continues with a series of affecting moments in which Douglass seems to apply the republican lessons learned from the *Orator*. Brutally beaten by Mr. Covey, Douglass decides to go ask his master, Thomas Auld, for protection. Assuming Auld's perspective, he describes his bloody hair and limbs after a seven-mile walk, "an appearance enough to affect any but a heart of iron," and gives an account of his pleading. Even though Auld ultimately sends him back, Douglass "seemed," as he spoke, "at times to affect him" (48). According to William S. McFeely, this moment is emotionally complex. After coming back from Baltimore to St. Michaels, Douglass and Auld found themselves negotiating the feelings they had for each other: "Frederick loved Thomas, and that love was returned" (41). When Douglass realizes that Auld is not willing to save him from Covey's clutches, "love turned to hatred that evening" (45). Inspired by his republican view of homosocial bonding and exchange, Douglass had hoped that Auld, maybe in a scene mirroring the dialogue between master and slave in the *Orator*, would respond to his double (physical and oratorical) appeal, but he leaves disappointed—and with an empty stomach.

When he resolves to fight Covey, he asserts he does not know "from whence came the spirit" (50); intimating a vague connection between the medicinal root Jenkins has given him and his sudden power of resistance, Douglass is thus careful to avoid any parallel with the liberal "spirit" of 1776. Indeed, the fight constitutes the culmination of his republican education, its description carefully registering each intervention by two bodies engaged in a sort of dialogue between equals. The fight transforms the slave into a man because it marks his entrance into a republican world. It later seems logical that Douglass' most effusive expression of love in the *Narrative* concerns his time at Mr. Freeland's, when he was "teaching these my loved fellow-slaves how to read" (55). His expression of feeling is strong and genuine: "I look back to those Sundays with an amount of pleasure not to be expressed. They were great days to my soul. The work of instructing my dear fellow-slaves was the sweetest engagement with which I was ever blessed. We loved each other. . . . They were noble souls; they not only possessed loving hearts, but brave ones. We were linked and interlinked with each other. I loved them with a love stronger than any thing I have experienced since" (55–56). In their nobility, their courage, their mutual love, these black men display the quintessential components of the ideal republic. Like the early speeches, the *Narrative* offers an insight into an emotional world Douglass is still holding on to before his clearer embrace of liberalism in the 1850s.

In Douglass' three most famous texts from the 1850s, "What to the Slave Is the Fourth of July?" (1852), *The Heroic Slave* (1853), and *My Bondage and My Freedom* (1855), the liberal rhetoric of the Revolution has clearly taken over as an appeal to the reader's emotions. Because of, as we have seen, the complexity of the political thought underlying the American fight for independence, and because of the inevitable use of history for contemporary purposes, nineteenth-century appeals to the founding fathers and even to the idea of revolution do not have an automatically clear political meaning—republican, liberal, or otherwise. In fact, the heritage of the Revolution received sharply different assessments throughout the antebellum period, as the development of a market society heightened the tension between proponents of liberal commercial individualism, on the one hand, and of civic virtue on the other. One significant change in attitude around the middle of the first half of the nineteenth century was that "the nation shifted its interest and emphasis . . . from the Declaration of Independence to the Constitution, from the more radical principles of 1776 to the consolidation of power that occurred in 1787" (Kammen 28). By the middle of the nineteenth century, says James Jasinski, "a reified tradition had been constructed" in which the "underlying vision of the Revolution was clear: the Revolution was rational, inevitable, natural, orderly, and conservative; the Revolution had become, in a word, domesticated" (78). At the same time, though, marginal groups would keep referring to the Declaration in order to vindicate their rights. Any literary use of the Revolution, the Declaration, or the Constitution would thus find meaning in context.

At the time Douglass was writing, he had just gone through significant ideological changes. Between 1841, the year he gave his speech at an abolitionist convention on the island of Nantucket, and 1847, the year he moved to Rochester, New York, at his return from Great Britain and started his own abolitionist paper, the *North Star*, Douglass adhered to Garrisonian tenets, especially the refusal to participate in the political process and a reading of the Constitution as proslavery. By the time he wrote his Fourth of July speech, he had come into contact with political abolitionists, especially Gerrit Smith, and after a long process of reflection he had reversed himself on those two positions. Any text about slavery in the 1850s, moreover, had to contend with the two milestones that were posed at the beginning of the decade, the Fugitive Slave Law and Harriet Beecher Stowe's *Uncle Tom's Cabin*. Everything in Douglass' new context pushed him in an increasingly liberal direction.

The Fourth of July speech marks his first appeal fully based on a vision of the founding texts as anchored in natural rights. Gerrit Smith adhered to the views about the Constitution expounded by William Goodell and Lysander Spooner in their respective treatises. In *The Unconstitutionality of Slavery* (1845), Spooner stated that "all law is grounded in the natural rights of individuals," and that this principle should prevail; any law or contract inconsistent with it is not binding; only the elements of the Constitution "*consistent with natural law, and man's natural rights*" (qtd. in Kraditor 191) are valid. Spooner also pointed out that slavery was never positively legalized and, even if it had been, the Declaration of Independence abolished it. And even if slavery was positively mentioned in state constitutions, it was not legitimate because it "is so entirely contrary to natural right" (qtd. in Kraditor 192). The Constitution itself, said Spooner, certainly does not make it legal either, since its wording is so ambiguous, and anything so contrary to natural right as slavery would need a clear and unambiguous statement. These ideas obviously inform Douglass' speech. He points out the "great principles of political freedom and of natural justice" ("What" 115) embodied in the Declaration, and states he does not even need to argue that "the slave is a man" (117) or that "man is entitled to liberty" (118) since those are natural, self-evident truths on which the United States was founded. Indeed, the Constitution is a "GLORIOUS LIBERTY DOCUMENT" (127) that nowhere mentions the word "slave" or "slavery." There was a glaring inconsistency in a country whose founding fathers had fought in the name of liberty, yet which still held people in bondage.

But Douglass was wrong. At this point he had sharply diverged from Garrison, who maintained that the Constitution condones slavery, and who had officially advocated disunionism ever since a decisive vote at the 1844 meeting of the American Anti-Slavery Society. In 1967 Aileen S. Kraditor was already pointing out that "Garrison's interpretation of the Constitution is now regarded as the correct one" (216), though many historians "have felt more kinship with the middle-of-the-road liberal abolitionists" (217), hence showing more openness to their interpretation. More recently, Charles W. Mills has argued that Douglass' focus on the contradiction between America's theory and practice was naïve. The framers of the Constitution used "euphemistic language," but "everybody knew what they were talking about" (180); moreover,] white supremacy was reflected in various laws and legal decisions, from the original Naturalization Act of 1790 to the Dred Scott decision of 1857. To Mills, Douglass' approach typifies the "conceptual apparatus of liberalism and its blocking from sight of certain embarrassing historical truths" (182). The color-blind reading of the Declaration not only ignored that humanism was always already raced; it remained oblivious to the fact that changes would need to be "much more radical, and the obstacles to be overcome in the white psyche . . . much more formidable" (192), and that "individual acts of sympathy and friendship" (196) were far from enough.[3]

Of course, Douglass too aimed at an eradication of systemic white prejudice and privilege. But one could argue that the liberal approach proved weak in the face of proslavery forces and arguments. By emphasizing their rights as individual states, and brandishing the "union" as the all-encompassing principle, the "slave states" of the South enlisted the founding texts and formulas in defense of their institution. Individualist humanism became easily engulfed in their white supremacist view of the nation. By emphasizing disunion, on the other hand, Garrison meant to propagate a different view of the nation, one where inclusive egalitarianism could not be erased. While humanism was certainly part of his credo, his image of mutual acknowledgment and national regeneration forced his readers and listeners to envisage the totality of the republic as multiracial, and to reject any part of the union that did not fit this republican vision. Declaring the Constitution to be proslavery forced a recognition of the hold that racism had over liberal humanism. When Douglass praised the founding fathers for laying "the corner-stone of the national superstructure" ("What" 114), he did not anticipate that not just the superstructure but the stone itself would need to be changed.

Douglass' liberal approach is confirmed in *The Heroic Slave* where, in a fictional mirror of the strategy used in the speech, the rebellious slave justifies his resistance by appealing to the founding fathers and the ideals of the Revolution. From the first paragraph, Douglass emphasizes Madison Washington's connection, through his birth in Virginia, to Patrick Henry and Thomas Jefferson, as well as to the man "who led all the armies of the American colonies through the great war for freedom and independence" (132). Washington's soliloquy shows he is directly inspired by the liberal ideals of the American revolutionaries. Asserting his own courage and decisiveness in the face of oppression, he cries out: "No,—no,—I wrong myself,—I am no coward. *Liberty* I will have, or die in the attempt to gain it. . . . What others have done, I will do. . . . If I get clear, (as something tells me I shall,) liberty, the inalienable birthright of every man, precious and priceless, will be mine" (133–34). The term "birthright" recalls the first paragraph, in which the narrator stressed the importance of "birth" in Virginia, where "even a man of ordinary parts, on account of the general partiality for her sons, easily rises to eminent stations"; indeed, many people aspiring to a higher status have "sighed and repined that they were not born in Virginia," where people escape "obscurity" simply "by the fact of their birthplace" (132). The term "birthright" connotes particular forms of privilege due, not to being human, but to belonging to a particular family or clan. As a consequence, it seems almost as if Washington deserves liberty by virtue of being not just a man but a Virginian. In a slippage typical of the liberal mindframe, the rhetoric of inner humanity veers toward a discourse of similarity, which, because it thrives on notions of family or blood, runs head-on into the prejudices characteristic of biological racism. As we have seen, the focus on interiors can take on unwanted connotations.

Critics have sharply different takes on Douglass' use of the liberal rhetoric of the Revolution. Maggie Sale calls his parallel between the 1841 rebellion of black slaves on the *Creole* and the rebellion of Americans against Britain "radical," "explosive," "oppositional," and "disruptive" (26). This was a time period when conservative interpretations of the Revolution prevailed.[4] To Sale, Douglass' rhetoric assailed the racial hierarchy as well as "the identity of US Americans as national subjects" (38). Yet as her research shows, during congressional? (U.S.) debates Southerners, invoking the "'rights of the South,'" turned the issue of the *Creole* rebellion into a dispute between the United States and Great Britain (the rebels had sailed the ship to the British Bahamas, where the authorities had set them free). Moreover, "writers for the slaveholding press entered the debate occasioned by the *Creole* rebellion by invoking a trope of revolutionary struggle in the service of the slave owners' property rights" (30). Sale argues that, when "Douglass asserts the equivalence of the struggle of the enslaved with that of revolutionary republicans," he "recasts the legacy of the Revolution from an oppositional perspective," positing that "the community of the nation needs to be reconceptualized in order not only to include but to serve African-American men" (41). His "rhetorical strategy reimagines the history of the Revolution in the service of a radical agenda, one that projects not just freedom but equality for enslaved men as the goal of the original fight for liberty" (46).[5] Richard Yarborough, on the other hand, offers an extensive critique, acknowledging the "conceptual briar patch" Douglass was caught up in, but interpreting the parallels with the founding fathers as a way "to gain reader approval" (175). In this reading, *The Heroic Slave* turns from a "radical" or "explosive" text into one that has basically sold out.

Did Douglass aim to elicit his readers' sympathy by using an ideology that he thought was sure to resonate with them, or did he mean to shock them by means of an "oppositional" and "disruptive" text? One important issue here is the political evaluation of rebellious violence. Understandably, many critics assume that a positive representation of rebellion and revolution makes a text more radical. Sundquist presents an image of an increasingly radicalized Douglass, based on his references to Nat

Turner, Joseph Cinque, Madison Washington. Indeed, by the 1850s Douglass had moved to a more explicit advocacy of slave violence. As Leslie Friedman Goldstein explains, Douglass had never been totally nonresistant in the first place, as exemplified by his glorified depiction of his fight against Covey in the 1845 *Narrative*. As he was becoming impatient with seemingly useless moral suasion, and after spending several years lecturing and facing the antagonism of white mobs (and suffering a personal assault in Pendleton, Indiana), he became more open to violent means. Then he met John Brown at the end of the 1840s, and "his rhetoric and reasoning regarding violence changed correspondingly." A major change "involved a shift from the tactic of discouraging slave revolts to encouraging them" (Goldstein 66).

Interestingly, though, he developed his position from a liberal perspective, using "the Locke-style explanation that slaveholders, by their behavior, had forfeited all right to be numbered with the human family" (67). The rights of slaves were not protected by the government, and so "were thrown back upon the original law of nature," which "gives men their natural rights of life and liberty." Hence, "by the natural, God-given law of self-preservation, slaves are bound to defend themselves against those who would deprive them of their liberty" (69). This Lockean take on violence explains why, just like the American Revolution, it a slave rebellion cannot properly be called radical. Concerned with discrete acts of resistance, Douglass' encouragement of rebellion tallies with an individualist vision founded in an inner right to personal liberty. Indeed, Goldstein makes an important distinction:

> Paradoxically, as Douglass moved away from the Garrisonians in their support for non-violence, he also was moving away from their essential tenet—a revolutionary rejection of the American Constitution—and toward the position that slavery could be abolished within the American system through the conventional channels of political reform. That is, Douglass moved from the position of a revolutionary who opposed violence to that of a reformer who favored violence. (62)

The early description of Madison Washington's physical appearance, almost devoid of racial characteristics, makes it clear to the reader that the context of *The Heroic Slave* needs to be understood as liberal humanist. Douglass' avoidance of race in *The Heroic Slave* is all the more striking in that it contrasts sharply with his earlier depiction of Washington in an April 1849 speech, "Slavery, the Slumbering Volcano." There he presents Washington as "a black man, with woolly head, high cheek bones, protruding lip, distended nostril, and retreating forehead" (*FDP* vol. 2, 155). In the novella, the hero is "tall, symmetrical, round, and strong": "His torn sleeves disclosed arms like polished iron. His face was 'black, but comely.' His eye, lit with emotion, kept guard under a brow as dark and as glossy as the raven's wing. His whole appearance betokened Herculean strength" (*Heroic Slave* 134). In an April 1849 review published in the *North Star*, Douglass had pointed out that "Negroes can never have impartial portraits, at the hands of white artists. It seems to us next to impossible for white men to take likenesses of black men, without most grossly exaggerating their distinctive features" (*Life and Writings* [hereafter *LW*] vol. 1, 380). Yet according to Yarborough, in the novella Douglass "retreats from his attack upon the racist stereotypes that he had earlier successfully undercut" (173). It seems as if every statement of blackness contains a suggestion that beauty, harmony, strength, and "glow" (*Heroic Slave* 135) compensate for that blackness. While the association with classic sculpture does force the reader to look at the black hero's body, the possible republican connotations remain limited to an indication of neutral male beauty. Rather than a realistic description, they imply a body that needs to be "read," its external attractiveness symbolic of inner qualities that can appeal to the white reader.

Not just his body but also his love story with liberty tends to mark Washington as an inheritor of individualism. When he tells his story of running away and having to come back to the plantation after a week, he "saw my fellow-slaves seated by a warm fire, merrily passing away the time, as though their hearts knew no sorrow." As a consequence, he "despised the cowardly acquiescence in their own degradation which it implied"; indeed, "where there is seeming contentment with slavery, there is certain treachery to freedom." The notion of slave contentment had always been a sore point with Douglass; in the *Narrative* he highlighted his tragic isolation from his fellow slaves because of his knowledge of, and longing for, freedom. But increasingly during this decade, Douglass seems to connect slaves' contentment with responsibility for their victimhood. In an August 1857 speech celebrating the anniversary of West Indian emancipation, Douglass complains about "the stolid contentment, the listless indifference, the moral death which reigns over many of our people." When Senator Toombs declared that blacks were "mentally and morally inferior," "of course the slaveholder uttered a falsehood, but to many it seemed to be a truth." Indeed, "the general sentiment of mankind is, that a man who will not fight for himself, when he has the means of doing so, is not worth being fought for by others, and this sentiment is just" (*LW*, vol. 2, 435). All seems to be connected in Douglass' natural rights ideology: sympathy can arise only for people who already have a sense of their natural right to freedom, and who can thus inwardly connect with the sympathizer. This closed circle apparently excludes the wretched who, without a clear notion of their own individual self-worth, cannot make that connection and, in their difference, do not deserve liberation.

In Douglass' novella, Washington manages to transform his white observers precisely through the power of his belief in liberty. The first time Listwell hears him, "the speech of Madison rung through the chambers of his soul, and vibrated through his entire frame." As in a number of previous slave narratives, a process of almost magical or sublime inner correspondence links the sympathizer and the object of sympathy. When they properly meet five years later, Listwell tells the fugitive that ever since he saw him, "'you have seldom been absent from my mind,'" and "'from that hour, your face seemed to be daguerreotyped on my memory.'" Washington "looked quite astonished, and felt amazed" (*Heroic Slave* 138). This moment is not about republican homosocial love or about mutual recognition, but about an internal transfer made possible by a convergence of ideology. This convergence reaches a metaphorical climax when Washington describes the fire that made him leave the woods where he had been hiding for several years. He uses images of the sublime to convey his experience, calling it "horribly and indescribably grand," "awful, thrilling, solemn, beyond compare," "overwhelming, stunning" (141). It seems as if only a rhetorical flight toward the sublime can establish the most reliable connection between Washington and his listeners. Later, when he tells the story of the rebellion on board the *Creole*, Tom Grant describes a similar feeling he had when observing the rebellion's leader at the helm: "'I forgot his blackness in the dignity of his manner, and the eloquence of his speech. It seemed as if the souls of both the great dead (whose names he bore) had entered him'" (161). Grant is impressed by what he imagines inhabits Washington's interior realm; this inner connection makes him forget the blackness of Washington's body. By participating in this strategy of "obliteration," Douglass anchors his text most solidly in the politics of liberalism.

Just as Douglass' Fourth of July speech may seem naïve, one wonders at the emotional and ideological effect on his readers of his adherence to raceless liberalism. Tom Grant's monologue concludes the *Heroic Slave* story, leaving unknown how it has affected the racist Jack Williams, who had just argued precisely the opposite, that blacks do not want freedom. The question of how to confront racism remained at the heart of what strategy would best affect readers. In the North, liberal individualism could foster antislavery sentiment, but it remained weak in the face of prejudiced views of free blacks, which led many abolitionists to emphasize self-help and the development of bourgeois values in order to prove that free blacks deserved equality. In the South, liberal individualism and the spread of democracy to previously disenfranchised whites during the Jacksonian era had led to a belief that keeping blacks in bondage created the possibility of an egalitarian and democratic society for whites. By making an appeal to readers' affect based on liberalism, abolitionists hoped to bypass the reality of race, and speak at the level of a common human core. But as George M. Fredrickson points out, this approach prevented abolitionists from "perceiving the full dimensions of the American race problem." It led them to an "underestimation of the force of color prejudice" (Fredrickson 40), and it could not prevent profound reactions among whites to "a racial visibility, a palpable physical difference" (40–41). In *The Heroic Slave* Douglass appeals to "a unified national identity" (Walter 237) through Washington's adherence to an American notion of liberty, but to Jack Williams, "'a nigger's a nigger, on sea or land'" (158): to him, racial considerations always trump national ones. As long as someone like Williams was not forced into an intersubjective recognition of a black person, into an acknowledgment of equality within difference, appeals to an individual right to freedom would not suffice.

Douglass' revision, in *My Bondage and My Freedom*, of salient scenes from his *Narrative* reveals a by now comfortable appeal to the reader's liberal sympathies. In his discussion of the slave songs, Douglass quotes the moment of insight and sympathy from the *Narrative*. To Sundquist, "the passage on the slave songs insists that we read the new autobiography . . . as a sign of Douglass's recognition that in the *Narrative* he stood 'within the circle'—not of the total institution of slavery, as in the first instance, but of Garrison's radical antislavery and the defined self of the platform storyteller it provided" (92). Douglass' act of self-quoting is significant, especially since it is exceptional in a book where sentences and passages from the *Narrative* are routinely and silently integrated into the text, but it can be seen as emotionally and politically more complex. Prefacing the quote with the announcement that "I cannot better express my sense of them now, than ten years ago" (*My Bondage* 65), Douglass is acknowledging his present inability to recapture the peculiar sense of black culture he conveyed in the *Narrative*. Rather than celebrating the distance he has achieved from his former self, he may be expressing some nostalgia about a time when he was able to feel and to elicit sympathy for a cultural expression that retained its racial uniqueness. The story of his awakening to literacy contains a few added details that place it in the context of his new strong adherence to natural rights. Relating his conversations with the white boys who give him his new knowledge, he expresses his "satisfaction in wringing from the boys, occasionally, that fresh and bitter condemnation of slavery, that springs from nature, unseared and unperverted" (99). Such additions throughout the autobiography make it an official declaration of his move to liberalism. Douglass has come a long way since he escaped from slavery, and his emotional appeals to the reader mirror those changes.

Epilogue: Transnationalism and Black Studies

In a thought-provoking essay, Ann duCille addresses the relative critical silence about William Wells Brown's 1853 novel *Clotel; or, The President's Daughter: A Narrative of Slave Life in the United States*, attributing this neglect to a dislike of the bourgeois politics of the book. She quotes Addison Gayle, who in *The Way of the New World: The Black Novel in America* rejected the novel for not adhering to black nationalist demands for fiction. DuCille recommends that African-Americanists take a step back and re-evaluate works previously rejected for mirroring white models. Her plea is important, and she gives at least two reasons for it. On the one hand, she prefers to consider the book "half-open" rather than "half-closed," seeing Brown's "mastery of neo-classical diction," for example, as "a subversive deployment of the King's English to tell the slave's story" (456). On the other hand, she acknowledges Brown's bourgeois inclinations, and concludes with an appeal for more generous reading practices:

> Yes, these novels are almost as concerned with color, class, and upward mobility as their detractors say they are, but is it possible to look at that concern not simply as an anxious emulation of the values of the dominant society but as a more honest engagement with the chromosomes of culture than many writers and critics are willing to make today? Is it the embar-

rassment of our own black middle-class riches that makes this earlier pursuit of the American Dream look so bankrupt? What did it mean for a people, impoverished by slavery and denied the inalienable right to life, liberty, and the pursuit of wealth and property, to claim a middle-class persona? (460)

Rather than encouraging readers to see the novel as subversive, here she recommends a more genuine assessment of what she calls the "chromosomes of culture," as part of her DNA metaphor about the African American literary tradition and its "biological" entanglements with the white tradition. After all, she says, bourgeois liberalism did constitute an important and liberating ideology for blacks at the time.

One could contrast this position with that of Joanna Brooks, who in her review of *Genius in Bondage: Literature of the Early Black Atlantic*, a collection of essays about the eighteenth-century slave narrative, chides the editors and the contributors for not adhering to the deeper meaning of Paul Gilroy's Black Atlantic, which he defines as a "counterculture of modernity." She argues that the collection's repeated emphasis on "individualistic self-fashioning obscures the crucial importance of the late eighteenth century as a time when peoples of African descent in England and the Americas cultivated common Black identities and built new post-slavery Black communities." The notion of Black Atlantic "honors this creative, conscientious, and oppositional construction of Blackness." She is particularly aggrieved that the editors of the collection "resist the positioning of early Black literature in relation to an African-American literary tradition" (358). In doing so, they seem to behave as a new generation of insensitive intruders: "The foundational and ongoing efforts of African-Americanists have brought legitimacy, respect, and resources to the study of Black literature and culture; the attraction of early Americanists and eighteenth-century British literature specialists to early Black Atlantic literature is a comparatively recent phenomenon" (359). Were she to use the same DNA metaphor as duCille—and if chromosomes could really carry indicators of race—Brooks would see the chromosomes of the early texts primarily as indicating blackness.

This book agrees more with duCille than with Brooks, and for two reasons. First, the cosmopolitanism I observe in the black writers I discuss is, apart from a few gestures toward black nationalism among the Freemasons, of an expansive, cross-racial character. Second, this book shows the extent to which those texts were inspired by the culture of modernity. The stigmatizing of black texts as mere imitations of white texts has a long and ugly history. That critical trend fortunately died down several decades ago, thanks to calls by such critics as Henry Louis Gates, Jr., to abandon sociological reductionism for thorough and independent close readings.[1] In this book, I have revisited the notion of white influence, but this time with more sophisticated tools. The editors of *Genius in Bondage*, Vincent Carretta and Philip Gould, actually aim at underlining "the creative engagement between black and white languages in the eighteenth century" (4). They use the example of Belinda's petition to the Massachusetts legislature for her freedom, with which I start my introduction. Belinda's appeal, they observe, uses the "language and tropes of the seduction novel" (4). While this form can be seen as subversive, it can also signify a degree of ideological immersion: "Does her handling of seduction challenge racial stereotypes by incorporating black women—African women—into the world of western sympathy? Does it reproduce these stereotypes by merely victimizing them as objects of sympathetic identification? Or does it do both?" (4–5). The critics argue that we should resist "positioning early black writing within the larger, national 'story' of African American literary history" because it necessarily leads to "teleological distortions" (11). My approach similarly, and partly, places black texts within their wider cultural and political context, and examines the nature of the interaction.

The depth and the complexity of this interaction need to be explored in a way that goes beyond simple metaphors. John Sekora has famously described the slave narrative as a "black message" in a "white envelope." Rafia Zafar begins her study by emphasizing that she wants to situate the work of black writers "in close and parallel relation to the work of their European-American contemporaries" (3), acknowledging that "not very long ago, to grant African American letters any consonance with American literature as a whole was seen as a kind of cultural treachery" (4). But then she goes on to portray her study as a survey of "African American literary masks, mimicry, and invisibility" (9), without theorizing or explaining the immediate passage from the concept of influence to that of masking. Images like "envelope" and "masks," through their implication of a clear-cut binarism, needlessly simplify the complex relationship between black and white cultures as expressed in the slave narrative, and particularly the extent to which the ideologies of modernity were absorbed by black writers.

I believe that this enterprise can be helped by the new emphasis on transnationalism, and in the next few pages I will focus on the trend that currently marks the field of American studies. There is a new awareness in the field of the need to expand critical readings beyond national borders, by emphasizing cross-national contact and influence. These new approaches force the critic to take a step back, and to examine American culture from a wider perspective. They offer a mine of possibilities for the study of African American texts, in that they encourage more systematic explorations of the role played by international cross-pollinations with African American literature and philosophy. The field is rich and promising. But transnationalism, through its anchoring in comparatism, can also lead to a surprisingly different kind of project. Indeed, it can help highlight aspects of African American literature that are specific to the national soil. When critics take a step back and try to adopt a wider, transnational perspective, they can use their comparative approach to showcase the very embeddedness of black literary traditions.

The turn toward internationalism has many causes, but certainly an important one has been the need once and for all to sound the death knell of American exceptionalism. In his introduction to the collection *Post-Nationalist American Studies*, John Carlos Rowe expresses the need for a field that is "less insular and parochial" (2), and that will mark a definite break with Cold War scholarship, which tended to reproduce American myths, such as the myths of superiority and of homogeneity. He proposes a new emphasis on transnationalism and comparatism, which will focus on the ways in which different cultures are transformed by mutual contact, not only in the United States but all over the Americas and, beyond that, in the Atlantic and the Pacific worlds. American historians have been moving in a similar direction. Ian Tyrrell makes the case for a more transnationally oriented practice of American historical scholarship, urging historians to move beyond "the primacy of the national focus" (1032) and suggesting a look at the ways in which U.S. history displays variations on transnational themes. He suggests alternative approaches such as a more regional analysis, on the model of the French Annales school or studies of the Atlantic world, or a turn to a global perspective, as in the world-systems theory promoted by Immanuel Wallerstein. In order to avoid some of the weaknesses displayed by those approaches, he makes specific suggestions on international analyses in the fields of economics and trade, the environment, and organizations and movements.

American exceptionalism has traditionally been put to patriotic or conservative uses. The myth-and-symbol school brandished glorified concepts like the frontier, manifest destiny, the American dream. However, we need to look closely at what role those myths have played in cultural criticism, and to ask whether, in our current rush to go global, we are not unnecessarily throwing overboard all notions of national difference. While we are fortunately moving (and have been, slowly, since the 1960s) beyond homogenized visions of American historical and ideological formations, we should not lose sight of the specific experiences and ideas that have made the United States into what it is today.[2] Even if we may wish that there were no nations at all, and look forward to a world less defined along national lines, as scholars we cannot deny that the idea of national identity and difference has shaped the cultures we are studying for more than two centuries. The identification of difference does not need to be celebratory. In a response to the Tyrrell article, Michael McGerr asks why we need to get rid of all notions of American difference; indeed, Tyrrell "does not deal with the evidence for American national exceptionalism or distinctiveness" (1056). Even the world-systems theory, he says, combines transnationalism with the concept of national uniqueness. Heinz Ickstadt points out that the rage for transnationalism in American studies seems to come from American more than from European scholars; he quotes Rob Kroes, a Dutch Americanist, who recently wondered whether we are moving toward a critical split, with transnational American studies in America and national American studies in Europe.[3]

A productive paradigm is offered by Paul Giles in his book *Virtual Americas: Transnational Fictions and the Transatlantic Imaginary*. Giles advocates a transnational approach to American literature and culture. By looking at cultural formations from a transnational, comparative angle, or by locating such comparative moments within those formations, the critic is able to highlight "the assumptions framing these narratives and the ways they are intertwined with the construction and reproduction of national mythologies" (Giles, *Virtual* 2). Such a method brings forward dimensions that had heretofore remained "virtual" or suppressed. In its consistently transnational perspective, Giles' project moves the angle of vision outside national boundaries, making the act of looking inside more unsettling, defamiliarizing, and ultimately critical, than previous approaches had allowed. What does the transnational approach consist in, and who could practice it? In a *Journal of American Studies* essay, Giles points out the potential for defamiliarization inherent in the foreign perspective, its possible ability to explode old assumptions, to undermine "the validity of rhetorical claims to speak from a privileged position 'within' any given culture" ("Reconstructing" 354). He speaks as a British scholar, but he reminds us that he is not advocating essentializing or privileging one's marginal positions. The demystification of cultural assumptions is first and foremost a question of methodology, of a willing suspension of belief, not of the critic's identity.

Comparatism is of course not new—indeed, it is a precondition for all forms of American exceptionalism. In the first chapter of *The Liberal Tradition in America*, Louis Hartz pointed out that American historians had not sufficiently been grounding their analyses in a contrastive approach with European history and politics. He asked: "How can we know the uniqueness of anything except by contrasting it with what is not unique?" (4). It was his "journey to Europe and back" (5) that allowed him to build his case: that the United States is and has always been grounded in the political philosophy of liberalism. While his stance may sound like run-of-the-mill Cold War nationalism, Hartz actually practiced exceptionalism-with-a-difference. Just as Richard Hofstadter had tried, in *The American Political Tradition*, to open the nation's eyes to its long-standing commitment to self-interest, Hartz partly argued that ambient liberalism had always crippled the development of a genuine left-wing tradition on American soil. But exceptionalism it remained, with its tendency to whitewash conflicts and suppress contradictory evidence. I would say that Giles echoes Hartz precisely because he remedies this major weakness, throwing away the bathwater but keeping the baby. They both use international comparatism to uncover ideologies that are too ambient to be noticed, a bit like the oxygen we breathe.

This transnational perspective offers a new paradigm for the study of African American and Afro-British texts. Here the method of estrangement involves a double movement rather than a simple one. Let's take African American texts, for example. For a long time they have been assumed to occupy an ideological position vis-à-vis a transcendent American spirit. A transnational, comparatist approach can help throw light, not just on the subversiveness or oppositionality of those texts, but also on currently underemphasized aspects, such as their actual reflection of American culture. While I have identified important forms of radicalization, I have also emphasized the subtle but very American nature of political ideology in those texts, compared with the different forms taken by liberalism and republicanism in European, in this case British, political traditions. Internationalism works here as a hermeneutic device for the critic, and can partly help highlight, besides their subversiveness and international dimension, the national embeddedness of texts.

Giles points out, regarding his comments on Henry Thoreau, after he has underlined Thoreau's participation in the capitalist economy, that this is not to "recapitulate that too familiar critical move where a text that appears oppositional is said ultimately to be complicit with the culture that frames it" (*Virtual* 13). Ever since Michel Foucault, and Foucault-inspired critics such as Ross Chambers, it has indeed become a critical commonplace that oppositional texts work from within the culture they oppose rather than as utopian outsiders. The aim here has been to examine the perpetual give-and-take in those texts, and partly to underline the ways in which they were fed by the soil in which they grew. This approach, born of a comparatist sensibility, has helped me complicate our readings of texts that, if they describe black experiences, also participate in the discourses of modernity.

Notes

Preface (pages ix–10)

1. Little has been written about the influence of sentiment on the slave narrative. Books about the slave narrative have usually extracted it from its political and philosophical context in order to emphasize a genealogical line connecting all slave narratives, as well as linking that genre with subsequent African American fiction. With her pioneering study, Marion Wilson Starling established the slave narrative as a major genre. Robert B. Stepto elaborated an interesting theory that African American narrative is based on the role of authentication and narration in the original slave narrative. William L. Andrews traced the evolution of an increasingly free and independent narrator's voice. Frances Smith Foster's book went the furthest in situating the slave narrative within its social and cultural context. The sentimental novel is often mentioned in discussions of Harriet Jacobs' narrative, but with the implication that sentiment is confined to seduction plots and to melodramatic appeals to the "dear reader."

2. It does play a role in debates taking place among contemporary political philosophers, though, such as Quentin Skinner and Charles Taylor.

Introduction (pages 1–32)

1. Since this document is most likely a transcription of an oral narrative, the question of attribution is thorny. According to Sharon M. Harris, Belinda's text "was narrated to an unidentified transcriber, but he or she *translated* this African woman's oral narrative into conventional late eighteenth-century discourse that romanticizes the autobiographical elements of Belinda's early life and invokes the language of the law that has perpetuated the system of slavery-at the same time that it seeks recourse from that system" ("Whose Past" 178). Roy E. Finkenbine highlights the radical idea of reparation at the heart of the petition.

2. John Saillant draws attention to the erotic dimension of the text, comparing the struggle to "a morbid travesty of sexual intercourse" ("Black Body" 97).

3. The current American meaning of "liberal" as left-leaning or progressive is much more recent, and particular to the United States and Britain.

4. Ann Douglas and Jane Tompkins sparked a lively debate on the progressive or the conservative dimensions of the American turn to sentiment in the eighteenth century, and of its entrenchment in American culture in the nineteenth. More recently, Michelle Burnham, Bruce Burgett, and Julia Stern have shown links between feeling and politics in American texts from the colonial period to the Civil War. Markman Ellis has offered a critique of British sensibility along similar lines.

5. Antislavery has also been subjected to political assessments. Ever since the end of the Civil War, the historiography of abolitionism has moved back and forth between praise for the abolitionists' revolutionary activities, and an emphasis on their social and political conservatism. Recently Thomas L. Haskell and David Brion Davis conducted a robust exchange about the complex processes that connected humanitarianism to capitalism in the age of the Enlightenment. Philip Gould, Vincent Carretta, and Srinivas Aravamudan have explored some political nuances of eighteenth-century antislavery texts, and a recent study by Brycchan Carey offers a rhetorical analysis of sentiment in abolitionism.

6. These are the terms commonly used in the debate, even though *liberalism* is technically an anachronism, since its use as a term designating a specific political ideology only appeared in the first half of the nineteenth century. *Republicanism* has the specific meaning of civic humanism or neo-Roman thought. Much writing about the period uses the term *republicanism* in a broader fashion.

7. The writers range from Henry Neville, Algernon Sidney, and James Harrington in the seventeenth century to John Trenchard, Thomas Gordon, and Richard Price in the next.

8. As Drew R. McCoy points out, this new interest helped place the Revolution within its idiosyncratic ideological context, and helped scholars to understand "the integrity of a political culture whose differentness, even 'foreignness,' twentieth-century scholars had generally underestimated or failed to recognize" (13).

9. To Bailyn, though, the opposition thinkers' key concepts, such as "natural rights, the contractual basis of society and government, the uniqueness of England's liberty-preserving 'mixed' constitution" were "commonplaces of the liberal thought of the time" (45).

10. In their eagerness to find an alternative to liberalism, many critics have embraced republicanism as the welcome missing link. As Mark Hulliung puts it, they have "conjured up a history of the United States wherein moral and rooted republicans once held sway until amoral and uprooted liberals gained the upper hand" (xi).

11. My argument does not use the opposition of the public and the private, or of the abstract and the concrete, that have become predominant in definitions of liberalism and republicanism by literary critics. Inspired by Jürgen Habermas' book on the liberal public sphere, many critics associate this sphere with republicanism, even though he clearly distinguishes his model from the classical one, in which human identity takes its source in "the public sphere itself" (*Structural Transformation* 51). What ultimately distinguishes a liberal from a republican public sphere has to do less with its superficial structure than with its inner dy-

namics. Since both republicanism and liberalism involve imagination and transcendence, the presence of one particular political vision can best be detected when we focus on content, or on the question of whose interests are being served. Elizabeth Maddock Dillon states the issue clearly: "Given that entry into the print public sphere (republican or liberal, public-minded or privately oriented) requires an act of imagination, what would seem to distinguish the two acts is the content of what is imagined rather than the active or passive nature of the engagement" (*Gender* 39). In liberalism, "the intimate sphere becomes both the origin and the telos of liberal subjectivity" (28); republicanism, on the other hand, "sees the public sphere as telos-as the site where virtue is established through concern with the public good (rather than with private property)" (262). All the texts I discuss entered the "public sphere," but they still have discrepant political messages. Michael Warner argues that Americans in the eighteenth century associated print culture with a republican message, but several eighteenth-century texts discussed in this book show that both political outlooks were present in the public sphere.

12. Many agree, for example, on a chronological transition from republicanism to liberalism, even if they disagree on the timing of that shift. Wood, for example, sees the shift happening during the debates on the Constitution, as he sees a change in notions of political representation, which led to the innovative concept of a separation of powers. Other historians place it later. See Rodgers.

13. Lee Ward points out, for example, that "the colonists held traditional British liberties like habeas corpus and jury trials not as products of custom and prescription but as individual natural rights, and saw the Glorious Revolution of 1688 as a popular revolution against tyranny" (17).

14. James T. Kloppenberg, who argues for the presence of three major ideologies during the Revolution-liberalism, republicanism, and Protestant Christianity-says that these "three streams almost immediately diverged" (10). There is general agreement on the increased predominance of liberalism in antebellum America, in parallel with the expansion of capitalism.

15. In the rest of the essay, Laqueur does show how various discourses on the body, such as forensic analysis, could serve a number of social goals.

16. Paracelsus found, for example, that "a festering sore on the foot . . . was best cured by finding a plant resembling the foot" (Male 20). Digby proposed applying plasters and salves to the instruments responsible for the bruise or cut.

17. The growing importance of inner space can be more generally considered part of the rise of modernity. David J. Denby argues that the sentimental text was based on an axis between interiority and exteriority, and that descriptions of suffering bodies functioned to "extérioriser une expérience intérieure" (378). This general emphasis on interiority and individualism in the culture of sensibility has also been tied to the rise of consumerism. G. J. Barker-Benfield argues that, because of a variety of improvements in the satisfaction of everyday needs and a consequent rise in living standards, the British middle class slowly developed a different attitude toward suffering and bodily pain. The new consumerism, while it provided for the body, allowed what he calls "the 'luxury' of feelings" (xxvi). At the same time, just as commercial capitalism fostered skepticism about an increasingly materialistic culture (what Simon Schama, referring to Holland, has

punningly called an "embarrassment of riches"), the middle class tried to detach itself from the materialist underpinnings of sensibility, in order to promote its more refined dimensions. Because "transcendence of subsistence" (56) became possible, society developed more concern with morals, respectability, and reform. Barker-Benfield refers to the thesis of Norbert Elias, who in *The Civilizing Process* highlights increasingly abundant Western standards of shame, delicacy, and self-control. Indeed, in her discussion of Laurence Sterne, Van Sant points out that the combination of microscopic analysis of the organs of sensibility with growing standards of refinement "paradoxically became the basis for an imagined immateriality of the body" (105). Sensibility thus slowly came to be "opposed to the material and sensual" (106). In Henry Mackenzie's novel *The Man of Feeling* (1771), for example, the main character "hardly has a body" (110).

18. Smith's philosophy was clearly anchored in processes of imagination and interiority, yet much has been made of his repeated use of the term "spectator." David Marshall, for example, argues that the theatrical nature of the situation of sympathy "becomes not only explicit but problematic for Smith" (594). But theatricality has an elastic meaning in Marshall's essay, referring to anything from the mere act of looking to the notion of spectacle. Smith was trying to strike a balance. The situation of sympathy necessitates the staging of the body, which involves a moment of spectatorship. But the body seems to act as a mere prop, as a pretext for the vital act of imaginative identification. Smith does not really bemoan the impossibility of total identification since, as Marshall points out, it would lead to a loss of the self. Sympathy makes possible a merging of selves, while preserving their integrity. The process can derail, through either excessive distance or excessive immersion. To Smith, proper balance is the key.

19. It is also quite probable that it is this aspect, more than Smith's civic humanist streak, that became associated with his philosophy in the wider culture.

20. *Self-control* is another one of those terms that was used freely in the service of either liberal or republican views, and whose meaning thus depends on context.

21. The modern equivalent for this form of political sentiment would be something along the lines of solidarity. Jürgen Habermas tries to develop such a concept, in his response to Lawrence Kohlberg. According to Kohlberg, sympathy "understands that one's perception of persons and their construction of interests in terms of life plans are not independent of contingencies such as psychological, social, structural, historical, and cultural factors" (166). Engaging in sympathy in this case definitely goes beyond the interior connection depicted by Smith. But Habermas still deems this insufficient. He develops the concept of solidarity, which maintains "the integrity of the lifeworld that makes possible their shared interpersonal relationships and relations of mutual recognition" (243). "Empathy" (247) is preserved, but as it plays a role in elements of the good in his concept of solidarity. Amanda Anderson has criticized Habermas for a perspective she deems too universal. Approving of Seyla Benhabib's analysis in *Critique, Norm, and Utopia*, she points out how "the perspective of the concrete other introduces the more concretely realized ethical principle of care, friendship, empathy, solidarity, and intimacy" (83). But if Habermas may be said to ignore

racial issues in his abstract concept of solidarity, Anderson's ethics of care look to me too much like punctual liberal sympathy.

22. Anthony Ashley Cooper, 3rd Earl of Shaftesbury, is usually considered the founder of the moral sense school. For an overview, see Janet Todd.

23. The phrase "sentimental novel" conjures up a wide variety of configurations, such as heterosexual seduction plots à la Samuel Richardson, tales of sentimental travelers encountering various suffering beings along their way, or stories of lovely natives sold into slavery by their ungrateful lovers. The genre extends into tales of resistance to various forms of seduction, such as sex or alcohol, or of oppression and slavery. Sentiment and sensibility, moreover, suffused many works that did not fit the narrow definition of novel of seduction or sentimental novel. In the United States, the theme of seduction gave way to domestic fiction or to what Nina Baym has called "woman's fiction," in both of which sympathy continued to play an important role, and feeling was an explicit theme in works by both male and female writers about a wide range of topics. Taken together, these works may seem like a succession of attempts to deal with a wide variety of issues by applying one formula, always the same-the attempt to make readers relate to particular characters and their tribulations in exclusively emotional terms.

24. See, for example, work by Nancy Armstrong, Elizabeth Barnes, Bruce Burgett, Elizabeth Maddock Dillon, Julie Ellison, Glenn Hendler, Jane Tompkins, Julia A. Stern, all of whom I will refer to in the following chapters.

25. Douglas condemned sentimentalism because it "provided the inevitable rationalization of the economic order" (12) and was a poor substitute for what she saw as the virile power of Calvinism. She deplored its anti-intellectualism, its trite historical consciousness, its focus on the particular and the individual. Tompkins argued that *Uncle Tom's Cabin*, hence the sentimental novel, used sentimentalism in order to "work in, and change, the world" (130): by "resting her case, absolutely, on the saving power of Christian love and on the sanctity of motherhood and the family, Stowe relocates the center of power in American life, placing it not in the government, not in the courts of law, nor in the factories, nor in the marketplace, but in the kitchen" (145).

26. Marriage and heterosexual love played an important role in both visions. Because of an increased emphasis on love and consent, marriage became imbued with notions of agency and freedom, even as its sexist ideology ensured the stability of a conservative order. While for all practical purposes both political ideologies kept women second-rank citizens, and so may not seem to have been that far apart on the subject (see Dillon), in marriage the substance of feeling changed, reflecting the gradual shift in emphasis from civic to private values, from republicanism to liberalism.

27. Douglas also points out differences between forms of sentiment in British and American Victorian culture, and underlines a greater "cohesiveness" (6) in Victorian England.

28. As Cathy N. Davidson points out, when discussing the early American novel, many characters liberated themselves in a way that "takes on many of the features of classical liberalism of the Adam Smith variety." By doing so, they rep-

resent the energy and the new feeling of freedom engendered by individualism and rebellion. But liberalism was also the "bugaboo" because "liberalism, far from mandating a revolutionary restructuring of society, merely opens the way for a different social hegemony with its own possibilities for oppression and exploitation" (*Revolution* 217). Liberal sentiment imposed an inner form of discipline meant to replace the sort of order previously imposed by an overtly patriarchal society. Increasingly as the nation moved toward the Civil War, this "bugaboo" became predominant.

29. The main argument is that liberalism's anchoring in rationality invites exclusion of what does not qualify as rational.

30. Rogers M. Smith defends a "multiple traditions view" (6), ascribing racism to "inegalitarian ascriptive traditions of Americanism" (3) that are autonomous from the two predominant moral and political visions that are liberalism and republicanism. Hulliung also argues that racism and illiberalism stand on the outside of each political tradition even as they perpetually infiltrate it.

31. In her introduction to *The Culture of Sentiment*, Shirley Samuels poses the issue of embodiment in the literature of sentiment as unresolved. She takes as an example the deaths of Eva and of Tom in *Uncle Tom's Cabin*, where Eva is "radically spiritualized," and Tom shown to go through "an escape from or transcendence of the body." Critical commentary has swerved between "a *dismissal* of the sentimental move outside or beyond the boundaries of a gendered or racialized body," and "a celebration of the emancipatory strategies of a sentimentality that *rescues* subjects from the unfortunate essentializing that the fact of having a body entails" (5). This book neither dismisses nor celebrates the attempted escape from the body. It presents liberal appeals as partly liberatory and partly oppressive.

32. As Rogers M. Smith puts it, "democratic republican conceptions of civic identity . . . can also have strongly egalitarian implications" (37). Smith argues that the ascriptive, inegalitarian tradition in America provided a civic myth that nurtured civic pride in a way that the hard-to-achieve goals of liberalism and republicanism could not. My argument is that, overall, liberalism is less well equipped than republicanism to counter that ascriptive tradition.

33. From this perspective, it is interesting to note that the growth of liberalism in the young United States went parallel with a stronger institutional effort to define the nation in terms of race and gender, as can be seen in the Naturalization Act of 1790 and the Alien and Sedition Acts.

34. Identification constitutes a major, and controversial, concept in the fields of psychology and psychoanalysis. Diana Fuss points to the problem of linking the process of identification with politics, reminding us that "the unconscious plays a formative role in the production of identifications, and it is a formidable (not to say impossible) task for the political subject to exert any steady or lasting control over them" (9). But she also highlights the many uncertainties around that very process, asking (and not answering) such questions as: "Are identifications conscious or unconscious? active or passive? immediate or belated? creative or lethal?" (10). While these issues constitute an important dimension of any form of identification, they do not in any way determine an analysis of the political subtleties involved in the process.

35. Saidiya V. Hartman shows the workings of liberal sympathy when she analyzes the way John Rankin, a white commentator on American slavery, imagines a scenario in which his wife and children are enslaved. As she points out, "the phantasmic vehicle of this identification is complicated, unsettling, and disturbing" (18). Part of what makes it disturbing is the way Rankin needs to project himself into the racial other in order to feel sympathy, thus exacerbating "the idea that black sentience is inconceivable and unimaginable." It shows that white sympathy "requires that the white body be positioned in the place of the black body in order to make this suffering visible and intelligible" (19).

36. Burgett's book similarly complicates the role of the body in sentimentalism, but his focus is more on its contradictory uses for private and public purposes.

37. "One sometimes uses this word in jest, to mean a man who has no fixed abode, or a man who doesn't feel a stranger anywhere." The entry refers the reader to the word "philosophe," implying a direct connection between cosmopolitanism and Enlightenment ideals.

38. I do not want to associate black writers with what Kwame Anthony Appiah calls "cosmopolitan patriots," who "can entertain the possibility of a world in which everyone is a rooted cosmopolitan, attached to a home of his or her own, with its own cultural particularities, but taking pleasure from the presence of other, different, places that are home to other, different, people" (22). Many of the writers discussed here do not have such a "home," and their brand of cosmopolitanism is marked by this unique characteristic.

39. That cosmopolitanism is a dynamic concept open to different interpretations is emphasized by the collection of essays edited by Gillian Brock and Harry Brighouse. As they put it in the introduction, the "precise content" of the "responsibilities" implied by the term is "widely disputed among cosmopolitans." They consequently distinguish between "*weak*" and "*strong*" (3) cosmopolitanism.

40. So I make a distinction that Appiah does not make. Appiah defines liberal cosmopolitanism, which he opposes to humanism, as follows: "So long as these [cultural] differences meet certain general ethical constraints-so long, in particular, as political institutions respect basic human rights-we are happy to let them be" (26). I introduce the concept of republican cosmopolitanism as the extension into the global arena of the alternative to this liberal "hands-off" approach.

41. In the rest of the book, Robbins discusses a number of issues and texts that to him illustrate his theory. The fact that internationalists of all stripes still recognize the importance of the welfare state, for example, proves that we need an alliance between cosmopolitanism and the new nationalism. In another example, he quotes from Andrew Ross's attack on ecological internationalism where, in language that could have been lifted from the pages of the *Economist,* Ross dismisses the "scarcity, voluntary poverty, and asceticism" that mark the "fierce evangelical tendency among environmentalists" (qtd. in Robbins 58) as a bad strategy in the face of Western "hedonism." While Robbins acknowledges the existence of "objective daily scarcity in the world beyond our borders" (58), he is still looking for an alternative to "quasi-religious fervor" that could "win broad U.S. support" (59). In another discussion, he questions the assumption that "all feeling is national feeling." He is puzzled by Benedict Anderson's distinction between the

"'deep, horizontal comradeship'" (69) of the nation and his colder assessment of international involvement-who would want to die for the European Union, asks Anderson? Robbins then asks how Anderson then accounts for the existence of the Abraham Lincoln Brigade or Médecins sans Frontières. If feelings are produced at the national level, what prevents us from extending them beyond the national borders? He asks: "If there can be an 'emotion of national pride,' then why not emotions of international pride, based on a horizontal comradeship across the formal equality of nations?" (70). Even Martha Nussbaum, he points out, in her 1994 essay "Patriotism and Cosmopolitanism," finds herself having to acknowledge the importance of love for the building of internationalism.

42. Similarly, Anderson's national model might not be extensible precisely because it is based on the sort of liberal transcendence that makes nationalism problematic in the first place.

43. In her "Reply," Nussbaum notes that many of her critics find universalism "boring," and states: "I am astonished that so many distinguished writers should make this suggestion" (139).

44. See "Beyond the Social Contract," in which Nussbaum defends "fellowship" against the "self-interest" inherent in social-contract theories (198), and offers a thicker or more positive description of international duty. Our goal, she says, "is not merely 'negative liberty'" (211).

45. The decision of which texts qualify as African American and which ones as Afro-British is sometimes difficult. My main criterion has been the amount of time a writer resided in a particular country. Vincent Carretta calls them all Afro-Britons because "all were subjects of the British monarch before the American Revolution, and many chose to remain so during and after that event, continuing to identify themselves as Afro-Britons rather than embracing the new political identity of African-Americans subject to the government of the United States." Still, he acknowledges that some of them "accepted, with varying degrees of enthusiasm, the new status of being African-Americans" ("Phillis Wheatley" 201). On the basis of that distinction, our differences are that I classify Gronniosaw and Marrant as African American.

Chapter 1: Interiority, Aesthetics, and Antislavery Sentiment (pages 33–83)

1. See, for example, Ian Hunter, who places aesthetics within a history of "'practices of the self'" (359), as part of a new "inwardness" and "attention to subjective states" (360).

2. The progressive potential of aesthetics (long relegated to the realm of bourgeois ideology) has been recently revived by some critics. See the special issue of *American Literature* edited by Christopher Castiglia and Russ Castronovo.

3. "Did not her fingers trace these beautiful, expanding flowers?-Did not she give to this carnation its animated glow, and to this opening rose its languishing grace?" (W. Brown 31).

4. Thanks to physiognomy, "the sentimental fictions of the 1760s and 1770s turn-or return-empiricism to a mystical system of interpretation" (Benedict 312).

5. Together they form what Nancy Armstrong calls the "household" ("Why Daughters" 11), which is open to extraneous elements, as opposed to the "patrilineal family," which "abhors a mixture" (12).

6. Ellen Pollak also links the predominance of incest narratives in the eighteenth century to the rise of liberalism, as the patriarchal social order is replaced by an apparently "'affective'" (13) nuclear family, where gender inequality subsists on other, more biological, grounds. To Barnes, what is presented as a seductive but dangerous element in the early national novel will turn into the "positive model of familial bonding" in the nineteenth-century domestic novel (15).

7. Ruth Bloch traces the development of the concept of virtue from this republican meaning to an increasingly feminine quality, with attributes like "'modesty,' 'tenderness,' 'delicacy,' and 'sensibility'" (51), in tune with a liberal focus on internal morality.

8. For more on Sterne, see the section on Ignatius Sancho below.

9. Critics have recently shown more interest in early American interiority, as shown by a special issue of *Early American Literature* edited by Christopher Castiglia and Julia Stern.

10. Similarly, Joy S. Kasson shows how commentators on Hiram Powers' sculpture *The Greek Slave* directed the gaze away from bodily beauty to emphasize moral values.

11. Aesthetic theory as a discipline was born in Germany, where the philosopher Alexander Gottlieb Baumgarten coined the word *aesthetic*. The first few decades of the eighteenth century "have a real claim to be the moment of the origin of modern aesthetics" (Guyer 15). As Paul O. Kristeller showed a few decades ago, dominating concepts of modern aesthetics such as "taste and sentiment, genius, originality and creative imagination did not assume their definite modern meaning before the eighteenth century" (497), and the very idea of fine arts as constituting a separate system appeared at the same time.

12. The rise of evangelicalism in the course of the eighteenth century considerably strengthened the religious focus on interiority.

13. This opening is a translation from William Ames' *De conscientia, et eius iure, vel casibus* (1623).

14. He seems to oppose "outward Comforts of Life" to what would be an interior quality of liberty.

15. "Extravasat" blood means "blood forced out of its proper vessels" (20).

16. Because of their many transatlantic contacts the Quakers form an idiosyncratic group in terms of national identity. Both John Woolman and Anthony Benezet are discussed in other parts of this book.

17. Jordan points out that "as a people set apart from others they were inclined to dwell introspectively on their own peculiarities" (272).

18. According to J. Herbert Fretz, the real motivation for this petition "is a moot question." While he thinks it most likely that the petitioners were inspired by their Mennonite background, he also offers the possibility that they may have had discussions while staying with Benjamin Furley, William Penn's agent in Rotterdam, who was "influenced by continental influences" (53).

19. For a specific account, see Henry J. Cadbury.

20. See Joanna Brooks, *American Lazarus* 29–30.

21. Interestingly, Brooks attributes this weakness to a "negative valuation of race: it did not signify salvation or damnation; it did *not* matter to God" (*American Lazarus* 31). It is tempting to see a parallel with the negative definition of freedom that is the hallmark of liberalism.

22. In a 1773 letter to Robert Pleasants, for example, the famous Patrick Henry deplores the existence of slavery "at a time, when the rights of Humanity are defined" (221), yet acknowledges that "I am drawn along by the general inconveniency of living without them [the slaves]" (222).

23. He refers to "a late decision in favor of a Virginia slave, at Westminster-Hall" (Rush 229).

24. As we will see in chapter 3, a black Methodist such as John Marrant also transformed the stress on interiority, by developing a more republican, black-identified theology.

25. See John Saillant's *Black Puritan, Black Republican* for a thorough discussion of the belief in a new dispensation, which offered a new interpretation of the Old Testament anchored in things spiritual.

26. The combination of rights with the idea of security marks the text as republican. See Philip Pettit, who makes a distinction between liberal freedom, which means being free from interference, and republican freedom, for which "what is also necessary is that the agent be protected against interference, that she be given guarantees which help to ensure against interference" (165).

27. The date is not quite certain.

28. Henry Louis Gates, Jr., famously identified the trope, which made its first English appearance in this text, and reappeared with revisions in subsequent narratives.

29. For more on the republican world of the ships, see chapter 2.

30. John Shields follows a more radical interpretation, but is at pains to explain why London reviewers did not remark on the poem: "Perhaps the reviewers, as most of her critics and commentators have been, were too bedazzled by the 'improbability' that a black woman could produce such a volume to take the content of her poetry seriously" (235). But Wheatley and her publisher found it likely that the critics would take her seriously when they decided to remove several political poems mentioned in the 1772 proposal, such as "On the Arrival of the Ships of War, and Landing of the Troops," and "On the Affray in King-Street, on the Evening of the 5th of March." More probably the reviewers felt a tone of reconciliation in the Dartmouth poem.

31. Kendrick sees a connection between Wheatley and Emmanuel Lévinas' theory of ethics, which emphasizes a real look at the face of the other: "Like Lévinas, Wheatley will not allow the reader to reduce her alterity by seeing her as within mastery's frame of the Same, nor will she allow her audience to reduce her to the radically absolutely Other" (51).

32. John C. Shields aptly refers to this trait as to the desire to "unbody [one's] own mind" (252).

33. See also Shields.

34. This poem was listed in the 1772 proposal she ran in the Boston newspapers, and dated 1768. The hymns were not listed in the 1772 proposal.

35. In her distinction between the sublime and the beautiful, she may also be said to anticipate Immanuel Kant. In his aesthetics, Kant distinguishes the beautiful, which derives from "a satisfaction in the Object," from the sublime, anchored "in the extension of the Imagination by itself" (108): it is "the state of mind produced by a certain representation with which the reflective Judgment is occupied, and not the Object, that is to be called sublime" (110). The Kantian sublime occurs whenever the imagination, faced with extreme magnitude or with infinity, tries to comprehend it and almost simultaneously recoils from the impossible task: "the feeling of sublime is therefore a feeling of pain, arising from the want of accordance between the aesthetical estimation of magnitude formed by the Imagination and the estimation of the same formed by Reason," so that "there is at the same time a pleasure thus excited" (119). Shields also sees Wheatley's attempt to portray immensity and her play between reason and imagination as an anticipation of the Kantian sublime. I want to emphasize that she is also interested in the other side of the equation, beauty.

36. They include "On Imagination," "To Maecenas," "To S.M. a Young African Painter, on Seeing His Works," "To the Rev. Dr. Thomas Amory, on Reading His Sermons on Daily Devotion," "Niobe in Distress for Her Children Slain by Apollo, from Ovid's Metamorphoses, Book VI. and from a View of the Painting of Mr. Richard Wilson," and "Isaiah LXIII.1-8." These poems were not included in the 1772 proposal.

37. This ethos comes up in her writing. Reading her letters, for example, tells us that Wheatley worked with the commercial ideology of her time. A Boston businessman commented that she was an "'artful jade'" (Grimsted 351), and a 1773 letter says about her poems that she was "'stopped by her friends from printing them here and was made to expect a large emolument if she sent the copy home'" (352). Especially after her return from England in the fall of 1773, she displayed a new awareness of the commercial possibilities of her recently published book, *Poems on Various Subjects, Religious and Moral*. Her third letter to her friend and fellow slave Obour Tanner, with whom her exchanges had until then remained on high, spiritual grounds, offers a surprising alternation of high-flown religious declarations with material considerations. After referring to "our dependence on the Deity," she mentions the "Benevolent conduct" and "the unexpected, and unmerited civility and Complaisance" (Mason 198) with which she was received in England. Then she switches back to the "sufferings of the Son of God" but, responding to a remark by Obour, expands on Esau's story, concluding: "Dear Obour let us not sell our Birth right for a thousand worlds," as if she were particularly aware of that danger at that time in her life. After closing, she adds: "I enclose Proposals for my Book, and beg youd use your interest to get Subscriptions as it is for my Benefit" (199). Another letter addressed to Obour from May 6, 1774, displays a similar mix. Obviously Wheatley is developing a consciousness of herself as a participant in liberal market exchanges, and the fact that she was emancipated during this period certainly enhanced that feeling.

38. A British reviewer states the following: "We are much concerned to find

that this ingenious young woman is yet a slave. The people of Boston boast themselves chiefly on their principles of liberty. One such act as the purchase of her freedom, would, in our opinion, have done more honour than hanging a thousand trees with ribbons and emblems" (Robinson 31). Obviously Wheatley is here used as a pawn in the confrontation between Britain and its rebellious colony.

39. See chapter 3 for parallels between brotherhood, homosocial friendship, and republicanism.

40. Hutcheson deplores that "innocent children of captives in war, or of men of a different complexion, are detained as slaves for ever, with all their posterity, upon no other pretence of right than this claim upon them for their maintenance; as if such were not of our species, and had not bodies and souls of the same feelings with our own" (vol. 2, 81).

41. John Witherspoon, for example, president of the College of New Jersey, gave lectures inspired by Hutcheson's moral sense philosophy, as well as by his concept of natural liberty. David Fate Norton singles out Francis Alison, chair of moral philosophy at the College of Philadelphia, as an adept and propagator of Hutcheson's theory. Many historians have emphasized the long-lasting impact of the Scottish Enlightenment in Britain and America, through philosophers such as Lord Kames and Thomas Reid. As Terence Martin points out, such influence operated as "a philosophy of containment" (11); it can explain how James Wilson, an active participant in the Revolution, could also be characterized as "a leader of the conservatives during 'the counter-revolutionary period'" (9), combining his sense of liberty with his devotion to social order. Antislavery thought on both sides of the continent originally owed much to the idea of benevolence as expounded by Hutcheson.

42. Much also depended on the question whether the Joint Opinion was valid: two legal officials who had been invited to a dinner at Lincoln's Inn in 1729 had asserted that a slave remained a slave, even in England.

43. Interestingly, Northern free states, which had abolished slavery on the basis of natural rights, did not go as far as the Somerset case in their handling of cases where Southern slaves reached Northern territory. Indeed, for a few decades, "Northern and Southern courts reached a not uncomfortable accommodation; slaves who lived permanently in a free state were free, Northern judges declared, but slaves who lived temporarily in a free state remained slaves." It seems that the theory of natural rights could not trump this "spirit of comity" (Wise 202). But those laws were gradually repealed, often by judges who invoked the Mansfield decision. For a different assessment of Mansfield's decision, which alleges that it was not as far-reaching as most people thought, see Jerome Nadelhaft.

44. This kind of passage could certainly fuel David Brion Davis' contention that abolitionism indirectly helped muddle the issue of capitalist exploitation at home.

45. Prince Hoare points out that Sharp "contends against the doctrine of *self-love* being the sole ruling principle in the human mind," and that he considers "the knowledge of good and evil" and "the principle of *reciprocal consideration*" (514) at least equally strong. Liberty was "his darling object," but as "regulated

by the view of his religious and social obligations." His law was that of "the liberty of mutual beneficence" (516).

46. In a later discussion about a different book, Ellis writes a similar sentence, but ends with a variation: the trite element-in this case, a lapdog-"leads nowhere: it is a closing-off device, diffusing enquiry into an amiable and placid equanimity approaching quietism" (*Politics* 98).

47. Unlike Ellis, I do not necessarily oppose this to the sublime. As we saw with Wheatley, the sublime can be anchored in interior, individual emotion.

48. Sterne's Anglican religious vision similarly blends personal feeling with a more portentous sense of duty. In fact, according to Tim Parnell, Sterne's Anglican theology constitutes the "most fruitful context" in order to understand his sentimentalism. Ever since the publication of R. S. Crane's article in 1934, the religious foundations of sentimentalism have been associated with latitudinarianism and its supposed rejection of Puritan dogma. But as Donald Greene points out, latitudinarians were neither Pelagians (justification comes by works alone) nor Arminians (opposed to the idea of predestination), and they did believe in original sin. "Far from endorsing the naïvely optimistic view of the fundamental goodness of human nature that is often attributed to them," Parnell continues, "Sterne and his fellow Anglicans, throughout the long eighteenth century, recommended the social virtues in a way that was both tough-minded and 'sentimental.'" Indeed, throughout the eighteenth century, "the Anglican insistence on the importance of pity, sympathy and philanthropy had as much to do with the effort to stir and cajole congregations into the kind of 'right' belief and 'right' behaviour that would most conduce to society's 'Happiness and Defence' as it did with the recommendation of certain virtues for their own sake" (124). The Anglican emphasis on benevolence involved less the celebration of fellow feeling than the hope to achieve an orderly and morally reformed society. Madeleine Descargues points out that Anglicans/latitudinarians wanted to distinguish themselves both from Catholics, who risked cutting themselves off from spirituality, and from dissidents like Methodists, who relied exclusively on an interior, individual experience. Anglicanism was "hostile aux radicalismes et aux excès" (330). That Sterne adhered to these positions reinforces the idea that he contributed to an attempt at political balance in British sentimental texts.

49. The fact that he recommends Bossuet to several correspondents shows an interesting desire to spread visions of universal rather than of national history.

50. Interestingly, Sancho does not refer to the Somerset decision that took place only a few months before he wrote this letter. We have only a few letters from 1772, the year over which the trial extended. Possibly Sancho sees that the condition of blacks has not changed much despite the decision (quite a few masters forced their slaves to sign contracts of indentured servitude), or his cross-national consciousness prevents him from celebrating a decision limited to Great Britain.

51. The painter William Stevenson says of him in an 1814 letter that "few men had seen more of human life, in all its varieties, from the Prince to the Beggar; and no one, I will venture to assert, ever made a better use than he did, of the knowledge resulting from his observations" (Sancho 269).

52. Sukhdev Sandhu emphasizes Sterne's dislike of "linearity," in that he "felt that we must look around us, be prepared to halt, to be diverted by what is going on in the corners, the crevices, the byways of life" (14). One could say that Sancho is extending this concern into interracial realms.

53. In a revised assessment, Ellis says that "by rendering distinctions between high and low culture unstable and unclear, Sancho's *Letters* possess within their mode of address a dangerous subversive quality" ("Ignatius Sancho's *Letters*" 211).

Chapter 2: Trade, Sailors, National Agency, and World Citizenship (pages 84–138)

1. Through this inclusiveness and sense of democratic equality, they broadened the concept of "citizen of the world," which had had elitist connotations ever since its development in classical thought.

2. Hammon's national identity is hard to categorize. My analytical framework shows him to present American characteristics, but his narrative also refers to him as an "Englishman." Vincent Carretta calls him a "Creole Black" ("Phillis Wheatley" 201).

3. The novel as a genre was also much debated at the time. Critics, for example, expressed clear worries that the novel spelled the advent of radical democracy; these misgivings represented "an attempt by an elite minority to retain a self-proclaimed role as the primary interpreters of American culture" (Davidson, *Revolution* 42).

4. Armstrong argues that the British domestic novel "antedated-was indeed necessarily antecedent to-the way of life it represented" (*Desire* 9). As such, it promoted a middle-class ethos based on gender division, and on an individual regulation of desire.

5. Evans uses a different vocabulary, and equates middle-class values with republicanism.

6. As Michael Warner says about the republican and the liberal models, "in the 1780s and 1790s the two lead a tense coexistence in the American novel" (174).

7. These figures struggle with the possible constraining effect of the common good, but also with the treacherous nature of a liberalism outwardly committed to individual freedom, but potentially equally coercive. That is why, as Davidson points out, the early sentimental novel cannot be reduced to a "simple formula." Even as they present themselves as educational works in defense of virtue, "many of the novels question the efficacy of the prevailing legal, political, and social values" (*Revolution* 140). In the process they get enmeshed in post-revolutionary debates about the nature of the new nation's social and political project.

8. See Jan Lewis and Linda K. Kerber.

9. Elizabeth Maddock Dillon, pushing Armstrong's argument, shows in great detail that the marriage contract under liberalism has the double, paradoxical effect of granting women an identity as seemingly consenting subjects even as it relegates them to an oppressive private sphere.

10. Unlike George, Lucy's tragic brother, Montraville receives a commission from his father.

11. Marion Rust argues convincingly that *Charlotte Temple* is primarily about agency.

12. Leslie Fiedler treats dismissively the fact that, when sentiment crossed the Atlantic, it fell into the hands of female authors, who expurgated the heterosexual encounter of both sex and class conflict, and turned the novel into "a moral struggle ending in the moral dominance of woman" (90). But moral struggle was an essential dimension of Richardson's novels-a reason why R. F. Brissenden calls them "novels of sentiment" rather than "sentimental novels"-and the issue of social class, though it took on different shapes, certainly did not disappear in the American novels.

13. According to Jan Lewis, "American republicanism offered women a role as wives," while liberalism was left "to extol the political dimensions of motherhood" (690). She points out that Kerber herself, who popularized the idea of republican motherhood, has warned against overinterpreting her point.

14. Stern opposes a positive view of liberalism, represented by Eliza's hankering for freedom, to a vision of republicanism as oppressive, and as leading to Eliza's "self-immolation" (75). This interpretation is close to that of Sharon M. Harris. Stern also views republican sympathy as underwritten by violence, and liberal sympathy as the expression of true compassion, as it "imaginatively leaps toward and embraces the other, domesticating difference under the larger umbrella of a common humanity" (95). I am more concerned with the negative implications of such a process. My interpretation is closer to that of Carroll Smith-Rosenberg, who argues that Foster is ambivalent, as she represents the desires of a new, individualistic, freedom-loving class but also worries about the consequences for the social order. Kristie Hamilton similarly highlights the conflict in the novel between republicanism and the instability engendered by rising liberal attitudes, particularly in an urban context. Bruce Burgett also underlines doubleness, by focusing on what he sees as the simultaneous republican appeal to disembodiment and the liberal anchoring in the body, ending up in "an ambiguous model of identification" (102). But because the novel is a published item, he says, its republican dimension predominates: "the novel interpellates readers, first, as republican citizens of the literary public sphere and, only second, as gendered subjects of the nation-state" (109). I made clear in the introduction my reservations about the automatic association of the literary public sphere with republicanism.

15. In his famous play *The Contrast,* performed for the first time ten years before the publication of *The Algerine Captive,* Tyler had presented a subtle debate between republicanism and liberalism, the winner of which was not republicanism as might at first appear. See John Evelev.

16. Patrick Parrinder points out that in the eighteenth century already, "criticism of the novel almost invariably entailed an awareness of the role of nationality in fiction" (25).

17. R. F. Brissenden points out that sentimental ideas "all derive from one basic notion," that "the source of all knowledge and all values is the individual human experience" (22). I argue that the degree to which this experience was individualized had political implications.

18. Fiedler calls *Clarissa* "the first sacred book of the bourgeoisie" (65), partly because her "virginity is the emblem of the ethical purity of her class" (67).

19. Even as she describes the sentimental novel's liberal appeal, Festa also indirectly describes its limitations. Her discussion of why the French Committee of Public Safety censored a French version of *Pamela* leads her to broad conclusions about the instability of interpretation, but the more specific issues at stake involve a reaction on the part of Robespierre and the commissioners to a liberal individualism that eschews the concept of republican equality. Their attitude evinced an awareness that the particular in this case might not reflect the universal.

20. Margaret Cohen represents this opposition as the conflict between "negative" and "positive" (109) rights in the sentimental novel. Cohen argues that there is a difference between the French sentimental novel, which stages a clear conflict between the two equally strong forms of freedom, and the Anglo-American sentimental novel, which shows a clearer, typically Anglo predilection for the former. I argue for a further distinction between the British and the American novel.

21. "I have never found the word *yeoman* in Jefferson's writings" (259), Appleby points out.

22. Armitage convincingly shows that in the developing ideology of the British Empire, the most salient question was how to reconcile empire (and classical notions of the res publica) with liberty.

23. For a specific analysis of this argument, see Philip Gould. See John Gallagher and Ronald Robinson for a classic description of how free-trade policies almost inevitably led to imperial conditions.

24. Cathy D. Matson and Peter S. Onuf show that in the United States the ideology of economic freedom as anchored in self-interest, as opposed to mercantilist imperialism, was prevalent, even if the debate with republican virtue had not totally disappeared and Americans had to resort to interventionist practices for pragmatic reasons. Their main argument is that mercantilist impulses were channeled in the service of production rather than consumption (in the form of promoting American manufactures), which still implied the main motive of wealth creation, and a rhetoric of dynamic and entrepreneurial economy.

25. The Continental Congress in October 1774, for example, decided to stop the importation of slaves, but nothing came of it.

26. As is well known, the principle of slavery itself was never debated during the convention, even though slavery was the elephant in the room during all the important negotiations. When Gouverneur Morris did broach the concept of "'human nature'" (Finkelman 204) during discussion of the three-fifths clause, the clause failed momentarily, not because he had convinced anybody, but because three slave states deemed it too much of a compromise. On the other hand, the awareness that the notion of "common good" could also threaten slavery interests came out when the delegates discussed a possible clause giving Congress the "power to legislate where the states were 'incompetent'" (208). Southern states voted against it, "opposed to allowing the national government to legislate for the '*general interest* of the Union,'" as they "suspected that such language might somehow be used to harm slavery" (209).

27. Similarly, "when emancipation came, it was an act of coercive power, of sheer Parliamentary supremacy" (D. Davis, *Age of Revolution* 162).

28. Davis also implies that, because the West Indies enjoyed only "virtual rep-

resentation" in Parliament, their power was much more vulnerable than that of the Southern states in Congress. Ironically, then, the less democratic system made the abolition of the trade, and of slavery, easier.

29. Gould shows how, at a very basic level, "sentiment saturates this era's literature against slave trading," as it keeps using terms such as "inhuman," "abominable," and "vile" (*Barbaric* 4).

30. See introduction.

31. Antislavery was a "means of reasserting their influence, of vindicating their reputation, and of restoring cooperative ties with Revolutionary patriots like Franklin and Rush" (D. Davis, *Age of Revolution* 222).

32. He was originally from France, and came to America from London at eighteen. His tracts reveal his immersion in European travel narratives, as well as in the writings of Francis Hutcheson and Scottish jurist George Wallace. He was widely read in philosophy and science, and conducted much transatlantic correspondence. See Maurice Jackson.

33. Interestingly, it is the notion of a group or corporation as a person that will lead to the freedom of modern corporations to, or not to, assume responsibility toward workers and the environment.

34. His discourse on slavery and freedom shows a not unconditional adherence to freedom. In a 1773 letter to John Fothergill, Benezet says that "the obtaining their freedom & indeed the freedom of many even amongst us, is by no means the object of my concern." His desire to see freedom reined in also comes out in his frequently expressed concern about slave rebellions. When he envisages the future of freed slaves, he displays an original mixture of segregationist and integrationist impulses. He suggests that the blacks could live out west, beyond the Allegheny Mountains. But, he adds, "it is clear to me that when ever a manumission of the bulk of the Negroes takes place, the thought of setting them in a body, by themslves [sic], will be found as impossible as it would be dangerous both to blacks & whites." Indeed, he continues, "the only rational, safe & just expedient both natural and religious would, I think, be that they may be mixed amongst the whites & by giving them a property amongst us, make them parties & interested in our welfare and security" (268).

35. One independent offshoot of this culture was the pirate ship, a "world turned upside down," in that it maintained "a multicultural, multiracial, multinational social order" (Linebaugh and Rediker 162).

36. As Linebaugh and Rediker put it, "the real citizens of the world, of course, were the sailors and slaves who instructed Philmore, Paine, Jefferson, and the rest of the middle and upper-class revolutionaries" (246).

37. See W. Jeffrey Bolster's *Black Jacks*. Most of the information in this and the next paragraph comes from this book.

38. See chapter 3 for a focus on that sort of black nationalism, among the Freemasons.

39. Indeed, the only real outsider here is the passenger, whom Hammon does not even count amongst the lost lives the first time he mentions the episode, when he announces that the captain, by throwing some of the wood overboard, could have saved "his own Life, as well as the Lives of the Mate and Nine Hands."

40. Opinions are divided on whether Hammon was a slave or a servant.

41. Vincent Carretta points out in a footnote that the passage seems inspired by a similar one in John Wesley's *Thoughts on Slavery* (1774).

42. Later on he also suggests that slightly more expensive commodities may be a small price to pay for the abolition of slavery-an argument that still resonates today, when we need to be reminded of "the high cost of low price."

43. Roxann Wheeler discusses Cugoano's discourse about color in detail, and sees problematic implications in his mixed use of color symbolism to refer to both skin complexion and moral value: "Rehearsing color stereotypes of blackness and whiteness at the same time that he tries to reject them, Cugoano's *Thoughts and Sentiments* moves with difficulty through the many registers of meaning in which black and white complexion signifies in a binary logic" (31).

44. I use the term *proletarian*, though the extent of the existence of a proletariat at the turn of the century is uncertain.

45. For discussions of Equiano's book tours, see Vincent Carretta (*Equiano the African*) and John Bugg.

46. Adam Potkay and Sandra Burr note that, in the original letter addressed to Lord Hawkesbury on which this passage is based, Equiano added a caveat that might detract from his belief in "the ideals of international commerce." He originally wrote that "'the Abolition of Slavery would be in reality an universal Good, and for which a partial Ill must be supported" (20). I would assume, though, that Equiano is here referring to the possible damage to "property" and livelihoods the abolition of slavery would entail.

47. For more details, see G. I. Jones.

48. In his biography, Carretta follows the gradual apparition of African references in Equiano's public statements, and links it to the simultaneous organization of the abolitionist movement and various activities in Parliament concerning the trade.

49. Another sentimental moment is his quoting from *The Dying Negro* when describing the moment he is sold by Pascal into the West Indies, showing his attachment not just to liberty but also to Britain.

50. As Geraldine Murphy points out, Equiano's Africa is "neither demonic nor Edenic" (561).

51. He says that the soil "'produces spontaneously, and almost without cultivation, all the necessaries of life, grain, fruit, herbs, and roots'" (Equiano 12), and describes some miraculous fishing, or the speed with which trees recover from the damage wrought by crickets.

52. "One can say that the Negroes of Senegal are the most beautiful among black men. Their size is above average, well formed and without defect. It is exceptional to see crippled, humped, or deformed ones, unless they had an accident."

53. "bouse de vache" (Adanson 44).

54. In his 1734 book, William Snelgrave does use such political references, but negatively. His account of how the king of Dahomey conquered the kingdom of Whidah makes fun of a people who, through the riches of trade, had become so "proud, effeminate, and luxurious" (3) that their town was easily invaded by two hundred soldiers. Both the soldiers and the whites in the town are "amazed, to see

the great Cowardice of these People" (15). Here the republican ethos is invoked to ridicule the Africans. (Only later do we find out in an aside that these people especially fear their assailants' cannibalism.)

55. Equiano also cites a number of authors to corroborate these claims (44).

56. Mary Beth Norton shows how, mostly because of racial discrimination, very few black loyalists received a pension or compensation for lost property.

57. See Carretta's biography for an excellent overview of the events.

58. Equiano's muster lists for the three transport ships at one point included 344 blacks and 115 whites (Carretta, *Equiano* 381).

59. The government would end up spending more than fifteen thousand pounds on the project.

60. Deirdre Coleman mentions that "most commentators agree that coercion was used to get London's blacks on board the Royal Navy ships for Sierra Leone" (202).

61. Trafford had a plan to relocate all colonial crops to Africa, which he contended was best situated and offered the best environment. As Deirdre Coleman says, his plan was representative of "the period's many European inscriptions on the tabula rasa of the African continent" (15).

62. Equiano's ideas thus differ strikingly from those of the original conceiver of the settlement, Smeathman, who imagined the black emigrants' community as a form of "dependency, leading them to agree 'to be governed by what they term WHITE-MANS's fashion" (D. Coleman 30).

Chapter 3: Brotherhood, Radicalism, and Antislavery (pages 139–189)

1. The terms *conservatism* and *radicalism* are somewhat anachronistic here, in that they acquired their specific political meaning in the nineteenth rather than in the eighteenth century.

2. This is one opposition among many others, since that time period was marked by political upheaval, such as conflicts between Whigs and Tories, or Country and Court.

3. See Freeman.

4. Several critics tend to present Brown as fundamentally radical, as he was surrounded with political radicalism in the 1790s. I agree with Wim Verhoeven that he is "at once radical and conservative" (11).

5. Henry Pleyel represents a balanced mix of belief in liberal freedom, as when he praises German "security of civil rights," with a republican outlook, as when he notes about the German government that "the evil flowing from this power, in malignant hands, was proportioned to the good that would arise from the virtuous use of it." Wieland sounds republican himself when he describes "wealth and power" as "two great sources of depravity" (C. Brown, *Wieland* 43), but his reasons for refusing them have nothing to do with the common good.

6. The first time Clara hears his voice, it "seemed as if an heart of stone could not fail of being moved by it." It imparts such an emotion that "I dropped the cloth that I held in my hand, my heart overflowed with sympathy, and my eyes

with unbidden tears" (C. Brown, *Wieland* 59). After seeing him, she "could not resist the inclination of forming a sketch upon paper of this memorable visage" (61). Carwin does not just seduce through his voice; he compels a full look at his body and face, a full recognition that demands memory and reproduction.

7. Shirley Samuels points out that, if the retreat of the friends' circle symbolizes the late-eighteenth-century "fear of contamination from the outside world" (*Wieland* 53), Carwin's intrusion is less to blame than "the interior of the home itself" (52); the violence seems "immanent rather than intrusive" (54).

8. Jay Fliegelman highlights this phenomenon of dark transformation as the downside of Lockean liberalism, whose upside is Benjamin Franklin's "process of self-creation" ("Introduction" xiii).

9. Besides several allusions to incestuous love, Clara mentions "a passion more than fraternal" (C. Brown, *Wieland* 211).

10. Pleyel warns against this danger when he argues that "to make the picture of a single family a model from which to sketch the condition of a nation, was absurd" (C. Brown, *Wieland* 34). While Brown might be indirectly discouraging a political reading of the novel, he could also be warning against building a nation on relationships akin to those that bind a family. Clara later realizes that "had I been a stranger to his blood" (216), Wieland would not constitute a menace.

11. Mary Chapman points this out in my edition of the novel.

12. Greven asks: "How transgressive can homosocial brotherhood actually be, when it was *itself* a socially engineered, deeply endemic aspect of culture? A deep yet underexplored tension exists between models of utopian homosocial brotherhood and the widespread compulsory fraternity of nineteenth-century life" (100).

13. Both the African Union Society, created in Newport, Rhode Island, in 1780, and the African Society in Providence advocated emigration and looked into the possibility of removing to Africa, but both plans were scuttled.

14. In France, the presence of the third item in the national motto "Liberté, Egalité, Fraternité" sounds like the apex of an ascending egalitarian line.

15. See Nicholas Hudson for an overview of how the concept of race gradually took on its modern connotations over the course of the eighteenth century.

16. This way it can "at best remain parallel to politics, in an adjacent sphere of life which affects politics only peripherally and makes no demands on it; the most salient example is the apolitical 'fraternity' of the lodges and clubs of modern America" (McWilliams 183).

17. According to Hugh Honour, "the minutes of the committee do not name the artist who designed and engraved the seal," and "the cameo has usually been attributed to William Hackwood" (314).

18. A somewhat eccentric Quaker, Woolman applied his convictions with a thorough literalness. When he traveled through the Southern states, visiting slave owners for purposes of observation and discussion, he would pay for his stay in order to compensate for the slave labor his visit must have occasioned. When he considered visiting the West Indies, he thought of how to avoid benefiting the slave trade by his visit. He refused to eat sugar, drink rum, wear dyed clothes, all products of the hated institution. He felt that his mission in life was to represent

the oppressed, and as Michael Meranze reminds us, he "experienced and articulated this mission through his body" (74). Meranze addresses the problematic implications of this use of the body. By "materializing conscience," Woolman's body "drew the spirit inextricably into the world of things" (75), running the danger that this singularity would keep alive the connection between conscience and his worldly self, as well as the world of things, of commodities, and, more generally, of capital. Meranze suggests that Woolman's asceticism shares its logic of control and of accounting with capitalism. To Margaret E. Stewart, however, this familiar condemnation of asceticism does not apply to Woolman, because it was not connected to domination. The importance to him of "kindness beyond expression" implies a balance of identity and difference, all life being "'of a kind'" while at the same time "one feels 'kindness' *toward* all life, being separable enough to be in a warmhearted relationship with it" (Stewart 268). To me, he goes even further. Woolman does indeed not place his boycott within the logic of capitalism. He envisions a moral community of which he and different others are a part, and combines feelings of compassion with a sense of responsibility toward members of that community. His gestures are more republican than liberal.

19. At one point, Nelson seems willing to open up her thesis, when she mentions the "arguably contradictory (democratic?) impulses of fraternal bonds" (13). Whether the uncertainty reflects hers or Rush's, it hints at the skepticism I emphasize about the democratic possibilities inherent in the concept of brotherhood itself.

20. For New York, there are three strikes on record before 1788 (Wilentz 56).

21. The motivations underlying the various forms of crowd activity that took place in the revolutionary period are notably hard to untangle.

22. As Foner points out, "it is one of the more tragic ironies of this complex debate that, in the process of attempting to liberate the slaves, the abolitionists did so much to promote a new and severely truncated definition of freedom for both blacks and whites." Indeed, "abolitionists understood slavery not as a class relationship, but as a system of arbitrary and illegitimate power exercised by one individual over another." This approach "cut abolitionists off from the labor movement" ("Abolitionism" 260).

23. Susan M. Ryan points out that benevolent societies reinforced the racial separation of American society, and relieved the whites' guilty conscience. They also worked to "defuse the symbolic power of the self-reliant, free black individual" (102). What I emphasize in this chapter are the possible benefits of moving away from that ideology of individualism.

24. For an interesting discussion of that motif in Marrant's *Narrative,* see Benilde Montgomery. For an analysis of the parallels with Christ, see Angelo Costanzo.

25. It seems that what Brooks calls the "Lazarus theology" (*American Lazarus* 106) fuses the Lazarus myth with the notion of the covenant.

26. As Saillant points out, these colonization schemes "betray the fear and disgust they [whites] felt at the prospect of a continued black presence in the United States" ("Slavery" 596).

27. The recognition by the sister also resembles what Marrant describes in his

Funeral Sermon, in which he quotes from 1 Corinthians 13:12 that "now we see through a glass darkly, but then face to face." Unlike the rest of the family, who have only an "imperfect insight into the glory of God," the sister experiences an "open vision of glory" (*Funeral Sermon* 170), a "clear sight" (171), an "immediate sensation" (172). Though he uses images related to the face and to vision, he is describing a more interior, intuitive feeling.

28. Acculturation, the "transformation by immersion into an alien culture accompanied by ritualized adoption into that culture," is typical of the captivity narrative (Vanderbeets 554).

29. Marrant says in a footnote that he was absent "'near twenty-three months'" (*Narrative* 241).

30. The 1785 edition of the *Narrative* expands on the previous ones by including this episode.

31. Cedrick May points out how Marrant's stance here is neither proslavery nor antislavery, showing Marrant's shrewd awareness of his audience. The Countess of Huntingdon was proslavery, and had been through what was to her an unfortunate experience when one of her black ministers, David Margate, who had been sent to a community in South Carolina, ended up fomenting a rebellion.

32. For this information and samples of correspondence by Hall, see Harry E. Davis.

33. A comparison of the texts reveals many similarities in the descriptions of the ancient dispersion of Masonic knowledge. The aspects I discuss in the following paragraphs, though, are specific to Marrant's sermon.

34. Muraskin's working definition of the black middle class includes not just socioeconomic status but also an adherence to the values associated with public respectability.

35. Herbert Aptheker does not include the signatures. For a copy of the petition, see Charles H. Wesley (65).

36. For example, they did not defend the cordwainers on trial for "conspiracy" in 1806 in Philadelphia and 1809 in New York. The judges ruled that journeymen might ask for better wages individually, but not in combinations.

37. Rohan McWilliam shows how revisionist historians' have brought nuances to the historiography anchored in the work of E. P. Thompson, by dissociating class or economics from political ideology.

38. For biographical information on Wedderburn, see Iain McCalman's book, article, and introduction to *The Horrors of Slavery and Other Writings by Robert Wedderburn*.

Chapter 4: Blood, Bodies, and the Antebellum Slave Narrative (pages 190–225)

1. In "The Identity of Slavery," Shirley Samuels points to the fraught choice between "reclaiming and denying the body" (160) typical of nineteenth-century sentimental culture.

2. For a good overview of the genre, see Herbert Ross Brown.

3. Both novelists, for example, seem to delight in doctrinal disputations be-

tween their characters, as if, to some extent, they were mourning the "loss of theology" so eloquently described by Douglas, who associates this loss with the onslaught of liberal sentimentality.

4. Gould, *Covenant and Republic*, analyzes the role of androgyny in both novels.

5. Charles Nichols seems to feel that way, as he variously refers to Grimes as "a disorganized and unsettled personality," typical of slaves who were "poorly integrated persons-permanently damaged souls" (554), "a restless and rather pathetic man" whose behavior was partly "pathological" (560).

6. As Andrews points out, the narrative pictures the South "in what would become a standardized image in abolitionist propaganda: the plantation as rural chamber of horrors, a nightmare world presided over by demonic whites as capricious as they were sadistic" (*To Tell* 78).

7. The major African episode he recalls, in which the invaders of his village "pledged their faith and honor that they would not attack" (V. Smith 7) if the villagers paid the amount required, only to turn on them anyway, initiates the theme of (un)kept promises and (un)fair dealing. For a discussion of how Smith's worldview may have been influenced by his African roots, see Robert E. Desrochers, Jr., "'Not Fade Away'".

8. The 1896 edition reproduced by Arna Bontemps contains various witness accounts and traditional tales on Smith's physical feats. According to one, Smith "weighed over three hundred pounds and measured six feet around his waist" (Bontemps 27).

9. There is of course the possibility that the word was added by his amanuensis, in which case the awareness of difference has different implications.

10. The veracity of the narrative has been thoroughly questioned, but as Charles T. Davis points out, "what was in question was Williams's facts; no one denied that Williams had uttered them or that they had emerged, without outside provocation or distortion, from his own imagination" (87). Factual or not, then, the narrative reflects his ideology.

11. Christopher Castiglia, for example, examines the "rhetorics of interiorization" (33) at work in the writings of William Lloyd Garrison, emphasizing his sympathy's encouragement of black interior discipline, and concurrent building of white interior civic depth. Consequently, Castiglia associates Garrison with the typical form of benevolence anchored in an individualistic, antisystemic approach. For an analysis of the link between benevolence and self-interest, see introduction.

12. In her perceptive discussion, Jenny Sharpe reminds us that the white abolitionists who wrote down and sponsored her tale actively promoted "ideals of obedience, self-discipline, hard work, and moderation" (123). To a certain degree, indeed, it is impossible to distinguish Prince's intent from theirs.

Chapter 5: The Case of Frederick Douglass (pages 226–240)

1. James Matlack, for example, finds the *Narrative* superior. Douglass "avoids the stylistic and emotional excesses common in the slave narrative

genre," the text is marked by "calm control and calculated understatement," and the writing is "firm, lucid, and brisk" (19).

2. Peter Walker has argued that Douglass was moved by a "hopeless secret desire to be white" and to "blot out his blackness" (247), but if that is the case, maybe the later Douglass was projecting that desire onto his earlier self. It seems more likely that in this passage Douglass was projecting a desire for racelessness.

3. Mills' position is similar to that of Rogers M. Smith, mentioned in the introduction. They both emphasize the existence of a separate and fundamental illiberal component in the American ideological makeup.

4. In a July 3, 1845, address the Massachusetts senator Rufus Choate warned that "true wisdom would advise to place the power of revolution, overturning all to begin anew, rather in the background, to throw over it a politic, well-wrought veil, to reserve it for crises, exigencies, the rare and distant days of great historical epochs" (Jasinski 77). Jasinski comments in a footnote that "Choate would probably have been pleased when the Declaration of Independence was removed from public display in 1894 and locked in a safe until 1924" (87–88).

5. Sundquist's argument is the closest to Sale's, asserting that even though Douglass knew he was using "the tools of the master," he considered them "a liberating ideology." "The notion," Sundquist points out, "that the language of the Revolution was but a new form of totalizing imprisonment, a thorough mockery of freedom, is a view that would have been anathema to Douglass" (121). Andrews leaves the question open, emphasizing that such a text is bound to make us look in two opposite directions at once, one toward liberation, the other toward the "mythology of an oppressive culture" (*To Tell* 187).

Epilogue (pages 241–247)

1. In *The Signifying Monkey,* Gates himself developed a theory about the difference of black texts.

2. In a recent issue of *American Quarterly,* Winfried Fluck reminds us that there is still a lot of work to be done on what constitutes the "historically unique constellations" (29) of American culture.

3. In their introduction, Christine Bolt and Seymour Drescher remind us that "comparative studies tend to bring out what is distinctive in the communities being compared," and that if "*international* attitudes toward blacks and slavery" changed through the eighteenth century, "local political and economic considerations still largely determined how far and how fast these changes would be acted upon" (3).

Works Cited

Adanson, Michel. *Voyage au Sénégal*. Ed. Denis Reynaud and Jean Schmidt. Saint-Etienne: Publications de l'Université de Saint-Etienne, 1996.
Addison, Joseph. *Cato*. *The Miscellaneous Works of Joseph Addison*. Ed. A. C. Guthkelch. Vol. 1. London: G. Bell and Sons, 1914. 330–420.
Anderson, Amanda. "Cryptonormativism and Double Gestures: The Politics of Post-Structuralism." *Cultural Critique* 21 (Spring 1992): 63–95.
Andrews, William L. *To Tell a Free Story: The First Century of Afro-American Autobiography, 1760–1865*. Urbana: U of Illinois P, 1988.
———, ed. *The Oxford Frederick Douglass Reader*. New York: Oxford UP, 1996.
Anstey, Roger. *The Atlantic Slave Trade and British Abolition, 1760–1810*. Atlantic Highlands, NJ: Humanities Press, 1975.
Appiah, Kwame Anthony. "Cosmopolitan Patriots." J. Cohen 21–29.
Appleby, Joyce. *Liberalism and Republicanism in the Historical Imagination*. Cambridge, MA: Harvard UP, 1992.
Appleton, Nathaniel. "*Considerations on Slavery, 1767*." Bruns 128–37.
Aptheker, Herbert, ed. *A Documentary History of the Negro People in the United States*. New York: Citadel Press, 1968.
Aravamudan, Srinivas. *Tropicopolitans: Colonialism and Agency, 1688–1804*. Durham, NC: Duke UP, 1999.
Arendt, Hannah. *On Revolution*. New York: Viking Press, 1965.
Armitage, David. *The Ideological Origins of the British Empire*. Cambridge: Cambridge UP, 2000.
Armstrong, Nancy. *Desire and Domestic Fiction: A Political History of the Novel*. New York: Oxford UP, 1987.
———. "Why Daughters Die: The Racial Logic of American Sentimentalism." *Yale Journal of Criticism* 7.2 (1994): 1–24.
Arner, Robert D. "Sentiment and Sensibility: The Role of Emotion and William Hill Brown's *The Power of Sympathy*." *Studies in American Fiction* 1.2 (Autumn 1973): 121–32.
Bailyn, Bernard. *The Ideological Origins of the American Revolution*. Cambridge, MA: Harvard UP, 1992.
Baker, Houston A., Jr. *Blues, Ideology, and Afro-American Literature: A Vernacular Theory*. Chicago: U of Chicago P, 1984.

———. *The Journey Back: Issues in Black Literature and Criticism.* Chicago: U of Chicago P, 1980.
Balibar, Etienne. "Is a Philosophy of Human Civil Rights Possible? New Reflections on Equaliberty." *South Atlantic Quarterly* 103.2–3 (Spring/Summer 2004): 311–22.
Ball, Charles. *Slavery in the United States: A Narrative of the Life and Adventures of Charles Ball, a Black Man.* Taylor (vol. 1) 259–486.
Barker-Benfield, G. J. *The Culture of Sensibility: Sex and Society in Eighteenth-Century Britain.* Chicago: U of Chicago P, 1992.
Barnes, Elizabeth. *States of Sympathy: Seduction and Democracy in the American Novel.* New York: Columbia UP, 1997.
Barrio-Vilar, Laura. "Narrating the African Self in the Late Eighteenth Century: Issues of Voice, Authority, and Identity in Gronniosaw's 1770 *Narrative.*" *Journal of Kentucky Studies* 20 (Sept. 2003): 117–22.
Baym, Nina. *Woman's Fiction: A Guide to Novels by and about Women in America, 1820–1870.* Ithaca, NY: Cornell UP, 1978.
Belinda. "Petition of an African Slave." Carretta 142–44.
Bender, Thomas, ed. *The Antislavery Debate: Capitalism and Abolitionism as a Problem in Historical Interpretation.* Berkeley: U of California P, 1992.
Benedict, Barbara. "Reading Faces: Physiognomy and Epistemology in Late Eighteenth-Century Sentimental Novels." *Studies in Philology* 92.3 (Summer 1995): 311–28.
Benezet, Anthony. "Anthony Benezet to John Fothergill, April 28, 1773." Bruns 267–69.
———. *Some Historical Account of Guinea: Its Situation, Produce, and the General Disposition of Its Inhabitants with an Inquiry into the Rise and Progress of the Slave Trade, Its Nature, and Lamentable Effects.* London: Frank Cass, 1968.
———. "Unpublished Notes on Thomas Thompson's Proslavery Pamphlet, 1772." Bruns 216–20.
Berlant, Lauren. "National Brands/National Body: *Imitation of Life.*" *Comparative American Identities: Race, Sex, and Nationality in the Modern Text.* Ed. Hortense Spillers. New York: Routledge, 1991. 110–40.
Berlin, Isaiah. "Two Concepts of Liberty." *Four Essays on Liberty.* London: Oxford UP, 1969.
Bestes, Peter, et al. Petition. Aptheker 7–8.
Bhattacharya, Nandini. *Slavery, Colonialism, and Connoisseurship: Gender and Eighteenth-Century Literary Transnationalism.* Hants, England: Ashgate, 2006.
Bibb, Henry. *Narrative of the Life and Adventures of Henry Bibb, an American Slave. Written by Himself.* Taylor (vol. 2) 1–101.
Bingham, Caleb, ed. *The Columbian Orator.* Ed. David W. Blight. New York: New York UP, 1998.
Blassingame, John. Introduction. *The Frederick Douglass Papers.* Series 1, vol. 1. Ed. Blassingame. New Haven, CT: Yale UP, 1979. xxi–lxix.
Bloch, Ruth H. "The Gendered Meanings of Virtue in Revolutionary America." *Signs* 13.1 (1987): 37–58.

Bogues, Anthony. *Black Heretics, Black Prophets: Radical Political Intellectuals.* New York: Routledge, 2003.
Bolster, W. Jeffrey. *Black Jacks: African American Seamen in the Age of Sail.* Cambridge, MA: Harvard UP, 1997.
Bolt, Christine, and Seymour Drescher, eds. *Anti-Slavery, Religion, and Reform: Essays in Memory of Roger Anstey.* Folkestone, England: Dawson, 1980.
Bontemps, Arna, ed. *Five Black Lives.* Middletown, CT: Wesleyan UP, 1971.
Breen, T. H. "Subjecthood and Citizenship: The Context of James Otis's Radical Critique of John Locke." *New England Quarterly* 71.3 (Sept. 1998): 378–404.
Brissenden, R. F. *Virtue in Distress: Studies in the Novel of Sentiment from Richardson to Sade.* London: Macmillan, 1974.
Brock, Gillian, and Harry Brighouse, eds. *The Political Philosophy of Cosmopolitanism.* Cambridge: Cambridge UP, 2005.
Brooks, Joanna. *American Lazarus: Religion and the Rise of African-American and Native American Literatures.* Oxford: Oxford UP, 2003.
———. Review of *Genius in Bondage: Literature of the Early Black Atlantic. Early American Literature* 37.2 (2002): 354–59.
Brooks, Joanna, and John Saillant, eds. *"Face Zion Forward": First Writers of the Black Atlantic, 1785–1798.* Boston: Northeastern University Press, 2002.
Brown, Charles Brockden. *Edgar Huntly or Memoirs of a Sleep-Walker.* Ed. David Lee Clark. New York: Macmillan, 1928.
———. *Ormond.* Ed. Mary Chapman. Orchard Park, NY: Broadview P, 1999.
———. *Wieland and* Memoirs of Carwin the Biloquist. Ed. Jay Fliegelman. New York: Penguin, 1991.
Brown, Herbert Ross. *The Sentimental Novel in America, 1789–1860.* Durham, NC: Duke UP, 1940.
Brown, Laura. *English Dramatic Form, 1660–1760: An Essay in Generic History.* New Haven, CT: Yale UP, 1981.
Brown, William Hill. *The Power of Sympathy.* New York: Penguin Books, 1996.
Bruns, Roger, ed. *Am I Not a Man and a Brother: The Antislavery Crusade of Revolutionary America, 1688–1788.* New York: Chelsea House Publishers, 1977.
Bugg, John. "The Other Interesting Narrative: Olaudah Equiano's Public Book Tour." *PMLA* 121.5 (Oct. 2006): 1424–42.
Bullock, Steven C. *Revolutionary Brotherhood: Freemasonry and the Transformation of the American Social Order, 1730–1840.* Chapel Hill: U of North Carolina P, 1996.
Burgett, Bruce. *Sentimental Bodies: Sex, Gender, and Citizenship in the Early Republic.* Princeton, NJ: Princeton UP, 1998.
Burke, Edmund. Philosophical Enquiry into the Origin of Our Ideas of the Sublime and Beautiful *and Other Pre-Revolutionary Writings.* Ed. David Womersley. Harmondsworth, England: Penguin, 1998.
Burnham, Michelle. *Captivity and Sentiment: Cultural Exchange in American Literature, 1682–1861.* Hanover, NH: UP of New England, 1997.
Cadbury, Henry J. "Negro Membership in the Society of Friends." *Journal of Negro History* 21.2 (Apr. 1936): 151–213.

Caldwell, Tanya. "'Talking Too Much English.'" *Early American Literature* 34.3 (1999): 263–82.
Carey, Brycchan. *British Abolitionism and the Rhetoric of Sensibility: Writing, Sentiment, and Slavery, 1760–1807*. Houndmills, England: Palgrave Macmillan, 2005.
Carretta, Vincent. *Equiano the African: Biography of a Self-Made Man*. Athens: U of Georgia P, 2005.
———. "Phillis Wheatley, the Mansfield Decision of 1772, and the Choice of Identity." *Early America Re-explored: New Readings in Colonial, Early National, and Antebellum Culture*. Ed. Klaus H. Schmidt and Fritz Fleischmann. New York: Peter Lang, 2000. 201–23.
———. "Possible Gustavus Vassa/Olaudah Equiano Attributions." *The Faces of Anonymity: Anonymous and Pseudonymous Publication from the Sixteenth to the Twentieth Century*. Ed. Robert J. Griffin. New York: Palgrave Macmillan, 2003. 103–39.
———. "Questioning the Identity of Olaudah Equiano, or Gustavus Vassa, the African." *The Global Eighteenth Century*. Ed. Felicity Nussbaum. Baltimore: Johns Hopkins UP, 2003. 226–35.
———, ed. *Unchained Voices: An Anthology of Black Authors in the English-Speaking World of the Eighteenth Century*. Lexington: UP of Kentucky, 1996.
Carretta, Vincent, and Philip Gould, eds. *Genius in Bondage: Literature of the Early Black Atlantic*. Lexington: UP of Kentucky, 2001.
Castiglia, Christopher. "Abolition's Racial Interiors and the Making of White Civic Depth." *American Literary History* 14.1 (Spring 2002): 32–59.
Castiglia, Christopher, and Russ Castronovo, eds. *American Literature* 76.3 (2004).
Castiglia, Christopher, and Julia Stern. Introduction. *Early American Literature* 37.1 (2002): 1–7.
Castillo, Susan, and Ivy Schweitzer, eds. *A Companion to the Literatures of Colonial America*. Malden, MA: Blackwell, 2005.
Castronovo, Russ. "Compromised Narratives along the Border: The Mason-Dixon Line, Resistance, and Hegemony." *Border Theory: The Limits of Cultural Poetics*. Ed. Scott Michaelsen and David E. Johnson. Minneapolis: U of Minnesota P, 1997.
Child, Lydia Maria. *Hobomok and Other Writings on Indians*. Ed. Carolyn L. Karcher. New Brunswick, NJ: Rutgers UP, 1986.
Clark, Elizabeth B. "'The Sacred Rights of the Weak': Pain, Sympathy, and the Culture of Individual Rights in Antebellum America." *Journal of American History* 82.2 (Sept. 1995): 463–93.
Clarke, Lewis and Milton. *Narratives of the Sufferings of Lewis and Milton Clarke, Sons of a Soldier of the Revolution, during a Captivity of More than Twenty Years among the Slaveholders of Kentucky, One of the So Called Christian States of North America. Dictated by Themselves*. Taylor (vol. 1) 601–72.
Clarkson, Thomas. *An essay on the impolicy of the African slave trade. In two parts. By the Rev. T. Clarkson, M.A.* London, 1788. Based on information

from *English Short Title Catalogue. Eighteenth Century Collections Online.* Gale Group.
Clawson, Mary Ann. *Constructing Brotherhood: Class, Gender, and Fraternalism.* Princeton, NJ: Princeton UP, 1989.
Clemit, Pamela. *The Godwinian Novel: The Rational Fictions of Godwin, Brockden Brown, Mary Shelley.* Oxford: Clarendon P, 1993.
Cohen, Joshua, ed. *For Love of Country: Debating the Limits of Patriotism.* Boston: Beacon P, 1996.
Cohen, Margaret. "Sentimental Communities." Cohen and Dever 106–32.
Cohen, Margaret, and Carolyn Dever, eds. *The Literary Channel: The InterNational Invention of the Novel.* Princeton, NJ: Princeton UP, 2002.
Coleman, Deirdre. *Romantic Colonization and British Anti-slavery.* Cambridge: Cambridge UP, 2005.
Coleman, Elihu. *"Testimony against Making Slaves of Men, 1733."* Bruns 39–45.
Costanzo, Angelo. *Surprising Narrative: Olaudah Equiano and the Beginnings of Black Autobiography.* New York: Greenwood P, 1987.
Coviello, Peter. "Agonizing Affection: Affect and Nation in Early America." *Early American Literature* 37.3 (2002): 439–68.
Crain, Caleb. *American Sympathy: Men, Friendship, and Literature in the New Nation.* New Haven, NJ: Yale UP, 2001.
Crane. R. S. "Suggestions toward a Genealogy of the 'Man of Feeling.'" *English Literary History* 1.3 (Dec. 1934): 205–30.
Cugoano, Quobna Ottobah. Thoughts and Sentiments on the Evil of Slavery and Other Writings. Ed. Vincent Carretta. Harmondsworth, England: Penguin, 1999.
Davidson, Cathy N. Introduction. *Charlotte Temple.* By Susanna Rowson.
———. *Revolution and the Word: The Rise of the Novel in America.* New York: Oxford UP, 1986.
Davis, Charles T. "The Slave Narrative: First Major Art Form in an Emerging Black Tradition." *Black Is the Color of the Cosmos: Essays on Afro-American Literature and Culture, 1942–1981.* Ed. Henry Louis Gates, Jr. New York: Garland, 1982. 83–119.
Davis, David Brion. "The Perils of Doing History by Ahistorical Abstraction." Bender 290–309.
———. *The Problem of Slavery in the Age of Revolution, 1770–1823.* New York: Oxford UP, 1999.
———. *The Problem of Slavery in Western Culture.* New York: Oxford UP, 1966.
———. "Reflections on Abolitionism and Ideological Hegemony." Bender 161–79.
Davis, Harry E. "Documents Relating to Negro Masonry in America." *Journal of Negro History* 21.4 (Oct. 1936): 411–32.
Denby, David J. "La Modernité du Sentimentalisme." *Eighteenth-Century Fiction* 7.4 (July 1995): 373–92.
Descargues, Madeleine. "Les Sermons de Sterne ou l'Ecriture Recréée." *Bulletin de la Société d'Etudes Anglo-Américaines des XVIIe et XVIIIe Siècles* 49 (Nov. 1999): 325–40.

Desrochers, Robert, Jr. "'Not Fade Away': The Narrative of Venture Smith, an African American in the Early Republic." *Journal of American History* 84.1 (June 1997): 40–66.

———. "'Surprizing Deliverance'? Slavery and Freedom, Language and Identity in the *Narrative* of Briton Hammon, 'A Negro Man.'" Carretta and Gould 153–74.

Dietz, Mary G. "Citizenship with a Feminist Face: The Problem with Maternal Thinking." *Political Theory* 13.1 (Feb. 1985): 19–37.

Dillon, Elizabeth Maddock. *The Gender of Freedom: Fictions of Liberalism and the Literary Public Sphere*. Stanford, CA: Stanford UP, 2004.

———. "*Slaves in Algiers*: Race, Republican Genealogies, and the Global Stage." *American Literary History* 16.3 (2004): 407–36.

Dillwyn, William. "*Brief Considerations on Slavery*, 1773." Bruns 270–78.

Douglas, Ann. *The Feminization of American Culture*. 1977. New York: Noonday P, 1998.

Douglass, Frederick. *The Frederick Douglass Papers*. Series 1, vols. 1 and 2. Ed. John Blassingame. New Haven, CT: Yale UP, 1979.

———. *The Heroic Slave*. Andrews 131–63.

———. *Life and Writings of Frederick Douglass*. Ed. Philip S. Foner. Vols. 1 and 2. New York: International Publishers, 1950.

———. *My Bondage and My Freedom*. Ed. William L. Andrews. Urbana: U of Illinois P, 1987.

———. *Narrative of the Life of Frederick Douglass, an American Slave, Written by Himself*. Ed. William L. Andrews and William S. McFeely. New York: Norton, 1997.

———. "What to the Slave Is the Fourth of July?" Andrews 108–30.

duCille, Ann. "Where in the World Is William Wells Brown? Thomas Jefferson, Sally Hemings, and the DNA of African-American Literary History." *American Literary History* 12.3 (2000): 443–62.

Dwyer, John. "Enlightened Spectators and Classical Moralists: Sympathetic Relations in Eighteenth-Century Scotland." *Eighteenth-Century Life* 15.1–2 (Feb. and May 1991): 96–118.

Ellis, Markman. "Ignatius Sancho's *Letters*: Sentimental Libertinism and the Politics of Form." Carretta and Gould 199–217.

———. *The Politics of Sensibility: Race, Gender and Commerce in the Sentimental Novel*. Cambridge: Cambridge UP, 1996.

Ellison, Julie. *Cato's Tears and the Making of Anglo-American Emotion*. Chicago: U of Chicago P, 1999.

Equiano, Olaudah. *The Interesting Narrative and Other Writings*. Ed. Vincent Carretta. New York: Penguin Books, 1995.

Evans, Gareth. "Rakes, Coquettes and Republican Patriarchs: Class, Gender and Nation in Early American Sentimental Fiction." *Canadian Review of American Studies/Revue canadienne d'études américaines* 25.3 (Fall 1995): 41–62.

Evelev, John. "*The Contrast*: The Problem of Theatricality and Political and Social Crisis in Postrevolutionary America." *Early American Literature* 31.1 (1996): 74–97.

Fanuzzi, Robert. *Abolition's Public Sphere*. Minneapolis: University of Minnesota Press, 2003.

Felix. Petition. Aptheker 6–7.

Festa, Lynn. "Sentimental Bonds and Revolutionary Characters: Richardson's *Pamela* in England and France." Cohen and Dever 73–105.

Fichtelberg, Joseph. "Word between Worlds: The Economy of Equiano's *Narrative*." *American Literary History* 5.3 (Fall 1993): 459–80.

Fiedler, Leslie. *Love & Death in the American Novel*. 1960. New York: Anchor Books, 1992.

Figlio, Karl M. "Theories of Perception and the Physiology of Mind in the Late Eighteenth Century." *History of Science* 13.3 (1975): 177–212.

Finkelman, Paul. "Slavery and the Constitutional Convention: Making a Covenant with Death." *Beyond Confederation: Origins of the Constitution and American National Identity*. Ed. Richard Beeman, Stephen Botein, and Edward C. Carter II. Chapel Hill: U of North Carolina P, 1987. 188–225.

Finkenbine, Roy E. "Belinda's Petition: Reparations for Slavery in Revolutionary Massachusetts." *William and Mary Quarterly* 64.1 (2007): 95–104.

Fladeland, Betty. *Men and Brothers: Anglo-American Antislavery Cooperation*. Urbana: U of Illinois P, 1972.

Fliegelman, Jay. Introduction. Brown, *Wieland* xii–xliv.

———. *Prodigals and Pilgrims: The American Revolution against Patriarchal Authority, 1750–1800*. Cambridge: Cambridge UP, 1982.

Fluck, Winfried. "Inside and Outside: What Kind of Knowledge Do We Need? A Response to the Presidential Address." *American Quarterly* 59.1 (2007): 23–32.

Foner, Eric. "Abolitionism and the Labor Movement in Antebellum America." Bolt and Drescher 254–71.

———. *Tom Paine and Revolutionary America*. New York: Oxford UP, 1976.

Foster, Frances Smith. *Witnessing Slavery: The Development of Ante-Bellum Slave Narratives*. 2nd ed. Madison: U of Wisconsin P, 1994.

Foster, Hannah Webster. *The Coquette*. Ed. Cathy Davidson. New York: Oxford UP, 1986.

Fredrickson, George M. *The Black Image in the White Mind: The Debate on Afro-American Character and Destiny, 1817–1914*. Hanover, NH: Wesleyan UP, 1971.

Freeman, Lisa A. "What's Love Got to Do with Addison's *Cato*?" *SEL: Studies in English Literature, 1500–1900* 39.3 (1999): 463–82.

Fretz, J. Herbert. "The Germantown Anti-slavery Petition of 1688." *Mennonite Quarterly Review* 33.1 (Jan. 1959): 42–59.

Fuss, Diana. *Identification Papers*. New York: Routledge, 1995.

Gallagher, John, and Ronald Robinson. "The Imperialism of Free Trade." *Economic History Review* 2nd ser. 6.1 (1953): 1–15.

Ganter, Granville. "The Active Virtue of *The Columbian Orator*." *New England Quarterly* 70.3 (Sept. 1997): 463–76.

Gates, Henry Louis, Jr. "James Gronniosaw and the Trope of the Talking Book." *African American Autobiography: A Collection of Critical Essays*. Ed. William L. Andrews. Englewood Cliffs, NJ: Prentice Hall, 1993. 8–25.

Gates, Henry Louis, Jr., and William L. Andrews, eds. *Pioneers of the Black Atlantic: Five Slave Narratives from the Enlightenment, 1772–1815*. Washington, DC: Counterpoint, 1998.

"Germantown Friends' Protest against Slavery, 1688." Bruns 3–5.

Giles, Paul. "Reconstructing American Studies: Transnational Paradoxes, Comparative Perspectives." *Journal of American Studies* 28.3 (1994): 335–58.

———. *Virtual Americas: Transnational Fictions and the Transatlantic Imaginary*. Durham, NC: Duke UP, 2002.

Gilroy, Paul. *Against Race: Imagining Popular Culture beyond the Color Line*. Cambridge, MA: Harvard UP, 2000.

———. *The Black Atlantic: Modernity and Double Consciousness*. Cambridge, MA: Harvard UP, 1993.

Godwin, William. *Enquiry concerning Political Justice*. Ed. K. Codell Carter. Oxford: Clarendon P, 1971.

———. *Things as They Are; or, The Adventures of Caleb Williams*. Ed. Maurice Hindle. London: Penguin, 2005.

Goldstein, Leslie Friedman. "Violence as an Instrument for Social Change: The Views of Frederick Douglass (1817–1895)." *Journal of Negro History* 61.1 (Jan. 1976): 61–72.

Gould, Philip. *Barbaric Traffic: Commerce and Antislavery in the Eighteenth-Century Atlantic World*. Cambridge, MA: Harvard UP, 2003.

———. *Covenant and Republic: Historical Romance and the Politics of Puritanism*. New York: Cambridge UP, 1996.

———. "'Remarkable Liberty': Language and Identity in Eighteenth-Century Black Autobiography." Carretta and Gould 116–29.

Greene, Donald. "Latitudinarianism and Sensibility: The Genealogy of the Man of Feeling Reconsidered." *Modern Philology* 75.2 (1977): 159–83.

Greven, David. "Troubling Our Heads about Ichabod: 'The Legend of Sleepy Hollow,' Classic American Literature, and the Sexual Politics of Homosocial Brotherhood." *American Quarterly* 56.1 (2004): 83–110.

Grimes, William. *Life of William Grimes, the Runaway Slave. Written by Himself*. Taylor (vol. 1) 181–233.

Grimsted, David. "Anglo-American Racism and Phillis Wheatley's 'Sable Veil,' 'Length'ned Chain,' and 'Knitted Heart.'" *Women in the Age of the American Revolution*. Ed. Ronald Hoffman and Peter J. Albert. Charlottesville: UP of Virginia, 1989. 338–444.

Gronniosaw, James Albert Ukawsaw. *A Narrative of the Most Remarkable Particulars in the Life of James Albert Ukawsaw Gronniosaw, an African Prince, as Related by Himself*. Gates and Andrews 30–59.

Guyer, Paul. "The Origins of Modern Aesthetics: 1711–35." *The Blackwell Guide to Aesthetics*. Ed. Peter Kivy. Malden, MA: Blackwell, 2004. 15–44.

Haakonssen, Knud. "From Natural Law to the Rights of Man: A European Perspective on American Debates." *A Culture of Rights: The Bill of Rights in Philosophy, Politics, and Law—1791 and 1991*. Ed. Michael J. Lacey and Knud Haakonssen. Cambridge: Cambridge UP, 1991. 19–61.

Habermas, Jürgen. "Justice and Solidarity: On the Discussion Concerning Stage 6." Wren 224–51.

———. *The Structural Transformation of the Public Sphere: An Inquiry into a Category of Bourgeois Society*. Cambridge, MA: MIT Press, 2001.

Hall, Prince. *A Charge Delivered to the African Lodge June 24, 1797 at Menotomy*. Brooks and Saillant 199–208.

———. *A Charge Delivered to the Brethren of the African Lodge on the 25th of June, 1792. At the Hall of Brother William Smith, in Charlestown*. Brooks and Saillant 191–98.

Halttunen, Karen. *Confidence Men, Painted Women: A Study of Middle-Class Culture in America, 1830–1870*. New Haven, CT: Yale UP, 1982.

Hamilton, Kristie. "An Assault on the Will: Republican Virtue and the City in Hannah Webster Foster's *The Coquette*." *Early American Literature* 24.2 (1989): 135–51.

Hammon, Briton. *Narrative of the Uncommon Sufferings, and Surprizing Deliverance of Briton Hammon, a Negro Man*. Carretta 20–25.

Harris, Robert L., Jr. "Early Black Benevolent Societies, 1780–1830." *Massachusetts Review* 20.3 (Autumn 1979): 603–25.

Harris, Sharon M. "Hannah Webster Foster's *The Coquette*: Critiquing Franklin's America." *Redefining the Political Novel: American Women Writers, 1797–1901*. Ed. Harris. Knoxville: U of Tennessee P, 1995. 1–22.

———. "Whose Past Is It? Women Writers in Early America." *Early American Literature* 30.2 (1995): 175–81.

Hartman, Saidiya V. *Scenes of Subjection: Terror, Slavery, and Self-Making in Nineteenth-Century America*. New York: Oxford UP, 1997.

Hartz, Louis. *The Liberal Tradition in America*. San Diego: Harcourt, Brace & Company, 1991.

Haskell, Thomas L. "Capitalism and the Origins of the Humanitarian Sensibility." Bender 107–60.

———. "Convention and Hegemonic Interest in the Debate over Antislavery." Bender 200–59.

Hayden, Lucy K. "Classical Tidings from the Afric Muse: Phillis Wheatley's Use of Greek and Roman Mythology." *CLA Journal* 35.4 (June 1992): 432–47.

Haynes, Lemuel. *Black Preacher to White America*. Ed. Richard Newman. Brooklyn, NY: Carlson, 1990.

Hendler, Glenn. *Public Sentiments: Structures of Feeling in Nineteenth-Century American Literature*. Chapel Hill: U of North Carolina P, 2001.

Henry, Patrick. "Patrick Henry to Robert Pleasants, January 18, 1773." Bruns 221–22.

Hepburn, John. "*The American Defence*, 1715." Bruns 16–31.

Hinds, Elizabeth Jane Wall. "The Spirit of Trade: Olaudah Equiano's Conversion, Legalism, and the Merchant's Life." *African American Review* 32.4 (Winter 1998): 635–47.

Hoare, Prince. *Memoirs of Granville Sharp*. London: Henry Colburn, 1820.

Hobbes, Thomas. *Leviathan*. Oxford: Oxford UP, 1996.

Hollis, Patricia. "Anti-slavery and British Working-Class Radicalism in the Years of Reform." Bolt and Drescher 294–315.
Honour, Hugh. *The Image of the Black in Western Art.* Part 4: From the American Revolution to World War II. Cambridge, MA: Harvard UP, 1989.
Hopkins, Samuel. "A Dialogue on Slavery, 1776." Bruns 397–426.
Hudson, Nicholas. "From 'Nation' to 'Race': The Origin of Racial Classification in Eighteenth-Century Thought." *Eighteenth-Century Studies* 29.3 (1996): 247–64.
Hulliung, Mark. *Citizens and Citoyens: Republicans and Liberals in America and France.* Cambridge, MA: Harvard UP, 2002.
Hunter, Ian. "Aesthetics and Cultural Studies." *Cultural Studies.* Ed. Lawrence Grossberg, Cary Nelson, and Paula A. Treichler. New York: Routledge, 1992. 347–72.
Hutcheson, Francis. *A System of Moral Philosophy.* Vols. 1 and 2. Glasgow: Foulis, 1755.
Ickstadt, Heinz. "American Studies in an Age of Globalization." *American Quarterly* 54.4 (Dec. 2002): 543–62.
Jackson, Maurice. "The Social and Intellectual Origins of Anthony Benezet's Antislavery Radicalism." *Pennsylvania History* (1999): 86–112.
Jacob, Margaret, and James Jacob, eds. *The Origins of Anglo-American Radicalism.* London: George Allen & Unwin, 1984.
Jasinski, James. "Rearticulating History in Epideictic Discourse: Frederick Douglass's 'The Meaning of the Fourth of July to the Negro.'" *Rhetoric and Political Culture in Nineteenth-Century America.* Ed. Thomas W. Benson. East Lansing: Michigan State UP, 1997. 71–89.
Jefferson, Thomas. *Notes on the State of Virginia.* Ed. William Peden. Chapel Hill: U of North Carolina P, 1955.
Jones, G. I. "Olaudah Equiano of the Niger Ibo." *Africa Remembered: Narratives by West Africans from the Era of the Slave Trade.* Ed. Philip D. Curtin. Madison: U of Wisconsin P, 1967. 60–69.
Jordan, Winthrop D. *White over Black: American Attitudes toward the Negro, 1550–1812.* Chapel Hill: U of North Carolina P, 1968.
Kammen, Michael. *A Season of Youth: The American Revolution and the Historical Imagination.* New York: Knopf, 1978.
Kant, Immanuel. *The Critique of Judgment.* Amherst, NY: Prometheus Books, 2000.
Kasson, Joy S. "Narratives of the Female Body: *The Greek Slave.*" Samuels 172–90.
Kazanjian, David. "Mercantile Exchanges, Mercantilist Enclosures: Racial Capitalism in the Black Mariner Narratives of Venture Smith and John Jea." *New Centennial Review* 3.1 (Spring 2003): 147–78.
Keith, George. "Pamphlet against Slavery, 1693." Bruns 5–8.
Kelly, Gary. *English Fiction of the Romantic Period, 1789–1830.* London: Longman, 1989.
Kendrick, Robert. "Other Questions: Phillis Wheatley and the Ethics of Interpretation." *Cultural Critique* 38 (Winter 1997–98): 39–64.
Kerber, Linda K. "The Republican Ideology of the Revolutionary Generation." *American Quarterly* 37.4 (Fall 1995): 474–95.

Klein, Milton M., et al., eds. *The Republican Synthesis Revisited: Essays in Honor of George Athan Billias*. Worcester, MA: American Antiquarian Society, 1992.

Kloppenberg, James T. "The Virtues of Liberalism: Christianity, Republicanism, and Ethics in Early American Political Discourse." *Journal of American History* 74.1 (1987): 9–33.

Kohlberg, Lawrence, Dwight R. Boyd, and Charles Levine. "The Return of Stage 6: Its Principle and Moral Point of View." Wren 151–81.

Kraditor, Aileen S. *Means and Ends in American Abolitionism: Garrison and His Critics on Strategy and Tactics, 1834–1850*. 1967. Chicago: Elephant Paperback, 1989.

Kramnick, Isaac. *Republicanism and Bourgeois Radicalism: Political Ideology in Late Eighteenth-Century England and America*. Ithaca, NY: Cornell UP, 1990.

Kristeller, Paul O. "The Modern System of the Arts: A Study in the History of Aesthetics, Part I." *Journal of the History of Ideas* 12.4 (Oct. 1951): 496–527.

Laqueur, Thomas W. "Bodies, Details, and the Humanitarian Narrative." *The New Cultural History*. Ed. Lynn Hunt. Berkeley: U of California P, 1989. 176–204.

Lawrence, Christopher. "The Nervous System and Society in the Scottish Enlightenment." *Natural Order: Historical Studies of Scientific Culture*. Ed. Barry Barnes and Steven Shapin. Beverly Hills, CA: Sage Publications, 1979. 19–40.

Lay, Benjamin. "*All Slave-keepers . . . Apostates*, 1737." Bruns 46–64.

Lee, Arthur. "'Address on Slavery,' March 19, 1767." Bruns 107–11.

Lee, Nathaniel. *Lucius Junius Brutus*. Ed. John Loftis. Lincoln: U of Nebraska P, 1967.

Levernier, James A. "Phillis Wheatley and the New England Clergy." *Early American Literature* 26.1 (1991): 21–38.

———. "Style as Protest in the Poetry of Phillis Wheatley." *Style* 27.2 (Summer 1993): 172–93.

Lewis, Jan. "The Republican Wife: Virtue and Seduction in the Early Republic." *William and Mary Quarterly* 44.4 (Oct. 1987): 689–721.

Linebaugh, Peter, and Marcus Rediker. *The Many-Headed Hydra: Sailors, Slaves, Commoners, and the Hidden History of the Revolutionary Atlantic*. Boston: Beacon P, 2000.

Locke, John. *The Second Treatise on Civil Government*. Amherst, NY: Prometheus Books, 1986.

MacFarquhar, Larissa. "The Populist: Michael Moore Can Make You Cry." *New Yorker* (February 16 and 23, 2004): 133–45.

Mackenthun, Gesa. "The Transoceanic Emergence of American 'Postcolonial' Identities." Castillo and Schweitzer 336–50.

Macpherson, C. B. *The Political Theory of Possessive Individualism: Hobbes to Locke*. Oxford: Clarendon P, 1962.

Male, Roy R. "*Sympathy*—a Key Word in American Romanticism." *Emerson Society Quarterly* 35 (1964): 19–23.

Marrant, John. *A Funeral Sermon Preached by the Desire of the Deceased, John Lock; The Text Chosen by Himself, from the Epistle of St. Paul to the Philippians, Chap i., Ver. 21. And Was Preached According to Promise, before His*

Father and Mother, Brothers and Sisters, and All the Inhabitants round the Neighbouring Village, By the Rev. John Marrant (1790). Brooks and Saillant 161–76.

———. *A Journal of the Rev. John Marrant, from August the 18th, 1785, to the 16th of March, 1790 (1790)*. Brooks and Saillant 93–160.

———. *A Narrative of the Lord's Wonderful Dealings with John Marrant, a Black, (Now Going to Preach the Gospel in Nova-Scotia) Born in New-York, in North-America. Taken Down from His Own Relation, Arranged, Corrected, and Published by the Rev. Mr. Aldridge. The Fourth Edition, Enlarged by Mr. Marrant, and Printed (with Permission) for His Sole Benefit, with Notes Explanatory (1785)*. Brooks and Saillant 47–75.

———. *A Sermon Preached on the 24th Day of June 1789, Being the Festival of St. John the Baptist, at the Request of the Right Worshipful the Grand Master Prince Hall, and the Rest of the Brethren of the African Lodge of the Honorable Society of Free and Accepted Masons in Boston (1789)*. Brooks and Saillant 77–92.

Marshall, David. "Adam Smith and the Theatricality of Moral Sentiments." *Critical Inquiry* 10.4 (June 1984): 592–613.

Martin, Terence. *The Instructed Vision: Scottish Common Sense Philosophy and the Origins of American Fiction*. Bloomington: Indiana UP, 1961.

Mason, Julian D., Jr., ed. *The Poems of Phillis Wheatley*. Chapel Hill: U of North Carolina P, 1989.

Matlack, James. "The Autobiographies of Frederick Douglass." *Phylon* 40.1 (1979): 15–28.

Matson, Cathy D., and Peter S. Onuf. *A Union of Interests: Political and Economic Thought in Revolutionary America*. Lawrence: U of Kansas P, 1990.

May, Cedrick. "John Marrant and the Narrative Construction of an Early Black Methodist Evangelical." *African American Review* 38.4 (Winter 2004): 553–70.

McCalman, Iain. "Anti-slavery and Ultra-radicalism in Early Nineteenth-Century England: The Case of Robert Wedderburn." *Slavery and Abolition* 7 (Sept. 1986): 99–117.

———. *Radical Underworld: Prophets, Revolutionaries and Pornographers in London, 1795–1840*. Cambridge: Cambridge UP, 1988.

McCann, Andrew. *Cultural Politics in the 1790s: Literature, Radicalism and the Public Sphere*. New York: St Martin's, 1999.

McCoy, Drew R. Introduction. Klein et al. 11–17.

McFeely, William S. *Frederick Douglass*. New York: Simon & Schuster, 1991.

McGerr, Michael. "The Price of the New 'Transnational' History." *American Historical Review* 96.4 (Oct. 1991): 1056–67.

McWilliam, Rohan. *Popular Politics in Nineteenth-Century England*. New York: Routledge, 1998.

McWilliams, Wilson Carey. *The Idea of Fraternity in America*. Berkeley: U of California P, 1973.

Meer, Sarah. "Sentimentality and the Slave Narrative: Frederick Douglass' *My Bondage and My Freedom*." *The Uses of Autobiography*. Ed. Julia Swindells. London: Taylor & Francis, 1995. 89–97.

Meranze, Michael. "Materializing Conscience: Embodiment, Speech, and the Experience of Sympathetic Identification." *Early American Literature* 37.1 (2002): 71–88.
Meyer, Michael. "An African's Troubles with His Masters' Voices." *The Politics of English as a World Language: New Horizons in Postcolonial Cultural Studies*. Ed. Christian Mair. Amsterdam: Rodopi, 2003. 209–17.
Miller, Floyd J. *The Search for a Black Nationality: Black Emigration and Colonization, 1787–1863*. Urbana: U of Illinois P, 1975.
Miller, Peter N. *Defining the Common Good: Empire, Religion and Philosophy in Eighteenth-Century Britain*. Cambridge: Cambridge UP, 1994.
Mills, Charles W. "Whose Fourth of July? Frederick Douglass and 'Original Intent.'" *Blackness Visible: Essays on Philosophy and Race*. Ithaca, NY: Cornell UP, 1998.
Montesquieu. *The Spirit of the Laws*. Ed. Anne M. Cohler et al. Cambridge: Cambridge UP, 1989.
Montgomery, Benilde. "Recapturing John Marrant." *A Mixed Race: Ethnicity in Early America*. Ed. Frank Shuffelton. New York: Oxford UP, 1993. 105–15.
Mullan, John. *Sentiment and Sociability: The Language of Feeling in the Eighteenth Century*. Oxford: Clarendon P, 1988.
Muraskin, William A. *Middle-Class Blacks in a White Society: Prince Hall Freemasonry in America*. Berkeley: U of California P, 1975.
Murphy, Geraldine. "Olaudah Equiano, Accidental Tourist." *Eighteenth-Century Studies* 27.4 (Summer 1994): 551–68.
Nadelhaft, Jerome. "The Somersett Case and Slavery: Myth, Reality, and Repercussions." *Journal of Negro History* 51.3 (July 1966): 193–208.
Nelson, Dana D. *National Manhood: Capitalist Citizenship and the Imagined Fraternity of White Men*. Durham, NC: Duke UP, 1998.
Nichols, Charles. "The Case of William Grimes, the Runaway Slave." *William and Mary Quarterly* 8.4 (1951): 552–60.
Norton, David Fate. "Francis Hutcheson in America." *Studies on Voltaire and the Eighteenth Century* 154 (1976): 1547–68.
Norton, Mary Beth. "The Fate of Some Black Loyalists of the American Revolution." *Journal of Negro History* 58.4 (1973): 402–26.
Nussbaum, Felicity A. "Being a Man: Olaudah Equiano and Ignatius Sancho." Carretta and Gould 54–71.
Nussbaum, Martha. "Beyond the Social Contract: Capabilities and Global Justice." Brock and Brighouse 196–218.
———. "Patriotism and Cosmopolitanism." *Boston Review* 19.5 (Oct./Nov. 1994): 3–6.
———. "Reply." J. Cohen 131–44.
Nwankwo, Ifeoma Kiddoe. *Black Cosmopolitanism: Racial Consciousness and Transnational Identity in the Nineteenth-Century Americas*. Philadelphia: U of Pennsylvania P, 2005.
Ogude, S. E. "Facts into Fiction: Equiano's Narrative Reconsidered." *Research in African Literatures* 13.1 (Spring 1982): 31–43.

Otway, Thomas. *Venice Preserved*. Ed. Malcolm Kelsall. London: Edward Arnold, 1969.
Ovid. *Metamorphoses*. Trans. A. D. Melville. New York: Oxford UP, 1986.
Parnell, Tim. "A Story Painted to the Heart? *Tristram Shandy* and Sentimentalism Reconsidered." *Shandean* 9 (1997): 122–35.
Parrinder, Patrick. *Nation & Novel: The English Novel from Its Origins to the Present Day*. Oxford: Oxford UP, 2006.
Pearce, Roy Harvey. "The Significances of the Captivity Narrative." *American Literature* 19.1 (Mar. 1947): 1–20.
Pennington, James W. C. *The Fugitive Blacksmith; or, Events in the History of James W. C. Pennington*. Taylor (vol. 2) 103–58.
Pettit, Philip. "Liberalism and Republicanism." *Australian Journal of Political Science* 28 (1993): 162–89.
Philmore, J. *Two Dialogues on the Man-Trade*. London, 1760.
Piles, Robert. "Paper about Negroes, 1698." Bruns 9–10.
Pocock, J. G. A. "Conservative Enlightenment and Democratic Revolutions: The American and French Cases in British Perspective." *Government and Opposition* 24.1 (1989): 81–105.
———. *The Machiavellian Moment: Florentine Political Thought and the Atlantic Republican Tradition*. Princeton, NJ: Princeton UP, 1975.
Pollak, Ellen. *Incest and the English Novel, 1684–1814*. Baltimore: Johns Hopkins UP, 2003.
Porter, Dorothy, ed. *Early Negro Writing, 1760–1837*. Baltimore: Black Classic P, 1995.
Porter, Roy. *Enlightenment: Britain and the Creation of the Modern World*. London: Allen Lane/Penguin P, 2000.
Potkay, Adam. "History, Oratory, and God in Equiano's *Interesting Narrative*." *Eighteenth-Century Studies* 34.4 (2001): 601–14.
Potkay, Adam, and Sandra Burr, eds. *Black Atlantic Writers of the Eighteenth Century: Living the New Exodus in England and the Americas*. Basingstoke, England: Macmillan, 1995.
Prince, Mary. *The History of Mary Prince, a West Indian Slave, Related by Herself*. Ed. Moira Ferguson. Ann Arbor: U of Michigan P, 2000.
Quarles, Benjamin. *Black Abolitionists*. New York: Da Capo P, 1969.
Quilley, Geoff. "Duty and Mutiny: The Aesthetics of Loyalty and the Representation of the British Sailor c. 1789–1800." *Romantic Wars: Studies in Culture and Conflict, 1793–1822*. Ed. Philip Shaw. Aldershot, England: Ashgate, 2000. 80–109.
Richards, Phillip M. "Phillis Wheatley, Americanization, the Sublime, and the Romance of America." *Style* 27.2 (Summer 1993): 194–221.
———. "Phillis Wheatley and Literary Americanization." *American Quarterly* 44.2 (June 1992): 163–91.
Robbins, Bruce. *Feeling Global: Internationalism in Distress*. New York: New York UP, 1999.
Robbins, Caroline. *The Eighteenth-Century Commonwealthman: Studies in the Transmission, Development, and Circumstance of English Liberal Thought*

from the Restoration of Charles II until the War with the Thirteen Colonies. Indianapolis: Liberty Fund, 1987.
Robinson, William H., ed. *Critical Essays on Phillis Wheatley*. Boston: G. K. Hall & Co., 1982.
Rodgers, Daniel T. "Republicanism: The Career of a Concept." *Journal of American History* 79.1 (1992–93): 11–38.
Roper, Moses. *A Narrative of the Adventures and Escape of Moses Roper, from American Slavery*. Taylor (vol. 1) 487–521.
Rousseau, G. S. "Nerves, Spirits, and Fibres: Towards Defining the Origins of Sensibility." *Studies in the Eighteenth Century III: Papers Presented at the Third David Nichol Smith Memorial Seminar, Canberra 1973*. Ed. R. F. Brissenden and J. C. Eade. Toronto: U of Toronto P, 1976. 137–57.
Rousseau, Jean-Jacques. *Emile or On Education*. Trans. Allan Bloom. New York: Basic Books, 1979.
Rowe, John Carlos. Introduction. *Post-Nationalist American Studies*. Ed. Rowe. Berkeley: U of California P, 2000. 1–21.
Rowson, Susanna Haswell. *Charlotte Temple*. Ed. Cathy Davidson. New York: Oxford UP, 1986.
———. *Slaves in Algiers; or, A Struggle for Freedom: A Play Interspersed with Songs, in Three Acts*. Philadelphia: Wrigley and Berriman, 1794.
Rubin-Dorsky, Jeffrey. "The Early American Novel." *The Columbia History of the American Novel*. Ed. Emory Elliott. New York: Columbia UP, 1991. 6–25.
Rush, Benjamin. "Address to the Inhabitants of the British Settlements in America upon Slave-Keeping." Bruns 224–31.
Russell, Gillian. *The Theatres of War: Performance, Politics, and Society, 1793–1815*. Oxford: Clarendon P, 1995.
Rust, Marion. "What's Wrong with *Charlotte Temple*?" *William and Mary Quarterly* 60.1 (Jan. 2003): 99–118.
Ryan, Susan M. *The Grammar of Good Intentions: Race and the Antebellum Culture of Benevolence*. Ithaca, NY: Cornell UP, 2003.
Saillant, John. "The Black Body Erotic and the Republican Body Politic, 1790–1820." *Sentimental Men: Masculinity and the Politics of Affect in American Culture*. Ed. Mary Chapman and Glenn Hendler. Berkeley: U of California P, 1999. 89–111.
———. *Black Puritan, Black Republican: The Life and Thought of Lemuel Haynes, 1753–1833*. New York: Oxford UP, 2003.
———. "Explaining Syncreticism in African-American Views of Death: An Eighteenth-Century Example." *Culture & Tradition* 17 (1995): 25–41.
———. "Slavery and Divine Providence in New England Calvinism: The New Divinity and a Black Protest, 1775–1805." *New England Quarterly* 68.4 (1995): 584–608.
———. "'Wipe Away All Tears from Their Eyes': John Marrant's Theology in the Black Atlantic." *Journal for Millennial Studies* 1.2 (Winter 1999): http://www.mille.org/publications/journal.html
Sale, Maggie. "To Make the Past Useful: Frederick Douglass' Politics of Solidarity." *Arizona Quarterly* 52.3 (Autumn 1995): 25–60.

Samuels, Shirley. "The Identity of Slavery." Samuels 157–71.
———. "*Wieland*: Alien and Infidel." *Early American Literature* 25.1 (1990): 46–66.
———, ed. *The Culture of Sentiment: Race, Gender, and Sentimentality in Nineteenth-Century America.* New York: Oxford UP, 1992.
Sánchez-Eppler, Karen. *Touching Liberty: Abolition, Feminism, and the Politics of the Body.* Berkeley: U of California P, 1993.
Sancho, Ignatius. *Letters of the Late Ignatius Sancho, an African.* Ed. Vincent Carretta. New York: Penguin, 1998.
Sandel, Michael J. *Liberalism and the Limits of Justice.* Cambridge: Cambridge UP, 1982.
Sandhu, Sukhdev. "Sterne and the Coal-Black Jolly African." *Shandean* 12 (2001): 9–21.
Sandiford, Keith A. *Measuring the Moment: Strategies of Protest in Eighteenth-Century Afro-English Writing.* Selinsgrove, PA: Susquehanna UP, 1988.
Sedgwick, Catherine Maria. *Hope Leslie, or, Early Times in the Massachusetts.* Ed. Mary Kelly. New Brunswick, NJ: Rutgers UP, 1987.
Sekora, John. "Black Message/White Envelope: Genre, Authenticity, and Authority in the Antebellum Slave Narrative." *Callaloo* 10.3 (Summer 1987): 482–515.
Sewall, Samuel. *The Selling of Joseph: A Memorial.* Ed. Sidney Kaplan. Cambridge, MA: U of Massachusetts P, 1969.
Shalhope, Robert E. "Republicanism, Liberalism, and Democracy: Political Culture in the Early Republic." Klein et al. 37–90.
Sharp, Granville. *An essay on slavery, proving from Scripture its inconsistency with humanity and religion; in answer to a late publication, entitled, "The African trade for Negro slaves shewn to be consistent with principles of humanity, and with the laws of revealed religion." By Granville Sharp, Esq. With an introductory preface, containing the sentiments of the monthly reviewers on that publication; and the opinion of several eminent writers on the subject. To which is added, an elegy on the miserable state of an African slave, by the celebrated and ingenious William Shenstone, Esq.* Burlington [N.J.], 1773. Based on information from *English Short Title Catalogue. Eighteenth Century Collections Online.* Gale Group. http://galenet.galegroup.com/servlet/ECCO
———. *A Short Sketch of Temporary Regulations (until Better Shall Be Proposed) for the Intended Settlement on the Grain Coast of Africa, near Sierra Leona.* London: H. Baldwin, 1786.
———. *Tracts on Slavery and Liberty.* Westport, CT: Negro Universities P, 1969.
Sharpe, Jenny. *Ghosts of Slavery: A Literary Archaeology of Black Women's Lives.* Minneapolis: U of Minnesota P, 2003.
Shields, John C. "Phillis Wheatley's Struggle for Freedom." *The Collected Works of Phillis Wheatley.* Ed. Shields. New York: Oxford UP, 1988. 229–70.
Shuffelton, Frank. "On Her Own Footing: Phillis Wheatley in Freedom." Carretta and Gould 175–89.
———. "Phillis Wheatley, the Aesthetic, and the Form of Life." *Studies in Eighteenth-Century Culture.* Vol. 26. Ed. Syndy M. Conger and Julie C. Hayes. Baltimore: Johns Hopkins UP, 1998. 73–85.

Smith, Adam. *The Theory of Moral Sentiments*. Amherst, NY: Prometheus Books, 2000.
Smith, Rogers M. *Civic Ideals: Conflicting Visions of Citizenship in US History*. New Haven, CT: Yale UP, 1997.
Smith, Venture. *A Narrative of the Life and Adventures of Venture, A Native of Africa, but Resident above Sixty Years in the United States of America. Related by Himself*. Bontemps 1–34.
Smith-Rosenberg, Carroll. "Domesticating 'Virtue': Coquettes and Revolutionaries in Young America." *Literature and the Body: Essays on Populations and Persons*. Ed. Elaine Scarry. Baltimore: Johns Hopkins UP, 1988. 160–84.
Snelgrave, William. *A New Account of Some Parts of Guinea and the Slave-Trade*. London: Frank Cass, 1971.
"The Sons of Africans: An Essay on Freedom, with Observations on the Origins of Slavery." D. Porter 13–27.
Sontag, Susan. "'There' and 'Here': A Lament for Bosnia." *Nation* 261.22 (Dec. 25, 1995): 818–20.
Spence, Thomas. *Pigs' Meat: The Selected Writings of Thomas Spence, Radical and Pioneer Land Reformer*. Ed. G. I. Gallop. Nottingham, England: Spokesman, 1982.
Starling, Marion Wilson. *The Slave Narrative: Its Place in American History*. Washington, DC: Howard UP, 1988.
Stepto, Robert B. *From Behind the Veil: A Study of Afro-American Narrative*. 2nd ed. Urbana: U of Illinois P, 1991.
Stern, Julia A. *The Plight of Feeling: Sympathy and Dissent in the Early American Novel*. Chicago: U of Chicago P, 1997.
Sterne, Laurence. *A Sentimental Journey through France and Italy by Mr. Yorick*. New York: Penguin Books, 2001.
Stewart, Margaret E. "John Woolman's 'Kindness beyond Expression': Collective Identity vs. Individualism and White Supremacy." *Early American Literature* 26.3 (1991): 251–75.
The Story of Quashi; or, The Desperate Negro. Newburyport, MA: W. & J. Gilman, 1820.
Sundquist, Eric. *To Wake the Nations: Race in the Making of American Literature*. Cambridge, MA: Harvard UP, 1993.
Sypher, Wylie. "Hutcheson and the 'Classical' Theory of Slavery." *Journal of Negro History* 24 (July 1939): 263–80.
Taylor, Yuval, ed. *I Was Born a Slave: An Anthology of Classic Slave Narratives*. 2 vols. Chicago: Lawrence Hill Books, 1999.
Thomas, Hugh. *The Slave Trade: The Story of the Atlantic Slave Trade: 1440–1870*. New York: Simon & Schuster, 1997.
Thompson, Thomas. *The African trade for Negro slaves, shewn to be consistent with principles of humanity, and with the laws of revealed religion. By Tho. Thompson,* . . . Canterbury, [1772?]. Based on information from *English Short Title Catalogue*. Eighteenth Century Collections Online. Gale Group. http://galenet.galegroup.com/servlet/ECCO
Todd, Janet. *Sensibility: An Introduction*. London: Methuen, 1986.

Tompkins, Jane. *Sensational Designs: The Cultural Work of American Fiction, 1790–1860*. New York: Oxford UP, 1985.
Twomey, Richard J. *Jacobins and Jeffersonians: Anglo-American Radicalism in the United States, 1790–1820*. New York: Garland, 1989.
Tyler, Royall. *The Algerine Captive; or, The Life and Adventures of Doctor Updike Underhill, Six Years a Prisoner among the Algerines*. Walpole, NH: David Carlisle, 1797.
———. *The Contrast: A Comedy in Five Acts*. Boston: Houghton Mifflin, 1920.
Tyrrell, Ian. "American Exceptionalism in an Age of International History." *American Historical Review* 96.4 (Oct. 1991): 1031–55.
Valeri, Mark. "The New Divinity and the American Revolution." *William and Mary Quarterly* 46.4 (Oct. 1989): 741–69.
Vanderbeets, Richard. "The Indian Captivity Narrative as Ritual." *American Literature* 43.4 (Jan. 1972): 548–62.
Van Sant, Ann Jessie. *Eighteenth-Century Sensibility and the Novel: The Senses in Social Context*. Cambridge: Cambridge UP, 1993.
Verhoeven, W. M. "'This Blissful Period of Intellectual Liberty': Transatlantic Radicalism and Enlightened Conservatism in Brown's Early Writings." *Revising Charles Brockden Brown: Culture, Politics, and Sexuality in the Early Republic*. Ed. Philip Barnard, Mark L. Kamrath, and Stephen Shapiro. Knoxville: U of Tennessee P, 2004.
Walker, James W. St. G. *The Black Loyalists: The Search for a Promised Land in Nova Scotia and Sierra Leone, 1783–1870*. New York: Dalhousie UP, 1976.
Walker, Peter. *Moral Choices: Memory, Desire, and Imagination in Nineteenth-Century American Abolition*. Baton Rouge: Louisiana UP, 1978.
Wallace, Maurice O. *Constructing the Black Masculine: Identity and Ideality in African American Men's Literature and Culture, 1775–1995*. Durham, NC: Duke UP, 2002.
Walter, Krista. "Trappings of Nationalism in Frederick Douglass's *The Heroic Slave*." *African American Review* 34.2 (Summer 2000): 233–47.
Walvin, James. "The Impact of Slavery on British Radical Politics: 1787–1838." *Comparative Perspectives on Slavery in New World Plantation Societies*. Ed. Vera Rubin and Arthur Tuden. New York: New York Academy of Sciences, 1977. 343–55.
Ward, Lee. *The Politics of Liberty in England and Revolutionary America*. Cambridge: Cambridge UP, 2004.
Warner, Michael. *The Letters of the Republic: Publication and the Public Sphere in Eighteenth-Century America*. Cambridge, MA: Harvard UP, 1990.
Wedderburn, Robert. *The Horrors of Slavery and Other Writings by Robert Wedderburn*. Ed. Iain McCalman. Edinburgh: Edinburgh UP, 1991.
Wesley, Charles H. *Prince Hall: Life and Legacy*. Washington, DC: United Supreme Council Southern Jurisdiction, Prince Hall Affiliation, 1977.
Weyler, Karen A. "Race, Redemption, and Captivity in *A Narrative of the Lord's Wonderful Dealings with John Marrant, a Black* and *Narrative of the Uncommon Sufferings and Surprizing Deliverance of Briton Hammon, a Negro Man*." Carretta and Gould 39–53.

Wheeler, Roxann. "'Betrayed by Some of My Own Complexion': Cugoano, Abolition, and the Contemporary Language of Racialism." Carretta and Gould 17–38.
Wilcox, Kristin. "The Body into Print: Marketing Phillis Wheatley." *American Literature* 71.1 (1999): 1–29.
Wilentz, Sean. *Chants Democratic: New York City & the Rise of the American Working Class, 1788–1850*. New York: Oxford UP, 1984.
Williams, James. *Narrative of James Williams, an American Slave, Who Was for Several Years a Driver on a Cotton Plantation in Alabama*. New York: American Anti-Slavery Society; Boston: Isaac Knapp, 1838. Used with permission of The University Library, The University of North Carolina at Chapel Hill.
Williams, Loretta J. *Black Freemasonry and Middle-Class Realities*. Columbia: U of Missouri P, 1980.
Winthrop, John. "A Model of Christian Charity." *The Norton Anthology of American Literature*. Vol. 1. Ed Nina Baym et al. New York: Norton, 1998. 214–25.
Wise, Steven M. *Though the Heavens May Fall: The Landmark Trial That Led to the End of Human Slavery*. Cambridge, MA: Da Capo P, 2005.
Wood, Gordon S. *The Creation of the American Republic: 1776–1787*. Chapel Hill: U of North Carolina P, 1969.
Woodard, Helena. *African-British Writings in the Eighteenth Century: The Politics of Race and Reason*. Westport, CT: Greenwood P, 1999.
Woolman, John. *The Journal and Essays of John Woolman*. Ed. Amelia Mott Gummere. New York: Macmillan Company, 1922.
Wren, Thomas, ed. *The Moral Domain: Essays in the Ongoing Discussion between Philosophy and the Social Sciences*. Cambridge, MA: MIT Press, 1990.
Wright, D. G. *Popular Radicalism: The Working-Class Experience, 1780–1880*. London: Longman, 1988.
Yarborough, Richard. "Race, Violence, and Manhood: The Masculine Ideal in Frederick Douglass's 'The Heroic Slave.'" *Frederick Douglass: New Literary and Historical Essays*. Ed. Eric J. Sundquist. New York: Cambridge UP, 1990. 166–88.
Young, Alfred F. *The American Revolution: Explorations in the History of American Radicalism*. DeKalb: Northern Illinois UP, 1976.
———. *Beyond the American Revolution: Explorations in the History of American Radicalism*. DeKalb: Northern Illinois UP, 1993.
Zafar, Rafia. *We Wear the Mask: African Americans Write American Literature, 1760–1870*. New York: Columbia UP, 1997.
Ziff, Larzer. "A Reading of *Wieland*." *PMLA* 77.1 (Mar. 1962): 51–57.
Zuckert, Michael P. *Natural Rights and the New Republicanism*. Princeton, NJ: Princeton UP, 1994.

Index

Abolitionism: adoption of equality goal in 1840s, 214; American vs. British, 98–100; conservatism of, 180; contrary positions on Constitution, 232–33; Douglass' eventual adoption of, 228; Garrisonian, 232, 233, 234, 240; lack of egalitarianism in, 39–40, 42; lack of true sympathetic connection with slaves, 42–43, 212–13; and national identity, 46; and natural rights theory, 34, 38–40, 41, 99, 190–91, 202–3; political assessment of, 250n5; Quaker, 41, 42, 99–103; raceless goal of, 239; racial prejudice among white abolitionists, 39–40, 43, 265n34; vs. radicalism, 178, 180; religious underpinnings of, 39–40, 41–42; transnationalism in, 4–5. *See also* American antislavery texts; British antislavery texts

Adanson, Michel, 128–29

Address to the Inhabitants of the British Settlements in America upon Slave-keeping (Rush), 44–45

Aesthetic sensibility (exteriority): introduction, 33–34; origins of theory, 257n11; in Sancho, 34, 73–74, 76–83; in sentimental novel, 35–38; in slave narrative, 34, 47, 50–52; in Wheatley, 61–67; in white antislavery writing, 34, 38–45, 69–73

Africa: emigration to, 152, 156–57, 158–60, 173–74; sailors' consciousness of, 107; in slave origin stories, 51, 56, 61–62, 68–69, 122–23, 124–30

African Americans: adoption of liberal perspective, 6–7; appeal of Freemasonry, 172–73; body and recognition of difference, 191; and brotherhood concept, 152–57; and desire to participate in capitalism, 199–201, 203; transnational perspective, 244. *See also* American antislavery texts

African diasporic identity: Cugoano, 85, 111–20; Equiano, 121–33; Hammon, Briton, 108–11

Afro-Britons, 6–7. *See also* British antislavery texts

Agrarian radicalism and Wedderburn, 183, 184–85, 187

Algerine Captive, The (Tyler), 91, 92–93

Alienating text, slave narrative as, 198–99, 208–11

America: vs. Britain on abolition, 98–100; brotherhood in, 144, 146–51; communitarian sensibility, 12–13, 34, 48, 216, 219; democracy as political focus, 179; exceptionalism concept, 244–45, 246; fraternity in, 152–55; freedom concept in, 96–97, 179, 202–3; individualism's appeal for, 6, 15, 34; interiority in, 34, 38–48, 152; liberal triumph in, 5–6, 12–13, 22, 171, 178–79, 192–93, 251n12; national identity in, 85–93, 192; natural rights theory and abolitionism, 34, 38–40, 190–91, 202–3; opposition of liberalism with republicanism in, 12–13, 14, 146–48, 204; political and

America—*continued*:
economic developments in 1840s, 213–14; and radicalism, 144, 155, 178–80; self-reliance focus in, 193, 216–17; value of transnational perspective on, 244–45. *See also* American antislavery texts; Antebellum slave narrative
"America" (Wheatley), 54
American and Foreign Anti-Slavery Society, 214
American antislavery texts: and Adam Smith's economic views, 104; Ball, 205–8; Bibb, 216–19; bodies in, 208–13; brotherhood in, 152–78; decrease in international consciousness, 192; Douglass, 226–40; and global trade considerations, 96; Grimes, 198–202, 205; Gronniosaw, 34, 49–52, 119; Hall, 139, 164–65, 164–78; Hammon, 108–11; interiority in, 34, 37–38; liberal/republican tensions in 19th century, 213–20; Pennington, 219–20; Roper, 208–11, 228; Wheatley, 34, 52–69, 164, 258–60nn30–38; Williams, J., 209, 211–13. *See also* Marrant, John
American Methodists, 42
American Political Tradition, The (Hofstadter), 246
American Revolution, 12–13, 15, 231–32, 250n8
American Slavery as It Is (Weld), 190
Anderson, James, 165
Andrews, William L., 162, 198, 205–6, 208, 209, 213, 226
Anglo-American liberalism and republicanism, 12–15. *See also* Black Atlantic texts
Anstey, Roger, 70
Antebellum slave narrative: body in, 208–13; cosmopolitanism of Mary Prince, 220–25; introduction, 190–93; republicanism and liberalism in, 198–208, 213–20
Anticolonialism, Cugoano's, 113–14
Antinomianism, Wedderburn's, 189
Appeal in Favor of that Class of Americans Called Africans (Child), 190

Appleby, Joyce, 13–14, 95–96, 179
Appleton, Nathaniel, 99
Armitage, David, 96
Armstrong, Nancy, 85
Arner, Robert D., 37
Artisans and brotherhood, 164–78, 179, 181
Assertives in Ball's narrative, 205–6
Association Movement, 180
Auld, Thomas, 230–31
Axe Laid to Root, The (Wedderburn), 182–83, 184–85, 186–87

Bailyn, Bernard, 12, 13
Baker, Houston A., Jr., 121, 230
Ball, Charles, 205–8
Barnes, Elizabeth, 36
Bavarian Illuminati, 147
Baym, Nina, 193
Beauty: in American texts, 34, 35, 45, 50–52, 61–63, 67; in British texts, 82–83; as interiority, 38
Belinda (Edgeworth), 95
Benevolence: Godwin on, 144–45; Hall on, 169; and Hutcheson, 20–21, 38, 69–70, 72; individualistic, 41–42, 147; republican version, 166; Sancho on, 73–74, 77, 79; Sharp's use of, 72
Benevolent societies, black, 152, 269n23
Benezet, Anthony, 100–103, 128, 265n34
Berlant, Lauren, 23
Berlin, Isaiah, 9
Bibb, Henry, 216–19
Bill of Rights, English, 10
Bingham, Caleb, 229–30
Black Atlantic, The (Gilroy), 8
Black Atlantic texts: ambiguities in American or British labels, 256n45; Ball, 205–8; Bibb, 216–19; body treatment in, 192; Clarkes, 214–16; cosmopolitanism of, 25–30, 34, 84–85, 106–8, 192, 255–56nn38–41; Cugoano, 85, 111–20, 136; Douglass, 226–40; as focus of book, 3–4; Grimes, 198–202, 205; Gronniosaw, 34, 49–52, 119; Hall, 139, 164–65, 168–78; Hammon, 108–11; liberalism and republicanism overview,

1–2, 24, 47–48; national identity in, 26; Pennington, 219–20; Prince, 192, 220–25; radicalization of ideas, 7–8; Roper, 208–11, 228; Sancho, 34, 53, 73–74, 76–83; scholarly debate on concept, 242–44; sentiment and politics in, 5–7, 15, 22–25; value of comparatist approach, 246–47; Wedderburn, 139, 181–89; Wheatley, 34, 52–69, 164, 258–60nn30–38; Williams, J., 209, 211–13. *See also* Equiano, Olaudah; Marrant, John

Black nationalism: among sailors, 107; in Equiano, 134; in Hall, 165; historical introduction of, 152; in Marrant, 158, 165; and New Divinity movement, 160; republicanism as precursor to, 178; and Sierra Leone emigration project, 136

Blackness, scholarly analysis of, 242. *See also* Body

Blacks. *See* African Americans; Afro-Britons

Blassingame, John, 227

Blood (genealogical connection), 191, 201–2, 209–10, 211. *See also* Familial ties

Body: in Clarke, L., 216; in Douglass, 228, 231, 236–37; equality of, 2, 150; in Grimes, 201–2; in Hammon, 109–10; liberal objectification of, 191–92, 210–11; in Marrant, 160–62; overview, 190–92; and political sentiment, 16–17; in Prince, 221–22; republican vs. liberal views of, 6, 19–20, 23, 24, 191–92; as resistance symbol, 231; in Roper, 208–11; in Sancho, 81; in sentimental novel, 35–36, 254n31; in Smith, V., 204–5; in Sterne, 75–76; and sympathy, 17–18, 20; in Wheatley, 67; and whites' inability to care about black bodies, 42–43; in Williams, 211–13

Bogues, Anthony, 120

Bolster, W. Jeffrey, 106, 108, 110

Book of Constitutions (Anderson and Desauliers), 165

Breen, T. H., 12

Brief Considerations on Slavery (Dillwyn), 104

Britain: vs. America on abolition, 98–100; blending of liberalism and republicanism in, 5–6, 10–12, 15, 22, 70–73, 94–95, 96, 103, 124, 141; brotherhood in, 140–45, 178–89; and elimination of slave trade, 96, 97–98; Enlightenment in, 11, 70; imperial destiny of, 97–98, 103–4, 108, 113–15, 123–24, 224; sentimental novel in, 93–95, 197, 262n4; working class in, 178, 180

British antislavery texts: Cugoano, 85, 111–20, 136; and global trade considerations, 96; interiority and aesthetic balance in, 34, 38, 69–73; Prince, 192, 220–25; radicalism in, 144–45, 178–89, 180; Sancho, 34, 53, 73–74, 76–83; transnational focus of, 192; Wedderburn, 139, 181–89; Wheatley's contribution to, 64–65, 68. *See also* Equiano, Olaudah

Brooks, Joanna, 158, 242

Brotherhood: American, 146–51, 152–78; British, 140–45, 178–89; introduction, 139–40

Brown, Charles Brockden, 144, 145–51

Brown, John, 236

Brown, William Hill, 35–37

Brown, William Wells, 241–42

Bullock, Steven C., 171–72

Burke, Edmund, 63

Burney, Fanny, 197

Burnham, Michelle, 161

Caldwell, Tanya, 123

Capitalism: African American desire to participate in, 199–201, 203; and class-spanning by Freemasonry, 170–71; and freedom of selling one's labor, 207; inherent inequalities in, 207–8; and interiority focus, 251–52n17; and manipulation of others for gain, 199–201, 203–4; and triumph of liberalism, 232. *See also* Trading economy

Captivity narratives, 108–9, 110, 160–62
Carretta, Vincent, 125, 135, 136, 243
Castronovo, Russ, 192
Cato (Addison), 142–43
Chain metaphor in Marrant, 166, 170
Charge (Hall), 168–71
Charlotte Temple (Rowson), 87–88
Child, Lydia Maria, 190, 194–97
Civic duty/virtue: and acceptance of difference, 23; artisans' view of, 156; in commercialism, 95–96; and cosmopolitanism, 28, 29; in Douglass, 229; duties vs. rights, 10–11; as pillar of republicanism, 9, 10; in sentimental novel, 89–90; in Wheatley, 53–54
Civic humanism, 3, 10, 43, 83, 88–90, 179
Civilizing mission of British Empire. *See* Imperialism, British
Clarissa (Richardson), 93, 94
Clark, Elizabeth B., 190
Clarke, Lewis, 214–16
Clarke, Milton, 214–16
Clarkson, Thomas, 103–4
Class: abolitionists' avoidance of, 201; fraternal orders' consciousness of, 171; Freemasonry's spanning of, 170–71; proletarianism in British slave narrative, 223; racial vs. class solidarity, 172–73; solidarity among artisans, 156; Wedderburn's consciousness of, 184, 186. *See also* Middle class; Working class
Clawson, Mary Ann, 170–71
Clotel (Brown, W. W.), 241–42
Columbian Orator (Bingham), 229–30
Commercialism. *See* Capitalism; Trading economy
Committee for the Relief of the Black Poor, 133
Common good: and antislavery position, 100–101, 103–4; artisans' commitment to, 175–76; British balance with interiority, 34, 38, 69–73; British Empire's duty to serve, 114–15, 124; as constraint on liberalism, 262n7; in Cugoano, 115–16; at expense of individual sympathy,

196; and freedom, 69–70, 72–73, 183; vs. individualism, 143–45; and moral limitations, 101–2; Native American commitment to, 194; and natural rights, 182; as pillar of republicanism, 3, 9, 11–12; in Prince, 224; in Sancho, 76, 77–78, 80; in sentimental novel, 89–90, 95, 262n7; and shared property, 185; and trade, 113, 121, 123–24; in Wheatley, 53–54
Communism in Wedderburn's text, 139, 181, 182, 184–85, 186, 189
Communitarian sensibility: in America, 12–13, 34, 48, 216, 219; among sailors, 104–6; and black antislavery texts' appeal, 46, 47; in black Freemasonry, 172–73; in Cugoano, 118; in Douglass, 229; in Equiano, 127–28, 129; in Marrant, 158, 165–66; in Sancho, 78–79; in sentimental novel, 88–90, 196–97; in Sharp, 71, 72; and workings of sympathy, 20
Comparatism, 246–47
Compassion, individual, as substitute for republican sentiment, 87, 88, 196. *See also* Sympathy
Conservatism, 180, 267n1
Considerations on Slavery (Appleton), 99
Constitution, abolitionists' contrary views of, 232–33
Contentment, concept of slave, 202, 237–38
Contractarianism: and abolitionist position, 39–40; in black antislavery writing, 46–47; Cugoano's restrictions on, 113; and freedom as negotiable, 70, 71, 100–101; and liberalism, 9
Coquette (Foster), 88–90
Corporeality. *See* Body
Cosmopolitanism: among sailors, 106–7; in Black Atlantic texts, 25–30, 34, 84–85, 106–8, 192, 255–56nn38–41; cross-racial character of, 242; in Equiano, 120–38, 183; in Gronniosaw, 52; liberalism, 26–29, 92; overview, 3–4, 25–30,

84–85; in Prince, 220–25; and republicanism, 7–8, 26–29, 47, 91; in sentimental novel, 91–92, 94–95; in Wheatley, 63–65, 68–69. *See also* Transnationalism; World citizenship
Costanzo, Angelo, 159
Covenant and Republic (Gould), 194
Coviello, Peter, 53, 54
Creole (ship), rebellion aboard, 235, 238–39
Cugoano, Quobna Ottobah, 85, 111–20, 136
Cursory Remarks upon the Reverend Mr. Ramsay's Essay (Tobin), 117

Davidson, Cathy N., 36, 85
Davis, Charles T., 211
Davis, David Brion, 98, 180
Declaration of Independence, American, 10, 232–33
Democracy as American political focus, 179
Desaguiliers, Jean Théophile, 165
Desire and Domestic Fiction (Armstrong), 85
Desrochers, Jr., Robert, 110, 111
"Dialogue on Slavery, A" (Hopkins), 160
Diasporic identity among blacks. *See* World citizenship
Difference, racial: ambiguities in, 202, 209–10, 214–15, 218–19; and American fraternal desire for similarity, 153; in Bibb, 218–19; civic virtue and acceptance of, 23; and criticism of whiteness, 214; in Douglass, 227–29; Douglass' later avoidance of, 236–37; in Grimes, 201–2; in Gronniosaw, 50, 52; and homosocial relationships, 151; humanism's lack of recognition, 43; and interracial consciousness, 221–22; liberalism's avoidance of, 22–25, 40, 41–42, 191; and national identity, 245; republican perspective, 6, 23–25, 109–10; in Sancho, 82–83; and separatism of benevolent societies, 269n23; in Smith, V., 204–5; Woolman's call for accepting, 154. *See also* Body

Dillon, Elizabeth Maddock, 92, 93, 149–51
Dillwyn, William, 104
Double consciousness, 8
Douglas, Ann, 21–22, 193, 253n25
Douglass, Frederick, 226–40
Doux commerce, 121
DuCille, Ann, 241–42
Dwyer, John, 19

Ecological internationalism, 255n41
Edgar Huntly (Brown), 148–51
Edgeworth, Maria, 95, 197
Education, Hall's support for black, 174, 176–77
Edwards, Jonathan, 153
Egalitarianism: in American slave narrative, 204; among sailors, 106–8, 110; in appreciation of black bodies, 45; in Cugoano, 115–17, 120; in Douglass, 228–29; in Equiano, 122, 135; fraternity's avoidance of, 155; and homosocial friendship, 145; lack of in abolition movement, 39–40, 42; and liberalism, 22–23, 40, 88, 147; radicals' approach in Britain, 180; in religious abolitionism, 40, 155; and republicanism, 13, 14, 25; in Wheatley, 68
Ellis, Markman, 75
Embodiment. *See* Body
Emigration to Africa: black reluctance concerning, 134–35; black societies' advocating of, 152; as escape from solidarity responsibility, 156–57; Hall's petition for, 173–74; and Marrant, 158–60; overview, 46–47; Sierra Leone project, 126, 133–38
Emotional and political discourse, integration of. *See* Sentiment, politics of
England. *See* Britain; British antislavery texts
Enlightenment: Britain's version of, 11, 70; and cosmopolitanism, 26; and Cugoano's antislavery argument, 112–13; and Hall's Freemasonry, 173; and interiority focus in America, 37; Wedderburn's use of, 183

Enquiry Concerning Political Justice (Godwin), 144–45
Environmentalism, cultural, 43, 76, 183–84
Equality: as abolitionist goal in 1840s, 214; bodily, 2, 150; fraternity's difficulties with, 152–54, 155, 170; and freedom, 39–40, 47; as goal of black antislavery writing, 47; in Hall, 170, 174; in Sancho, 82–83; in Wedderburn, 181. *See also* Egalitarianism
Equiano, Olaudah: and Cugoano, 112; exposure to radicalism, 180; introduction, 85; Sierra Leone emigration project, 133–38; slave narrative of, 120–33; transnationalism of, 120–38, 183
Essay Concerning Human Understanding (Locke), 17
Essay on Sharp (Hutcheson), 72
Essay on the Impolicy of the African Slave Trade, An (Clarkson), 103–4
Evans, Thomas, 181, 182
Exceptionalism, American, 244–45, 246
Expressives, 206, 226
Exteriority. *See* Aesthetic sensibility

Familial ties: and appeals to universal brotherhood, 153; in Bibb, 216–19; and blood connection in 19th-century slave narratives, 191, 201–2, 209–10, 211; and fraternity's inequality, 152–54; in Hall, 173; liberalism's focus on, 143, 146–47, 195; in Prince, 221. *See also* Brotherhood
Fear, politics of, 215–16
Feeling and politics. *See* Sentiment, politics of
Feeling Global: Internationalism in Distress (Robbins), 27–29
Festa, Lynn, 93–94
Fichtelberg, Joseph, 121
Fiedler, Leslie, 151
Fisher, Isaac, 205
Fliegelman, Jay, 94
Foner, Eric, 8, 156
Foster, Hannah Webster, 88–90
Foucault, Michel, 247

Fraternity: American development of, 152–55; Brown's complex, 150–51; class consciousness in, 171; and craft societies, 156; Freemasonry, 164–78; inequality in, 152–54, 155, 170; normalizing influence of, 151. *See also* Brotherhood
Frederickson, George M., 239
Freedom: American version, 96–97, 179, 202–3; as balance between natural law and common good, 69–70; in Benezet, 100–103, 265n34; British version, 179; commercial benefits of, 115, 207, 264n24; and common good, 69–70, 72–73, 100–103, 183; in Cugoano, 120; in Douglass, 228; and equality, 39–40, 47; fragility of vs. commercial interest, 96–97, 99; and land redistribution, 184–85; liberal concept of, 3, 9, 104, 263n13; moral qualifications for, 101–4, 113; as negotiable in contractarianism, 70, 71, 100–101; in Prince, 223, 225; racial restrictions on, 91–92; republican concept of, 101–2, 263n13; of selling one's labor, 207; as sourced in community belonging, 71; as transcendent of personal attachment, 218; in Wheatley, 58–59
Freemasonry, 164–78
Friendship and common good, 78. *See also* Homosocial friendship
Fugitive hero, cult of, 213

Gallop, G. I., 182
Garrison, William Lloyd, 190, 214, 271n11
Garrisonian abolitionism, 232, 233, 234, 240
Gates, Henry Louis, Jr., 50, 243
Gayle, Addison, 241–42
Gender issues, 4, 86–88, 193, 217–18, 263n13
Genius in Bondage (Carretta and Gould), 243
Giles, Paul, 245–46, 247
Gilpin, William, 38
Gilroy, Paul, 8, 242

Global consciousness. *See* Transnationalism
Godwin, William, 144–45
Goldstein, Leslie Friedman, 236
"Goliath of Gath" (Wheatley), 60
Goodell, William, 232
Gould, Philip, 5, 14, 194, 243
Great Britain. *See* Britain; British antislavery texts
Greven, David, 151
Grimes, William, 198–202, 205
Gronniosaw, James Albert Ukawsaw, 34, 49–52, 119
Grotius, Hugo, 10, 39

Haakonssen, Knud, 10–11
Hall, Prince, 139, 164–65, 168–78
Halttunen, Karen, 37–38
Hammon, Briton, 108–11
Hanway, Jonas, 135
Hardy, Thomas, 178, 180
Harrington, James, 10
Hartz, Louis, 13, 246
Haskell, Thomas L., 24, 99
Hayden, Lucy K., 66
Haynes, Lemuel, 47–48
Hendler, Glenn, 24
Heroic Slave, The (Douglass), 231, 234–39
History of Mary Prince, The (Prince), 192, 220–25
History of Mason and Dixon's Line (Latrobe), 192
Hobbes, Thomas, 199–200
Hobomok (Child), 194–97
Hofstadter, Richard, 246
Hollis, Patricia, 178
Homer and Wheatley, 65–66
Homosocial friendship: in America, 144, 218–19; in Britain, 144; in Brown's novels, 146–48, 149–51; and Douglass, 231; and egalitarianism, 145; and republicanism, 139, 142–43. *See also* Brotherhood
Hope Leslie (Sedgwick), 194–97
Hopkins, Samuel, 160
Horrors of Slavery, The (Wedderburn), 183–84

Humanism, civic, 3, 10, 43, 83, 88–90, 179
Humanitarian narrative, 16, 24, 152
Human nature, Hobbesian version, 199
Hume, David, 38
Huntingdonian Connexion, 42, 157–58, 159
Hutcheson, Francis, 20–21, 38, 69–70, 72
"Hymn to Evening, A" (Wheatley), 61, 62
"Hymn to Morning, A" (Wheatley), 61

Ickstadt, Heinz, 245
Identity, and Romanticism in slave narratives, 213. *See also* Cosmopolitanism; National identity
Imagination and sympathy, 18–19
Imperialism, British: and anti-slave trade movement, 97–98, 103–4, 123; in British slave narrative, 224; and Cugoano, 113–14, 115; duty to serve common good, 114–15, 124
Individualism: American appeal to, 6, 15, 34; artisans', 156; and benevolence, 41–42, 147; in Bibb, 216–17; as boon for women, 86–88; in Britain, 6; vs. common good, 143–45; and Douglass' radicalism, 236; in Freemasonry, 172; in Gronniosaw, 50; as pillar of liberalism, 3; in Prince, 222; of religious experience, 160–63, 188–89; of sentimental moment, 75; in sentimental novel, 86, 93, 193, 197; and stoicism as prerequisite for sympathy, 19–20; as struggle for survival, 200; and sympathy toward oppressed, 98–99; Wedderburn's criticism of, 183–84; in Wheatley, 54; and white supremacy, 234
"Injustice and Dangerous Tendency of Tolerating Slavery" (Sharp), 71
Interiority: in America, 34, 37–48, 152; in Black Atlantic writings, 24; British balance with common good, 34, 38, 69–73; and capitalism, 251–52n17; in Douglass, 235; of emotional processes, 18; and familial ties, 195;

Interiority—*continued:*
 in Gronniosaw, 49–52; introduction, 33–34; in liberalism, 18–20, 191; in Marrant, 160, 161–62; as modern phenomenon, 251–52n17; religion as sign of, 34, 39, 48, 49–50, 56–58, 157; in Sancho, 34, 73–74, 76–83; of sensibility in 18th century, 74–76; in sentimental novel, 35–38, 145, 146–48; and sublime, 261n47; in Wedgwood's medallion, 154; in Wheatley, 34, 52–69; in white anti-slavery texts, 34, 38–45, 69–73
International identity. *See* Cosmopolitanism
Internationalism. *See* Transnationalism
Irwin, Joseph, 134

Jacob, James, 178
Jacob, Margaret, 178
Jacobinism, 179–80, 182–83
Jasinski, James, 232
Jefferson, Thomas, 52–53, 95–96, 97
Jordan, Winthrop D., 40
Journal (Marrant), 157, 158–59, 160
Jubilee (religious concept), 189
"Just Limitation of Slavery, The" (Sharp), 71–72

Kazanjian, David, 203
Keith, George, 41
Kelly, Gary, 197
Kendrick, Robert, 55
Knowledge exchange and Freemasonry, 174–75, 176, 177
Kraditor, Aileen, 214, 233
Kramnick, Isaac, 10
Kroes, Rob, 245

"Lament for Bosnia, A" (Sontag), 27
Land redistribution, 181, 184–85, 189
Laqueur, Thomas W., 16
Larrimore, George, 211
Latrobe, John, 192
"Law of Liberty, The" (Sharp), 73
"Law of Passive Obedience, The" (Sharp), 72–73
Lee, Arthur, 44
Lee, Nathaniel, 140–41

Levernier, James A., 55
Liberalism: in America, 5–7, 12–13, 14, 22, 146–48, 171, 178–79, 192–93, 251n12; in Black Atlantic texts, 1–2, 24, 47–48; and body, 6, 19–20, 23, 24, 191–92, 210–11; in Britain, 5–6, 10–12, 15, 20–21, 22, 70–73, 94–95, 96, 98, 103, 124, 141; classic vs. modern left-wing, 249n3; and cosmopolitanism, 26–29, 92; in Cugoano, 112–13; dangers for society, 151; definitional issues, 250–51n11, 250n6; and difference/racism, 6, 22–25, 40, 41–42, 109–10, 191, 233–34, 238–39; Douglass' development of, 226–27, 232–40; and egalitarianism, 22–23, 40, 88, 147; in Equiano, 127; evolution overview, 7, 8–9; and familial ties, 143, 146–47, 195; freedom concept in, 3, 9, 104, 263n13; in Grimes, 200–201; in Gronniosaw, 49; in Hammon, 108–11; in Jefferson, 95–96; as middle-class ideal, 86, 87, 93, 165; national focus of, 91–92; nineteenth-century transition to, 190–91, 193–208, 213–20; normative image of citizen, 84; overview, 3; in Prince, 220, 223; radical possibilities of, 13–14; rationality as anchor for, 254n29; vs. republicanism, 8–15; in Roman plays, 140–42, 143; in Sancho, 77; scholarly need for alternative to, 250n10; in sentimental novel, 85–90, 93–94, 193–97, 253–54n28, 262n7, 264n19; and similarity, 23; in Sterne, 74–75; and sympathy, 20, 41, 89–90, 127, 195, 263n13; in Wheatley, 54–55. *See also* Capitalism; Contractarianism; Individualism; Interiority; Natural rights
Liberal Tradition in America, The (Hartz), 13, 246
Libertarianism as American political focus, 179
Liberty. *See* Freedom
"Liberty Further Extended" (Haynes), 47–48
Life (Grimes), 198–202

Linebaugh, Peter, 104–5, 189
Literacy, importance for Douglass, 230
Locke, John, 3, 9, 10, 13, 17, 236
London Corresponding Society, 178, 180, 183
Lucius Junius Brutus (Lee), 140–41

Mackenthum, Gesa, 91
Macpherson, C. B., 199
Madison, James, 97
Mansfield, Lord, 71
Marrant, John: chain metaphor in, 166, 170; communitarian sensibility, 159, 163–64; and Freemasonry, 139, 165–68, 174–75, 176; religious foundation for, 157–58, 159–63, 165–66; slave narrative, 157–58, 160, 167–68
Masculinity and sentimental fiction, 140
Mather, Cotton, 153
May, Cedrick, 159
McCalman, Iain, 182, 188, 189
McFeely, William S., 230–31
McGerr, Michael, 245
McWilliams, Wilson Carey, 152–53
Mercantilist imperialism, absence of in America, 264n24
Metamorphoses (Ovid), 66–67
Methodism, 42, 157–58, 181, 187–88, 189
Middle class: and desire for social respectability, 165; and Freemasonry's appeal for blacks, 172; and liberalism, 86, 87, 93, 165; and Wheatley's republican influences, 55; working class alliance with, 180
Millenarianism, Methodism's, 188, 189
Miller, Peter N., 11–12
Mills, Charles W., 233
Modernity, 242–43, 251–52n17
Montesquieu, Baron de (Charles de Secondat), 44
Moral limitations and common good, 101–2
Moral problem, slavery as, 214
Mullan, John, 94
Muraskin, William A., 172
Mutual improvement societies, black, 152
My Bondage and My Freedom (Douglass), 226–27, 231, 239–40
Myth-and-symbol school of American culture, 244–45

Narrative (Clarke, L.), 214–16
Narrative (Clarke, M.), 214–16
Narrative (Douglass), 226, 227, 228–31
Narrative (Equiano), 120–33
Narrative (Gronniosaw), 49–52
Narrative (Marrant), 157, 160, 167–68
National agency in sentimental novel, 85–93
National identity: in America, 85–93, 192; in Black Atlantic texts, 26; British, 80, 93, 108; Douglass' raceless, 239; in Equiano, 132, 137–38; introduction, 84–85; and liberal abolitionist appeal, 46; liberalism vs. republicanism, 23–24; and racial difference, 245; in Sancho, 80; and transnational connections, 5; as undermining international solidarity, 28; and value of difference, 245
Native Americans, 160–62, 194–97
Natural law theory, 10–11, 44, 71, 72, 159–60
Natural rights: abolitionism as based in, 38–40, 41, 43–44, 99, 190–91; artisans' view of, 156; coupling with common good focus, 182; in Cugoano, 112–13; in Douglass, 232–33, 238; and Hutcheson on liberty, 69–70; and interiority, 34; as pillar of liberalism, 3; in Smith, V., 202–3
"Nature and Importance of True Republicanism, The" (Haynes), 48
Negative freedom, 9, 104
Nelson, Dana D., 155, 172
New Divinity school, 42, 159–60
Newport African Union Society, 152
Nichols, Charles, 192
"Niobe" (Wheatley), 66–67
Noble-savage mystique in Equiano's story, 128–29
Northern work ethic, and criticism of Southern plantation life, 207
North Star, 232
Notes on the State of Virginia (Jefferson), 52–53

Nova Scotia, black community in, 157, 159
Novel as genre, 262n3. *See also* Sentimental novel
Nussbaum, Martha, 29
Nwankwo, Ifeoma Kiddoe, 220–21

Oceana (Harrington), 10
Ogude, S. E., 125, 126
"On Being Brought from Africa to America" (Wheatley), 56, 61–62
"On the Death of a Young Gentleman" (Wheatley), 58
"On the Death of General Wooster" (Wheatley), 58–59
"On the Death of the Rev. Dr. Sewell" (Wheatley), 55–56
"On the Death of the Rev. Mr. George Whitefield" (Wheatley), 57–58
Oppositional texts, function of, 247. *See also* Black Atlantic texts
Origins of Anglo-American Radicalism, The (Jacob and Jacob), 178
Ormond (Brown), 147–48
Otis, James, 43–44
Otway, Thomas, 141–42
Ovid, 66–67

Paine, Thomas, 180
Pamela (Richardson), 93–94
"Paper about Negroes" (Piles), 41–42
Parker, Theodore, 213
Passing as white, effect on slave narrative, 202, 209–10, 214–15, 218–19
Pearce, Roy Harvey, 161
Pennington, James W. C., 219
Peters, Thomas, 159
Philmore, J., 106
Philosophical Enquiry into the Origin of Our Ideas of the Sublime and Beautiful (Burke), 63
Physicality. *See* Body
Picturesque, the, 38
Piles, Robert, 41–42
Plan of a Settlement to Be Made Near Sierra Leone (Smeathman), 134
Plays, Roman, 140–44
Plebian culture, British vs. American, 179

Pocock, J. G. A., 9–10, 11, 13
Poetic expression, Wheatley's, 52–69
Politics and feeling. *See* Sentiment, politics of
Porter, Roy, 11, 37
Possessive individualism, 200
Possessive market model, 199
Postlethwayt, Malachy, 102–3
Potkay, Adam, 126
Power of Sympathy, The (Brown), 35–37
Prejudice, racial. *See* Racism
Prince, Mary, 192, 220–25
Proletarianism in British slave narrative, 223. *See also* Working class
Property: abolition of private, 181, 182, 184–85, 189; artisan vs. merchant views of, 156; Hall on, 176; in liberalism, 9, 46; in republicanism, 10
Pufendorf, Samuel, 39
Puritan republican ethos, 194

Quakers: abolitionist position of, 41–42, 99–103; Benezet, 100–103, 128, 265n34; transnationalism of, 257n16; Woolman, 153–55, 268–69n18
Quashi, 2
Quilley, Geoff, 108

Racism: in abolitionists, 39–40, 43, 265n34; on board ships, 107; Cugoano on, 117–18; and economic restrictions on free blacks, 203–4; Jefferson's, 53; liberalism's inability to transcend, 233–34, 235, 238–39; slave narratives consideration of widespread, 191
Radicalism: vs. abolitionism, 178, 180; and artisan republicanism, 176; body as symbol of resistance, 231; in British antislavery texts, 178–89; in Brown's novels, 145, 149–50; in cosmopolitanism of blacks, 25–30; in Cugoano, 112, 117, 118–20; in Douglass, 227, 229–30, 235–36; in Godwin, 144–45; in Hall, 169–70, 175–76; in Hammon, 110; introduction, 139–40; lack of in America,

155; and liberalism vs. republicanism, 7–8, 13–14; and sailor solidarity, 104–5, 107; in Sancho, 74, 79, 80–81; term usage, 267n1; in Wedderburn, 181–89; in Wheatley, 63–64; in Woolman, 153–55
Rationality, liberalism's anchoring in, 254n29
Real Whigs, 9–10, 12
Rediker, Marcus, 104–5, 189
Religious belief: in Cugoano, 119–20; and egalitarianism, 40, 155; in Gronniosaw, 49–50; interiority of, 34, 39, 48, 49–50, 56–58, 157; and liberal abolitionism, 39–40, 41–42; in Marrant, 157–58, 159–63, 165–66; Methodism, 42, 157–58, 181, 187–88, 189; in Sancho, 76; and sentimentalism, 261n48; in Sharp, 71–72; and slavery acceptance, 39; and universal brotherhood, 153, 166–67; in Wedderburn, 186, 187–89; in Wheatley, 56–58, 62, 63. *See also* Quakers
Republicanism: in America, 12–13, 14, 146–48, 204, 213–20; among artisans, 175–76; benevolence in, 166; in Black Atlantic texts, 2, 24, 47–48; and black nationalism, 178; and body, 6, 19–20, 23, 24, 191–92; British blending with liberalism, 5–6, 10–12, 15, 20–21, 22, 70–73, 94–95, 96, 103, 124, 141; and brotherhood, 139, 142–43, 152, 157; civic humanism, 3, 10, 83, 88–90, 179; and cosmopolitanism, 7–8, 26–29, 47, 91; in Cugoano, 115–17, 120; definitional issues, 9, 250–51n11, 250n6; as devoid of personal feeling, 195–96; and difference/racism, 6, 23–25, 109–10; in Douglass, 226, 228–31, 237; in Equiano, 130; evolution overview, 7, 9–11; and freedom definition, 101–2, 263n13; and Freemasonry, 168; Garrisonian, 214, 234; and global trade, 96; in Hall, 168, 174, 177–78; in Hammon, 109–10; horizontal approach to nationhood, 84; in Jefferson, 53, 54; vs. liberalism, 8–15; in Marrant, 163; overview, 3; in Pennington, 219–20; in Prince, 224; and radicalism, 7–8, 13–14, 176; in Roman plays, 140–41, 142–43; in Sancho, 78; scholarly focus on, 250n10; in sentimental novel, 37, 86, 88–90, 93–94, 146–47, 148, 149–50, 193, 194–97; and sympathy, 20, 41, 89–90, 127, 195, 196, 263n13; in Wheatley, 53–54, 55–56, 59–61, 63–64, 65–66; in white antislavery writing, 44–45. *See also* Aesthetic sensibility; Body; Brotherhood; Civic duty/virtue; Common good; Communitarian sensibility; Egalitarianism
Revolution, American, 12–13, 15, 231–32, 250n8
Revolutionary: Douglass as, 235–36; Wedderburn as, 181, 184, 187
Richards, Phillip M., 54–55, 64
Richardson, Samuel, 37, 93–95
Rights of Man (Paine), 180
Rights of the British Colonies Asserted and Proved, The (Otis), 43–44
Rights vs. duties, 10–11. *See also* Natural rights
Robbins, Bruce, 27–29, 223
Robbins, Caroline, 10
Robinson, William H., 64
Rodgers, Daniel T., 13, 14
Roman plays in Britain, 140–44
Romanticism and slave narratives, 213
Roper, Moses, 208–11, 228
Rousseau, G. S., 17
Rowe, John Carlos, 244
Rowson, Susanna Haswell, 87–88, 91
Rubin-Dorsky, Jeffrey, 85–86
Rush, Benjamin, 43, 44–45, 155
Russell, Gillian, 108
Ryan, Susan M., 24

Saillant, John, 25, 158
Sailors: common ground with slaves, 104–8; Equiano's story, 124; Hammon's story, 108–11; impressment of as slavery, 80; Marrant's story, 157; Wedderburn's experience, 181
Sale, Maggie, 235
Sánchez-Eppler, Karen, 191

Sancho, Ignatius, 34, 53, 73–74, 76–83
Sandiford, Keith A., 79, 102
Scottish moral sense school, 20–21
Searle, John, 205–6
Second Treatise of Government, The (Locke), 9
Sedgwick, Catharine Maria, 194–97
Segregation and abolitionists' prejudices, 42
Sekora, John, 243
Self-control and British sentimental novel, 197
Self-improvement, 156, 172
Self-interest: in Ball, 206–7; benevolence as serving liberal, 41–42; in Equiano, 123; as foundation of American freedom, 264n24; and internationalism as liberal, 28; and manipulation of others for gain, 199–201, 203–4
Self-reliance, American focus on, 193, 216–17
Sensibility in Anglo-American culture, 16–18, 36, 74–76. *See also* Aesthetic sensibility; Interiority
Sentiment, politics of: Black Atlantic overview, 5–7, 15, 22–25; Douglas's condemnation of, 253n25; introduction, 15–22; nineteenth-century developments, 190; overview, 2–4; in slave narratives, 1–2, 249n1. *See also* Liberalism; Republicanism
Sentimental Journey, A (Sterne), 74–76
Sentimental novel: American, 85–93, 145–51, 193–97; British, 93–95, 197, 262n4; common good vs. liberalism in, 89–90, 95, 262n7; cosmopolitanism in, 91–92, 94–95; definition of genre, 253n23; gender issues in, 263n12; interiority and aesthetics in, 35–38, 145, 146–48, 254n31; liberalism in, 85–90, 93–94, 193–97, 253–54n28, 262n7, 264n19; national agency in, 85–93; radicalism in, 145, 149–50; republicanism in, 37, 86, 88–90, 93–94, 146–47, 148, 149–50, 193, 194–97; and slave narrative, 249n1
Sewall, Joseph, 154
Sewall, Samuel, 39–40

Sharp, Granville, 70–73, 104, 134
Sherman, Roger, 97
Short Sketch of Regulations (Sharp), 134
Shuffelton, Frank, 64, 69
Sierra Leone emigration project, 126, 133–38
Similarity: dangers for America's egalitarian ideal, 147; and Douglass' interiority, 235; and fraternity in America, 153, 168; liberal attachment to, 90; in national identity focus, 93. *See also* Familial ties
Sincerity and interiority, 37–38
Skin color, 215–16. *See also* Difference, racial
Slave narratives: avoidance of bodily difference in, 24; Ball, 205–8; Bibb, 216–19; Clarkes, 214–16; Douglass, 226, 227, 228–31; Equiano, 120–33; Grimes, 198–202, 205; Gronniosaw, 49–52; Hammon, 108–11; Marrant, 157–58, 160, 167–68; nineteenth-century liberal transformation of, 213; overview, 191–92; Pennington, 219–20; politics of sentiment in, 1–2, 249n1; Prince, 220–25; Roper, 208–11, 228; scholarly analysis of, 243; Smith, V., 202–5; Williams, J., 209, 211–13
Slavery: British abolition of, 71; impressment of sailors as, 80; as moral problem, 214; philosophical perspectives, 38–39, 44, 70; slave trade, 96–104, 113, 123–24, 154. *See also* Abolitionism; American antislavery texts; British antislavery texts
Slavery in the United States (Ball), 205–8
Slaves in Algiers (Rowson), 91–92
Slave trade, 96–104, 113, 123–24, 154
Smeathman, Henry, 134
Smith, Adam, 18–20, 104, 123, 252nn18–19
Smith, Gerrit, 232
Smith, Venture, 202–5
Smithian sympathy, 40, 49, 73, 75, 145
Society for Effecting the Abolition of the Slave Trade, 154

Society of Spencean Philanthropists, 181
Sociological reductionism, 243
Solidarity: among sailors, 104–5, 107; class, 156, 172–73; and cosmopolitanism, 28, 29; emigration to Africa as escape from, 156–57; in Equiano, 136; Hall, 165; interracial, 185–87; in Marrant, 159, 165; national vs. international, 28; in Prince, 221; racial, 157, 163, 165, 169, 172–73; in Smith, V., 204–5; and sympathy, 252–53n21; in Williams, J., 211–12. *See also* Brotherhood
Some Considerations on the Keeping of Negroes (Woolman), 153–55
Some Historical Account of Guinea (Benezet), 101–2, 128
Somerset decision, 71
"Sons of Africans: An Essay on Freedom, The," 47
Sontag, Susan, 27, 28
Spence, Thomas, 181, 182
Spencean thought, 181
Spirit of the Laws (Montesquieu), 43, 44
Spooner, Lysander, 232–33
Status society, slave society as Hobbesian, 199–200
Stern, Julia A., 87, 263n14
Sterne Laurence, 37, 74–77
Stoicism, 19–20, 140–41
Story of Quashi, The, 2
Stowe, Harriet Beecher, 4, 40, 191
Subjecthood, 12
Sublime, 238, 259n35, 261n47
Sundquist, Eric, 226, 235–36
Sympathy: in Benezet, 102; and body, 17–18, 20; in Douglass, 227–28; eighteenth century conceptual development, 17–19; individual, 19–20, 98–99, 195, 196; liberal vs. republican views of, 20, 41, 89–90, 127, 195, 196, 263n13; nineteenth-century American developments, 190; in sentimental novel, 36; Smithian (liberal), 40, 49, 73, 75, 145; and solidarity, 252–53n21; in Woolman, 155

System of Moral Philosophy, A (Hutcheson), 20–21, 69–70

Theory of Moral Sentiments (Smith), 18
Things as They Are (Godwin), 145
Thompson, E. P., 179
Thompson, Rev. Thomas, 100
Thompson, Thomas Boulden, 135
Thompson, William, 13
Thornton, John, 59–60
Thoughts and Sentiments on the Evil of Slavery (Cugoano), 111–20
"Thoughts on the Works of Providence" (Wheatley), 58
Tobin, James, 117
"To Maecenas" (Wheatley), 65–66
Tompkins, Jane, 21–22
"To the Right Honourable William, Earl of Dartmouth" (Wheatley), 53–54
"To the University of Cambridge, in New-England" (Wheatley), 56
Trading economy: and common good, 113, 121, 123–24; Equiano on, 120–21, 122–24; liberal and republican acceptance of, 95; and national vs. international identities, 85, 95–104; in sentimental novel, 92; slave trade, 96–104, 115, 123–24; and world citizenship of sailors, 104–8, 124
Transnationalism: in abolitionist movement, 4–5; and black studies, 241–47; and body treatment in slave narratives, 192; in Cugoano, 85, 111–20, 136; and Freemasonry, 168; in Gronniosaw, 52; in Hammon, 110–11; in Marrant, 164; of Quakers, 257n16; and radicalization of ideas, 7–8; in Wedderburn, 181, 183, 186; in Wheatley, 64–65, 67–69. *See also* Cosmopolitanism; Equiano, Olaudah
Transracial social consciousness, 74
Truth Self-Supported (Wedderburn), 188–89
Two Dialogues on the Man-Trade (Philmore), 106
Twomey, Richard J., 179–80
Two Treatises of Government (Locke), 10

Tyler, Royall, 91, 92–93
Tyrrell, Ian, 244, 245

Uncle Tom's Cabin (Stowe), 4, 40, 191
Unconstitutionality of Slavery, The (Spooner), 232–33
United States. *See* America
Universal Dictionary of Trade and Commerce (Postlethwayt), 102–3
Universality in Hall's brotherhood, 168–70

Valeri, Mark, 159
Van Sant, Ann Jessie, 16–17, 74
Venice Preserved (Otway), 141–42
Virtual Americas (Giles), 245–46
Voyage au Sénégal (Adanson), 128–29

Walker, James W. St. G., 159
Wallace, Maurice O., 172
Wallerstein, Immanuel, 244
Walvin, James, 178
War in state of nature, 199–200, 236
Warner, Michael, 149
Way of the New World, The (Gayle), 241–42
Wealth of Nations (Smith), 104
Wedderburn, Robert, 139, 181–89
Wedgwood, Josiah, 154
Weld, Theodore, 190
Wesleyan Methodism, 158, 189
Weyler, Karen A., 161
"What to the Slave Is the Fourth of July?" (Douglass), 231, 232–33
Wheatley, John, 68
Wheatley, Phillis, 34, 52–69, 164, 258–60nn30–38
Wheatley, Susanna, 68
Whigs, 9–10, 12, 179, 182
Whitefield, George, 42, 160–61
White supremacy as integral to Constitution and law, 233–34
White texts: avoiding of radicalism, 178, 180; Benezet, 100–103, 128, 265n34; British vs. American on abolition of slave trade, 98–99; on brotherhood, 140–51; Garrison, 190, 214, 271n11; Godwin's radicalism, 144–45; Hutcheson, 20–21, 38, 69–70, 72; interiority vs. aesthetic sensibility in, 34, 38–45, 69–73; Roman plays, 140–44; Whitefield, 42, 160–61; Woolman, 153–55, 268–69n18. *See also* Sentimental novel
Wieland (Brown), 146–47
Wilberforce, William, 180
Wilentz, Sean, 155–56, 175–76
Williams, James, 209, 211–13
Williams, Loretta J., 172–73
Willis, Thomas, 17
Wingrave, Jack, 76
Winthrop, John, 153
Wise, Steven M., 71
Wood, Gordon S., 12, 13
Wood, John A., 224
Woodard, Helena, 79
Woolman, John, 153–55, 268–69n18
Working class: American lack of focus on, 179–80; and artisan republicanism, 176; black abolitionists' relationship to, 156; in Britain, 178, 180; common ground with slaves, 185, 186–87; Wedderburn's use of tactics from, 184
World citizenship: and Christian benevolence, 72; Cugoano's, 111–20; Equiano's, 120–33, 183; Hammon's, 110–11; introduction, 84–85; of sailors, 104–8, 124. *See also* Transnationalism
World-systems theory, 245
Wright, D. G., 180

Yarborough, Richard, 235, 237
Young, Alfred F., 13, 155, 179

Zafar, Rafia, 243
Ziff, Larzer, 145–46
Zuckert, Michael P., 10